Sailors on the Rocks

Maritime titles by the same author:

Destroyer Leader: The Story of HMS Faulknor *1934–46*
Task Force 57: The British Pacific Fleet 1944–45
Hard Lying: The Birth of the Destroyer
British Battle Cruisers
Heritage of the Sea
Royal Navy Ships' Badges
Battles of the Malta Striking Forces
Per Mare, Per Terram
Fighting Flotilla
Arctic Victory
The Great Ships Pass
The Battle-Cruiser HMS Renown *1916–48*
Destroyer Action
Critical Conflict: The Royal Navy's Mediterranean War 1940
Cruisers in Action
Naval Warfare in the English Channel
HMS Wild Swan
Battleship Royal Sovereign
Eagle's *War: the Diary of an aircraft carrier*
Into the Minefields
Midway – Dauntless Victory
Sailors in the Dock: Royal Navy Courts Martial down the centuries
Cruise Ships: The World's Most Luxurious Vessels
Cruise Ships: The Small Scale Fleet
Offshore Ferry Services of England & Scotland

Sailors on the Rocks

Famous Royal Navy Shipwrecks

Peter C. Smith

Pen & Sword
MARITIME

First published in Great Britain in 2015 by
Pen & Sword Maritime
an imprint of
Pen & Sword Books Ltd
47 Church Street
Barnsley
South Yorkshire
S70 2AS

ISBN 978 1 78340 062 1

See all Peter C. Smith's books at www.dive-bombers.co.uk

A CIP catalogue record for this book is available from the British Library

Typeset in Ehrhardt by
Mac Style Ltd, Bridlington, East Yorkshire
Printed and bound in the UK by CPI Group (UK) Ltd,
Croydon CRO 4YY

Pen & Sword Books Ltd incorporates the imprints of Pen & Sword
Archaeology, Atlas, Aviation, Battleground, Discovery, Family History,
History, Maritime, Military, Naval, Politics, Railways, Select, Transport,
True Crime, and Fiction, Frontline Books, Leo Cooper, Praetorian Press,
Seaforth Publishing and Wharncliffe.

For a complete list of Pen & Sword titles please contact
PEN & SWORD BOOKS LIMITED
47 Church Street, Barnsley, South Yorkshire S70 2AS, England
E-mail: enquiries@pen-and-sword.co.uk
Website: www.pen-and-sword.co.uk

Contents

Introduction and Acknowledgements   vi

Chapter 1   Wrecked off Rame   1

Chapter 2   Destroyed by Plague – The *Winchester*, 24 September 1695   8

Chapter 3   The Great Storm – The *Mary, Mortar, Northumberland,
                  Restoration & Stirling Castle*   22

Chapter 4   A Navigational Inexactitude   37

Chapter 5   A Melancholy Echo   51

Chapter 6   Unlucky Horseshoe   71

Chapter 7   The *Birkenhead* Drill   83

Chapter 8   Violating *Tapu*   114

Chapter 9   Ashore on Lundy   132

Chapter 10   'An Unreliable Fix'   151

Chapter 11   Sole Survivor   159

Chapter 12   The Wrecking of **Raleigh**   177

Chapter 13   Short-cut to Nowhere   194

Chapter 14   On No Account Leave the Ship!   217

Chapter 15   Who has the Helm?   235

Further Selected Reading on Royal Navy Shipwrecks   251
Index   252

Introduction and Acknowledgements

This book was written as a companion volume to my earlier *Sailors in the Dock: Naval Courts Martial Down the Centuries* (The History Press, Stroud, 2011) and follows a similar format. Fifteen cases of Royal Navy ships becoming victims of shipwreck are detailed, with highlights of circumstances leading up to them, outline details of the ships themselves and the principal characters involved. The term shipwreck is also specific: many ships of the Royal Navy have foundered in storms or as a result of battle damage, or often as not, neglect, but only ships that have been driven ashore and lost on an unforgiving coast are included in this volume. However, some losses have a high degree of uncertainty about them, and are difficult to define without further evidence released to the public domain, and therefore are hard to so determine. So the *Association* features because fresh information is being suppressed at the time of writing, but the *Mary Rose* and the *Royal George* are *not* included, calamities though they were, as the ships did not go ashore.

Although all ships are Royal Navy vessels, the actual term HMS (His/Her Majesty's Ship) did not come into effect until 1789; before that the terms His Britannic Majesty's Ship, The King's Ship or just the name of the vessel herself sufficed. In this volume I have used the definitive article to cover all the permutations and present some uniformity. Likewise, the term battleship did not gain currency until around the middle of the nineteenth century, prior to which the terminology was 'line-of-battleship' or 'ship-of-the-line' (because line ahead had become the standard naval battle strategy from the time of the Second Dutch War (1665–67)), and these had various 'ratings' according to the guns and numbers of guns carried; however, I have used the word 'battleship' throughout to describe the main type of warships of the day. In a similar fashion the eyes of the fleet, the main light scouting ships, were for centuries known as 'frigates' – only in the mid-nineteenth century did this description change to 'cruiser' and then to various categories of cruiser, 'Armoured' or 'Protected' and, subsequent to the notorious Washington Naval Treaty of 1922, 'Heavy' or 'Light', with 'Scout' appearing briefly earlier for leaders of destroyer flotillas. I have used the term 'frigate' up to Victorian times and from then on the various cruiser terms.

Another explanation must be made, this time in terms of dates. In earlier chapters the contemporary chronicles, ships' log books, newspaper reports, personal correspondence, all use the old Julian calendar. Our foes, the Dutch, French, Portuguese and Spanish, had all changed to the Gregorian calendar, so-named as it was introduced in a Papal Bull by Pope Gregory XIII to redefine the earlier Julian Calendar, in 1582 but not the English who, with our usual stubbornness and individuality, held out against such change until 1752 (Great Britain was not alone, Russia not until 1918 while Greece waited until 1923 to make the switch). I have stuck with the dates exactly as recorded at the time and have not attempted to convert them and nor have I used the term OS (for Old Style). Also, the ships are *warships* and so, in the interests of continuity, the twenty-four hour clock has been adopted throughout as standard, even though it was not so utilised in the service for many years.

I would wish to thank the following individuals who have assisted me with their stories, knowledge, photographs and, above all, their enthusiasm for this project.

Dawn Gillian Springett, Erina, NSW, for great assistance – the daughter of a *Sturdy* survivor, Dawn has amassed a large quantity of first-hand information, eye-witness accounts and photographs. I am grateful to her for permission to quote from these. Evelyn Caulfield, for permission to quote from the memoirs of her father Stanley Ibbott; Duncan Sutton, Surrey History Centre, Woking, Surrey; Stephen Farish, Admin Co-ordinator, The Regimental Museum of The Royal Welsh, Brecon; Derek Fox, whose grandfather Ernest Fox was a crew member and who has amassed a large amount of information on the *Sturdy* for his in-depth study, *The Loss of the Sturdy*, published in *Warship World* in 2008, and which he kindly shared with me; Diana Manipud, Archives, King's College London Archives, for assistance with accessing the Memoirs of Captain John Montague Howson RN Rtd; Colin Bruce, Imperial War Museum Library Research Room, for assistance in accessing the Private Papers of Commander Stanley Herbert King Spurgeon DSO RAN; the staff of the National Archives, Kew, London, for their exemplary help over a period of many visits to access the Log Books and Reports of the ships as quoted within these pages; Ruairi McKiernan, *The Irish Examiner* Archives, Dublin, for assistance in tracing the letter from M. Alleande Bernard concerning Bandmaster Zwyker; John Wallace, National Reference Service, National Archives of Australia, Canberra ACT; Kory Penney, Archivist, Maritime History Archive, Memorial University of Newfoundland, St John's; J. N. Hans Houterman, for his unfailing and unstinting help in tracing officer details; Deon Francois Schonland Fourie SD SM MMM JCD, Professor of Strategic Studies, University of South Africa (Rtd), Pretoria, RSA; Rear Admiral Arne Söderland PS SM MMM SAN (Rtd); Allan Sinclair, Curator, Naval Collections, Ditsong Museum of Military History, Saxonwold, Johannesburg, RSA; Johan van der Berg, Chairman, Cape Town Branch, South African Military History Society; Major Colin Berowald Innes (Rtd), of the Black Watch Castle & Museum, Balhousie Castle, Perth; Major Antony George Drumearn Gordon, Royal Scots Fusiliers, Rtd, Cape Town Military History Society, Cape Town, RSA; Captain Francois Morkel, Castle of Good Hope, Military Museum, Cape Town, RSA; Esther Mann, Curator Corps of Army Music Museum, Twickenham; Justin Saddington, Collections Content Curator, Department of Collections Care, National Army Museum, Chelsea, London; Rod Mackenzie and May Mason of the Argyll & Sutherland Highlanders Museum, Edinburgh; Ian Williams, East Kent Society; Teunish Schol, Alan Mountain, Cape Town Military History Society Committee, RSA; Archivist Manjunath Neelam, Nelson Mandela Metropolitan University, Port Elizabeth, RSA; Allan Brodie,

Historic England; Amanda Martin, Curator, Isles of Scilly Museum; Alison Wareham FCLIP, Library Information and Enquiries Manager, National Museum of the Royal Navy, Portsmouth; Theresa Palfrey, Norfolk Record Office; Maggie Oulaghan; Kevin McIntyre and Kate Swann, Senior Public Information Curator, Department of Access & Outreach, National Museum of the Royal Navy; Neil Staples, Seafarers' Section, Maritime and Coastguard Agency, Registry of Shipping and Seamen (RSS), Cardiff; Mrs Heather Johnson, National Museum of the Navy, Portsmouth, Teresa Gray, Surrey History Centre, Woking; Stirling Castle; Pete Bullimore, thamestugs.co.uk; Anne Cowne, Information Officer, Information Centre, Group Communications, Lloyd's Register Group Services, London; Clare Gibson, The Army Children Archive (TACA); Alison Clarke, Navy Search; Jeanie Smith, Assistant Librarian, Guildhall Library, Aldermanbury, London; Ben Fellows, Royal Army Museum, Chelsea, London; I have used original spellings when compiling the list of *Birkenhead* survivors, of which so many variations of spellings and numbers abound, compounded by the fact that the ship's muster lists were incomplete and many names are still not fully located and recorded – such instances apply to many of the older or incomplete records so some tolerance is required here. I have done my best in the time allowed to track most of them down but many remain – and even present-day authors seem extremely shy about revealing their full names. Thanks also to Hans Nether, Anglo–Netherlands Society, London; Emma Hatford-Forbes, The Black Watch Museum; Joan Marsh, South African Military History Society, Kengray, RSA, Ken Panchen, Old Azorians Association, Worthing and Lloyds of London for permission to reproduce images. Last, but by no means least, my deep thanks to my most patient, experienced and dedicated editor Richard Doherty.

One final note, the footnotes, which I hope shine fresh light on some aspects of these histories, not least on the backgrounds of the participants, vessels and organisations involved, are firmly placed at the *foot* of each page (which might apparently come as a surprise to some American critics!) but any mistakes are my own and will be rectified in future editions.

Peter Charles Horstead Smith
Riseley, Bedford
October 2015

N.B. With regard to Official photographs and those taken by representatives of the United Kingdom Government prior to 1 June 1957, HMSO has declared that the expiry of Crown Copyright applies worldwide.

Chapter 1

Wrecked off Rame

The *Coronation*, 3 September 1691

The sea shanty *Spanish Ladies* used to be a well-known and loved song in the distant days when I was a schoolboy. It is now banished to the limbo land of 'political correctness' whereby it is deemed sinful by the BBC, education authorities and many other worthies to dare to celebrate anything that smacks of English tradition. It is with that banishment in mind that I reproduce the words in full here, and they are relative to our tale.

> Farewell and adieu to you fair Spanish ladies,
> Adieu and farewell to you ladies of Spain,
> For we're under orders for to sail to old England
> And we may never see you fair ladies again.
>
> So we'll rant and we'll roar like true British sailors,
> We'll range and we'll roam over all the salt seas,
> Until we strike soundings in the Channel of Old England:
> From Ushant to Scilly 'tis thirty-five leagues.
>
> The first land we made, it is called the Dodman,
> Next Rame Head off Plymouth, Start, Portland and Wight:
> And we sailed by Beachy, by Fairlight and Dungeness,
> Until we brought to by the South Foreland Light.[1]

The children's author, Arthur Mitchell Ransome, another boyhood favourite, who told splendid yarns that excited and enthralled, but never condescended to, his young audience, is also nowadays probably largely unknown to our schoolchildren, but he put his finger on the nub of these verses back in 1932. He had his fictional character, an old mariner named 'Peter Duck', comment that 'thirty-five leagues' between the Ushant light and the Isles of Scilly was a nonsense unless they were tacking hard up Channel in the face of a north-east gale and ticking off each of the legs as they sighted them.[2]

---

1. Traditional shanty. A League is 3 statute miles or 4.828032km.
2. Ransome, Arthur, *Peter Duck*, 1932: London. Jonathan Cape, p.428. The actual distance between the two places, which mark the extreme north and south positions of the western entrance to the English Channel, is approximately 100 miles, or 28.965 leagues.

The wars with the Dutch in the seventeenth century marked a time, very much like the present day, when the national defences had been allowed to lapse to a very low ebb indeed by an indifferent and inept government. Britain's enemies took little time to exploit the situation but their humiliations were added to by the intrusion of nature itself, which, as always, proved master of all. At the time of the Restoration of the Monarchy after the stern and severe restrictions of the Cromwellian Parliament, the renaming of warships was one of the most immediately obvious results of this return to normality. This should not be surprising, as it was aboard the *Naseby*, the only 1st-rate ship-of-the-line built by the Commonwealth, that King Charles II, accompanied by his brother James, Duke of York, Admiral Sir Edward Montagu and Samuel Pepys, Secretary to the Board of Admiralty, embarked on 23 May 1660 at The Hague in Holland. Named in honour of the Parliamentary forces' most famous victory, this great vessel's title was the subject of an after-dinner discussion, and, not surprisingly, it was decided that she should become *Royal Charles*, while the *Richard* (named after Cromwell's son – 'Tumble-down Dick') became the *Royal James* and *Resolution* reverted to *Prince Royal*. However, the king's self-indulgence and self-obsession soon reduced the nation's Navy to a pale shadow of its former self and, when the Dutch sailed up the Medway, all three vessels were captured, burnt or both. Funds which should have gone to the defence of the realm were squandered because of, in the measured words of Thomas Curson Hansard, when recording parliamentary debates, 'The loose dissipation of the King having still added to his great pecuniary difficulties'. Pepys had been dismissed and few new warships were built in this period. Not until after several wasted years was Pepys reinstated to his former official position by Admiral Edward Russell, 1st Earl of Orford, and matters were taken firmly in hand. With the growing maritime power of France and Holland menacing the nation more and more, and at the constant urging of Pepys and a few others, and against still massive indifference in Parliament, finally, on 23 February 1677, a fleet replacement programme was reluctantly funded, to the tune of £600,000.

The rebuilding of the fleet, 'The 30 great ships programme' of 1677, was recognised at the time, without exaggeration, as being, 'a great undertaking', and comprised a single 1st-rate, the *Britannia*, nine 2nd-rates, whose approved displacement of 900 tons was increased to 1,100 tons at the king's insistence on 17 May, and twenty 3rd-rates, most of them to be built in the King's shipyards of Deptford and Woolwich in London, and Chatham, Harwich and Portsmouth, under the master shipwright Daniel Furzer, the latter being selected to construct *Coronation*. King Charles also expressed the wish that the ships were undertaken as a coherent whole class, standardised, taking as the construction matrix not the length of the keel, as hitherto, but by their gun decks, and each new warship had her plans drawn up on vellum by Edmund Dummer.

Each vessel consumed 2,000 oaks and for such a large programme stocks proved scarce. A labour force of one hundred men per ship was also required, and included shipwrights, caulkers, ropemakers, scavelmen (who kept the drainage ditches and dykes of the dockyards clear) and general labourers.

It was not until 1682 that the keel of a new vessel was laid. Even then the money was not available, other than in fits and starts, and it took three further years before the ship, a 90-gun, three-decker ship-of-the-line, built in Navy Board style, was finally launched by Master Shipwright Isaac Betts at Portsmouth Dockyard on 23 May 1685. *Coronation* was one of nine such vessels constructed and she had a gun-deck of 160 feet 4 inches (48.8696m) which enabled her to carry such a heavy armament. Overall her keel was of 140 feet (42.672m) length with a beam of 44 feet 9 inches (13.6398m), a depth in hold of 18 feet 2 inches (5.5372m) and draught aft of 16 feet 4 inches (4.9784m) and she had a burthen of 1,427 tons. She conformed to the accepted 'Royalist' theme naming policy, and this 2nd-rated vessel was christened as *Coronation*. She lay idle and uncompleted for several more years, again principally due to lack of funding for the necessary fitments to complete her for sea. Her timbers rotted, fungi grew and she lay almost forgotten until the Treasury once more reluctantly supplied the money to see the job finished. Such neglect at Portsmouth, where the *Coronation*, *Ossory* and *Vanguard* were constructed, was blamed by Sir Anthony Deane on lack of maintenance, and the man on the spot, Sir Richard Beach, put it down to lack of ventilation due to laxity in obeying standing orders to open the gun ports every morning and close them every night and, later, shifted the blame to the use of unseasoned timber. With a new keel required before she could be finished, this cheese-paring policy cost more in the long run, but this has continued to be the peacetime norm of Government funding of British defence forces right up to the present day.

Even with an influx of money, it was highly suspected that not all the rotted sections of her hull were totally replaced and that she was not fully sound from the time when she did put to sea. Whether this was the case or not, finally her masting and sails were supplied, and her cannon were brought aboard and emplaced. Designed as a 90-gun ship, she actually carried more than this at the time of her loss – a mixed armament of twenty-two 32-pounder (14.5kg) British demi-cannon on her lower gun deck, twenty-six 17.5-pounder (7.9kg) ordinary culverins on her middle gun deck, with four more on her lower gun deck, twenty-six 9-pounder (6.8kg) British sakers on her upper gun deck, ten 6-pounder (3.8kg) British light sakers on her quarterdeck and a pair of British 3-pounders (1.36kg) in her roundhouse. Her major guns were cast by Thomas Westerne who, with Charles Harvie, leased the John Sackville foundry at Brede, Rother, East Sussex, from 1662 to 1673.

The *Coronation* was first commissioned on 14 February 1690 under the command of Captain John Munden, as Flagship of Vice-Admiral Sir Ralph Delavall. It was not only her construction that suffered such financial parsimony, however; designed to accommodate a wartime crew of around 660 officers and men, there were insufficient trained men and it was thought she sailed off to war short-handed.

Her only major naval action was the defeat at the Battle of Beachy Head on 30 June 1690 where an Anglo-Dutch Fleet under Admiral Arthur Herbert, Earl of Torrington, was soundly trounced by the numerically far superior French fleet under Admiral Anne-Hilarion de Contentin, Comte de Tourville.

Torrington all along counselled against battle lest undertaken in the most favourable condition and with the maximum strength. He maintained that by keeping the 'Fleet in being' until such an opportunity arose, its very presence would restrict and hamper the enemy and negate its aims and ambitions. However, after Queen Mary II, in the absence of King William III, had sought the counsel of Thomas Osborne, Marquess of Carmarthen, and Secretary of State Daniel Finch, Earl of Nottingham, Admiral Russell ordered Torrington to engage. Having notably failed to do so with much vigour, Torrington was flung into the Tower of London as a coward and forced to face a court martial for leaving his Dutch allies, under Admiral Cornelis Evertsen, to do most of the fighting. He was ultimately acquitted of the charges but the king was unimpressed and he was dismissed from his position as First Lord of the Admiralty.

Munden also left the *Coronation* and became captain of the 3rd-rate *Lenox*. Although a 'tarpaulin' (an officer of humble origins who had come up from the ranks in an age of mainly gentlemen commanders), John later went on to become an admiral. On 29 October 1690 a new officer was appointed to be the second officer to command the *Coronation*, this worthy being Captain Charles Skelton. He was an experienced mariner having commanded the 3rd-rate *Bedford* in 1689–90.

Coronation formed part of the Channel Fleet under Russell, who flew his flag aboard the 1st-rate ship-of-the-line *Royal Sovereign*.[3] Russell now adopted the more aggressive policy toward the enemy he had advocated of Torrington and sought to actively blockade their Channel bases. The fleet, having provisioned in Torbay, sailed on 28 August to resume their patrol, in heavy force, seventy major British and Dutch warships accompanied by a host of smaller vessels but while in the vicinity of Ushant on 1 September, an SSE gale began to develop and the fleet tried to run for the safety of Plymouth Sound. In order to avoid the notorious Eddystone Reef, Russell ordered the ships to steer along the southern coast of Cornwall and Devon but, as the wind continued to increase enormously, the fleet was soon in trouble here also. The Rame Peninsula in Cornwall acts as the western bulwark for the major naval port of Plymouth, Devon, and the anchorage of Plymouth Sound. In its centre is Rame Head with the fourteenth-century chapel at its peak. The notorious reef known as the Eddystone Rocks, on which many a vessel foundered down the centuries, is nine miles (14km) to the south but Rame comprises the same unyielding Precambrian metamorphic rock (*gneiss*) and is just as unforgiving. Penlee Point (*Penn Legh*) is at the eastern extremity, with Lady Cove to the west and Penlee Cove to the east.

On 3 September 1691 the whole fleet was caught by the now massive gale and many ships sought refuge in Plymouth, but to reach there they had to claw their way around Penlee Point. This proved a hazardous undertaking indeed and many a proud vessel failed to make it in the horrendous conditions prevailing. The 3rd-rate *Harwich* made a run for safety but was soon in trouble, then was rammed by the 3rd-rate *Elizabeth* and ended up smashed to matchwood on the rocks at Maker Point; the 3rd-rates

---

3. The former famed *Sovereign of the Seas.*

Northumberland and *Royal Oak* both went ashore, but were later refloated; some small vessels foundered in the Hamoaze or went ashore at Cattewater.

Witnessing several ships that attempted to reach Plymouth only to pay the ultimate price, the *Coronation* herself sought such shelter as she could close to the dangerous headland, putting down her best bower, the heaviest anchor aboard, a five-ton monster 16 feet 6 inches (5m) in length and 8.25 feet (2.5m) across the flukes, and hoping its cable would hold firm. The rocky seabed between Rame Head and Penlee offered little purchase, however, in the prevailing conditions. On such an open, lee shore, this attempt to hold her proved a false hope, the storm was too fierce and it is thought that while her cable was still being paid out water began pouring into her below. This was either due to a leak sprung in her rotten timbers, or because, as one account has it, that the crew had not closed the ship's gun ports or, according to one historian, that her ports were not caulked.[4]

Another authority claims that she 'rolled away her masts'.[5] All her three masts went overboard, though whether this was due to the ferocious gusts of wind snapping them off as by one account, or that Captain Skelton deliberately ordered them to be cut away in a last-ditch frantic effort to reduce the impact of the gale, bring the ship upright and so save his craft, as another version has it, are, like most of her final moments, unclear. One account stated that *Coronation* was 'Dismasted, with only an Ensign flying from her stern'. The Admiralty report stated that:

ye *Coronation* which was overset off ye Ramhead, on ye Coast of Cornwall. Resolved, the opinion of the Court is, that by a Butt-head starting, or some Planke giving way Shee spring a Leake, and thereby was lost.

In his journal, the Chief Mate of Russell's flagship, Edward Barlow, recorded:

A second-rate ship, the *Coronation*, coming into the Sound her anchors being let drop and veering out cable to her up, she took a Salley and sank down to righties in about 22 fathoms.[6]

Whatever the truth of the matter, all these last-minute desperate attempts to try and save her were too late and the *Coronation* capsized, whereupon the upturned wreck, went down in twenty-two fathoms (40m) in latitude 50° 18' 34.2" North, 04° 11' 58.8,"[7] East Lady Cove, the wreckage being driven close inshore by the southerly gale.

---

4. Hepper, David J., *British Warship Losses in the Age of Sail, 1650–1859*, 1994, Rotherfield,. Jean Boudriot Publications.

5. Page, William FSA (Editor) – *The Victorian History of Hampshire and the Isle of Wight*, Vol 5, Orig. 1912, Woodbridge, Boydell & Brewer.

6. Barlow, Edward, *Barlow's journal of his life at sea in King's ships: East & West Indiamen & other merchantmen from 1659 to 1703*, Hurst & Blackett, London.

7. Maritime & Coastguard Agency site location.

What man had laboured to construct over so many years, and the French had failed to harm in the heat of battle, nature had destroyed in a few brief moments.

The longboat was somehow launched into the maelstrom into which a few men scrambled, while others clung to the masts and spars. Only between seventeen and twenty-three of her ship's company (again accounts vary) of her nominal 600 officers and men survived and Captain Skelton was not among them.

The other ships of the fleet gave widely differing locations of the disaster, perhaps not surprisingly considering the ferocity of the elements at the time. The 2nd-rate *Ossory* recorded seeing the wreck 'on shore', while the 2nd-rate *Windsor Castle* reported that *Coronation* was 'overset three miles from shore'. One eyewitness to the disaster was Edward Clement, who was serving aboard the 2nd-rate *Duchess*. He later stated that, as he watched, 'the crew of the wrecked ship were swept off by twenties and they all sank at once'. He compared this to the death of those killed in battle, he having earlier served aboard the 3rd-rate *Cambridge* at the Battle of Beachy Head. At that action 'men who were shot and fell overboard, floated'; by contrast, in the case of the *Coronation*, 'Those who were drowned sank at once'.

Among the many good men lost that terrible day was John Sterry, the *Coronation*'s shipwright, who hailed from St Mary Overie, Southwark. His grieving mother, Elizabeth Sterry, presented the will of her son, drawn up on 6 February 1690 in London, on 1 October 1691 before the Worshipful Thomas Pinfold, Military Doctor of Laws Surrogate of the Venerable and Distinguished Richard Raines, Military Doctor of Laws, Master Keeper Commissary of the Prerogative Court of Canterbury. John, obviously a single man with no widow or children to consider, had made his mother his:

> true and lawfull Attorney to aske demand recover and receive for me and in my name and to my use as well as all money payable to me pursuant to their Majesties Declaration of the twenty third of May Eighty Nine and all and singular such wages same and sumes of money as now is or att any time hereafter shall grown unto me for my owne service or other wises in any of his Majesties Shipps ffriggotts or vessells or any Merchant Shipp or Shipps ...

As 'sole Executrix' Elizabeth was, after payment of 'my just debts fully satisifyed and funerall chargers if any paid', to receive everything. No funeral charges were forthcoming, his mother was duly 'granted of all and singular goods chattels and credits ...'. A shipwright, being a skilled man, who might earn £2. 10d per day[8] could accumulate a useful sum for a widowed mother.

Courts martial were held to enquire into the tragedy, both Captain Skelton and Lieutenant William Passenger being tried *in absentia* on the same date, 22 October 1691. The verdicts on both men were 'Not Guilty'.[9]

---

8. Equivalent to £153.43 in 2014 purchasing power.
9. NA Kew, ADM1/5252/106, ff 106 157, Captain Skelton & ff 107 157, William Passenger, Lieutenant, HMS *Coronation*, Royal Navy. Crime: Loss of HMS *Coronation*.

Today there remain two principal areas of wreckage from *Coronation*, now a Protected Site, broken into two segments some 2624.75ft (800m) apart.[10]

The inshore location had first been identified by fishermen George Sandford and Alan Down in 1967 among the jagged, kelp-covered rocks. Here were found no less than fifty-nine of the iron cannon and four anchors. The offshore location was first discovered in July 1977, by a team under Peter McBride, using a proton precession magnetometer (PPM) at a depth of between approximately fifty-nine and sixty-five feet (18-20m) and at that site a further seventeen guns and three ships' anchors have been found. Further survey work was conducted by Peter Holt in 1996, with the use of a magnetometer. One of these guns (number thirty-nine) was raised and moved to shallower water on the other side of the Sound at Fort Bovisand, Devon, in 1983. It was cleaned up and identified by Peter McBride and later moved in 1996 to the Breakwater Fort. Among the other artefacts discovered, and which confirmed the identity of the wreck, was a folded pewter plate marked with the crest of Captain Skelton.

In 2008 it was reported that unauthorised access had on two occasions caused damage to the site[11] but now the sites are under stricter control. A dedicated 'Diver Trail', with specific locations marked with numbered buoys, was inaugurated on 16 April 2011 by the British Sub-Aqua Club to provide a monitored undersea route to be followed.

---

10. Offshore Site 17 Designation Number 2 Order 1978/321 and Inshore, Site 33 Designation Number 1 order 1988/2138.
11. Cockcroft, Lucy, 'Top 10 Wreck Sites most at Risk of Falling Into Ruin', article in *Daily Telegraph*, 8 July 2008.

Chapter 2

Destroyed by Plague – The *Winchester*, 24 September 1695

'Scurvy Knave' is an epithet that, today, has almost comical connotations with references as such in many Hollywood films and cartoons but, for centuries, both at sea and ashore, there was no humour to be found whatsoever in that disease or the misery it brought in its wake.

Symptoms of scurvy included overwhelming fatigue and lethargy, the mouth developed ulcers, bones began to ache, breathing became difficult and the victim's tongue became white-coated. Toe fungal rot occurred and quickly deteriorated, requiring amputation in some cases, while the stomach became bloated and distended and the skin broke out in irritating sores and rashes. On long-distance voyages its potency was increased and resulted in a huge number of slow, lingering, but invariably certain, deaths. Although the beneficial effects of eating citrus fruits had been frequently noted from the fifteenth century onward, it was not until 1753 that a retired Royal Navy surgeon, Edinburgh-born James Lind, initially published the findings of his experiments with such fruits on combating scurvy.[1]

The issuing of lime juice to the crews of HM ships was sneeringly denigrated by the Americans who originated the term 'Limeys', a name that has endured ever since. However, if not the absolute solution, this move did much to curb the effects of scurvy at sea and was widely imitated by most other nations. However, when it came to spreading death, Yellow Fever was far deadlier, as was demonstrated by what happened to her crew prior to the dreadful loss of the battleship *Winchester*.

HMS *Winchester* (60) was a full-rigged, 934-ton, 146ft 2.5in (44.6m) long, 4th-rate battleship, with a keel length of 121ft (36.881m), a beam of 38ft 2 in (11.6m) and a draught of 16 ft (4.9m). She was designed by William Wyatt and constructed at his shipyard at Bursledon, Hampshire, at a cost of £9,140 (11,635.3€). She was launched on 11 April 1693 and originally had a crew of 285 officers and men. Her first commander was Captain Edward Bibb.[2] Her final voyage commenced from Southampton on 23 January 1695, as part of a fleet of nineteen ships to take part in what became known as 'King William's War' or more commonly the War of the League

1. Lind, James, *A Treatise of the Scurvy in Three Parts Containing an inquiry into the Nature, Causes and Cure of that Disease, together with a Critical and Chronological View of what has been published on the subject*, 1753, London, Andrew Millar.
2. Among Bibb's many previous commands had been the fire-ship *Hopewell*, from 19 January 1691, and the *James Galley*, 1692–93, the 4th-rates *Adventure* and *Weymouth* and the 3rd-rate *Swiftsure*.

of Augsburg or the War of the Grand Alliance (1689–97). King Louis XIV of France had commenced hostilities by forcibly annexing territory along the Rhine and this aggression so alarmed her neighbours that they formed the Alliance of The League of Augsburg in 1686 (The so-called Grand Alliance.) England, most unusually, found herself allied with Spain against France and, on at least three separate occasions, small British fleets had to be hastily despatched to protect the scattered British colonies in both the Caribbean and North America, whose defences (as per usual British practice, both before and ever since, right up to the present day) had been allowed to fall into an alarming state of disrepair and neglect. Much concern was expressed locally throughout these Caribbean colonies at this state of affairs; for example on 7 March the Agents for the Leeward Islands addressed the King himself stating that 'We are much alarmed at the advices from France of preparations of ships of war and land forces to be sent to the West Indies in order to attack the Leeward islands, which are not guarded at sea except by one ship of war, much out of repair.'[3] This assessment has an all too familiar ring to modern readers of course. They entreated His Majesty, 'We beg that you will order some ships of war and land-forces to be sent to the Leeward Islands.'[4]

In due course, the powers-that-be at home duly slowly began to stir themselves and, *pro-tem*, until the planned full squadron of warships and troops could be assembled, it was agreed that a single 5th-rate 32-gun frigate, HMS *Hastings*, (Captain John Draper) should be sent to relieve HMS *Chester* (Captain Thomas Heath) and convey twenty-five tons of naval stores to Barbados.[5] This appeared inadequate as there were reliable reports of at least twelve and maybe as many as nineteen well-armed French privateers, in addition to three warships, all ready for action at Martinique, plus news of a French war fleet preparing for sea at la Rochelle. All this was not just alarmist talk for the French Governor of Martinique, Jean-Baptiste du Cassee, did indeed mount a damaging raid on Jamaica on 27 June which caused great havoc ashore.[6]

The main British invasion convoy sailed from England for Hispaniola on 22 January, the 4th-rate 40-gun frigate HMS *Reserve* (Captain James Lance)[7] escorting fourteen transports, an ordnance store ship, a hospital ship and three civilian merchant vessels. Bad weather conditions earlier in The Downs caused their naval escorts to

---

3. This was the 4th-rate *Tyger*, (Captain Thomas Sherman) built in 1647 and rebuilt as a 44-gun frigate at Deptford Dockyard in 1681.

4. And *et seq*, Fortescue, John William, (editor), *Calendar of State Papers Colonial, America and West Indies, Volume 14: January 1693 – May 1696*,pp.434–52, 1903, London. Institute of Historical Research. J. W. Fortescue KCVO was a military historian, Librarian and Archivist of Windsor Castle and President of the Royal Historical Society.

5. The *Chester* was a 48-gun 4th-rate launched in 1691. She had fought at the Battle of Barfleur in 1692. The Governor of Antigua, Christopher Codrington, reported on 3 July that *Chester* 'has no recruit of naval stores or provisions from home since she came' two years earlier!

6. The similarities of the threat, and the British government reaction to it, to the Falklands scenario 300 years later, are all too evident.

7. This officer is so named in the logbooks of the period, but is also transcribed as Launce, Lawnce and even Lawrence in other contemporary records.

be delayed and they arrived off Falmouth the next day.[8] The 5th-rate 30-gun *Child's Play* (Captain Frederick Weightman)[9] was detached on 4 February to proceed ahead with despatches for St Domingo's governor and on 12 February the fleet anchored in the Funchal Road, Madeira. Here a ferocious storm broke over them which lasted for twenty-four hours; many were forced to slip their anchors and cables and these vessels became dispersed far and wide. Commissary John Murrey, embarked for the passage aboard the convoy's ordnance store ship, along with his two clerks, recorded that 'This afternoon only nine ships out of twenty were in sight. Our captain wished to sail for Jamaica as we could not see the Commodore, but to this I would not consent'.

Murrey's host ship was part of a group of five merchantmen separated from the bulk of the fleet and under escort of *Winchester* along with the 268-ton fireship *Firebrand* (6).[10]

Winchester herself had embarked 150 Royal Marines who were originally to be put ashore where they were to form part of a joint British and Spanish force assembling in Santo Domingo to assail the French in western Hispaniola (present day Haiti). On 17 February the *Winchester* began to beat back to Madeira with these strays to rejoin the fleet, but when, next day, the master of Murrey's ship resolved to proceed to Jamaica on his own, 'the men-of-war bore down and fired at us, so we brought to'. However, after a Council of War it was indeed decided to proceed to Savona, for the wind still remained against them turning back. Murrey wrote on 26 February, 'Four soldiers have died since we started, and twenty more are sick.' On 7 March Murrey transferred

---

8. HM Ships *Dunkirk* (Commodore Wilmot flying his broad pennant), *Winchester* (Captain Thomas Butler), the 5th-rate 24-gun *Ruby* (Captain Thomas Dilkes), the former French *L'Entrepreant*, taken as a prize earlier that year); the 24-gun 6th-rate *Swan* (Captain Timothy Bridges) and two 5th-rate fireships, the *Terrible* (Captain John Fletcher) and the *Firebrand* (Captain John Soule).

9. The former French *Les Jeux* taken as prize.

10. Fireships were originally just that, obsolete vessels filled with combustibles and set ablaze to drift down on anchored enemy fleets who refused to come out and fight. One contemporary description of their lethal cargo can be given here – 'At the bottom of the hold were a hundred barrels of powder; these were covered with pitch, sulphur, rosin, tow, straw, and faggots, over which lay beams bored through, to enable air to flow to feed the fire, and upon these lay three hundred carcasses filled with granadoes, chain-shot, iron bullets, pistols loaded, and wrapt in linen pitched, broken iron bars, amid the bottoms of glass bottles. There were six holes or mouths, to let out the flames, which were so vehement, as to consume the hardest substances, and could be checked by nothing, but the pouring in of hot water.' By the 17th-century they had been much refined from those origins and the Royal Navy was having warships specifically built as a highly-specialised type. They had gun-ports which were hinged along their bottom edges instead of along the top edge and a special fire-room stocked with flammable material and well ventilated for safety until needed. They were lavishly equipped with grapnelling irons to hold the enemy target fasts, and also had vents built in as trunking to spread the conflagration quickly to the ship's upperworks and masting, iron chambers stocked with gunpowder to blow the fireroom ports away and special escape routes, sally ports, aft so the crew could escape safely once the tinderbox had been ignited. Some twenty-three such ships were built from 1691 to 1694, but most served out their lives as conventional sloops-of-war. They were phased out from 1800 onward. See Coggershall, James Lowell, *The Fireship and its role in the Royal Navy. A Thesis*, 1997, Austin TX, University of Texas at Austin.

to the *Winchester*, due to 'the mutinous disposition' of some of the army officers and continued his diary from aboard her.[11]

On 20 March the fleet sighted land, with 'Mariegalante (*sic*) about three leagues distant, and Dominica to the south west. Steered towards Guadeloupe, hoisted French colours as we were among the French islands'. They arrived at Montserrat on 21 March and Nevis before dawn the following day before proceeding to Old Road, St Christopher's[12] in the afternoon, 'with the intention to get water, which is much wanted'. Two days later the *Terrible* and *Dunkirk* arrived and anchored; 'like us ... they had been unable to get back to Madeira and had therefore borne away.' Nine more ships came in on 25 March; 'this day the whole of our fleet was assembled with not one ship lost.'[13]

Ominously, the sloop *Swan* had already brought news to the citizens of Barbados from Bermuda of the state of the British relief fleet and she had reported that 'There was sickness on board of them'. Indeed Murrey's journal confirmed on 28 March that '130 have died since we came out'. There was also widespread sickness aboard the *Tyger* which much reduced her complement and also among the redcoats ashore.[14] Thus it can be seen, even at this early date, that being stationed in the Caribbean was already no sinecure, war or no war. On 29 June Governor Edward Cranfield at Barbados wrote to Charles Talbot, Duke of Shrewsbury, 'Now that we have entered the calm months the sickness increases, and, as the physicians report, with greater malignancy than ever.' Even the Governor of the Barbados succumbed, as also did the enemy; 'They have the distemper at Martinique as severely as we....' Of the other British warships on station the 4th-rate 50-gun, *Bristol* (Captain Edward Gurney) and the 30-gun *Play* (Captain Frederick Weightman) had but one day's provision and there were little or no stocks ashore. On 3 April the convoy sailed for Samana, escorted by the *Reserve, Ruby, Winchester* and *Firebrand*, while the Commodore was embarked aboard the *Dunkirk*, the 4th-rate *Hampshire* (Captain Thomas Symonds whose previous command had been the 8-gun fireship *Speedwell* at the Battle of Barfleur in 1692. Symonds was to die in October when he was replaced by Captain John Fletcher) which joined from Jamaica with its Governor, Colonel Peter Beckford, embarked), and the 6th-rate 24-gun *Swan* (Captain Captain Timothy Bridges). Bridges was to die in August and was replaced by Captain Thomas Kenney) and *Terrible* left for St Domingo to confer with the Spanish Governor, who had promised assistance.

---

11. Despite a joint briefing from the king prior to their departure, which included an entreaty to them to work together harmoniously, relations between the British Navy commander and the Army commander were bad almost from the beginning, and deteriorated rapidly into outright antagonism – which explained much about how the venture ultimately turned out.
12. St Kitts.
13. Sainsbury, William Noel (editor), *Calendar of State Papers Colonial*, 1693–1696, No. 198, *Commissary Murrey's Journal of the Expedition to Hispaniola*, pp.546–56, 1880, London, Institute for Historical Research.
14. A memo sent to the king from Colonel Henry Holt on 14 June, noted that: 'The regiment formerly commanded by Colonel Godfrey Lloyd and now by myself has been for five years abroad in a very unhealthy climate, and has suffered much ... by the pestilential diseases of the country ... whereby three-fourths of the Regiment have perished.'

War operations finally got underway with the landing of the soldiers and marines from the fleet which had sailed in two sections from St Christopher's and St Domingo on 26/28 March. The object of this sortie was a pre-emptive attack on the French before they could themselves mount a second raid, or even an all-out invasion of Jamaica. British naval forces under Commodore Robert Wilmot and the troops under Colonel Luke Lillingston,[15] with a little Spanish assistance, ('three very indifferent ships but well manned') had assembled on 8 May at Bayahá[16] and landed at Manchioneel Bay, seizing the most easterly French settlement in Hispaniola with the loss of just a single man, and then moved on overland to assail Port d'Espe. After a disastrous twelve-day march through the jungle and swamps, the headstrong Lillingston lost many of his men to sickness and had to be reinforced before he could resume hostilities. Commodore Wilmot's sailors and marines stormed and captured the fort at Port de Paix (Pòdepè) almost unaided, as well as taking possession of Fort Cap François.[17] Meanwhile Lillingston[18] had also fallen sick, as did his brother, Major Jarvis Lillingston, of the same regiment, while his regiment itself had been reduced to just a pitiful strength of forty fit men. Not surprisingly then the campaign stalled before Petit Guavas and Léogâne, the real objectives of the Allied invasion, could be assailed and taken. The Spanish proved themselves more concerned with the captured slaves 'and other plunder' than fighting, and refused to go any further. After much ill-tempered wrangling the Commodore decided to cut his losses and re-group and the fleet re-embarked the survivors on 17 July and left Hispaniola, arriving back at Port Royal on 23 July, but not before making one fatal decision.

Many of the ship's supplies and water had run out during the campaign and before they upped anchor the water stocks were replenished from sources on Hispaniola. *Winchester* re-joined the fleet and headed for Port Royal, Jamaica. But already all was far from well aboard the ship; scurvy had taken a hold and quickly spread. Worse still, the water that had been embarked at Hispaniola proved contaminated and soon deaths from plague began to occur. Commissioner Murrey recorded that both his assistants had also died by 27 July, while, on 24 August, Lieutenant-Governor Sir William Beeston was advising Secretary of State Sir John Trenchard that 'Colonel Lillingston is sick himself and so are his officers; about half his men are lost and the rest so unfit for further service that they are all very sickly and weak, and some die

---

15. Colonel Jonathan ffoulkes had died shortly after arrival in the West Indies and Lillingston assumed his command and rank. See Cannon, Richard, *Historical Records of the British Army: comprising the History of every Regiment in Her Majesty's Service*, 1837, London, Parker, Furnival and Parker.
16. Fort Dauphin
17. Known today as Cap Haïtien.
18. Major Lillingston finally died on 15 July but Colonel Luke survived to make sarcastic (and some say scurrilous) insinuations about Wilmot's behaviour as a likely contributory cause to the *Winchester*'s loss in 1702. It would appear that even the latter's demise had not mitigated the depth of detestation between the two men. Lillingston later became a brigadier general and died in April 1713.

daily'. Contemporary accounts concerning the *Winchester*, confirmed by other ships in the squadron,[19] give a grim account of a mounting death toll, one man per day succumbing to disease while being refitted at Port Royal – a number which was soon to begin to escalate rapidly.

It was decided that forces on hand were too slender to make a second attack and so the transports were discharged. Captain Bibb was sent ashore at Jamaica suffering from scurvy and sickness and Captain Thomas Butler took command of the sick and ailing crew for the voyage of the fleet back to England.[20]

What remained of the squadron set sail for home from Port Royal on 3 September 1695. Some ships had been so debilitated by the ravages of the disease that they were unable to sail and during the three long weeks it took the remainder (the 6th-rate *Terrible*, the 5th-rate *Experiment*, *Winchester* and the *Dunkirk*) to reach the vicinity of the eastern Florida coast, another 140 men had died aboard the British ships while many more lay either dying or listless and unable to fully function. The toll steadily mounted; *Winchester*'s log recorded how, on 9 September, three men were buried at sea, next day another four were put over the side and the following day another nine. On the last date, 11 September, the log recorded how, with moderate winds, 'we split our spreet sail (Spritsail), top sail and mizzentop sail, not having the men to tend our sails and not more than 10 well on their feet'. On 12 September *Winchester* buried a further seven of her crew at sea and on 13 September the log recorded, 'Our men die very fast. We buried 8 men'.

Other ships in company were suffering from the ravages of disease also; the *Terrible*, the flagship of the squadron with Commodore Robert Wilmot aboard, reported on 9 September, 'Our men begin to fall sick,' while on Saturday 14 September her entry read, 'Our men almost all sick'. On this latter date a long entry in *Winchester*'s captain's log recorded the mounting difficulties and problems of keeping the ships together and the mounting horror of deaths.

This 24 hours fair weather blowing fresh yesterday about 3 in the afternoon we made the Signall by hawling up Sailes and firing of Gunns for ye Squadron to stay for us, they running away and Left us Disabled we had not 7 men Well our Shipp increasing upon us by the water She made in the hold and we Left Destitute of all ability to pump it out our people being all dead and Sick and my Self with my Distemper and ye Griefe I entertained at these Dismall Calameties, was of the opinion of all a Dying Daily. In ye Night we made Severall false fires

19. Captains' Logs, including *Winchester*, 1693 April 11 to 1695 September 2, ADM51/4395; *Experiment*, 1694 September 6 to 1694, October 10, ADM51/328; *Terrible*, 1694 May 18 to 1694 May 23, ADM51/4367; and *Firebrand*, 1699 9 January to 1699 May 24, ADM51/355, held at National Archives, Kew, London.
20. Ill as he was, this saved Bibb's life and he survived to go on to command successively four 3rd-rate battleships – the *Norfolk* from October 1694; the *York* in 1697; the *Monck* in June 1699 off Great Yarmouth under Vice-Admiral John Benbow on the Dunkirk Station, (ADM106/482.106, National Archives, Kew, London) and the *Monmouth* in 1701. He died on 10 February 1701.

but had no Return to it this morning we Spreed our Ensigne[21] at the foretopmast Shrouds & fired Severall gunns but no Notice yett taken of us we than having 4½ foot Water in the hold our Gunner dyed this morning about 10 a clock we buryed 17 men.

Meanwhile the sloop–rigged fireship *Firebrand,* late out from Port Royal and escorting a brigantine bound for the Carolinas and New York, caught up with and joined the squadron on this day.

On 15 September *Winchester* buried a further dozen men but rank was no protection against 'Yellow jack' and on this self-same day the log of the *Terror* recorded that Commodore Wilmot 'parted this life and at 4 this afternoon was buried and Captain Lance hoisted the broad pennant on board the *Experiment*'. The *Firebrand* also recorded how 'at 4 they buried him overboard at which time his sloop fired 20 guns'. Significantly Wilmot is said to have expired 'of the fever'. The weather continued to deteriorate to add to their woes, *Winchester* recording on 16 September, 'Fresh gales this morning much rain and thunder. We buried 25 men'. The entry for the next day read 'Dark and blowing weather. At 10 at night we split our main topsail for want of strength and got them down. We buried 10 men' and on 18 September again, 'Fresh gales, we daily throwing our men overboard. Buried today 5 men'. Nor was the new Commodore to be spared, dying at 1400 that afternoon and being consigned to the deep four hours later, *Experiment* recording for her part that day, 'Captain Lance died this evening – we struck ye broad pennant'. Lance was replaced as captain by Lieutenant David Lloyd, but his demise left Captain Thomas Butler of the *Winchester* as Senior Officer. As recorded in her log, he duly tried to sort the commands out as best he could and explained their predicament in detail.

This 24 hours close weather with fresh gales. This morning I took possession of the *Dunkirk* and issued orders for ye rest of ye captains of ye squadron to obey what further orders they should receive from me from time to time. I then gave Captain Soule a commission to command ye *Winchester* for he having eldership and preference for it. I gave another to Captain Hickman[22] ye first lieutenant of ye *Dunkirk* to command the *Firebrand* Fireship.–I find by with examination having made it ye *Dunkirk* is almost in as bad and weak condition as I left ye *Winchester* in for want of men, her company being almost dead and sick. Insomuch it for my part with tears in my eyes & grief accompanying my West Indian distemper, I cannot see yet which way it is possible to save one of our ships, ye captains all sick, those yet are already dead, dayly *(sic)* dying & dropping ye poor seamen hourly thrown overboard insomuch yet ye living can scarcely bury ye dead. But this mortality cannot last long for God knows we are in a weak and miserable condition. I propose God willing when the weather will go to call a Council of

21. Hoisting the ship's flag upside down was the internationally recognised signal of distress.
22. Joseph Hickman, he continued to command the *Firebrand* until 1698.

War to determine what to do for the preservation through I see no place to go for us nearer than Virginia, which is above 300 leagues off.

At 0500 they had sighted another sail and the *Experiment* gave chase. On overhauling the vessel she proved to be a Spanish warship out from Cadiz and bound for Cuba. As the alliance was still officially in force, after staying overnight with the squadron, she was allowed to proceed about her business.

On 20 September Captain Butler further recorded events in one of the last entries in *Winchester*'s log (Captain John Soule's own personal log did not survive) in this manner:

'Yesterday on the decease of Captain Lance I was carried aboard the *Dunkirk* and took possession of her then gave Captain Soule a commission to command the *Winchester* having the next pretension.' *Dunkirk* then hoisted the Commodore's pennant.

The usual route for sailing vessels entailed passing Cape San Antonio, the westernmost tip of Cuba, and steering north-east sailing close to the Florida Keys in order to pick up Gulf Stream and the Trade Winds to take passage eastward across the Atlantic. This was the normal routine and on 21 September they caught a glimpse of the port of Havana, '5 leagues to the south-east'. The weather was fair but the gale veered from ESE to SSE but around 0100 veered more southerly, forcing them to tack to the east. Eventually they gave up the idea of reaching Cuba, the log of the *Firebrand* recording how they found, 'we could not go to Matanzas'.[23] With Cape Hafiaus some eight leagues off bearing SE by E the decision was that the wind gave them no choice but to press on to Virginia. A Council of War was duly called aboard the *Dunkirk* the next day which confirmed that decision: 'we resolved to go for Vergnia (*sic*), there to recruit what men we had left with fresh provisions and to wood & water our ships in which we were scant.' At 1800 the following day *Terrible* recorded the sighting of the Keys to the westward of the Cape Keys, 'so we tack and stands off till 2 a clock ye next morning'.

The hazards were clearly known but the weather remained adverse. On 23 September the *Experiment* logged how 'We have had ye wind from ye East to ye ENE, a small gale with fine weather' while *Terrible* was recording:

This 24 hours a fresh gale of wind this morning at two a clock we tacks and stands in till 10 then we saw the land bearing NNE we supposed to be near to Cape Keys we tacks and stands off till 4 in the afternoon and then bore away to leeward to a brigantine till near 6 at night and then the Keys bore N by W nearest distance 13 or 14 miles we tacks and stands away NNE the wind at East but about 9 or 10 a clock it veers to the ENE at 12 the Commodore fires 2 guns and puts

---

23. A harbour situated on the north-west coast of Cuba.

out his lights to go about we being a good bit of astern bears up and brings to the other way and lies by a glass in that time the Commodore comes up with us and presently we hear guns ...

The source of the firing was seen to be the *Winchester*.

This was the first record that the squadron was aware the *Winchester* was in trouble. In fact, she was doomed. It was said that only eight of *Winchester*'s crew, under First Lieutenant John Hisket and Sailing Master Andrew Mallard, remained healthy and able to operate the vessel by the time she met her fate at night off the Keys, 'ye rest being sick to ye number of 50 men and boys or thereabout'. These few were unable to prevent the *Winchester* from being lost, despite the fact that lead-line soundings were being taken hourly and no bottom being found at 2300 hours. But only a few hundred yards separated this deep water from the jagged reef offshore when, with the wind veering once more to the east, Butler ordered the squadron to head for the Bahama Channel. The skeleton crew of the *Winchester* attempted to comply but before she could be worn round Mallard recorded, she 'struck a ledge of rocks which lye about four leagues to ye north of ye Cape, and about ye like distance from ye shore'.

The date was 24 September and she had unexpectedly smashed herself into a coral reef off one of the northernmost islets and was there impaled on the Elkhorn and Staghorn pinnacles and holed (bilged). She was impaled there with her dead, sick and dying crew, estimated at three hundred originally but now very much reduced.

Mallard's memories of Tuesday 24 September gave stark witness of the swiftness of her end: 'before we could half wear her shee struck and sitt fast all the men we had could not furell the maintopsil.' The ship's yawl was lowered to ascertain whether she could be got off. A powerful south-western current made it all the four rowers could do to keep the boat adjacent to the ship, but soundings revealed that there was a depth of seven feet (2.1336m) above the reef, with sixteen feet (4.8768m) under her stern.[24]

We can also refer again to the logs of the closest surviving vessel to the *Winchester* for some subsequent clues as to her fate. The *Dunkirk*[25] recorded:

At 12 last night we Tack'd and stood to ye Leeward ye Weather fair but ye wind fresh wee mett ye *Winchester* standing to ye Florida shore Norward & sometime after heard Gunns fir'd without Intermission by wich wee apprehend a farther addition to our increasing sorrows for wee did believe ye *Winchester* was Run'd aground but could give them noe releife in ye night being very dark & ye wind blowing directly upon ye Shore ...

---

24. Master's Log HMS *Winchester*, 11 April to 24 September 1695 – ADM 52/120; Captain's Log HMS *Winchester*, 11 April to 20 September 1695 – ADM 51/4395; and Court Martial Enquiry , loss of HMS *Winchester*, 1680 – ADM 1/5256; all National Archives, Kew, London.
25. She was the former 60-gun battleship *Worcester*, which had been renamed in 1660, to honour the capture of that port in 1657.

The *Firebrand* noted:

> These past 24 hours we have had hazy weather intermittent with squalls blowing fresh at E and S to the NE by E. Last night at 12 a clock we tacked and stood to the northward for the Flaurady (*sic*) shore till 1½ past one in the morning and then the signal was made for the fleet to go about or toward and bring them about the other tack and in warning the *Winchester* run aground at which the *Winchester* fired several guns …

The log of the *Experiment* for this date had 'A fresh gale with squalls of rain. Ye fleet being by ye a count about 6 or 7 leagues from ye land & at 12 said night we all tacked & stood to ye south end'. However, 'in tacking ye *Winchester* running upon a reef that lies about 3 or 4 leagues from ye land & was lost & this day at noon I observed & found myself in ye latitude as margent ye *Winchester* for bearing from us at ye same time W by S distance 2 or 3 leagues ye land plain to be seen …!'

It transpired the *Winchester* had not gone aground on land but had come to grief on an unknown coral reef offshore. Situated six miles from the coast of North Key Largo on the Florida Keys, the Carysfort Reef is about six miles in length. One American scuba diver has described this reef as 'not only one of the largest, but one of the most mature reefs in the chain' and also 'one of the healthier reefs in the chain'.[26] The reef took its name from HMS *Carysfort*.[27]

At first light the *Dunkirk* hauled about and ventured back close to the land and found the *Winchester* pinned like a butterfly and beyond salvation.

> ab't break of day wee Tack'd & bore down & found ye *Winchester* biueldg (*sic*) on a reife ab't 3 Leagues from ye Main wee having w'th us a Brigantine bound to New Yorke I man'd him & sent him to ye *Winchester* by w'ch means sav'd about 100 sick and 10 well men wich were left of near 300 y't came from Jamaica we could save nothing of Stores it being too dangerous lying imbayed on a Lee Shore.

---

26. Bertelli, Brad, 'Snorkelling Into History: Carysfort Reef', article in *Keys.net Reporter*, 6 April 2012.
27. But, never, *ever*, as Bertelli would have it, *Carrysford*. HMS *Carysfort* as she always was, had in fact been named in honour of John Joshua Proby, the Whig politician and diplomat, who became 1st Baron, Lord Carysfort. The title originates with this Irish Peerage, but commemorates the far older fort built in County Wicklow and named after Henry Cary, 1st Viscount Falkland (1625–28), and named Cary's Fort (*Criesfort*).] She was a 118-feet long, 6th-rate 28-gun frigate, the first ship of that name of course, and had been launched at Sheerness in 1766. She saw successful service in both the American War taking several privateers. On 23 October 1770, while under the command of Captain William Hay, and working from Jamaica, she struck the then uncharted reef and the coral pierced her hull but she survived and got away. The reef was duly noted on the charts of the day and named after her near-victim. *Carysfort* later served throughout the French Revolutionary War, seeing action in both the East Indies and, again, the West Indies. Her most famous action was that in which she re-captured the larger frigate *Castor*, sailing under French colours, on 29 May 1794.

The *Experiment* stated that 'this morn ye brigantine went in & fasht (*sic*) off all ye men from ye *Winchester* for bearing from us at ye same time W by S distance 2 or 3 leagues'. The *Terrible* logged that:

> This 24 hours a fresh gale; as soon as it was day we saw the *Winchester* lie fast aground with her sails aback about 9m or 10m N of Cape Florida. We and the *Experiment* and a brigantine bore down to her as near as conveniently we could, and Captain Butler went on board with his boat and save the men for there was no hopes of ye ship, he came away and left her.

It was later alleged that not all that could have been saved were saved, even though the brigantine's crew were 'Under pain of death' to save all they could. One historian stated that 'Others were left to perish in the surf because they had broken into the spirit-room, and were hopelessly drunk!'[28]

The *Firebrand* recorded events thus: 'we stood off til 6 in the morning then we see her aground close by the shore so the Commodore sent the Brigantine down to her.' Both the *Terrible* and *Experiment* were signalled by Butler to join in the rescue operation, 'so they saved all the men only one and at noon she bear SW past about 4 or 5 degrees. The place where she run ashore lies in the latitude of 25.36.' Later she noted that the brigantine returned from the vicinity of the wreck and reported that 'the *Winchester* could not be got off so we made the best of our way for Vergnia'.

On the afternoon of 24 September, the survivors were transferred aboard the *Dunkirk* who, 'Gave them an entry on ye *Dunkirk* books'.

The squadron had managed to effect the rescue of 110 men including Captain Soule, along with his and the Master's logs, but Soule, unhappily, died later aboard his rescuer just as final safe-keeping was at hand. The *Dunkirk*'s log entry for 6 October recorded this final irony.

> At 8 this morning we came to sail, and by 11 anchored in 12 fathoms in James River, Point Comfort bore N E 2 miles. At 12 last night Captain Soule departed this life with very grief for the loss of ye *Winchester*. This morning we buried him on Point Comfort & fired 12 guns.

The *Dunkirk* herself had survived, although many of her own crew were also ill, as had the rest of the squadron. But, on dropping anchor in the James River, they found to their dismay their longed-for haven and sanctuary was much lacking in charity and offered only cold comfort after all their trials and tribulations. Not surprisingly,

---

28. Hannay, David, *A Short History of the Royal Navy 1217–1815*. 2 Vols. 1898 and 1909, London, Methuen & Co. Hannay was a highly respected writer on naval affairs of his day, a Lecturer at the Royal Naval College, Greenwich, and founding member of the Naval Records Society and contributor to their magazine *The Mariner's Mirror*. His allegation in this regard should therefore command respect as regards to authenticity.

perhaps, the locals were far from enamoured at having a squadron of plague-ridden ships arrive on their doorstep. *Dunkirk*'s log entry contains this plaintive notation for 8 October: 'We are daily endeavouring with the planters to get fresh provisions to recruit our poor men & sloops to fetch water but ye inhabitants are very unreasonable with us.' Not until a fortnight later was *Dunkirk* able to record that 'Our men begin to recruit having fresh provisions'.

Eventually the squadron was refreshed enough to risk the next leg of the journey back to England, but their ordeal was far from over for the weather and the sea had not done with them yet. Naturally, with so many men incapacitated, the deterioration of the ships in the earlier gales had been impossible to make good, and so it was that, after the squadron sailed from Cape Henry on 7 November, they were subjected to the full blast of winter in the North Atlantic. Storms were continuous and the ships became separated. All finally made port, but in an awful state.[29]

As for the unfortunate *Winchester* herself, she has since been awarded, by some at least, the dubious distinction of having the accolade (albeit of dubious validity) of the first recorded North American shipwreck. The crystal waters closed over the *Winchester* for two-and-a-half centuries and it was not until 1938 that traces of the wreck, in the form of a ship's cannon visible on the bottom through the clear waters, were stumbled upon, perchance, by two local fishermen, Sam Lynch and Jacob Monroe. These worthies realised that the find was a significant one and initially kept it to themselves while they debated how they could best avail themselves of their discovery. Soon after, they were out fishing again and ran out of fuel while close to Elliot Key.[30] They managed to pole themselves ashore and contacted local historian Charles Mann Brookfield at the Ledbury Lodge on Elliott Key, the most northerly of the keys and nowadays part of the Biscayne National Park. From what they learned from this encounter the pair decided that Brookfield was a man who would know best what to do with their find and the following day they duly informed him that they had seen many cannon on the seabed along the reef.

Brookfield was, naturally, excited at the news and in due course, with Attorney Hugh Merritt Matheson, hired professional divers and obtained the use of an ocean-going barge, the *Charles W. Baird*, and thus organised an impromptu salvage attempt. During the winter of 1938–39, and again in June 1940, this search duly located and

---

29. The fates of these surviving ships are as follows: *Dunkirk* (60) – was rebuilt as a 4th-rate at Blackwall on the Thames in 1704 and re-built for the second time in 1734 at Portsmouth; she survived until 1749 when she was broken up; *Terrible* – originally a fire-ship, re-rated a 6th-rate in 1696, as a fire-ship once more in 1703 and a 5th-rate in 1710. She met an ignominious end, surrendering to the Spanish off Cape St Vincent in 1710; *Experiment* (32) was a long-serving vessel, whose life was extended by being re-built in 1727. She was finally broken up in 1738; *Firebrand* – she served for a further twelve years before, while under the command of Captain Francis Percy, she herself was wrecked on the Outer Gilstone Rock, Isles of Scilly, on the night of 22 October 1707 as described in Chapter 4.

30. Weller, Robert 'Frogfoot', *Famous Shipwrecks of the Florida Keys; Volume I*, pp.29–33, 1990, Birmingham AL, EBSCO Media.

recovered no less than thirty-four cannon barrels, some ships' anchors, a few cannon balls, musket balls, some silver coinage and (it is said) parts of a Latin prayer book,[31] which had been lodged beneath one of the cannon and preserved by the sand. These finds were all located some mile-and-a-half south-west of Carysfort Reef Light in Latitude 25° 51' 10' North, Longitude 80° 44' 00" West, not too distant from present-day Turtle Harbor. These artefacts were salvaged but the precise identity of the ship remained unconfirmed. Later examination and detective work at the Admiralty back in London, revealed that the cannon had the Tudor Rose Crown cast in relief and the letters 'T', 'W' and 'H' engraved on their trunnions.[32] They also found coins dated 1694 with Britannia on them, which matched those known to have been carried aboard the *Winchester*. In January 1941 *National Geographic Magazine* published an article by Brookfield and his salvage efforts.[33]

The Second World War got in the way of further meaningful searches but in 1960 charter boat skipper Bobby Klein had divers locate further evidence: pewter plates and jugs, brass dividers for navigation, silver buckles, ballast stones common to the River Thames, and even a gold watch.

In 1962, after two decades had elapsed, *National Geographic* revived interest in the Brookfield story[34] which rehashed the *Winchester* sinking and featured Brookfield's theory that her loss was largely due to the debilitating effect of widespread scurvy among her crew. This, in turn, stimulated public action in exploring the site and further diving work was done. Across the Atlantic a British medical specialist examined all the evidence there was from three hundred years earlier. He concluded that both scurvy and dysentery had taken its toll of the crew, making them prone to all manner of disease, and that their condition had probably been compounded, while ashore in Haiti, by drinking water infested by mosquito larvae, with the result that many contracted Yellow Fever with resulting death.

Noted Miami historian, the late Dr William Marcellus Straight, was an acquaintance of Brookfield and he challenged the scurvy theory as being the sole cause of the disaster. He was challenged by Brookfield to advance an alternate theory and, after detailed examination of what evidence there was, came to a different conclusion.[35]

Straight concluded that, certainly, the standard provisions supplied to HM ships, beef, pork and pease pudding,[36] oatmeal, butter, cheese, bread and weevil-ridden

31. The *Litany of Loreto* dating from 1587 as approved by Pope Sixtus V.
32. These were the manufacturer marks of Thomas Westerne, who had a cannon foundry at Ashburnham, Sussex, between 1669 and 1688.
33. Brookfield, Charles M., 'Cannon on Florida Reefs Solve Mystery of Sunken Ship', article in *The National Geographic Magazine*, No. 80, dated December 1941, pp.807–24. See also Brookfield, *Personal papers*, (5 boxes); Miami Archives & Research Center, Reference 65, Miami Fla.
34. Brookfield, Charles M., 'America's First Undersea Park', article in *National Geographic Magazine*, No. 121, January 1962, pp.58–69.
35. Straight, Dr William M., 'The Bilging of the *Winchester*', article in *Tequesta: The Journal of the Historical Association of Southern Florida*, No. XLVIII, pp.25–35, 1988, Miami, HASF.
36. Pease pudding (pottage) was a savoury dish made from boiled legumes; it is apparently still popular in northern regions of England.

'hard-tack' biscuits, which, although seemingly a varied diet, 'supplied almost no Vitamin C and therefore were no barrier against scurvy'.[37] Vegetables and fruits were only available while the ships were in port, and, as they produced dysentery, were not much favoured even then. Diseases brought afloat included syphilis, smallpox and, above all, typhus spread by lice. The tropical West Indies harboured its own hazards of course, including malaria, but the real quick killer was Yellow Fever, colloquially known as 'Yellow Jack', caused by a virus spread by mosquitoes, and infected larvae infesting the lakes and pools from which the ships replenished their water casks.

Yellow fever was no slouch; it could kill a man in under a day, the first indications being extreme, the victim's pain becoming unbearable, head and back ache, the distinctive 'yellowing' of the body. In the final extremis red and blue spots appeared on the victim's wrists and torso and the agony became intense. It was indeed a ghastly death and in those days no cure was known.[38] While not dismissing out of hand the other suspects – scurvy, dysentery, malaria, all being killers – Straight considers that these were 'slow' killers, whereas the rate of death in the unfortunate *Winchester* was far from that and that, therefore, yellow fever was the most likely cause.

What remains of HMS *Winchester* lies about twenty-eight feet (9.1m) below the surface of the water and is totally encrusted with coral. Five of the salvaged cannon are on display at the Lignum Vitae Key Botanical State Park, near Tavernier Key, and part of Florida State Parks organisation, four in the park and one at the entrance. The site has now been absorbed into the Marine Preserve of the John Pennekamp Coral Reef State Park but currently there are no mooring buoys to give away the location to unauthorised scavengers. As an interesting side-line on total misinformation, according to Bob Weller, one of the cannon recovered by Art McKee (the so-termed 'Father of Modern Treasure Hunting') was shipped back to England, where it was melted down and used in the construction of a new HMS *Winchester*. However, sad to relate, there was **NO** new HMS *Winchester* and so that part of the story is pure fiction.[39]

The *Winchester* herself lies largely undisturbed again, with only blue parrot fish, surgeon fish, barracuda and moray eels to keep watch over her.[40]

---

37. Scurvy was a killer at sea. The fleet of Admiral of the Fleet George Anson (Lord Anson) which circumnavigated the world in 1740–44, was said to have lost more than half its total number of seamen to it.
38. Augustin, George, *History of Yellow Fever*, 1909, New Orleans, Searcy & Paff Ltd.
39. There was, however, an HMS *Westminster*, a Type 23 *Duke*-class frigate launched in 1992 and, at least at the time of writing, still in service with the Royal Navy despite the Cameron government's rapid rundown of the fleet – perhaps Weller was confused between the two different names and did not verify his information? However, many other American sources continue to claim this mythical ship as 'fact'.
40. See also Cohn, John & Russell, Jesse, (Editors), *HMS Winchester (1693)*, 2012, Seattle, Washington, Value Sensitive Design (VSD), University of Washington.

Chapter 3

The Great Storm – The *Mary, Mortar, Northumberland, Restoration & Stirling Castle*

24 November to 2 December 1703

There have been many 'Great Storms' which have burst and bullied their way across the British Isles during recorded history. Each generation had experienced its own demonstration of nature's indifference to the business of mere mortals and every such incident brings predictable media mania, coupled with the tooth-sucking scepticism of the older generation, who can always recall worse! It was the English mariner who had, for centuries, been more exposed than his land-based brethren to the worst excesses of Britain's notoriously miserable weather conditions, which themselves result from being a small group of islands off a huge continental land mass. We should of course be grateful that it is just our regular winter gales and 'blows' that we have to undergo and not the far more excessive ravages of Japan's *tsutsumi*, the monsoons that batter eastern India across the Bay of Bengal or the mighty and all-destroying hurricanes of the Caribbean (the notorious *gaffe* by BBC weather forecaster Michael Fish and the ferocious blow of October 1987 notwithstanding) that we have to contend with. Having said that, to be caught on a lee shore in a Force 9 in a little cockleshell of a ship, be it a wooden-hulled and masted sailing craft, a frail and slender little steel destroyer or even a fully-fledged battleship, is not to be recommended.

Many accounts of Royal Navy ships getting caught up in such maelstroms have been recorded in print down the years but some events stand out from the pack, terrible though these experiences may have been, by account of the sheer violence and longevity of the outbreak, and equally, by the number of shipping casualties that have resulted. One such notable occurrence, when the Royal Navy suffered the loss of not just one or even two of its warships, but thirteen, with damage to many more, was the storm which devastated the whole country between 24 November and 2 December 1703. It has been recorded as the most severe gale or natural disaster ever recorded in southern Britain. Its affect was stark and one historian described this storm as being 'without rival in the recorded history of our Island'.[1] Widespread devastation felled Winstanley's Tower,[2] damaged every steeple and spire in London, including the roof

---

1. Trevelyan, George Macaulay, *England Under Queen Anne*, 3 vols, 1930–34, London, Longmans, Green.
2. The original wooden Eddystone Lighthouse. The designer Henry Winstanley, along with five companions and keepers, all vanished without a trace with it.

of Westminster Abbey and the queen herself was forced to seek shelter in the cellar at St James's Palace; the winds also demolished 2,000 chimney stacks in the capital, wrecked more than 500 boats, barges and pinnaces[3] in the Pool of London, felled 4,000 oaks in the New Forest and destroyed 400 windmills. The *English Post* carried details of great carnage in the capital, including the:

> blowing in a multitude of Chimnys, Houses, and tops of Houses, whereby many People were kill'd in their beds, and several Wounded: It would be almost endless to enumerate the mischief occasioned thereby in and about this City, as the blowing down of Trees at St James's Park, the Inns of Court, Moor-Fields, and divers other Places, abundance being torn up by the Roots, and others of a great bigness broken off in the middle.[4]

Today such devastation would, almost unhesitatingly, all be blamed on 'Global Warming' due to man-made interference with the climate; three centuries ago they had to find other excuses for the carnage, of course, and an equally outlandish theory was propounded by the celebrated author of *Robinson Crusoe*, Daniel Defoe (Fox), who ascribed these misfortunes as a 'punishment' of the Royal Navy for their lamentable performance to date against France and Spain during the War of the Spanish Succession![5] Others, equally convinced of their own piety and sanctity, put it down to the Good Lord, who gets blamed for so many things, winnowing the sinners; but, as it always had been down the aeons, it was just a natural climatic event, albeit a most unpleasant one.[6] However, the University of East Anglia's Weatherquest, takes a more adult viewpoint; in the words of its Director, Jim Bacon, 'The 1703 storm was in a class of its own in terms of strong winds it brought with it', while climatologist Dr Charles Edward Pelham Brooks noted that two weeks before the storm hit England, there had been a hurricane off Virginia.[7]

Some other climate studies have described the events that led up to this cataclysmic event as 'a series of cyclones' originating in the western Atlantic but, equally, as is always the case with weather events, current or historical, other 'experts' have dismissed this out of hand due to lack of proof. But, whether its origins were tropical or extra-tropical, there was no doubting the ferocity with which the gales struck the south-western British Isles. From the middle of November onward the weather across the English Channel had been uniformly poor, with gale following gale in unremitting

---

3. Pinnace – a ship's boat of small dimensions.
4. *English Post*, 29 November 1703.
5. Defoe, Daniel, *The Storm; or a collection of the most dreadful Casualties and Disasters which happen'd in the late dreadful Tempest both by Land and Sea*, 1704, London, George Sawbridge.
6. Of course some modern Internet 'experts' will have none of this, alleging that these accounts were all 'hyped up' but such distain totally ignores the death count and also the recorded, officially-confirmed damage lists.
7. Brooks, Charles Edward Pelham MSc FRAI FRMst Soc, *Climate Through the Ages: A Study of the Climatic Factors and their Variations*, 1926, New York, Roy V. Coleman.

succession on a line from the Bristol Channel to the Thames, but none were to equal the ferocity of the hurricane that hit from the afternoon of 26 November 1703. The first inklings of this mighty wind had been felt some time before.

> After a slight break in the stormy weather of the foregoing fortnight it began to blow again in the afternoon of the 26th, and by dark was blowing a gale. The gale soon freshened to a storm, blowing with a force approaching seventy miles an hour, and so continued during the early hours of the night.[8]

The full force of this momentous storm reached the area of the Bristol Channel and it subsequently tore and ripped north-eastward across England, from south Wales to the Humber River, bringing with it a huge swath of destruction and devastation. By the time it had roared across London into Essex the barometric pressure had been recorded at 937 millibars (mb)[9] and indeed there is speculation it went lower than that in places. Wind speeds were recorded in excess of 100mph (160 km/h) in the same area.

Yet, notwithstanding all this carnage across the south of England, it is the effect it had on the Royal Navy that concerns us here. Engaged as they were with the enemy in the War of the Spanish Succession, some of the fleets had just returned from the Mediterranean and elsewhere and there was therefore a higher than normal concentration of warships strung along the southern coastlines of England and Wales, from Milford Haven in the west, round the Channel ports and up the North Sea as far as Great Yarmouth in Norfolk, which had squadrons plying to Scandinavia and the Baltic States.

Let us follow the storm's progression and the destruction it wrought. But first, as a kind of rehearsal for the havoc to follow, an early casualty came on 7 November, when the 10-gun bomb-ketch *Portsmouth* (Captain George Bawes) with a crew of forty-four souls, was lost in a gale off the Nore. They were still being mourned when events of even greater tragedy followed.

Bristol and the Avon

Several ships were driven ashore from their anchorage in the King and Hung Roadsteads,[10] including the former 3rd-rates, acting as store-ships, the *Canterbury* and *Suffolk*, along with the merchantman *Richard and John*, which had recently arrived from Virginia.

One worthy of that city, the Reverend Thomas Chest, wrote that from Arlingham

---

8. Carr Laughton, Leonard George & Heddon, Victor, *Great Storms*, 1927, London, Philip Allen & Co.
9. Reading taken at midnight by the Reverend William Derham, Vicar at St Laurence's Church, Upminster,and Fellow of the Royal Society (FRS), which was maintained for four hours.
10. A roadstead is a sheltered anchorage and, due to the huge rise and fall of the tidal Avon river, ships were left suspended, or 'hung' from their moorings, when the tide ebbed.

down to the mouth of Bristol River Avon, particularly from Aust Cliff to the River's Mouth all that Flat called the Marsh, was drowned. They lost many Sheep and cattle. About 70 Seamen were drown'd out of the *Canterbury* Store-ship, and other Ships that were Stranded or Wreck'd.[11]

The cost to the city from the storm was estimated at more than £100,000.

The 6th-rate 8-gun storeship *Canterbury* (Commander Thomas Blake) was lost at Bristol with the captain and twenty-five men lost from a crew of forty The ship was salvaged but ordered to be sold. The 4th-rate 48-gun *Vigo*, (Captain Thomas Long) with 212 crew[12] was lost off the Dutch Coast; four men were lost. The 6th-rate 10-gun *Suffolk* (Captain Richard Watkins) was lost at Bristol but all the eighty members of her crew were saved. The 5th-rate 32-gun *Arundel* (Captain Unton Deering) with a crew of 145 men was lost at Bristol, but all the crew were saved; the ship was salvaged and continued to serve until 1713

Milford Haven

A graphic account of events hereabouts was given by Captain Joseph Soanes, commander of the 5th-rate 28-gun *Dolphin*, which had been operating in the Irish Sea earlier. Soanes had under his command the 3rd-rate 80-gun *Cumberland* (Captain Samuel Martin), the 4th-rate 48-gun *Coventry* (Captain Kerrit Roffey), the 5th-rate 36-gun *Looe* (Captain Robert Arris) (later to be wrecked in Scratchwell Bay on 12 December 1705), the 5th-rate 34-gun *Hastings* (Captain John Draper) and the 5th-rate 42-gun *Hector* (Captain Jordan Sandys). They were joined by the 32-gun 6th-rate *Rye* (Captain James Carleton) and these warships were providing Royal Navy escort for an incoming convoy of 130 merchant vessels. The convoy had taken shelter in Milford Haven, but, even here they were not safe and thirty merchantmen were driven ashore or otherwise lost.

Captain Soanes related how, on 26 November:

at one in the afternoon, the wind came at S. by E. a hard gale, between which and N.W. by W. it came to a dreadful storm; at three the next morning was the violentest of the weather, when the *Cumberland* broke her sheet-anchor, the ship driving near this, and the *Rye* both narrowly escap'd carrying away; she drove very near the rocks, having but one anchor left, but in a little time they slung a gun, with the broken anchor fast to it, which they let go, and wonderfully preserved the ship from the shore. Guns firing from one ship or other all the night for help, though 'twas impossible to assist each other, the sea was so high, and the

---

11. Chambers, Robert, *The Book of Days: A Miscellany of Popular Antiquities in Connection with the Calendar, Including Anecdote, Biography, & History, Curiosities of Literature and Oddities of Human Life and Character*, 2 Vols, 1864, London, Chambers.

12. She was the former *Dartmouth*, taken as a prize, re-captured and re-named.

darkness of the night such, that we could not see where any one was, but by the flashes of the guns; when daylight appeared, it was a dismal sight to behold the ships driving up and down, one foul of another, without masts, some sunk, and others upon the rocks, the wind blowing so hard, with thunder, lightning, and rain, that on the deck a man could not stand without holding. Some drove from Dale, where they were sheltered under the land, and split in pieces, the men all drowned; two others drove out of a creek, one on the shore so high up was saved; the other on the rocks in another creek, and bulged; an Irish ship that lay with a rock through her, was lifted by the sea clear away to the other side of the creek on a safe place; one ship forced ten miles up the river before she could be stopped, and several strangely blown into holes, and on banks; a ketch, of Pembroke, was drove on the rocks, the two men and a boy in her had no boat to save their lives, but in this great distress a boat which broke from another ship drove by them, without any in her, the two men leaped into her and were saved, but the boy was drowned. A prize at Pembroke was lifted on the bridge, whereon is a mill, which the water blew up, but the vessel got off again; another vessel carried almost into the gateway which leads to the bridge, and is a road, the tide flowing several feet above the common course. The storm continued till the 27th, about three in the afternoon; that by computation nigh thirty merchant ships and vessels without masts are lost, and what men are lost is not known; three ships are missing, that we suppose men and all lost. None of Her Majesty's ships came to any harm; but the *Cumberland* breaking her anchor in a storm which happen'd the 18th at night, lost another, which renders her incapable of proceeding with us till supplied.[13]

Plymouth

The bulk of the fleet had moved up–Channel and only the 3rd-rate 64-gun battleship *Monck* (Captain Josiah Mighells), which was acting as the port guardship, and the 5th-rate 32-gun *Mermaid* (Captain Finch Riddle), preparing for service on the West Indies Station, were in the Sound when the storm struck but, while the latter managed to ride out the storm, the *Monck* was driven ever closer the coast. She cut away all her masts by the board and thus managed to avoid being wrecked.

Spithead

Captain Robert Fairfax in the 3rd-rate *Kent* was with the fleet that had returned home with Admiral Sir Cloudesley (Clowdisley) Shovel and Admiral Sir John Leake from the Mediterranean with their ships in good condition but with more than 1,500 of their crews dead from sickness while abroad. They first arrived at Plymouth Sound and then later they dropped anchor at Spithead.

---

13. Soanes, Captain Joseph, *The London Gazette,* No. 3972, 2 December 1703.

On the two previous days, November 24 and 25, there was fine weather, and the *Kent* loosed her sails to dry. On the 26th there was much wind with rain, and in the night the full fury of the storm burst over Spithead. At four in the morning of the 27th Fairfax let go his sheet anchor. Three-quarters of an hour afterwards the cable of the small bower parted in the hawse, and the long boat was swamped alongside. The force of the storm increased to a hurricane, with thick weather and small rain. The reports of guns from ships in distress could be heard when the roar of the wind lulled at intervals. It was a terrible night, but the good ship rode it out. At seven the full fury of the storm was passed, and when morning broke, thirteen ships were seen on shore. On 28th the *Kent* hove up her sheet anchor, and went into Portsmouth Harbour to refit.[14]

Other warships were not so fortunate, the *Lichfield*'s prize and the *Newcastle* both being victims and driven onto the Dean Sand, while the fireship *Vesuvius* went ashore near Southsea Castle and was stranded. In addition, another fireship, the *Firebrand* and a hospital ship, the *Jeffreys*, were driven onto the Spit, but managed to get themselves off again.

The 3rd-rate 70-gun battleship *Resolution* (Captain Thomas Liell) with a crew of 221, also from Spithead, with her crew bailing and pumping to keep her afloat, was wrecked at Pevensey, Sussex, but all her company were saved.

The 6th-rate 10-gun advice boat[15] *Eagle* (Captain Nathan Bostock) was lost at Selsey, with a crew of forty-five, all of whom were saved.

The 5th-rate 36-gun *Litchfield*, a Prize (Captain Peter Chamberlain) with a crew of 108, all of whom were saved, went ashore in Sussex and ship was salved. The 4th-rate 54-gun *Newcastle* (Captain William Carter) was blown across the Owers Shoal off Selsey Bill without grounding but the tide ensured she had sufficient water under keel to save from anything worse than some hard 'bumping' or she would have been lost for certain, but in vain, for she beached herself eventually. She had aboard a crew of 253 officers and men, of whom just twenty-four, including the ship's carpenter, were saved. On 27 November the 5th-rate 8-gun fireship *Vesuvius* (Captain Henry Paddon) with a crew of forty-eight, all of whom were saved, drifted from Spithead and was wrecked near Chichester. The ship was refloated on 12 March.

The Downs

The Downs is a famous roadstead that has for centuries been a noted haven for shipping off the Kent coast; the area is some eight miles long and six miles wide, roughly encompassed by the boundaries of the cliff of North Foreland, south of Kingsgate in

---

14. Markham, Clements Robert, CB FRS, *Life of Robert Fairfax of Steeton – Vice-Admiral, Alderman and Member for York AD1646–1725*, 1885, London, Macmillan & Co.

15. Terminology used between 1660 and 1680 for a fast vessel to convey messages around the fleet, later superseded by the term Despatch Boat.

Thanet, down past Deal to the Seven Sisters on the northern edge of Dover harbour. The elongated, and ever-shifting, sandbars of the Goodwins[16] present themselves as an 'island' albeit one that is divided by a narrow channel. However, when inundated, the sands become porous and unpredictable, constantly changing texture and location. The Goodwins have long served as a offshore shield, protecting masses of shipping huddled inside them from the full and direct force of gales breaking from the east and north. However, during the Great Storm the sands offered no such protection to the huddled fleets of shipping, both naval and mercantile, that had sought sanctuary while *en route* through the Straits for the wind rocketed in from the south-west.

High tide in the Downs was at midnight and the flood ran whipped up by a westerly wind off the shore and this combination saw a huge tidal surge. Now the Goodwins, as so oft before, became both an agent of destruction, the anvil on which the hammer of the gale crushed vessel after vessel, and, ultimately, a graveyard for an incomparable number of victims. Ashore at Whitstable, north Kent, a waterspout was generated that engulfed a small vessel, lifting her up and dropping her 800 feet (244m) inland from the coast. At sea off south-eastern Kent, the effect was more profound and no less devastating. In addition to Vice-Admiral John Leake's flagship, the 2nd-rate *Prince George*, there was the 60-gun 4th-rate *Mary* and others from Shovell's Mediterranean command, plus Vice-Admiral John Graydon's West Indies squadron, with his flag in the 3rd-rate 80-gun battleship *Lancaster*, all in the mix with an estimated 160 merchant vessels huddled for shelter off Deal itself. It was a recipe for a disaster, which swiftly ensured.

The 3rd-rate 80-gun *Shrewsbury* (Captain Josias Crow) survived by the skin of her teeth. Walter Jerrold recorded the following eyewitness account of what occurred, in a letter written by one Miles Norcliffe, a survivor from the *Shrewbury*, during the event.

These lines I hope in God will find you in good health; we are all left here in a dismal condition, expecting every moment to be all drowned: for here is a great storm, and is very likely to continue; we have here the real admiral of the blew in the ship call'd the *Mary*, a third rate, the very next ship to ours, sunk, with Admiral Beaumont,[17] and above 500 men drowned: the ship call'd the *Northumberland*, a third rate, about 500 men all sunk and drowned; and the ship call'd the *Restoration*, a third rate, all sunk and drowned; these ships were all close by us which I saw; these ships fired their guns all night and day long,

16. Once originally low-lying land protected by a seawall in the days of Edward the Confessor, and the tithe of Goodwyne (Godwin), Earle of Kent. After the Norman Conquest this area became the responsibility of the Abbot of St Augustine, Canterbury, who shamefully neglected the sea defences and the land reverted to the Channel.
17. Rear-Admiral Basil Beaumont. Beaumont, as a very youthful ship's captain, had survived the loss of his first command, the 5th-rate *Centurion*, to another bad storm in Plymouth Sound on Christmas Day 1689. He had only flown his flag aboard the *Mary* for a very short time in patrols in the North Sea and Baltic and, on returning home, had anchored in the Downs on 19 October and was still there when the storm struck.

poor souls, for help, but the storm being so fierce and raging, could have none to save them: the ship call'd the *Shrewsbury*, that we are in, broke two anchors, and did run might fierce backwards, with 60 or 70 yards of sands, and as God Almighty would have it, we flung our sheet anchor down, which is the biggest, and so stopt: here we all pray'd to God to forgive us our sins, and to save us, or else to receive us into his heavenly kingdom. If our sheet anchor had given way, we had been all drown'd: but I humbly thank God, it was his gracious mercy that saved us. There's one, Captain Fanel's ship, three hospital ships, all split, some sunk, and most of the men drowned. There are above 40 merchant ships cast away and sunk; to see Admiral Beaumont that was next to us, and all the rest of his men, how they climbed up the main mast, hundreds at a time crying out for help, and thinking to save their lives and in the twinkling of an eye were drown'd: I can give you no account, but of these four men-of-war aforesaid, which I saw with my own eyes, and those hospital ships, at present, by reason the storm hath drove far distant from one another: Captain Crow, of our ship, believe here in great danger, and waiting for a north-easterly wind to ring us to Portsmouth, and it is our praise to God for it; for we know not how soon this storm may arise, and cut us all off, for it is a dismal place to anchor in. I have not had my cloth off, nor a wink of sleep these four nights, and have go to my death with cold almost.[18]

Another historian noted that:

Rear-Admiral Beaumont, who was on Board the *Mary*, which he quitted when the Ship was breaking, got upon a Piece of her Quarter-Deck, but was soon wash'd off, and drown'd. A Sailor on board this Ship, the only Man[19] that was sav'd out of the *Mary*, was tost by the Waves into the *Sterling-Castle (sic)*, which perish'd immediately, and he was as miraculously sav'd a second Time, as I heard him tell the Story himself, but have forgot the Circumstances of his last Escape.[20]

Atkins was somehow washed to safety a second time, this time on to a ship's boat broken adrift from the *Stirling Castle* – he was the third man aboard and got ashore on the Kent coast. Despite the effects of exposure he survived to relate his tale.[21]

Clements Markham offered this description of that eventful night thus:

---

18. Jerrold, Walter, with Illustrations by Thomson, Hugh, *Highways and Byways in Kent*, pp.142–3, 1907, London. Macmillan & Co.
19. Thomas Atkins.
20. Somerville, Reverend Thomas, Doctor of Divinity; FRSE, *The History of ENGLAND during the Reign of Queen ANNE; with a dissertation concerning the danger of the Protestant Succession; and an Appendix containing Original Papers*, 1798, London, Andrew Strahan/Thomas Cadell/ William Davies.
21. See Laker, John, *History of Deal*, pp.251–3, 1917, Deal, Thomas Frederick Pain & Sons.

The storm seems to have spent its utmost fury at the Downs, blowing from the south-west and commencing at about one in the morning of the 27th. In the evening the Downs presented a forest of masts, at dawn it was a desert. The *Prince George*,[22] with the flag of Admiral Leake, held fast with all anchors down until three in the morning, when the *Restoration* was seen to be driving down upon her. She came so near that the *Prince George* had to brace her yards in the hopes of her going clear, but her anchor caught in the hawse of the *Prince George*, and she was brought to; thus two great ships were riding by the same cables. It seemed impossible that the ground tackle could hold, and there was no alternative but to cut the *Restoration* away. This, however, was no easy matter, and meanwhile their best bower came home. When hope was nearly gone, and every moment seemed likely to see both ships drift away to destruction, the *Restoration* suddenly got clear and disappeared in the gloom. She was lost, with every soul on board. At daylight twelve ships were seen on the Goodwins, which were all broken up by ten, and all hands perished, except about eighty from the *Stirling Castle*. The rest of the ships foundered at their anchors, only a very few escaping to sea and living out the gale.[23]

An account by the historian and relative Stephen Martin Leake reads thus:

About three o'clock, believing the storm to be at the worst, they were encouraged to hope they might ride it out; but just then, they discovered the *Restoration*, a third-rate ship, driving upon them, and presently came so near, they were forced to brace their yards to prevent her driving on board them -- however they hoped she might go clear of them; but whilst they flattered themselves with this expectation, her anchor came up to the hawse of the *Prince George*, and she stopt, riding fast by them. Now their fate seemed inevitable; for was it possible their ground tackle should hold two great ships; there was no means left but to cut her away. They endeavoured it, but could not do it. There were now no hopes, they waited their approaching fate, which every minute threatened their destruction. By the prodigious strain, their best bower was soon brought home, and their small bower brought a-head, and in this manner they rode for half an hour, the longest half hour that ever they knew, for every minute seemed to be the last; but when all human aids failed, and all expectations were vain, the invisible hand of providence relieved them, for whether the cable of the *Restoration* parted, or the anchor slipped, they knew not; but she drove away, and soon after was lost, with every living creature on board, by which means Vice-Admiral Leake happily survived the general devastation. This wonderful deliverance under providence was owing to a prudent foresight in the Admiral and his captain, Captain George

---

22. The former 90-gun 2nd-rate *Duke,* which had been rebuilt and renamed.
23. Markham, Clements Robert, CB FRS, *Life of Robert Fairfax of Steeton – Vice-Admiral, Alderman and Member for York AD1646–1725*, 1885, London, Macmillan & Co.

Martin,[24] by providing against the worst. The day before, when it blew very hard, and considering the time of the year, the place they were in, and what might happen, they made a snug ship, veering out their long service to two cables and two thirds, and doing everything that might enable them to ride out a hard storm, by which precaution they not only saved themselves, but the lives of seven hundred men under their care, with Her Majesty's ship; and all this without cutting away a mast, using any extraordinary means, or receiving any damage more than usual in a hard gale of wind.....[25]

Admiral Leake described the scene on the following morning.

When it was day they saw twelve sail ashore upon the Goodwin, Bunt Head, and Brake Sands, amongst whom was Admiral Beaumont in the *Mary,* the *Stirling Castle, Northumberland,* and *Restoration,* who were all to pieces by ten o'clock, and all the men perished, except one from the *Mary* and eighty from the *Stirling Castle.* It was a melancholy prospect to see between two and three thousand perish in this manner, without a possibility of helping them.[26]

Another ship's master described events in a similar manner.

By four o'clock we miss'd the *Mary* and the *Northumberland,* who rid not far from us, and found they were driven from their anchors; but what became of them, God knows. And soon after, a large man-of-war came driving down upon us, all her masts gone, and in a dreadful condition. We were in the utmost despair at this sight, for we saw no avoiding her coming thwart our haiser; she drove at last so near us, that I was just gowing to order the mate to cut away, when it pleas'd God the ship sheer'd contrary to our expectation to windward, and the man-of-war, which we found to be the *Sterling (sic) Castle,* drove clear of us, not two ships' lengths, to leeward.

It was a sight full of terrible particulars to see a ship of eighty guns and about six hundred men in that dismal case. She had cut away all her masts; the men were all in the confusion of death and despair; she had neither anchor, nor cable, nor boat to help her, the sea breaking over her in a terrible manner, that sometimes she seem'd all under water. And they knew, as well as we that saw her, that they drove by the tempest directly for the Goodwin, where they could expect nothing but destruction. The cries of the men, and the firing their guns, one by one, every

---

24. Later Commodore Martin.
25. Leake, Stephen Martin, *The Life of Sir John Leake, Knt. Admiral of the Fleet &c.,* 1750, London.
26. Clarke, James Stanier & McArthur, John, 'Biographical Memoir of the Late Sir John Leake, Knt. Admiral of the Fleet', entry in *The Naval Chronicle,* Volume 16, July–December 1806, pp.441–515.

half minute for help, terrified us in such a manner, that I think we were half dead with the horror of it.[27]

A rather more oblique approach to military history was revealed by Alan Woods. He wrote that:

In 1703 the sixty-gunned warship *Shrewsbury* was lost on the Goodwins, and is reported to reappear[28] on the anniversary of its (*sic*) sinking. On the wild and stormy night of 25/26 November, the Goodwins swallowed four navy frigates (*sic*), *Stirling Castle, Northumberland, Restoration* and *Mary*. 1,271 sailors perished in the cold waters.

Two (*sic*) survivors from the *Mary* were rescued, and stated that before they went on the deadly sands, they had seen a ghostly sixteenth-century warship with all guns firing, and afire from stem to stern, ram their ship, pass boldly through it without any feeling of impact, then disappear into the sands. The ghostly form of a frigate (*sic*) in distress was seen, two days later, by ships anchored well off the Goodwins to ride out the storm, her name read *Northumberland*, and she was out of control and heading straight onto the sands, where she disappeared once again.[29]

Fortunately scientists like Dennis Wheeler have provided rather less speculative presentations of events.[30]

Other victims included the 3rd-rate battleship *Northumberland* (70) (Captain James Greenway) with the loss of her entire crew of 220 officers and men, including twenty-four Royal Marines; the 3rd-rate battleship *Restoration* (Captain Fleetwood Emms (or Eames) with the loss of her entire crew of 387 officers and men and the 3rd-rate *Stirling Castle* (70) (Captain John Johnson), wrecked on the Goodwins with a crew of 446 officers and men of whom sixty were saved including the captain, the third lieutenant, the ship's cook, four Royal Marines and the chaplain, while the first lieutenant, Benjamin Barnett was lost.

The 4th-rate *Mary* (64) (Flag of Rear-Admiral Basil Beaumont, and commanded by Captain Edward Hobson) with a crew of 273 officers and men, had her entire

---

27. *Anon* ('An Ingenious Hand'), *An Exact Relation of the Late Dreadful Tempest; with, a Faithful Account of the Most Remarkable Disasters which happened on that occasion*, 1704, London, Ann Baldwin.

28. The writer does not reveal by whom.

29. Wood, Alan C., *Military Ghosts*, 2009, Stroud, Amberley Publishing. The author uses the term 'frigates' it would seem for *any* sailing warship (much like TV journalists today use the term 'battleship' when the last British such was scrapped in 1960) – for *Northumberland, Restoration* and *Stirling Castle* were all line-of-battleships of course, and ships are both 'it' or 'she' without specification either.

30. Wheeler, Dennis, 'The Great Storm of November 1703: A new Look at the Seamen's records'. Article in *Weather*, No.58, pp.419–27, 2006, Sunderland, University of Sunderland.

complement drowned on the Goodwins, except for just three men, these being the captain and purser (both fortunately being safe ashore at the time) and Thomas Atkins who had a remarkable story of survival to relate as noted earlier.

Today, the wreck of the *Stirling Castle*, herself one of the thirty 'Great Ships' of the 1677 Navy Programme of the King Charles II and Samuel Pepys era, is located off the north-west edge of the Goodwins, just over five miles (8.5 km), north-east of Deal, in position 51° 16' 46" N, 01° 30' 41" E. She was re-discovered at a depth of about 39 feet 3 inches (12 meters) in 1979 by a team of local divers from the Ramsgate Dive Club working off that town. She was described as being 'littered with human bones, organic artefacts, rope, intact gun carriages …'. But the shifting, elusive sands soon buried her once more and she did not re-emerge again until 1998 when parts were once more exposed. She is currently owned by the Isle of Thanet Archaeological Society and is one of sixty such wrecks included under the Protection of Wrecks Act (1973), five of which, including *Northumberland* and *Restoration*, are on the Goodwins.[31]

The Nore

The 2nd-rate 90-gun battleship *Association* (Captain Samuel Whitaker), with all her anchors down off the Gunfleet sands off the Essex coast, was nearly overwhelmed by the gale, but the main-mast was cut down by the board and she subsequently was blown from the Thames Estuary across the North Sea as far as Gothenburg, Sweden, with Norfolk-born Admiral Sir Cloudesley Shovell, a national hero, and Vice-Admiral Sir Stafford Fairborne, both aboard her and they were, for a while, posted as missing. It took a considerable time for her to be repaired for the voyage back home again. Her story is not without interest.

Admiral Shovell had left the Downs with most of his ships, seven three-decker battleships, one two-decker battleship and some smaller craft,[32] and anchored in the Black Deep, a channel into the Thames Estuary, placing them off Long Sand Head about fifteen miles from Harwich well inside, and at quite a distance from, the Galloper Shoal. A gale was already blowing here and so the battleships 'struck lower yards and top-masts' as was standard practice when taking bad weather precautions. But it did not save them on a pitch-black night with a WSW gale steadily increasing in intensity. The *Association* herself was taken away despite everything.

> She passed, entirely helpless, across the tail of the Galloper, in water deep enough for her not to strike but so shallow as to render the sea marvellously high and uneven. At this point she suffered severe damage, and came within an ace

---

31. Anon, Hampshire & Wight Trust for Maritime Archaeology, National Oceanography Centre, Southampton. *Stirling Castle: Archive Summary Report. Final Report. July 2009*, 2009, Fort Cumberland, Portsmouth, English Heritage.

32. He had earlier transferred from his previous flagship, the three-decker *Prince George*, in the Downs as she was to return to Portsmouth.

of foundering. The sea beat in the ports of her upper deck, which were almost twenty feet above the water-line, and the mass of water that came aboard caused her to lie down on her side in a most dangerous position. To right the ships, holes had to be cut in the decks, so that the water might run down into the hold, and be thence pumped out; but before they had succeeded thus in getting the water down to the bottom of the ship an immense weight of it collected on the lower gun-deck, only some three feet above the water-line had the ship been upright.

But the ship, in the first place, was not upright, and secondly, she was being flung this way and that by huge breaking seas, so that this great body of water went surging back and fore across the deck. It surged with such force that it burst the fastenings of two of the gun-ports-hinged lids opening outwards – and then the doom of the ship seemed certain. But meanwhile she had been driving over the narrow tail of the shoal, and under its lee found the sea easier; a high and dangerous sea, of course, in such a gale, but sufficiently regular to allow men to set to work. The admiral himself took charge, and under his direction the skill and courage of the crew prevailed, the ports were barred in, and almost against hope the ship was saved.[33]

The *Association* was not yet out of the woods, however; the storm took her toward the coast of Holland with its own reefs of sand aplenty. Fortunately the wind veered to the southward enabling her to steer along the coast rather than be driven upon it and she finally gained sanctuary in the mouth of the River Elbe. After emergency repairs she prepared to return home but yet another gale struck and she was forced north once more, *sans* her anchors, cables and sufficient provisions to maintain her crew, most of whom were in poor health. She eventually put into Gothenburg and returned to England via Copenhagen, and did not arrive in the Medway for two months after the storm had taken her. We shall meet her again soon and also Sir Cloudesley.

Her erstwhile companions mostly survived by getting clear of the shoals and away from land, and then fighting the gale out in the North Sea where they stood a better chance. The 3rd-rate 70-gun *Restoration* (Captain Fletchwood Eames) was wrecked on the Suffolk coast with all 387 crew lost, so there are no eyewitness accounts of her passing. The 5th-rate *Mortar* (12), a bomb (Captain Beaumont Raymond), with a crew of sixty officers and men, was blown across to Holland and there went ashore. The captain survived and later commanded the 4th-rate 60-gun *Exeter* in 1710 and died at Vera Cruz in 1717 in mercantile service. Only four crewmen were lost from a complement of fifty-nine.

Other ships suffered similar adventures, some surviving, some not. The 3rd-rate 70-gun battleship *Revenge* (Captain William Kerr) was forced off her anchors and drifted over to The Netherlands, as did the 3rd-rate *Russell* (Captain Isaac Townsend). The 3rd-rate *Dorsetshire* (Captain Edward Whitaker) was similarly taken by the gale

33. Laughton and Heddon, *op. cit.*

far from land but managed to fight the wind and waves in the southern North Sea before returning safely.

Chatham

The only casualty here was the 80-gun three-decker *Vanguard*. This 2nd-rate 90-gun battleship, laid up in the River Medway without any crewmen aboard her, was totally helpless when her moorings were broken by the sheer force of the wind and she soon drove ashore. Her old timbers dated back to 1678 and were so rotted that she proved very fragile and hard to salvage in one piece and subsequently foundered.[34]

Great Yarmouth, Norfolk

On the 27th the local press reported on the 'most dreadful storm last Night, no body knows what Ships are missing' but then added the fact that 'The *Reserve* to our great Surprise sunk down this Morning, and all her Men are lost. I cannot as yet give further particulars.' It was later reported in the *London Gazette* that:

> Her Majesty's Ships the *Portland, Advice, Triton* and *Nightingale*, which were in our Road in the late great Storm, have received no Damage, but the *Lyn* and *Margate* were obliged to cut all their Masts by the board, A Merchant Ship called the *Golden Peace of Dantzick*,[35] which was bound thither, was cast away on our Sands, but all her Men were saved.[36]

The 4th-rate 54-gun *Reserve* (Captain John Anderson), with a crew of 258 officers and men, was indeed lost at her anchors in the Yarmouth Roads. The entire crew was lost, save for the captain, the ship's master, the purser, the *Chyurgeon*[37] a clerk and sixteen sailors, all of whom happened to be ashore at the time she went down.

Postscript to the Storm

Just as there had been a preliminary loss, so the momentous events of those days included a final warning of the frailty of mankind. The 4th-rate 54-gun *York* (Captain John Smith), formerly known as the *Marston Moor*, was wrecked two days after the

---

34. However, she proved resilient for she was refloated the following year and returned to service after being twice rebuilt. She was renamed *Duke* in 1728 and she confounded all by remaining afloat until 1769 when she was finally broken up permanently.
35. Danzig, Prussia, nowadays Gdansk in Poland.
36. *The London Gazette*, No.3971, 29 November 1703, p.2. The British warships mentioned were *Advice*, 4th-rate (Captain Salmon Morris); *Portland*, 4th-rate (Captain James Jesson); *Triton*, 4th-rate (Captain Trudor Trevor); *Lynn*, 5th-rate (Captain Edmund Letchmere), *Margate*, 6th-rate (ex-*Jersey*, Captain John Chilley) and *Nightingale*, 6th-rate (Captain Seth Jermy).
37. Old English for Surgeon.

peak of the storm in 'hazy but moderate' weather, with the loss of just four of her crew of 332 officers and men, going down off the Shipwash in the Thames Estuary.[38] Her loss is often included in the accounting of the Great Storm but, technically, took place just outside the dates usually associated with it.

Summary

In all it was estimated that in excess of 1,500 Royal Navy officers, men and Royal Marines were killed by the storm.[39] If the civilian casualties afloat are added to the body count, then some 10,000 seamen were said to have been drowned that night.[40]

To replace the serious Royal Navy losses from the storm, including not just the ships and crews destroyed, but the widespread damage inflicted on those warships which did stay afloat, there was a widespread and determined drive to engage sufficient carpenters and joiners, and prisoners in jails and even foreign prisoners of war were drafted to make good the loss before our enemies could take advantage of our temporary weakness at sea. As usual in such extremes, the nation rallied round. A disaster fund was set up and special memorial services were held for those who died. In the event, both the Royal Navy and the Nation, as has always been the way, emerged from this disaster, stronger and more united than ever.

---

38. Smith survived and later became Captain of Greenwich Hospital.
39. Wheeler, Dennis, 'The Great Storm of November 1703: A new look at the seamen's records', article in *Weather*, Volume 58 (11), pp.419–27, Harvard University Press.
40. Lamb, Hubert, *Historic Storms of the North Sea, British Isles and Northwest Europe*, 1991, Cambridge, Cambridge University Press.

Chapter 4

A Navigational Inexactitude

The *Association*, 27 October 1707

For a month during the summer of 1707, between 29 July and 21 August, with the War of the Spanish Succession in full swing, an Allied army composed of Austrian, British and Dutch troops under command of Prince Eugene of Savoy, laid siege to the French port of Toulon. A British fleet commanded by the naval hero of the day, Admiral Sir Cloudesley Shovell, was also present blockading the harbour from the seaward side and managing to inflict considerable damage on French men-of-war.[1] Despite this, the land campaign was a failure and the fleet was called back home. A lieutenant's log for 1705 describes Sir Cloudesley Shovell's fleet as being thirty-nine ships of the line of battle, seven fireships and four bombs together with several light frigates and a great many transports and tenders.[2]

The composition of the principal warships of the British fleet heading thankfully back home was as follows. The flagship was the 90-gun 2nd-rate battleship *Association* (Flag of Admiral Sir Cloudesley Shovell, Commander-in-Chief, Captain Edmund Loades – Flag Captain, Captain Samuel Whitaker – ship's captain); the rest of the fleet comprised the 100-gun 1st rate battleship *Royal Anne* (Flag of Vice-Admiral Sir George Byng, Captain James Monypenny); the 80-gun 3rd-rate *Torbay*, (Flag, Rear-Admiral Sir John Norris, Captain William Faulknor); the 96-gun 2nd-rate *St George*, (Captain James, Lord Dursley); the 80-gun 3rd-rate *Somerset* (Captain John Price); the 64-gun 3rd-rate *Monmouth* (Captain John Baker); the 70-gun 3rd-rate *Eagle* (Captain Robert Hancock); the 70-gun 3rd-rate *Lennox* (Captain Sir William Jumper); the 64-gun 3rd-rate *Swiftsure* (Captain Richard Griffith); the 70-gun 3rd-rate *Orford* (Captain Charles Cornewall); the 54-gun 4th-rate *Romney* (Captain William Coney); the 54-gun 4th-rate *Panther* (Captain Henry Hobart); the 32-gun 5th-rate *Rye* (Captain Edward Vernon); the 24-gun 6th-rate *La Valeur* (Captain Robert Johnson); the 24-gun 6th-rate *Cruizer* (Captain John Shales)[3]; the 28-gun 5th-rate *Phoenix* – fireship (Captain Michael Sansom); the 28-gun 5th-rate *Firebrand* – fireship (Captain Francis Piercy);

---

1. Two 3rd-rates, the 52-gun *Le Fortune* and the 58-gun *Le Sage*, were set ablaze and sank, while frigates *L'Andromède* and *La Salamandre* were severely damaged.
2. Knowles, Lieutenant Thomas, Journal of Proceedings of HM fire-ship *Firebrand*, 6 January 1703 to 30 January 1704, ADM/F/L/138, National Archives, Kew, London.
3. *La Valeur* was a prize, a French corvette captured by the 54-gun 4th-rate *Worcester* (Captain Thomas Butler) in the English Channel on 4 February 1705 and added to the Royal Navy; the *Cruizer* was likewise yet another Prize, the former French *de Meric*.

the 28-gun 5th-rate *Vulcan* – fireship (Captain William Ockman); the 8-gun 5th-rate *Griffin* – fireship (Captain William Houlden); the 10-gun sloop *Weazel* (Captain James Gunman); and the 8-gun yacht *Isabella* (Captain Finch Reddall.)[4]

Having come from their hard stint of duty off the French Mediterranean naval base, Shovell's ships were in bad need of refurbishment and supply and the bulk of them were accordingly sailed for home, leaving a small portion behind to maintain the watch and blockade. The fleet touched at Gibraltar and sailed again from there on 29 September, destination Spithead, taking departure from Cape Spartel the next day. By early on Wednesday 22 October,[5] the ships were nearing the mouth of the English Channel. The waters around the Isles of Scilly were already notoriously dangerous and a lighthouse had been erected near St Agnes Island.[6]

Shovell was uncertain of his exact location and determined not to rush straight ahead without due care. According to Edmund Herbert he ordered the rest of the fleet to heave-to around midday on 21 October in order to make observations, 'the first he had been able to take for many days'.

Captain Finch Reddal of the yacht *Isabella* recorded in his log how:

This 24 hours hard gails of wind until 10 at night, (of the 22nd) then the wether somewhat moderate. At four in ye afternoon (of the 22nd) ye Admiral brought and sounded: we likewise sounded & had between 50 and 55 fathom water, a course sand intermixt wth shells.

Sir William Jumper's *Lennox* was at variance with the findings of the rest of the fleet, who agreed that they were in the latitude of Ushant, in that from his estimations, he 'believ'd 'em to be nearer Scilly'.[7] The fact that the sailing master of the *Lennox* alone of the entire assembly, made an almost correct positioning estimate appears to have been ignored as stated.[8] This worthy does indeed appear to have been in a minority of one, for the decision reached was that the fleet lay in the vicinity of Ushant, (48° 27′ 29″N; 5° 05′ 44″ W) rather than the Isles of Scilly (49° 56′ 10″ N; 6° 19′ 22″ W), and that therefore only open water lay ahead of them. By 1800, although the weather had closed down again and the wind was steadily rising, an easterly course was accordingly

---

4. The former property of Henry Fitzroy, Duke of Grafton, and named after his wife, Isabella Bennett, Second Countess of Arlington – used as a despatch boat.
5. This is the original, Old Style dating; under today's calendar this would be 2 November.
6. This edifice was constructed in 1680 by Captain Hugh Till and Captain Symon Bayly, assisted by one Thomas Eskins. It was white-painted and the lens-free lamp was coal-fired with a big open basket known as a *chauffer* and was claimed to be visible for six or seven leagues. It was certainly burning that night but apparently not seen by the ships until already too late.
7. Log of Captain Jumper, ADM 51/30, 1 January 1706 to 22 January 1708. National Archives, Kew, London.
8. At least one modern source (Commander William Edward May), however, attributes this almost correct observation to the sailing master of the *Panther* rather than the *Lennox*, stating that *Panther*'s sailing master was 'very nearly correct in his position and must have thought that the fleet was standing into danger'.

resumed in full confidence that they were clear, with the *Association* leading the way, but, tragically, they were far north of where they thought they were. Captain Jumper recorded in his log that 'Small winds N'rly ye former part but at Noone hard gales at SWBS and thick weather. At 11: y morning parted wy Fleet and bent good sailes home near ye length of Scilly w the *Valeur* + *Phoenix*'. They had been detached to Falmouth. Next day Jumper logged 'Fresh gales from noon yesterday at SSW but Clear till 2 steering NEBN then hazy and wett and the Gale freshing we altered our Course to E-ward'.

Herbert also recorded that, according to his sources, 'The next day, having soundings at 90 fathoms, he brought to and lay by about 12 o'clock and summoned all the sailing-masters of the various ships on board the *Association*, and consulted them as to the fleet's actual position'.

However, although the ships did indeed take soundings at various times, the idea of a meeting is dismissed out of hand by Peter McBride and Richard Larn,[9] who considered that the launching of various ships' boats to take soundings was subsequently misconstrued by historians as rowing to a meeting aboard the flagship, an event which none of the masters' journals record. All were of the opinion that they were in the latitude of Ushant and near the coast of France, except the master of Sir William Jumper's ship, the *Lennox*, who judged that they were nearer Scilly, and that three hours' sail would bring them in sight of the Scilly Lights, but, as the *Lennox* had already departed the area with a detached squadron, his information could not have been known to Sir Cloudesley. That worthy was therefore guided by the unanimous findings of the remaining ships of the fleet and his decision on the course was duly adopted with few, if any, qualms.

Normally the small, lighter-draught, vessels, would have led the fleet, and might have given some warning, but the *La Valeur*, *Lennox* and *Phoenix* were detached as a squadron by Shovell by the sounding of a signal gun aboard *Association* at 1100 with orders to proceed to Falmouth independently and there to pick up a convoy of merchant vessels which were due to be convoyed to the east. Thus it was the flagship that was left to lead the remaining ships of the fleet off on a north-easterly course at around 1800, with the *St George*, *Eagle*, *Romney*, *Royal Anne*, *Torbay*, *Monmouth* and *Swiftsure* in line behind her, and with the remaining smaller vessels, *Cruizer*, *Firebrand*, *Griffin*, *Weazel*, *Isabella*, in the great ships' train. They were steering into deadly peril, with visibility hampered by a black night and a rising gale with heavy rain squalls which made station-keeping difficult.

At 2000 the flagship, with little or no warning, struck the Outer Gilstone reef and the following waves 'beat out the *Association*'s lights'. The ships close astern of her either followed her to their doom, or had lucky, often near-miraculous, escapes from sharing the same fate.

---

9. McBride, Peter and Larn, Richard, *Admiral Shovell's Treasure and Shipwreck in the Isles of Scilly*, 1999, Penryn, Troutbeck Press.

The *Royal Anne* was only saved by the quick actions of her officers and men, who, the moment they realised the mortal danger they were in, set her topsails 'in an instant' and managed to just clear the rocks which were within 'a ship's length of them'.[10]

Torbay – The Journal of Lieutenant Arthur Field.

Oct. 23. Hard gales, with hazey weather and rain. At 6 the Gen[ll] made a signal to wear, w[c] we repeated; at 7 the *Monmouth* made the signal of danger; at ½ past 7 on our weather bow we unexpectedly see ye breakers on the Bishop & Clarks:[11] we immediately wore and made the signal of danger, which was very eminent, in which we had infallible demonstrations of Almighty Providence, first our wearing sooner than usual with main and fore-course, 2ndly when we judg'd ourselves inevitably on ye rocks, yett preserved from ye mighty danger; at 9 ye lights of Scilly bore E. by S ½ S, about 3 miles: we then steered between ye W[t] and ye N. W. till 7 this morning. At 9 sounded and had 60 fathom water, then told 11 sail who followed us 'God preserve the rest'!

St George – Journal of Lieutenant Benjamin Wiscard.

Oct 23. At ½ past 7 we heard several guns fired, and at 8 we discovered ye breakers off from ye island of Silley (*sic*), we wore ship and stood to ye estward; ye lighthouse of Silley bore E. S.E ½ S, dist[t] 6 miles at 7 in ye morning. Tackt and stood to ye S. at 9. Counted 6 sail. Admiral Shovell supposed to be lost.

The *St George* had, in fact, come dangerously close to sharing the fate of the *Association* for 'she struck the same ledge with the Admiral's ship', but the next wave somehow lifted her over the reef and into deep water.[12]

Somerset – Journal of Joseph Lyne, Master

Wensday Oct 22. 1707. Thick weather with small rain. At 8 we saw the westernmost of the Island of Scilly nearing N. At ½ an hour after 8 we lost sight of our Admiral's light at once, and saw Silley light bearing N.N.E. 3 miles. The ye *Royal Ann* who was ½ a mile to leeward of us, extinguisht her lights and did not light them again; in an hour we heard and saw a great many guns fir'd in several places, w[ch] we supposed to be from ships in danger.

---

10. *The London Gazette*, No 4380, 30 October to 3 November 1707.
11. This pair, the 'Outer Rocks' lie west of St Agnes with, just east of them, the 'Western Rocks and Gilstone Reef – their precise location is 48° 87' 02"N, 6° 40' 06"W.
12. Boyer, Abel, *The History of the reign of Queen Anne: digested into Annals, Vol. VI*, pp.241–5, 1707, London, Abel Roper.

Monmouth – Journal of Captain John Baker.

Oct. 22. At ½ past 5 ye signall was made to make sail wch we did , & endeavouring to get ye Flag's light ahead of us we discovered a rock to leeward of us; we immediately wore ship and got clear of it, & in wearing I discovered ye light of Silley bearing E by N^{dly}. So I made ye signal of Danger and repeated it several times, so y^t might be taken notice of, and made w^t saile I could to the westward, wch was wth my courses.

Swiftsure – Journal of Captain Richard Griffiths.

Oct.23. At 6 Sir Cloudesley Shovel made ye signal to war, at ye same time we all made saile, hauling up E. by S., E.S.E. and S.E. At ½ past 7 fell in with ye islands of Scilly; the Gen^{ll} fired one gun, as we plainly saw, and immediately lost sight of him; then Rear Admiral Norris fired four guns, hoisted several lights and wore, and put all his light out, at ye same time made the light on St Mary's under our lee bow. At 7 a.m. (on 23rd) saw seaven saile wch I judged to some of ye separated fleet.

Isbaella – Journal of Captain Finch Reddall.

We lay by til 6 foll. At which time we heard several guns fir'd to ye S°ward of us, supposing they had discovered danger; at 8 at night saw ye light of Scilly bearing S. E. by S. dist^t judgment about 4 miles. We took it to be one of our Admiral's lights; we steered after it till we perceived it to be a fixed light, it being very thick dark rainey wether, we perceived ye rocks on both sides of us; we being very near to them we immediately wore our yacht and layed our head to ye westward, crouding all ye saile we could to weather ye rocks under our lee; we filled full and full, & by God's mercy we got clear of them all, for wch deliverance God's holy name be blest and praised, wch caused a great separation in ye fleet, for happy was he that could shift for himself, some steering wth their heads to ye S°ward, and others to ye Northward, and those that lay wth their heads to the S°ward were most of them lost. In ye morning we saw 5 sail besides oursfelves, wch stood to ye westward as we did, the *Torbay*, Sir John Norris, the *St George,* my lord Dursley, the *Monmouth*, Captain Baker, the *Griffin*, fire-ship, Captain (William) Holden, the *Weasel*, Captain (James) Gunman.

Firebrand

Firebrand also struck the same Outer Gilstone rocks as the *Association* had, but she managed to get off again aided by a providential huge wave. Leaking badly, she bumped and scraped her way along the southern edge of the western rocks betwixt Annet and St Agnes until she eventually foundered in Smith Sound, hard alongside

Menglow Rock and taking two score of her crew down with her. Only twenty-five men, including Captain Frances Piercy, were able to scramble ashore and reach the safety of St Agnes. Over 1,300 men perished in this incident, making it one of the worst disasters in British naval history[13]

The *Firebrand*'s crew listing included her commander, lieutenants, a physician, a sailing master and midshipmen. She was armed with six minions and two falconettes.[14] According to a letter written by Captain Francis Piercey, dated 25 October 1707, '17 men were saved in the boat, with the Captain and five drove ashore on a piece of the wreck'. He recorded that Midshipman Edward Wilford did not survive the wreck but that Physician Charles Bradford, Lieutenant William Probyn and Midshipman Ben Marshall were among those who did survive.[15]

The fleet's distress was also witnessed by observers aboard another squadron of British warships (the so-termed 'Welsh Fleet') who had been sheltering in the Isles of Scilly from the 22nd and were still there that evening. These units were the four 4th-rates, the 54-gun *Antelope* (Captain Philip Cavendish), *Hampshire* (Captain Henry Maynard) and *Salisbury* (Captain Sir Francis Hosier) and the 50-gun *Southampton*, (Captain Joseph Soanes); two 5th-rates, the 32-gun *Arundel* (Captain Joseph Winder) and the 36-gun galley *Charles*, (Captain John Hager); and the 6th-rate 24-gun *Lizard* (Captain Josiah Mighells).[16] This squadron was escorting a large convoy of coasters eastward. A *Salisbury*'s lieutenant's log recorded that they heard the warning guns being fired out at sea and saw the signals of distress in the darkness, but that it was not possible to go to their aid.[17] From daylight onward huge quantities of flotsam and debris was seen drifting in toward the shore and the *Charles*, *Salisbury* and *Southampton* sent out their ships' boats to see whether they could find any survivors. The *Southampton*'s pinnace found a document addressed to a sailor aboard the *Association*, which gave the first clue of what fleet had been involved in the tragedy. Later they found the *Phoenix*, half-full of water, lodged on the rocks near New Grimsby, Tresco. [18]

What of the detached squadron? In truth, they fared little better than their erstwhile companions. Heading north-east-by-north toward Falmouth to pick up their convoy they experienced much the same horrible weather conditions. Rather than risk running ashore on the southern coast of Cornwall, they trimmed their course twice during the

---

13. Larn, Richard (Editor), *Poor England has lost so many men*, 2006, St Mary's, The Council of the Isles of Scilly.
14. NMM ADL/H/222, National Maritime Museum, Greenwich, London.
15. ADM 39/789 & ADM 33/257, ADM 106 3069 2, National Archives, Kew, London.
16. The *Arundel*, *Lizard* and *Southampton* had arrived from Milford Haven, while the *Antelope*, *Charles*, *Hampshire* and *Salisbury* which had been cruising to the west, put in seeking shelter at 1600 on the 22nd.
17. Styles, Master Thomas, Journal, HMS *Salisbury* 1707–1710, dated 1 January 1707 to 31 December 1710, ADM/L/S/II, National Maritime Museum, Greenwich, London.
18. There is a deep-water sound here between Tresco and Bryher, which is described as being well-sheltered from the East and West, 'but awful in SSE & NNE winds' and there is the added 'treacherous hazard of the rocky reef at Kettle Bottom'.

afternoon and by evening were heading east-south-east at three knots.[19] And, like the main body, the three little ships were likewise confounded (with the exception maybe of *Lennox*'s sailing master, who was tragically vindicated) to find themselves sighting the Scilly Light some five miles off. Before they realised it they were in among the rocks and reefs south-west of Scilly and were in mortal danger.

The lieutenant of the *Phoenix* later recorded in his journal the horrible dilemma they found themselves in, recording how the ship's master 'ran forward and called out there's a ship ahead we will go under her stern and know who they are; but we soon found the mistake, it being a rock'. They wore round a second time to avoid this hazard but in doing so hit another, and found themselves 'struck fast on a sunken rock and continued there for some minutes but a great sea that almost filled us hove us off in 9 fathom'.[20] Captain Michael Sansom similarly described events thus:

> We were shot so far in that we could not weather the Smith Rock but was forced to ware ship and brought too with our heads to the northward and set our mainsail and we laid up NW the wind at WSW. We wore loosing our maintop-sail but the wind veered to the WNW so could not weather the NW Rocks: we put our ship to stays but would not so that we put our helm a weather and endeavouring to ware here she struck the leeward part of the rock & received a sea which almost filled her, but hove her off into 9 fathoms astern.

The *Phoenix* was heavily damaged by the rock off Samson Island and the ship so compromised that the crew could only save themselves by running her ashore on the sands between Tresco and Bryher.

> We fired several guns: a boat came from the shore, advising with the pilot finding my ship very leaky & that we could not free her with 2 pumps & having also 8ft of water in the hold: We brought all our stream cable for a spring to cast her & cut our best bower cable away, and run in between Samson and Bryer Islands, and laid her ashore upon the sand, it being then about half flood, it was a quarter flood when we struck first upon the rock. We unbent our sails and unrigged our topmasts and got them ashore.

Here they were found by the *Salisbury*, out searching for survivors. Her sailing master recorded how they boarded the *Phoenix*: 'She comes almost full of water in her hold by striking against one of the rocks but got safe into Grimsby.'[21] The *Phoenix* had certainly survived, but hardly intact. Her crew was forced to forage among the wreckage being washed ashore from the big ships that had gone down, in order to

---

19. Captain's Journal, HMS *Lennox*, ADM51/4238, National Archives, Kew, London.
20. Master's Journal, HMS *Phoenix*, ADM51/4290, National Archives, Kew, London.
21. Master's Journal HMS *Salisbury*, ADM52/28, National Archives, Kew, London. This port being New Grimsby, where she finally arrived on the 25th.

effect some sort of repairs to her starboard hull where the rocks had stove her in, just to enable her to complete her voyage to a better-equipped port to be fixed properly. With next to no facilities this proved a protracted affair, made no easier by the repeated gales that struck her continually. The pumps were manned throughout and the ship's carpenter and crew worked stolidly at their task during calm intervals throughout November, being assisted by those sent by the *Arundel, Lizard* and *Southampton* from 27 November. Not until 16 January were they able to get her safely afloat, and anchor her in 10 feet of water off Hangman's Island, while it was not until 8 February, with the storms almost continuous, that she was moved to an anchorage off St Mary's in seagoing condition. She sailed from the Isles of Scilly three days later and arrived in Plymouth Sound on 20 February.[22]

Both *La Valeur* and the *Lennox* were more fortunate. They managed to struggle through to the relative safety of Broad Sound where they anchored overnight. On the following morning both these vessels got underway once more and arrived at Falmouth on the 25th, bringing with them some scant outline of the disaster that had struck the fleet, but they could only hint at heavy losses without knowing precisely which ships had gone down.

The aftermath came a few days later and, after they had sorted themselves out, some of the survivors exchanged views. Joseph Lyne, the sailing master of the *Somerset*, recorded:

> Satterday 25th. At 8 o'clock we came up with ye *Royal Ann*, ye *Orford* and a fire ship. Our Captain went on board Sir George Byng, who gave them an account of Sir Clousesley being lost on Scilly last Wensday night, and that ye *Royal Ann* hardly escaped.

There was only one survivor from the three big ships – the *Association*, with 702 souls aboard, went down with all hands; likewise the *Eagle* was lost with every man-jack man of her more than 377-man crew, when she smashed up on the aptly-named Tearing Ledge, close to Bishop Rock sinking, ironically enough, in 130 feet of water; the *Romney* went down with every man aboard, 236 officers and men, save one, having struck the Crim Rocks.[23] Finally, the little *Firebrand*, with a crew of four dozen, was

---

22. The *Phoenix* was laid up for many years at Plymouth and was then rebuilt in Woolwich Dockyard between June 1728 and 1731 at a cost of £4,752, 19 shillings and 11 pence! She served in the West Indies from 1732 and off Carolina and then Georgia between 1838 and 1740. On return home in 1742 she was surveyed, hulked, and finally sold in June 1744 for £201. Captain Sansom meanwhile went on to command the 32-gun 5th-rate *Lyme*, the 42-gun *Mary Galley* and then the 54-gun 4th-rate *Moor* until November 1711.

23. The precise locations of *Eagle* and *Romney* are still uncertain and the recorded sites given on Gostelo Chart, prepared by the famed London Cartographer Walter Gostelo, and dedicated to Sidney the 1st Earl of Godolphin, and Governor of Scilly. This worthy died in 1712 so the chart is almost contemporary, the original being held in the British Library at St Pancras. However, its accuracy has been much questioned of late, with the revisionist theory, based on what cannon and artefacts have been recovered, that the sites of the two shipwrecks may possibly have been inadvertently transposed.

also lost, but twenty-two men survived her wrecking, including her captain and lieutenant. The *Phoenix* also went ashore, as related, but no man died and she was later salvaged. In all there were some 1,340 fatalities that night.

The lone survivor was George Lawrence, an able seaman from the *Romney*, described as 'a North country-man from near Hull, a butcher by trade, a lusty fat man but much battered wth ye rocks'. He was found hanging on the rocks close to the Gilstone. It was recorded by Herbert that Lawrence was closely interrogated: 'ye Captains, Lieutenants, Doctors &c of ye Squadron came on shoar and ask'd him many questions in relation to ye wreck' but that he was treated callously by these naval officers:

> not one man took pity on him, either to dress or order to be dress'd his brusises &c., wherefore had persish'd had no Mr Ekins, a Gent^n of ye Island,[24] charitably taken him in; and a doctor of a merchant ship then in ye road under convoy of *Southampton* &c, search'd his wounds and applied proper remedies.

However, Thomas Styles, ship's master of the *Salisbury*, recorded that Lawrence was 'entered on the books' of that ship on 26 October, along with the survivors of the *Firebrand,* the day after the wreck.[25] Lawrence could not recall much of what had occurred to him, but he did apparently inform his rescuers that 'Sir Cloudesley was to the windward of all the ships, and fired three guns when he struck, and immediately went down, as the *Romney* a little after did'.[26]

The *Salisbury* transported her rescued men to Plymouth, arriving there on 28 October. They were duly cared for at the naval hospital at Stonehouse, Plymouth, and by 8 November Lawrence himself had recovered from his ordeal sufficiently to be discharged, being taken to London to give his brief and sketchy account of events to Their Lordships' representatives at the Admiralty. By 19 December he had been promoted boatswain's mate and appointed to the 26-gun 5th-rate fireship *Terrible* (Captain William Jameson).

Of the 1,315 men aboard the *Association, Romney* and *Eagle* there was, as related, only one survivor, Lawrence from the *Romney*. Sir Cloudesley Shovell, his two stepsons (John and James, the sons of his wife's late husband Admiral Sir John Narborough), Henry Trelawney, the second son of the Bishop of Winchester, Captain Edmund Loades (his wife's nephew), Captain Samuel Whitaker, the ship's captain, and Peter Pury, ship's chaplain, were among those who perished. The body of Sir Cloudesley Shovell was found apparently washed ashore at Porth Hellick Bay, a tidal inlet on the south-eastern coast of St Mary's in the Isles of Scilly.

---

24. Thomas Ekins, Stewart to Godolphin.
25. Master's Journal, HMS *Salisbury*, ADM52/282, National Archives, Kew, London.
26. Letter from John Ben, St Hilary, Cornwall, dated 16 November 1707 concerning the finding of the body to Bishop Sir Jonathan Trelawny, Vice-Admiral for Shipwrecks, South Coast of Cornwall – cited in *Penzance Natural History and Antiquarian Society, Volume 2*. 1864: Penzance. PNH&AS.

Other bodies that came ashore here included Admiral Narborough and his brother, Trelawney, Captain Loades and Shovell's pet Newfoundland dog, Mumper.[27] The battered stern of Shovell's barge, bearing the Admiral's coat of arms, was also washed up at the same spot and it was assumed that many of his entourage managed to get aboard the barge and sought safety, but that the barge was dashed on the rocks in sight of salvation. Cooke surmised that:

> This supposition seems to be strengthened by the fact that the Guilstone (*sic*), upon which the *Association* was lost, is at least seven miles S. W. of Porthellick Bay where the body came ashore; and it does not seem likely that it could have drifted such a distance amongst rocks and sands and have been taken up, as Mr Herbert Notes, with scarcely a scratch upon it.[28]

There was a very strong suspicion that the Admiral, and maybe the others, may have, in truth, still been alive and that he was washed ashore semi-conscious, but had been subsequently foully murdered by local women who had noticed the valuable rings he was wearing, which included a large emerald- and diamond-encrusted ring presented to him by his very good friend, James, Lord, Dursley.[29]

According to a letter written in 1709 by Edmund Herbert[30], Sir Cloudesley's body was first found by two women, 'stript of his shirt' and 'his ring was also lost off his hand, which however left ye impression on his finger'. Sir Cloudesley's widow, Elizabeth, who had lost so many of her family that night, had already offered a large reward for the recovery of any family property. According to Henry Sidney, Earl of Romney, and Robert Marsham-Townshend in a letter dated 31 May 1792 to Captain William Lockyer, and quoted by Cooke, shortly after Lady Shovel herself died in 1732, a St Mary's woman confessed to her clergyman on her own deathbed that the Admiral had indeed been alive when first found, 'exhausted and faint' and that she had murdered him for his valuables. The Admiral had been buried hastily by the Reverend Henry Penneck, but located and unearthed by Mr Paxton. The dying woman,[31] duly

---

27. Pattison, Samuel Rowles, FGS, 'Sir Cloudesley Shovell', article in *Journal of Royal Institute of Cornwall*, Volume 1, October 1864, Truro, James R. Netherton.
28. i.e. the Admiral's body itself, which was largely free of wounds. See Cooke, James Herbert, FSA, 'The Shipwreck of Sir Cloudesley Shovell on the Scilly Islands, in 1707: from original and contemporary documents hitherto unpublished'. (First read at a Meeting of the Society of Antiquaries, London, 1 February 1883*)*, 1883, Gloucester, John Bellows. The *Arundel*'s ship's purser, Thomas Paxton, is described by Edmund Herbert as stating that Shovell 'was as fresh when his face was washt as if only asleep; his nose likewise bled as tho' alive ...'.
29. Dursley was later titled Earl of Berkeley.
30. Herbert was a young man sent to the Isles of Scilly by the family to help locate 'property' belonging to the Admiral; he later became Deputy Paymaster of the Marines' Regiments.
31. Unnamed, but McBride and Larn, *op. cit.*, assert that one Mary Mumford, 'is the most likely candidate'.

produced the ring and handed it to the vicar, seeking last-minute atonement, and thereby it eventually found its way to the Berkeley family.[32]

The body was formally identified by the purser of the *Arundel* who had been well-acquainted with Sir Cloudesley earlier and he recognised a distinctive 'black mole under his left ear, and also by the fact that the first joint of one of his forefingers being broken inwards. He had likewise a shot in his right arm, another in his left thigh'.

Not surprisingly, today's Scilly Islanders reject any such slur on their distant forebears. They much prefer the alternate version of Shovell's demise as described by Edmund Herbert.

Sir C. S. was found on shoar (at Port Hellick Cove) in St Mari's Island, stript of his shirt, which by confession was known, by 2 women, which shirt had his name at ye gusset at his waist; (where by order of Mr Harry Pennick was buried 4 yards off ye sands; which place I myself view'd, & as was by his grave, came by said woman that first saw him after he was stript; His ring was lost from off his hand, which however left ye impression on his finger, as also of a second. The Lady Shovel offered a considerable reward to anyone should recover it for her, & order thereto wrote Captain Benedick, Deputy Governor & Commander in Charge of the Islands of Scilly (giving him a particular description thereof), who used his utmost diligence both by fair and foul means, though could not hear of it. Sir Cloud, had on a pair of thread stockings and a thread waistcoat. (Others say a flannel waistcoat and a pair of drawers). Mr Child (Mr Paxton) Purser of ye *Arundel* caused him to be taken up and knew him to be Sir Cloudesley by a certain black mould [mole] under his left ear, as also by the first joint of one of his forefingers being broken inwards; he has likewise a shot in his right arm another in his left thigh). Moreover he was well satisfied 'twas him, for he was a fresh when his face was washed as if only asleep; his nose likewise bled as tho' alive, which Mr Child (Paxton) said was bec(ause) of himself, For Sir C. had preferred him to Purser of *Arundel* and was his particular friend. Many that saw him said his head was the largest that ever they had seen, and not at all swell'd with the waters, neither had he any bruise or fear about him, save only a small scratch above one of eyes like that of a pin. He was a very lusty comely man, and very fat.

Sir Cloudesley was initially buried in the sand near where he was discovered, at Porth Hellick Cove, but was soon disinterred and his body was later brought back to Plymouth aboard the *Salisbury*, where it was embalmed. It was later carried in state to London with much mourning of a popular hero *en route*. During the journey from the West Country large crowds turned out to pay their respects to the Admiral.

---

32. Marsham-Townsend was a direct descendant of Shovell and the text of their letter was published in Charnock, John, *Biographia Navalis; or, Impartial memoirs of the lives and characters of officers of the navy of Great Britain, from the year 1660 to the present time, drawn from the most authentic sources, and disposed in chronological arrangement.* 4 Volumes, 1794/5, London, Robert Faulder.

On 22 December 1707 the Admiral was given a state funeral, as befitting an English naval hero, at Westminster Abbey. At the instigation of Queen Anne, a twenty-foot-high memorial, designed and sculpted by Grinling Gibbons was commissioned, which carried the following inscription:

Sr CLOUDESLY SHOVELL Knt Rear Admirall of Great Britain and Admirall and Commander in Chief of the Fleet: the just rewards of his long and faithfull services. He was deservedly beloved of his Country and esteem'd, tho' dreaded, by the enemy who had often experienced his conduct and courage. Being shipwreckt on the rocks of Scylly in his voyage from Thoulon the 22d of October 1707, at night, in the 57th year of his age his fate was lamented by all but especially the sea faring part of the Nation to whom he was a generous patron and a worthy example. His body was flung on the shoar and buried with others in the sands; but being soon taken up was plac'd under this monument which his Royall Mistress has caus'd to be erected to commemorate his steady loyalty and extraordinary vertues.

Other memorials were erected including one to the Norfolk-born admiral at Narborough, and there is a bust of him in the Castle Museum at the county town of Norwich, while the Narborough family victims are commemorated both at Knowlton Church, Deal, Kent and at nearby Knowlton Court, the family seat.

A court martial was subsequently held on the survivors from the two salvaged vessels. The court martial of the surviving officers of the *Firebrand* took place on 21 November 1707. It was held aboard the 80-gun 3rd-rate *Somerset,* which at that time was laid up under repair at Blackstakes on the River Medway, Kent, and had Captain John Price as Court President.

The court's findings were:

The court having strictly enquired into the matter it appeared to the court by evidence upon oath of the surviving officers, that they were in their proper station and fell in amongst the rocks with the rest of the ships, and that both before and after she struck they used the utmost endeavours for saving the ship: the court not finding the said Fireship was lost through any neglect of duty in the officers of her. The court does acquit the said Captain Frances Piercy and the other officers as to the loss of the said Fireship the *Firebrand*.[33]

Following the wreck of the *Association* and the other ships, the Admiralty instigated the search for a way of accurately calculating longitude. A recent BBC television documentary ascribed the motivation for this research to loss of treasure to the City of London, rather than much concern for the loss of life, a seemingly jaundiced viewpoint apparently ascribing to a modern political agenda. Nor are rumours

33. ADM1/5266 Court Martial, National Archives, Kew, London.

of vast treasure any more accurate, although this lure of fortune at the rainbow's end (in these cases, of course, the wreck site) has always been a prime motivation for the pillage of sunken ships down the centuries. Attempts at locating some of Shovell's ships have continued almost since they first went down, with the lure of Defoe's 'immense riches' being the spur. Certainly the *Association* was known to be carrying funds for the maintenance of both the Duke of Savoy's troops and also the Coldstream Guards but, as Toulon did not fall, there was not much actual loot to bring back from there, so persistent legends of the drowned admiral's reputed 'ten chests of gold' seemed rather good motivation, and most certainly English gold sovereigns, and Portuguese *Reis*, along with various silver coinage, have been recovered in goodly amounts. Since serious diving on the wrecks commenced back in the 1960s there have been many attempts on the Outer Gilstone site and cannon and other artefacts were brought up by a naval team operating from the inshore minesweeper *Puttenham* in July 1966, with two private teams hovering in the wings waiting their opportunities. Two further inshore minesweepers, the *Odiham* and *Shipham*, joined the hunt the year after but, from 1968 onward, the Royal Navy was ordered to be withdrawn and private companies took over, salvage work continuing for two more decades.

Treasure or not, the earlier loss of the *Coronation* and continuing similar disasters, made accurate navigation one of the Admiralty's most taxing problems. Given the technology of the day, it is not surprising that the emergence of a solution took so long. This problem was eventually solved by the Barton-upon-Humber clockmaker John Harrison who invented the H-4 marine chronometer in 1772 and claimed the £20,000 prize money.

Historically, it was always assumed to have been the difficulty of ascertaining the correct longitude that has been cited as the principal reason for the disaster that overtook Shovell's command; however, more recently, some more diligent and knowledgeable researchers have cast considerable doubt on the veracity of this oft-quoted 'given'. Retired Royal Navy commander, the late William Edward May, whose credentials and research are considered by most, including myself, to be exemplary, was one such doubter. He analysed all forty-four of the logs and journals that still survive from the estimated total of sixty-one from twenty-one of the ships that were involved. He found there were some duplications, including Lieutenant Thomas Jacobs and Walter Lashbrooke of *St George*, Lieutenants John Furzer and Streynsham Master of *Monmouth*, Captain Richard Griffiths and Lieutenant Andrew Horseman of *Swiftsure* and Lieutenants Thomas Graves and Arthur Field of *Torbay*. That still left him forty original references from which to draw his conclusions.

He considered the measurements taken by the *Orford*, as recorded by her Lieutenant Anthony Lochard, rather than those recorded by the *Lennox*, as being the most accurate of the bunch. Indeed the captain of the *Lennox* himself was to record that 'I was surprised to find my ship so far to the northward and indeed can impute it to nothing but the badness of the compass which was very old and full of defects'.[34] May noted of Lochard's entries:

> Each noon he gives the bearing and distance of Spartel, the departure and difference of longitude from it, the D.R.[35] latitude and, when he got one, the observed latitude, and the course and distance made good from the previous noon.[36]

Significantly, however, May also noted that there were 'a few obvious mistakes'. Commander May's studied conclusion was that it was more due to the precise *latitude* that was the more significant factor in this incident than the generally-touted reason of an imprecisely estimated longitude. He made clear that, at the time, neither the longitude *nor* the latitude of the Isles of Scilly was precisely recorded in the 1697 edition of the *Seaman's New Kalendar* by Nathaniel Colson ('Student in Mathematics'), which was the standard navigation guide in use by the fleet at that time.

Nonetheless, if the loss of 'so many men' did spur the advancement of naval navigation it could be said that, from this catastrophic event, good did eventually come. It inspired the mathematician William Whiston and led to the involvement of Parliament and their *Act for the Discovery of Longitude* of 1714 with the establishment of the Board of Longitude with the results that, eventually, ensued. It is also fact that warships with technology beyond any imagining in the eighteenth century did not prevent ships continuing to be lost by wrecking in the centuries that followed, no matter how culpable Shovell has been made out to be in 1707 and since.

---

34. Marcus, Geoffrey Jules, 'Sir Clowdisley Shovell's Last Passage', article in *The Journal of the Royal United Services Institute*, Volume CII, p.547, 1957, London, RUSI.
35. Direct (or Deduced) Reckoning.
36. May, Commander William Edward RN, 'The Last Voyage of Sir Clowdisley Shovel', National Maritime Museum, reproduced in *Journal of Navigation*, Volume 13, No. 3, July 1960, pp.324–32, 1960, London, Royal Institute of Navigation.

Chapter 5

A Melancholy Echo

The *Lutine* – 9 October 1799

In the third quarter of the eighteenth century the French *Marine Nationale* laid down a series of 5th-rate 26-gun frigates designed by acclaimed shipwright Joseph-Marie-Blaise Coulomb and known as the *Magicienne* class. One of these was *La Lutine*.[1] She was ordered on 23 October 1778, laid down at Toulon shipyard in March 1779, launched on 11 September of the same year and commissioned for service in November 1779. She had a gun-deck length of 143 feet 3 inches (46.662metres), an overall length of 145 feet (44.2metres), a beam of 37 feet (11.2metres), a draught of 17 feet (5.2metres) and was armed with twenty-six 12-pounder long guns and six 6-pounder long guns.

On 1 February 1793 the French had invaded the Low Countries and declared war on Great Britain. Once again a British fleet, under Vice-Admiral Sir Samuel Hood (with the assistance of a Spanish squadron under Admiral Juan de Lágara) invested the Mediterranean naval base of Toulon, held by French Royalist forces which had declared for the young King Louis XVII and which were being assailed by the bloodthirsty armies of the Republican Nationalist Convention for their temerity. The brief campaign was not conducted well by the Allied armies ashore and eventually the port was abandoned. When the siege was nearing its end, the French Royalists handed over their whole fleet to the British rather than allow them to fall into Republican hands. It has been recorded that this fleet comprised no fewer than seventeen active battleships, five frigates and eleven corvettes with four battleships and a frigate refitting in the New Basin; and four battleships, five frigates and two corvettes in the Old Basin, one of the latter being *La Lutine*.[2] Other sources assert, in contradiction, that *La Lutine* was not handed over to Vice-Admiral Hood's representatives until 18 December.

More reliably, the records of The National Maritime Museum at Greenwich, vouchsafe the fact that control of *La Lutine* had been handed over to Hood on 29 August and that she had been converted by the British into a bomb vessel equipped with mortars. In that state she was engaged in duels with the French artillery ashore commanded by a certain Colonel Napoleon Bonaparte. The final outcome was that *La Lutine* was found to be in good condition and was adopted into the Royal Navy

---

1. Which can be translated as the *Teaser, Temptress* or *Sprite.*
2. Ireland, Bernard, *The Fall of Toulon: The Last Opportunity to Defeat the French Revolution,* p.301, 2005, London, George Weidenfeld & Nicolson.

as the *Lutine* with immediate effect. Not all the French ships were as worthy and, on their departure from that base, the Allies burnt nine battleships and five frigates, while taking away three battleships, six frigates and several smaller vessels. This was a crippling blow to the fledgling Revolutionary Navy.

Under the White Ensign as the *Lutine,* her first commanding officer was Commander James Macnamara from October 1793 and a year later he was succeeded by Captain John Monckton. *Lutine* arrived at Woolwich Dockyard on 8 November and in 1795 she was re-sheathed in copper up to the waterline and listed for conversion as a 5th-rate frigate and meanwhile she was employed as a static guardship in 1796. In 1797 she commenced this modification at Woolwich Dockyard, which was not finally completed until January 1798 at a cost of £8,643.0s.0d. The *Navy List* of 15 August 1799, amended by Captain Henry Duncan,[3] lists her armament as twenty-six 12-pounders on her main deck, four 24-pounder carronades and four 6-pounders on her quarterdeck, two 24-pounder carronades and two 6-pounders on her foredeck, a total of thirty-eight guns.

Meanwhile the War of the First Coalition continued and the French Republican armies had invaded the Low Countries, Belgium and the Dutch Republic in 1794. The Revolutionary General Jean-Charles Pichegru's troops duly marched into Amsterdam, intent on spreading the poison of the Directory and then, later, the Consulate. This aggression had the effect of compelling the Prince of Orange, *Stadtholder* William V, to flee to exile in the sanctuary of England. A Revolutionary Batavian Republic was announced and they promptly switched their allegiance to their French invaders.[4] It was this unprovoked aggression by the French and subsequent actions by those sections of the Revolutionary Dutch, the so-called 'velvet revolution', that directly forced the abandonment of Amsterdam as the principal European centre of capital and trade. A new centre for free trade was essential and it was the independent Hanseatic City-State of Hamburg to which both refugees from 'The Terror', and their considerable money and trading expertise, then flowed. Hamburg thrived as never before for five years on this influx of talent, trade and cash.

This defection by the Dutch led seamlessly on to the War of the Second Coalition, and the British Fleet under Admiral Adam Duncan, flying his flag aboard the 74-gun 3rd-rate *Venerable*, duly trounced the Dutch Navy in the shallows of their own waters at the Battle of Camperdown on 11 October 1797. The Allies joined with the Russians and mounted an invasion of northern Holland in August 1799 with the landing at Callantsoog under Lieutenant-General Sir Ralph Abercromby. Unfortunately, although there were high expectations of an easy land victory and the hope of being welcomed as liberators, both of these ambitions failed dismally to materialise. However, the British, enforcing a blockade of Amsterdam, in which the *Lutine* duly played her part, had discovered considerable sympathy for the Orange cause in what remained of

---

3. The Deputy Controller, Navy Office to 1801.
4. When the French did this with the Germans in 1940 it was termed 'collaboration' – the effect was much the same.

the Batavian fleet, and some defeatism, if absent in those ashore. The Anglo-Russian invasion fleet of 200 warships and transports duly arrived off the Texel roadstead on 26 August 1799, and commenced landing Abercromby's and the Russian troops. The Den Helder forts quickly surrendered and the Dutch fleet withdrew and took up position at Vlieter.

On the 30th Vice-Admiral Sir William Mitchell took in a squadron comprising nine British and two Russian two-deckers and five British frigates, standing in toward the Texel via the Mars Diep, where the 64-gun *America* and the Russian 66-gun *Ratwiesan*, along with the 38-gun frigate, *Latona*, all went aground, the latter soon getting off and joining Mitchell's command which had passed Helder Point and steered into the Vleiter Channel.[5]

The Batavian commander, Rear-Admiral Samuel Story, tried to gain time by a parley but Mitchell was not fooled and gave the Dutchman one hour to surrender or fight, and mutinies began in several ships, while some high commanders were secretly Orange sympathisers. On the surrender the British took over these ships and put prize crews aboard and sent them back to England. Mitchell accepted the surrender of the remains of the Batavian Republic Navy on 30 August. Ashore, however, the Batavian and French armies, with the support of the 'occupied' Dutch populace, were more successful and they forced the Allies to withdrew their troops in October. The Royal Navy continued operations, the whole affair being termed the 'Vlieter Incident'.[6]

The Royal Navy therefore began to exercise its age-old policy of close blockade and the *Lutine* was among the squadrons of British warships that mainly served in the North Sea and took part in the blockade of Amsterdam and Mitchell's aggressive actions in the islands. In May 1799 Monckton was moved on to command the 98-gun 2nd-rate battleship *Formidable*, under Admiral Sir Charles Thompson, and his successor as commander of the *Lutine* was 32-year-old Captain Lancelott Skynner. He was immediately thrust into the actions and patrols off the Dutch coast and the naval sorties of August 1799 in support of the Duke of York's fresh land offensive against the Dutch and their French masters. Meanwhile, far away to the north, other momentous decisions were being made which would affect the fate of the little *Lutine* and her ship's company.

By 1799 hitherto booming Hamburg was teetering on the edge of financial disaster. Wild speculation had fuelled a buying frenzy centred on West Indian imports – sugar,

---

5. The Allied Fleet formed up with *Glatton* (64) ahead, then followed *Romney* (50), *Isis* (60) Flag, *Veteran* (64), *Ardent* (64), *Belliqueux* (64), *Monmouth* (64), *Over yssel* (64) – a Prize taken from the Dutch earlier, *Mistisloff* (66) and the frigates *Melpomene* (38), *Shannon* (32) *Juno* (32), with the *Lutine* under Captain John Monckton at the rear of the line. The 18-gun sloop *Victor* was used as a despatch vessel.

6. The ships which mutinied and then gave in to the British ultimatum, were the 74-gun 2nd-rate *Washington*, the 64-gun 3rd-rates *Cerberus*, *De Ruyter*, *Gelderland*, *Leyden* and *Utrecht*, the 50 gun 4th rates *Batavier* and *Beschermer*, the 44-gun *Mars*, the 40-gun *Amphitrite* and 32-gun *Ambuscade*, 5th-rates, and the 16-gun brig *Galathea*. For the military side of this operation see *A Subaltern* (pseudonym) – *The Campaign in Holland 1799*, pp.16–17, 1861, London, William Mitchell Military Publishers.

coffee and spices – but it was now feeling the ravages of the Continent-wide war and this led to a run on the markets and an increasing and alarming number of bankruptcies of famous trading houses. When the Elbe froze up and imports could not reach their markets this made things worse. A familiar enough tale to modern ears of course and, as usual, the finances of the whole of Europe were threatened by economic meltdown. The growing power of Britain was then, as now, fuelled by the City of London, and when the British ambassador at Hamburg, Sir James Craufurd, sent an urgent appeal to the British Government in London for financial help on 20 September the response was instant.[7]

On receipt of this appeal from the Government it appeared self-evident to a group of merchants, led by the Goldsmid Company in the City, that it was in their own interests not to let a crash occur in Hamburg lest it lead to serious ramifications in London, and they quickly set about assembling a vast sum of gold and silver in a bid to stave off the looming crisis. The Royal Navy was ordered to convey this treasure, conservatively estimated at £1,200,000[8] in bullion, destined for Hamburg via Cuxhaven. At this point it should be noted here that all Lloyd's records were destroyed in a fire in 1838 that started with an overheated stove in Lloyd's room and which spread until it totally destroyed the Royal Exchange, including the historic Lloyd's coffee house itself. The precise quantities of the various quantities of specie that the Bank of England sold to the merchant gentlemen are on record at the Bank of England, but how much of this the *Lutine* actually carried can never be known for certain and therefore all estimates down the years have been pure conjecture.[9]

It was recorded that the bullion was packed in relatively flimsy casks which were bound with iron hoops, while the silver was carried in similar casks but with wooden hoops. Neither form of container proved strong enough to last long in conditions such as they were soon to find themselves in and quickly disintegrated, leaving the coins themselves to be randomly distributed or sucked down into the silt with each successive tide.

---

7. As an aside it should be noted that both Craufurd in Hamburg and William Wickham, the British *Chargé d'Affaires* in Berne, Switzerland, were secretly running networks of spies and were in close contact with William Granville, 1st Baron Grenville, the British Foreign Secretary: see Sir James Craufurd, *Foreign Office and Predecessors: Political and other Departments: General correspondence before 1906, Bremen, Hamburg & Lubeck, 1781–1870*; FO33, National Archives, Kew, London. Also William Wickham,*Correspondence with Sir James Craufurd at Hamburg, 1798–1801*, 38M49/1/66/1-40, Hampshire Archives and Local Studies, Winchester. HRO Library, Books 1138-a-b.

8. In excess of 12 million Dutch guilders, being the equivalent of approximately £103 million in 2015.

9. Although it is recorded that on the morning of 11 January, while still treating the Royal Exchange fire, they did manage to salvage the safe containing the Lloyd's secretaries' books, in addition to cheques and bank notes. When the drawers of the safe were opened outside this valuable find was immediately blown around but it was reputed that at least some were, 'collected carefully and the numbers and dates traced'. It is thought this included the Lloyd's Subscription Book of 1799. Likewise, the full passenger list was, most regrettably, apparently also destroyed in the same conflagration.

Admiral Lord Duncan, the Commander-in-Chief of the North Sea Fleet, with his flag flying in the 74-gun 3rd-rate, *Kent*,[10] and lying in the Yarmouth Roads off Great Yarmouth, Norfolk, was given the responsibility by Their Lordships at the Admiralty of conveying the Government payments destined for the troops ashore, but *additionally*, the civilian contribution also, along with thirty distinguished passengers, these worthies being mainly City of London merchants or their representatives. Initially a cutter was assigned to thus unusual task, it not being the Royal Navy's usual remit to use their warships as packet boats for civilian use.[11]

Duncan's instructions stemmed from a request initiated by the Secretary of State of the Treasury to the Lords Commissioners of the Admiralty dated 27 September which concerned the safe and urgent transportation of a sum of silver to the Texel 'for the use of the Army in Holland'. But they added a more unusual rider for this consignment stating that it would also include 'a quantity of bullion for Hamburg'. They requested that one or more naval vessels be put at their disposal for this conveyance as soon as possible.[12] The Admiralty replied the following day stating that they had ordered the new 36-gun 5th-rate frigate *Amethyst* (Captain John Cooke) to be made available for this task. The Secretary of State duly advised Their Lordships on 2 October that the silver coinage 'for the Army in Holland', had been safely loaded aboard the *Amethyst* at Gravesend, but that the Hamburg monies 'would not be ready until next week'. Due to the urgency it was requested that the Government monies be despatched at once and it was requested that a second vessel be made available for the latter consignment at that time. Admiral Duncan therefore allocated the 136-ton Hired Armed Cutter *Nile* (Lieutenant Richard Whitehead) for this duty. Meanwhile the *Amethyst* duly sailed from the Nore on 6 October, reaching Texel without incident three days later, where the Army funds were handed over safely; she left Texel again on the 20th and safely arrived back at the Nore on the 23rd.

By this time the initial monies of the City of London's bullion consignment destined for Hamburg had finally arrived at Gravesend where, on 12 October, Lieutenant Whitehead[13] had arrived in the *Nile*, and placed himself and his command at the Treasury's disposal. He notified his superiors on the Sunday that he had received aboard bullion from Messers Goldsmids & Co. and had duly sailed with it to the Elbe, and, like Cooke, he then carried out the mission without a hitch. In view of what happened to the subsequent shipment one would have thought Their Lordships

---

10. Confusingly, the Royal Navy was also employing another *Kent*, a former mercantile vessel, the 12-carronade, hired armed cutter commanded by Lieutenant William Lanyon and she was an active participant of the inshore squadron employed off the Dutch coast at this time.

11. How this came about has been most carefully documented in a recent excellent volume by Frederick Martin, who examined the entire surviving relevant correspondence; see Martin, Frederick, *The History of Lloyd's and of Marine Insurance in Great Britain*, 2004, Clark, New Jersey, USA, The Lawbook Exchange Ltd.

12. It does not appear that the fact that the Hamburg portion of these monies were *not exclusively* Government funds was made clear to the Admiralty in this initial note.

13. ADM9/6/1998, National Archives, Kew, London.

would have been pleased at his initiative and success, but all Whitehead received was a growl of admonishment from the Admiralty about sailing without authorisation!

In the interim, word had got around in the City that the Royal Navy was conveying the money to Hamburg, rather than it being sent via an ordinary packet boat. Instantly, considerably more funds suddenly became available and Vice-Admiral Duncan was therefore directly petitioned by the merchants to provide them with yet another vessel. Of towering physical statue, but notoriously short in temper, Adam Duncan was nearing the end of his tether on this unorthodox behaviour, but he had been a recipient of a Sword of Honour from the City for his victory at Camperdown and probably felt obliged to respond in return. He duly prudently cleared his yardarm by advising the Admiralty in the same 11 October epistle that 'Having received yesterday a pressing application from the merchants to convey a quantity of bullion lying here to Cuxhaven, I ordered Lieutenant Terrel (*sic*) of the hired Cutter *Courier* to proceed with it'.[14] Threlfall was duly alerted for the task but Duncan then had second thoughts and, on reflection, he now considered the little *Courier* a rather inadequate craft to convey so many important citizens to Holland. Considerations such as the bad weather at the time of year and the largeness of the civilian passenger complement pointed to the need for a more powerful and seaworthy vessel, coupled with the desire for a more senior captain as host, with knowledge of the area and a reliable crew to be entrusted with such a ticklish and unusual task.

Duncan therefore changed his plan and had both passengers and cargo offloaded and transferred aboard the *Lutine*, which was commanded by Captain Lancelott Skynner. This worthy was an experienced officer who had held a succession of commands and had previously been appointed as captain of the sloop *Zebra* in November 1794, the 5th-rate *Experiment* in January 1795, the 3rd-rate *Ganges* in 1796 and the 5th-rate *Beaulieu* in March the same year. He had been appointed to the *Lutine* in May 1795 and, just prior to his final voyage, the *Lutine* had already run this very same route, having, on 2 October, escorted the Packet Boat *Prince of Orange* from Yarmouth Roads to Cuxhaven with mails, passengers and a King's Messenger aboard. Skynner was therefore thoroughly acquainted with the route he was to retrace.

Lord Duncan duly advised Their Lordships about this diversion of *Lutine* from her normal duties in a letter dated 9 October:

The merchants interested in making remittances to the continent for the support of their credit, having made application to me for a King's ship to carry over a considerable sum of money, on account of there being no Packet for that purpose, I have complied with their request, and ordered the *Lutine* to Cuxhaven with the same, together with the mails lying there for want of conveyance; directing

---

14. This might possibly be a misinterpretation of Duncan's handwriting – in fact it was Ship's Master Arthur Threlfall who commanded the 122-ton, 12-gunned Hired Armed Cutter *Courier* at this time.

Captain Skynner to proceed to Stromness[15] immediately after doing so, to take under his protection the Hudson's Bay's ships and see them in safety to the Nore.

Also rumoured to be part of her unbelievably valuable cargo were the Dutch Crown Jewels, which had been re-set and polished by the long-established London Royal Jewellers and Goldsmiths, Rundell and Bridges of 32 Ludgate Hill, and were to be returned 'hermetically sealed in a strong iron chest'.[16] This tale was repeated in another newspaper as late as March 1869 but it is pure fiction because, although much individual jewellery featured in the court of King William I, and was certainly subsequently dispersed across Europe by the French invasion, the first 'official' regalia of Holland was not commissioned by King William II until 1840. 'It is thus,' lamented Frederick Martin, 'history is written – and copied.'

The famous Lloyd's firm of underwriters had its origins in the coffee house of Edward Lloyd in Tower Street in the late 1660s. Here the new fashion for the drink brought together merchants, traders, ship-owners, sea captains and businessmen to discourse on their doings and conduct informal transactions. The growing wealth of England and the expansion of her empire centred on sea power and there was an upsurge in the need for merchant ships at risk from the elements and our enemies alike, to have their valuable cargoes insured. As one merchant would not be able to cover the whole cost, 'brokers' took the risk from one to another until the whole risk was fully 'underwritten', i.e. covered. Should a loss occur they would, on their word and bond, be liable for the share of the cover they had committed to. In 1769 a group of these influential men established the New Lloyd's Coffee House in Pope's Head Alley and from there their business became more and more formalised, but still relied totally on the trust that, once a word was given, a debt would be paid.

Thus it was that in 1799 Lloyd's, as it had become, undertook to insure a portion of *Lutine*'s cargo. But it must be noted that this did not include all the monies embarked. The records of the various other parties that had made their own companies' individual contributions to the grand total have been scattered to the four winds down the centuries. It has been estimated, following examination of the sequence of the serial numbers stamped on the gold and silver ingots that have been recovered, that she embarked one thousand bars in all.

The *Lutine*, thus laden, duly sailed away off Great Yarmouth on 9 October, bound for Cuxhaven. Under Captain Skynner were First Lieutenant Charles Gastine Aufrere, Lieutenant James Jervis Kinneer,[17] Walter Montgomery who was the ship's surgeon and John Strong, ship's steward, a total crew complement of 240 officers and men. She also

---

15. Stromness, a port in the Orkney Islands, at this time a staging stop for merchant ships arriving from Newfoundland and northern Canada.

16. *Urban, Sylvanus*, Gent. (the editorial pseudonym of John Bowyer Nichols), *Gentleman's Magazine: and Historical Chronicle for the year 1799, Volume LXIX, November 1799*, pp.895–6, London, William Pickering.

17. The eldest son of Superannuated Captain James Kinneer who had previously commanded the fire-ship *Salamander*, and 6th-rates *Daphne* and *Hyaena* – and had then been retired.

carried thirty distinguished worthies to oversee the transport and transfer of the monies, among them being the 27-year-old Anne Henri René Sigismonde de Montmorency-Luxemboorg, Duc de Châtillon, as well as several women, an infant and many City of London worthies including 20-year-old Daniel Weinholt, conveying £40,000 for investment in the House of Parish and Co., Hamburg, whose body later came ashore at Hornum[18] and one other unfortunate, Hartog Isaac Levy Schabracq, representing the company of brothers Benjamin and Abraham Goldsmid of Capel Court.[19]

The last professional eyes to have observed her passage that night appear to have been from aboard the 32-gun 5th-rate *Blonde* (Captain Daniel Dobree), which had been alternately transporting Russian troops over to (unsuccessfully) fight the French and evacuating fleeing Dutch refugees. She was anchored off the island of Texel, where the then Lieutenant James Anthony Gardner later recalled, 'A short time before we sailed we saw the *Lutine*, 36, Captain Launcelot Skynner, at the back of the Haaks,[20] and if I am correct, the evening she was lost and only one saved, *who died soon after*.'[21]

On the evening of 9 October, a black night, a powerful north-westerly gale was encountered and the *Lutine* sought sanctuary but was swept by the tide into the *Ijzergat*,[22] a swirling deep-water channel between the muddy islands of Vlieland and Terschelling, with the smaller sandbar of de Richel to the south-east, off the Waddenzee region of the northern Dutch coast. Here, instead of safety, she was dragged by the strong tidal currents onto the notorious sandbanks off the islands. The first reports from the *Naval Chronicle* stated that 'a strong lee tide rendered every effort of Captain Skynner to avoid the threatened danger unavailable, and it was alike impossible, during the night, to receive any assistance from the *Arrow*, Captain Portlock, which was [by then] in company, or the shore, from whence several schoots (*sic*) were in readiness to go

18. Lack, Clem, BA Dip Jour. FRHistSQ, Vice-President, 'The Man Whom the Lion Bit', Address to the Royal Historical Society of Queensland, Newstead House, Brisbane, dated 24 April 1969; and, following, Siemon, Rosamund, *The Eccentric Mr Wienholt*, 2005, Brisbane, University of Queensland Press.

19. Fletcher, Johan J.,Typescript, 'Notes on the wreck of the *Lutine*: Some Materials for The true Story of the *Lutine*.' NOT/18. National Maritime Museum, Greenwich, London; also, 'Account of the *Lutine* and description of the salvage operations 1894–98 compiled by Johan J. Fletcher, in charge of operations, with diagrams, sketches and photographs', dated 1 January 1894 to 31 December 1898, FLE/8 & HIS/4 National Maritime Museum, Greenwich, London.

20. The Haaks was a dangerous shoal to the west of Texel. The 32-gun 5th-rate *Blanche* (Commander John Ayscough) had gone ashore there on 29 September and, although she was got off, she later sank in the New Deep as a result of her damage. No crew were lost and the subsequent court martial totally exonerated Ayscough. The Sailing Directions noted: 'In approaching the Haaks from the westward, great care is requisite', adding that, 'The Haaks are very dangerous sands, composed of many patches, which were ... frequently shifting.'

21. My italics. Gardner, Commander James Anthony RN, *Recollections of James Anthony Gardner – Commander RN (1775–1814)*, Hamilton, Admiral Sir Richard Vesey GCB & Laughton, John Knox MA, DLitt (Editors), 1906, London, Spottiswoode & Co for The Navy Records Society.

22. The *Ijzergat* or Iron Gate.

to her'.[23] One recent American pundit ignores any such mitigating evidence of effects of the north-westerly storm weather and tidal conditions in the dead of night on the *Lutine*'s misfortune, and instead asserts that the wind 'should have enabled him to give this perilous shore a wide berth and to keep to his course up the North Sea' and that, instead, Skynner 'plunged into a death-trap from which there was no escape'.[24] For a more realistic take on the route from Great Yarmouth to Cuxhaven, having the Dutch and German Friesland Island to your lee, there is an excellent description of these treacherous waters and evershifting bars which can be found in the famous novel by Erskine Childers, which, although fiction, is written from the author's own firsthand experience of small sail-boat work in the area.[25]

Once ashore there she was pounded by the breakers and quickly broke up. Here, amid the whirling currents and hidden shoals and hazards, the *Lutine*, like so many hundreds of ships before and after her, found that there was little opportunity or hope of salvation. Her cargo, her entire crew and every one of her passengers were drowned, save two men.[26]

Thorough research by Johan J. Fletcher had thrown up anecdotal evidence of actual eyewitness to the immediate aftermath of the disaster,[27] the written testimony of a local fisherman named Jan Folkerts Visser. It was not until July 1938 that Johannes Arnoldus Hermann Rijnders, Burgomaster of West Terschelling, had publicly revealed the continued existence of this document. Further research by Professor Sense Jan van der Molen, in conjunction with Hans Jan de Freyer, Curator of the Terschelling Museum, *Het Behouden Huis*, revealed the original which he duly transcribed and included in his comprehensive account of the disaster.[28]

From memory the eighty-year-old recalled that on that fateful night, at 0200, the brig-sloop *Wolverine* (Captain William Bolton) had arrived from the Vlieland Road with Captain Portlock aboard, and that the British reported that they had witnessed distress rockets being fired from the *Buitengronden*, indicating a vessel was in trouble there. All available mariners were ordered to man their craft immediately and head out there urgently to see if any rescue could be effected. Visser recalled that he joined his father in the pilot boat with six others and they put to sea around 0500:

---

23. My parentheses. Report, 'Loss of *La Lutine*', dated 12 October in *Naval Chronicle*, Volume II: from July to December MDCCXCIX, 1799, London, Bunney & Gold.

24. Paine, Ralph Delahye, *The Book of Buried Treasure: Being a True History of the Gold, Jewels, and Plate of Pirates, Galleons, etc., which are sought for to this day*, 2010, Chapel Hill, NC, Project Gutenberg – University of North Carolina.

25. Childers, Erskine Hamilton, *The Riddle of the Sands: A Record of Secret Service*, Chapter 12 *et al.*, 1903, London, Smith, Elder & Co.

26. Ruiter, Wijke, Feature, *The eternal mystery of lost gold*. Scribe Weekly.com.

27. *Logbook of* Lutine *Salvage*, translation from Dutch by Johan J. Fletcher, donated by his sister, Miss V. Fletcher to the National Maritime Museum 1940; FLE/3 & HIS/4, National Maritime Museum, Greenwich, London.

28. Van der Molen, Professor Sense Jan, translated by James Brockway, *The Lutine Treasure: The 150-year search for gold in the wreck of the frigate Lutine*, p.36, 1970, London, Adlard Coles Limited; original published in Rotterdam by Nijgh & Van Ditmar.

and there found many chattels and corpses, that they picked three corpses out of the water, one chest, a crate and two barrels containing flour, and afterwards came across a piece of the upper gun-deck of a ship, to which a man was clinging. That they thereupon immediately did all in their power to save him, that after much effort they succeeded in getting him aboard, after which they had returned to the waterway, since they saw nothing else other than all manner of goods and corpses. That they offered him some of the wine and bread (which they had taken from the sea), very little of which he used, and that he seemed to be out of his mind, seeing the commotion he made none of which they could understand.

On returning to the *Wolverine* the Dutch handed over three corpses 'which were clad in uniform: blue coat, trousers and white waistcoats: one with two epaulettes, the others each with one'. The *Wolverine*'s doctor went aboard the pilot boat to attend to the survivor, but while administering attention on the survivor

whereupon he swooned and was afterwards taken on board the warship, after which they returned to Vlieland and being on board the warship a day later, they then met the survivor, who was walking on a crutch since his leg was injured, and then learned that the survivor was the writer of the English frigate *Lutine*....

Visser also recalled that the three corpses, which were those of Captain Skynner and his two Lieutenants, Aufrere and Kinneer, were taken ashore and buried in Vlieland churchyard. This burial was also attested to by another veteran, one Willem Blom, who recalled that for several days after the incident corpses continued to be washed ashore and were also interred. The Dutch fishermen estimated that a total of eighty-seven bodies from the *Lutine* were thus recovered and, later joined by other grim recoveries, these were buried in massed, unmarked, graves reputedly close by the Brandaris light house.

Meanwhile the *Naval Chronicle* gave a different account of survivors, claiming that two men were 'picked up by the cutter *L'Espiegle* near Borkum, on their oars, one of whom expired soon after his arrival at Yarmouth. The other disposed that being under a press of sail, at about eight knots an hour, the vessel struck upon a rock and instantly upset',[29] having crossed the Enkhausen flat among the Dutch Islands at this period.[30]

29. The 17-gun Brig-Sloop *Espiegle*, (at first under Captain James Boorder and later under Captain James Slade) was certainly operating in the inner channels of the Zuyder Zee or *Zuiderzee* – translates as 'Southern Sea.'

30. She had originally been the French *L'Espiegle* (Master Joseph Henri Maxmin) which had been taken as a prize by the 5th-rate *Nymphe* (Captain Percy Fraser) and 6th-rate *Circe* (Captain Roberet Winthrop) in an action off Ushant on 30 November 1793, and added to the Royal Navy. HMS *Espiegle* Captain's Log 5 October 1799 to 30 September 1800, ADM51/1303; Master's Logs 2 March 1798 to 16 December 1801, ADM52/ 2972; Pay Books (Series III) 1 July 1779 to 15 December 1804, ADM35/586; Musters 1 October 1779 to 31 December 1801, Musters List 1 May 1799 to 31 October 1800, ADM 36/13463, National Archives, Kew, London.

The distance from West Terschelling to Borkum is fifty–seven miles (92km). Lest this is considered improbable, it should be remembered that the corpse of another victim, Daniel Wienholt, was eventually washed ashore on Sylt Island, some 350 miles farther north. His body was discovered by Herrn Straendvoyt Decker, and he was buried on 11 November at St Niels Church, Westerland, Isle of Sylt,[31] where his memorial tablet still exists. *The Chronicle* added:

> When the dawn broke, *La Lutine* was in vain looked for: she had gone to pieces, and all on board perished, except two men, who were picked up, and one of whom has since died from the fatigue he had encountered. The survivor is Mr Schabrack (Schabracq), a Notary Public. [32]

They estimated that £600,000 had sunk in the wreckage.

Captain Nathaniel Portlock, the commander of the British squadron based at Vlieland, which comprised the 28–gun sloop *Arrow* (with Lieutenant David Gilmour) and the 14–gun brig-sloop *Wolverine*,[33] was instructed by the Admiralty to see what could be recovered, and he duly surveyed the wreck site and informed the Admiralty of his impotency to deal with what he had found.

> Sir, It is with extreme pain that I have to state to you the melancholy fate of his majestys's Ship *Lutine*, which ship ran onto the outer banks of the Fly Island passage on the night of the 9th Inst. in a heavy gale of wind from the NNW, and I am much afraid the crew with the exception of one man, who was saved on a part of the wreck, have perished.

Of the alleged sole survivor Portlock wrote, 'This man when taken up was almost exhausted. He is of present tolerably recovered, and relates that the *Lutine* left Yarmouth Roads on the Morning of the 9th inst. bound for the Texel.' This latter statement was incorrect for her true and stated destination was actually the Elbe River and Hamburg – and his misapprehension on this score appears to indicate that, contrary to some more recent Dutch allegations, Portlock had no prior knowledge of the *Lutine*'s true mission, especially as she had been a last-minute substitution. Equally false, if persistent, was the similarly wrong press speculations of the day that the bullion which the *Lutine* carried was British Government money to pay for the British military operations in Holland against the French and Batavian Republic, for, as we have noted earlier, these strictly Government funds, for the Army payroll, had already been safely conveyed by the *Nile*, as was right and proper. By contrast, that

---

31. Sylt at that date was part of Denmark, not Germany.
32. A Notary Public is an individual with certain legal qualifications and usually solicitor experience who is fully authorised to certify or authorise particular documents attesting to their legitimacy especially when needed abroad.
33. She was the former mercantile collier *Rattler*.

money now loaded aboard the *Lutine* was an exclusively private and commercial cargo of specie funded by London merchants, a rather more unconventional arrangement and one that Their Lords Commissioners of the Admiralty, were soon to regret. He added that 'she had on board Considerable quantity of Money'.

This survivor specified by Portlock was not named in that initial report but Vincent Nolte later recorded that 'if I am not mistaken, the second mate was the sole survivor and the sorry bearer of these tidings'.[34]

Portlock added:

> The wind blowing strong from the NNW, and the lee tide coming on, rendered it impossible with Schowts[35] or other boats to go out to aid her until daylight in the morning, and that time nothing was seen but parts of the wreck. I shall use every endeavour to save what I can from the wreck, but from the situation she is lying in, I am afraid little will be recovered.[36]

Vice-Admiral Mitchell enclosed Portlock's letter with his report to the Admiralty in London, dated 15 October, which they received four days later. The wreck quickly broke in half.

Apart from Visser's testimony that the survivor was the ship's writer, nothing more was known of him for almost two centuries. However, as the bicentenary of the *Lutine* disaster approached, the islanders decided to mount a *Lutine* Commemoration year in 1999 and, in preparation, from 1997 further deep research was done. According to Mr Gerald de Weerdt, a later curator of Terschelling Maritime Museum, in 1997, the local Dutch historians were struck, as had been Der Molen earlier, by the scarcity of detailed information on the *Lutine*'s loss. The conclusions the team apparently reached were that 'the storm alone could not have caused the accident'.[37] They based their findings on three facts: (1) The *Lutine* had been fully overhauled the year before and her rigging renewed, she was therefore assumed to be 'in a perfect state of maintenance'; (2) The *Lutine* had been intensively employed in the area of the Friesland Islands where she was lost and therefore the crew from the captain down, were 'highly experienced' in both the navigational hazards and how their ship handled in such conditions; (3) The storm conditions encountered, did not present any more than 'a routine procedure' to a ship like the *Lutine*. They concluded that, *ergo*, the loss of the ship was 'human failure'.

---

34. Nolte, Vincent, *Vijftig jaren in de beide halfronden* (*Fifty years in the two hemispheres: memories of the life of a merchant voormaligen*.), p.21,1883, Leiden, D noothoven van Goor.

35. Dutch *Schuyts* or *Schuits* – flat-bottom sailing barges with leeboards for navigation of shallow channels.

36. Captain Nathaniel Portlock to Vice-Admiral Andrew Mitchell, aboard the 50-gun 4th-rate *Isis* in the Vlie Passage, dated 10 October 1799.

37. De Weerdt, Gerald A., 'Sinking of the *Lutine* 1799: The never-ending story of a shipwreck.' Address delivered to The Insurance Institute of London, 12 October 1999.

Whether this revisionist theory is accepted in total or not, the Dutch investigators went much further than that in their assertions. One excellent piece of detective work resulted, for, in examining the Muster and Paybook Lists of the *Isis*, Mitchell's flagship, they at last discovered the identity of the naval survivor.[38] An entry for 18 October recorded that Able Seaman John Rogers had joined the *Isis* with an entry stating he was 'from the *Arrow*, the late *Lutine*'. A clerk aboard *Isis* noted that Rogers was 'unserviceable'. An examination of the last available muster list for the *Lutine* confirmed that John Rogers had been a crew member of that vessel. This clue, which had previously always been overlooked, was dutifully followed up and it was found that the badly-injured Rogers was retained aboard the *Isis* until she returned home in January 1800, when the opportunity was taken to transfer him to the hospital ship *Spanker*.[39] All well and good, but when he was later deemed to have recovered Rogers was transferred to the *Grāna*[40] at Sheerness, the transfer taking effect on 17 February 1800. The last report on him from the *Grāna*, dated 14 May 1800, was that John Rogers, born in Newry, in what is now Northern Ireland, had 'run' (i.e. deserted).[41] Rogers thus disappears from known Admiralty records and one can imagine that he took on an alias to further escape detection.

The Dutch investigators allege that this evidence proves that someone 'tried to keep him out of sight, far away from, for example, the media. Probably his story about human errors would embarrass the Admiralty. Lloyd's would have refused to pay out the insurance money ...'. Quite how desertion leads to this assumption is tenuous in the extreme. Other Dutch sources appear to pursue some kind of dramatic 'cover-up' theory where none appears to exist.[42] To this author, all this speculation seems an awful lot of assumptions to make with little real proof. It was acknowledged that Rogers was badly injured in the wreck, with one, or both legs, damaged. As soon as convenient he was put aboard a hospital ship, which is logical rather than sinister, as is his subsequent transfer to a convalescent vessel for further recuperation. He then chose to desert, a

---

38. HMS *Isis* – Paybooks 1 May 1779 to 10 March 1880, ADM34/426 and Musters List (Series I) HMS *Arrow*, 1 October 1797 to 28 February 1800, ADM36/13367 National Archives, Kew, London.
39. *Spanker* had been built as a 24-gun floating battery but in 1795 had been converted to act as a hospital ship and at this date was commanded by Lieutenant William Caspal.
40. She was a 527-ton Spanish 30-gun 6th-rate, commanded by *El Capitán* Don Nicolás de Medina, which was taken as a prize after a battle with the British 32-gun 5th-rate *Cerberus* (Captain Robert Mann) on 25 February 1781. After some service as a 28-gun post ship in the Royal Navy, she had been converted at Sheerness to act as a convalescent ship from 1 January 1799, under the command of Lieutenant Daniel Gibson.
41. Admiralty: *Naval Hospitals' and Hospital Ships' Musters, and Miscellaneous Journals. Records of Medical and Prisoner of War Departments; Hospital Muster Books – Grāna (Ship) 1798 to 1800.* ADM102/246 and HMS *Grāna* May 1800 in ADM36/14708, National Archives, Kew, London.
42. See, for example, Huiskes, Robert, and de Weerdt, Gerald A., in co-operation with Museum 't Huys Preserve and Museum Tromp Huys. *De Lutine 1799–1999 de raadelachtige ondergang van een schip vol goud (The Lutine, 1799–1999: The mysterious sinking of a ship full of gold.)* 1999, Bossum, Thoth.

common enough practice at the time.[43] Maybe he didn't wish to face a similar ordeal again once fully recovered – and who could blame him! As for the allegation that all traces of Rogers have been deliberately expunged from the records, or 'systematically removed', then surely their own, and others' successful research findings demonstrates otherwise? So before we embrace yet another conspiracy theory, perhaps yet more facts need to be unearthed.

We now have yet another Dutch study, published in Belgium, this time by the novelist Martin Kendriksma,[44] but, as at the date of this book going to press, this has not yet been published in full in an English translation, so a meaningful comparison has not yet proved possible. In addition, I have been unable to obtain permission to read the full script of a lecture on the subject delivered by this gentleman in London in February 2015.

Captain Portlock's initial forebodings of the impracticability of any salvage seemed quickly vindicated. The *Wolverine* was joined by the *Arrow* and two *Conquest*-class shallow-draught gun-brigs, the *Pelter* (Lieutenant John Walsh) and the *Swinger* (Lieutenant John Lucas), from the Inshore Squadron, both of which had the advantage that they could be rowed into the shallow waters among the sandbars with eighteen oars if necessary, but this little flotilla could do little. On the 11th the wreck site was surrounded by fishing vessels and Portlock, knowing the tendency of islanders everywhere to take advantage of such situations, had immediately ordered Lieutenant Lucas to take precautions. Lucas duly complied and his action was recorded in the log of the *Swinger*: 'Sent the Cutter manned and armed with Lieutenant Braddel[45] to the wreck to Prevent the Dutch from Robbing Her'. Again this has been misconstrued; rather than being a simply preventative measure at unauthorised salvage of British goods from a British ship, which would have been taken as a routine and reasonable measure in *any* similar such situation, this order has nowadays been hinted at as having more sinister undertones,[46] as if Portlock and his local team were already privy and fully *au fait* with the enormity of the wealth carried by the *Lutine*.

The second survivor (which some historians have stated to have been Isaac Hartog Levy Schabracq), did not survive for very long.[47] He was cited in the contemporary

---

43. See Rodgers, Nicholas Andrew Martin, 'Stragglers and Deserters from the Royal Navy during the Seven Years War', *Bulletin of Institute of Historical Research LVII*, (Vol. 57), pp.56–79, 1984, London, University of London.
44. *Lutine: de spannendste Nederlandse goudjact ooit* (trans – *Lutine: the most exciting Dutch gold yacht ever.*) Martin Hendriksma. 2013: Brajek-Michelbeke. Uitgeverij De Geus.
45. Lieutenant John Tandy Braddell, who died 30 June 1811. See *A List of the Flag officers of His Majesty's Fleet with the dates of their First Commissions, as Admirals, Vice-Admirals, Rear-Admirals and Captains*, dated 1 January 1804, London, M. & Samuel Brooke. Also ADM6/348/13, pp.49–52, National Archives, Kew, London.
46. Wijke, *op. cit.*, following closely on de Weerdt, *op. cit.*
47. Amsterdam-born Schabracq was the fifty-one-year-old eldest son of Jewish parents, and was living in Lothbury, City of London. He had been granted a notarial faculty and worked with the Scriveners & Aelig Company. His niece had married into the Goldsmid family and the firm used him quite frequently on such missions.

press reports as being the 'sole survivor', which was untrue, but that 'he could give no coherent account, and he died while on the way to England before his shattered nerves had mended', which tallies very well with the description given by the fisherman Visser in his account of the behaviour of the man they had got aboard the pilot boat and also somewhat with Gardner's vague recollection. However, Schabracq had married a Christian girl, Frances Ling, and his widow duly had his will proved by Benjamin and Abraham Goldsmid, to which his friend Michael Bedford and Frances's mother Ann, added an account of how he had put his affairs in order prior to his departure should anything happen to him during his mission.[48] No mention of burial, or recovery of body, was recorded, which would have been the case had he returned to England aboard a British warship before he died. In fact, the note specifically states that he 'had not returned'. The 'ship's writer' mentioned by Visser being one and the same as the second mate mentioned by Gardner, a worthy hailing from Newry, County Down, is therefore the most likely candidate.[49]

The exact position of the *Lutine*'s wreck site was marked for some time by two very large *Rijkskapen* (National Markers) but the floods which engulfed the Noorsvaarder bank in 1863 swept these away. They were replaced with two *Lutinemerks* in 1874 in rather different positions and her wreck was cited as being 6,902 feet from Cape Field on Vlieland and 10,160 feet from the Brandans, Terschelling, from which a triangular 'fix' could be obtained where the bearings of the two markers made an intersection at 80° 46′ 36″. This placed the *Lutine* at 53° 21′ 33″ 974 North; 0° 10′ 41″ 804 East of the Amsterdam meridian, which is measured from the Westerkerk church spire in the heart of that city.

Concern was soon being expressed at the losses suffered by the wreck of the *Lutine*.[50] They need not have worried. John Julian Angerstein was a skilled underwriter,[51] who ensured that Lloyd's paid the claim in full within two weeks of this cataclysmic loss. By so doing the reputation of Lloyd's, one that endures to this day, for trust in paying valid claims, and the funding to do so, no matter how enormous the sum, was established.

Having insured the gold, and duly paid up promptly, Lloyd's underwriters considered, with considerable justification, that, under the rights of subrogation, they owned it and therefore had first rights of salvage. The Batavian Government was equally vocal in its own claim to the cargo but as legitimate war booty and they duly initiated a salvage operation headed up by a splendidly-titled Committee for the Public Properties of

48. *Akevoth*, Dutch Jewish Genealogical Data base, 2013.
49. HMS *Lutine*, Muster Lists 1 January 1799 to 30 September 1800, ADM36/14633; Pay Books (Series III) 30 October 1798 to 26 May 1802, ADM35/997 & 998, National Archives, Kew, London.
50. See, for example, *Letter from London Assurance Company to the Admiralty concerning the loss of the* Lutine, *frigate, dated 19 October 1799.* Document No: 18832, London Guildhall Library, Aldermanbury, City of London.
51. Although dismissed nowadays by modern-day Americans as 'the rate-setting moral icon of Lloyd's in the 1770s'. See for example – Martin, David, *One Stroke (in Time) of the Lutine Bell: an integrated economy – Integral Accounting*, October 2014, Charlotteville VA, Integral Accounting.

Holland. Back in London Their Lordships at the Admiralty had instructed Portlock to see whether any recovery could be made. When he duly filed his pessimistic report, the Admiralty lost little time in divesting themselves of the dubious web in which they had become unwittingly entangled. The captain of the *Arrow* was instructed to hand over the man who had been saved 'at the first opportunity' in order that any information he might have regarding the loss 'may be given to the persons concerned in the property as may be necessary for the benefit of the persons to whom it belongs'.[52]

One can imagine the relief felt at the Admiralty on receipt of a letter from Lloyd's on 22 October informing The Lords Commissioners that Mr Nepean[53] could confirm that 'a sum of money, equal to that unfortunately lost on *Lutine*, is going off this night to Hamburg'. Less welcome, the Committee requested that they 'trust Their Lordships will direct such steps as they may think expedient for its protection to be taken'. This the Admiralty most reluctantly agreed to, not wishing to be involved again in such contentious matters, but Admiral Duncan made it abundantly clear that this was to be the last time it would be done, warning the Committee 'not to expect the parcels can be again conveyed'.

Lloyd's despatched a team of experts to examine what remained of the wreck for themselves to see if any recovery was possible. They found her lying in two halves at a depth of 25 feet (7.5metres).

Between 1800 and 1801 the local populace, especially the fishermen from Wyck, ignored the legal niceties of all interested parties, and with the apparent philosophy of 'finders, keepers' and with the prime advantage of being the men on the spot, swarmed all over the wreck site after it had been abandoned by the Royal Navy. They worked under the nominal directorship of Frederik Pieter Robbé, the Terschelling Wreck Receiver. Robbé's team did manage to lift three intact casks, one containing seven gold bars and a chest with 4,606 Spanish *pistoles* before their attempts were, perforce, abandoned. Despite their primitive methods the Dutch locals were remarkably efficient, one estimated listing of the amount of loot they extracted from the shifting sands was recorded as fifty-eight gold bars totalling 64pounds 23 ounces; thirty-five silver bars of 1,756 pounds 8 ounces; 41,697 Spanish silver *pistoles*; 212 Spanish half-*pistoles*; 179 Spanish gold *pistoles*; twenty-nine Spanish gold half-*pistoles*; twenty-four Spanish gold quarter-*pistoles*; eighteen Spanish gold one-eighth *pistoles*; twenty-eight Spanish gold one-sixteenth *pistoles*; eighty-one double *Louis d'or*; 138 single *Louis d'or;* 138 single *Louis d'or*; four English guineas and

---

52. HMS *Arrow* ship's Log 18 July 1799 to 24 December 1799, ADM52/2718; Ship's Pay Books 1 January 1799 to 30 November 1800, ADM 35/18; Musters (Series I) 1 October 1797 to 28 February 1800, ADM 36/13367, National Archives, Kew, London.

53. Sir Evan Nepean, Secretary to the Board of Admiralty. He had formerly been purser to Captain John Jervis aboard the 3rd-rate *Foudroyant* but had, at the tender age of 29, proved himself so adroit and adept that he was made Permanent Under-Secretary of State for Home Affairs, at which time he had been responsible for naval and political intelligence.

two English half-guineas.[54] Also recovered was the ceremonial sword of Lieutenant Aufrere.

What of the banking crisis in Hamburg? One source states that the loss of the *Lutine*'s bullion 'caused the very crisis it had sought to avert' but, as we have seen, *some* of the monies, the initial loading, *had* been safely delivered by HMS *Nile*. By this time eighty-two banks had failed, and the panic had spread to Bremen and Frankfurt; however, funds came not just from London, but from Berlin also, and gradually normality was restored.

The sunken treasure is still hunted more than two centuries later. Estimated at €60 million of today's currency, about two-thirds, some €40 million, is officially noted as salvaged. Some 112 gold bars, from the 195 *Lutine* was reputedly carrying, and sixty silver bars are registered as recovered. The Ijzeregat itself has long since silted up and ceased to exist and, as early as 1804, primitive attempts to salvage from the wreck had been brought to a halt as the remains vanished from view.

Renewed salvage attempts were made in 1814 by Pierre Eschauzier from The Hague, who was appointed to replace Robbé as the wreck-receiver at Terschelling, and who later became the major there. Eschauzier was appointed by the Dutch King William I, who donated 300 guilders to him for the purpose of kick-starting a renewed salvage operation. Eschauzier's efforts produced just eight *Louis d'or* and seven Spanish *pistoles* for his trouble. Nothing daunted, Eschauzier enlisted the aid of the famous British engineer John Rennie and discussed using his two-ton diving bell from astern the schooner *Gelder*. Unfortunately Rennie died shortly after these discussions. Further attempts by Eschauzier followed in 1822, utilising the bell-equipped *klokduikers*, and continued unavailingly until 1829. When the silt moved again in 1835 further work was done but not pressed forward due to lack of funding.

In 1857 a chance discovery by fishermen Cornelus Wever and Jan Van Keulen found that the ever-shifting sands had once more uncovered some remains of the *Lutine* and commercial attempts were begun to find the reputed fortune. This time more flexible helmeted divers (*helmduikers*) were employed and some 20,000 guilders worth of coinage was recovered. Work continued in good weather periods at intervals between 1858 and 1860 and thirty-six gold and sixty-seven silver bars were brought up along with 3,500 *pistoles*. From then until 1860 Louis Jean Marie Taurel and Jean Pierre Brand-Eschauzier oversaw the raising of further artefacts, including cannon of which they had little or no interest as well as 41 gold and 64 silver bars and over 15,000 coins. After that supply petered out and the project was again abandoned in 1863.

Next came Wilhelm Hendrik ter Meulen, a Bodegraven-born engineer who approached the *Lutine* as a mechanical problem to be solved by logic.[55] He invented a

---

54. For the origins of how so much Spanish treasure was available for shipment from London see Thompson, James David Anthony, 'The Origin of Spanish Dollars Acquired by Britain, 1799–1805', article in *The British Numismatic Society Journal, Volume 38*, pp.167–73, 1969, London, British Numismatic Society, London.
55. ter Meulen, Francois Pieter, *Willem Hendrik ter Meulen in ziju werkzaamheid voor de 'Lutine' geschetst (A Portrait of Willem Hendrik ter Meulen and his work on the Lutine)* 1907, Amsterdam, Privately published.

zandboor (sand–drill) which he hoped would auger his way to the fortune. But again, success eluded him.

In 1871 Lloyd's Act was promulgated and it spelt quite clearly their position viz-a-viz the *Lutine*'s remaining fortune.

> The Society may from time to time do or join in doing all such lawful things as they think expedient with a view to further salving from the wreck of the *Lutine*, and hold, receive, and apply for that purpose so much of the money to be received by means of salving therefrom as they from time to time think fit, and the nett money produced thereby, and the said sum of twenty-five thousand pounds, shall be applied for purpose connected with shipping or marine insurance, according to a scheme to be prepared by the Society, and confirmed by Order of Her Majesty in Council, on the recommendation of the Board of Trade, after or subject to such public notice to claimants of any part of the money aforesaid to come in, and such investigation of claims, and any such barring of claims not made or not proved, and such reservation of rights (if any), as the Board of Trade think fit.

Further attempts followed, the most serious attempt being that mounted by the so-termed '*Lutine* Syndicate' between 1893 and 1898. The principal operatives behind this scheme were renowned Victorian civil engineer Walter Robert Kinipple (1832–1901), then residing at Brighton, and Johan J. Fletcher (1857–1940), a salvage expert, who took charge of the actual operation. They laid sandbags in a circle around the wreck site, reinforced by oak piling inside which protective circle divers went to work. Kinniple, born at Limehouse, was famed for his work creating London docks at Greenwich, Gravesend, Limehouse and Deptford in which he tamed the Thames. However, five years' dedication and application, often halted by appalling weather, produced very little other than a very steady income for the divers themselves and the loss of considerable capital to little avail by the Syndicate.[56]

In 1933 the Beckers' Tower, the brainchild of one Frans Beckers from Gennep, appeared. This apparatus was a steel diving dome lowered from a pontoon but it proved too heavy for the task. Only a few cannon balls and some coins were ever excavated. Five years later, in 1938, the Billiton Company brought their giant *Karimata* dredger, the largest then in existence, which had been built expressly to scoop up tin from the waters off the islands of Belitung and Bangka, near Sumatra in the Dutch East Indies.[57] Instead, it was towed out to the wreck site amid enormous publicity and commenced operations. Only one gold bar was ever recovered but whatever large segments of the *Lutine* that might have still survived were totally pulverised and smashed in the brutality of the process.

---

56. Fletcher's personal account, *HMS Lutine*, a manuscript book, with a 1925 provenance, which was bound between oak boards salvaged from the wreck, with a copper disc from the *Lutine*'s hull plating pinned to the front cover, and which was accompanied by a further letter, dated 1897 with details of the author, was sold at the London Auction House of Christie's on 11 May 2000 for £376.
57. Modern-day Indonesia.

In 1980 Henry Newrick, a New Zealand business publisher by profession, but a treasure hunter by inclination, managed to raise £500,000 from investors to make another attempt on the *Lutine*. The project failed totally, due, said Newrick to 'the worst weather in forty years'.[58] Later dives were made by Hille van Dieren from the *Wrakkenmueum* (Wreck Museum) at Terschelling.

The last attempt at salvage involved a certain Harlingen, West Friesland dentist, Anne Jan Duyf, working alone from a small anchored floating pontoon, moored above the wreck site from 2010. Apart from finding some nails, he remained tight-lipped on his success or otherwise.[59] After 2010 all further salvage attempts were banned by the Netherlands authorities.

Artefacts that *have* been salved include several cannon, one of which was presented to Queen Victoria in 1886 and now resides on the North Terrace of Windsor Castle, while another cannon was presented to the Corporation of London and is on display at the Guildhall. The Combined Military Services Museum at Maldon, Essex, houses a third. The Dutch have four *Lutine* cannon on display at Terschelling itself with a fifth in the Stedelijk Museum, Amsterdam, along with two 3.8-ton (3,900kg) bower anchors recovered in 1913. The rudder was brought up on 18 September 1858 and its timber was used to construct a chair and table for Lloyd's chairman, but is nowadays kept in the Old Library at Lloyd's. The National Maritime Museum holds a box of relics saved from the wreck of the *Lutine* which includes several naval buttons, a metal plaque marked 'ICM', eight lead shot, a piece of oak, a spoon, copper sheathing, nails and other sundries.[60]

One item that was recovered, and has earned undying fame as a Lloyd's icon, was the *Lutine*'s 106-lb (48kg) ship's bell. This was discovered on 17 July 1858 and was found tangled in the chains which had run from the ship's wheel to the rudder. It was recovered in this condition and brought back to London thus. The bell was disentangled and mounted on a rostrum in the Lloyd's Underwriting Room. Since then it has been moved several times, hanging in the Royal Exchange from early in the 1890s until 1928 when it was re-hung in the Lloyd's Leadenhall Street premises. In 1958 the bell was again re-sited to the Lime Street headquarters where it hung until 1986. Yet another shift of venue took place on 24th May 1986 when it was transferred on a 12-foot (3.657m) oar from a Thames barge by Lloyd Waiters, in their traditional red livery to the newly-opened Lloyds building across Lime Street, where it currently hangs inside the rostrum. When the new building was officially opened by Her Majesty Queen Elizabeth II on 18 November 1986 the bell was rung twice.

The 18-inch (46cm) diameter bronze bell itself has the Royal Crown and Arms of the House of Bourbon, in acknowledgement of her mentor, King Louis XVI, while on the rim is the legend 'Saint Jean' (St John the Baptist), under whose protection the ship and crew had been placed when she was launched.

---

58. Bowen, David, *Investors take a plunge, to the bottom of the sea* – article in *The Independent*, issue dated Sunday, 20 August 1995.
59. Wierninga, Feige, *'Smuggler' Anne Duyf and the Gold of the Lutine*, article on *Crimesite Camilleri*. 2011: Rotterdam.
60. National Maritime Museum, Greenwich, London, REL0282.

Popular tradition has it that the *Lutine* Bell is rung once every time that a ship known to be overdue has had her safe arrival confirmed, and twice when the loss of that ship has been confirmed. This enabled all the brokers and underwriters to be made aware of the news simultaneously. Unfortunately, down the decades the bell developed a crack and thus it is only rung sparingly, being now sounded only upon special occasions, and the last time this was done was on 9 November 1989 when wreckage from an overdue ship, the 228,000-ton *Berge Vanga,* a Norwegian bulk-ore carrier, was discovered in the South Atlantic.[61] For good news on shipping the last occasion on which the bell was rung twice was on 10 November 1981 to announce the safe arrival of the overdue Liberian motor vessel *Gloria.*

What Lloyd's regards as 'special' appears flexible but it even included, or so it is said, the sinking of the German battleship *Bismarck* in May 1941, this being the *only* time it was rung for this purpose during the Second World War with its thousands of ship losses, although it was frequently rung during the London Blitz as an air-raid warning. The passing of famous persons, royalty and politicians is also marked thus. When the much-loved Queen Elizabeth The Queen Mother, died on 30 March 2002, the *Lutine* Bell was rung; likewise on the death of Diana, Princess of Wales, when she was killed in a Paris car crash on 31 August 1997. Other notables thus honoured with a single toll of the *Lutine* Bell include the deaths of HM King George V on 20 January 1936, HM King George VI on 6 February 1952 and the American President Franklin Delano Roosevelt on 12 April 1945. The bell was also sounded on the assassination of American President John Fitzgerald Kennedy on 22 November 1963 and on the death of Sir Winston Leonard Spencer Churchill on 24 January 1965.

It has also been rung to commemorate the innocent civilian victims of al-Qaeda terrorist atrocities against the Twin Towers of the World Trade Center in New York City and the Pentagon, in the Commonwealth of Virginia, on 11 September 2001 and against the London Tube system on 7 July 2005. In a way, the bell represents a memorial to all the crew of the *Lutine* who failed to return.[62]

Thus we can record among them, William Aikenhead, James Aldridge, Goodall Tame Boult, George Christal, Timothy Collins, Jacob Dawson, John Dowdall, John Elliot, Henry Lawrence, James Hill, Thomas Holdgate, William Jones, Anthony Joping, William Lesk, Richard Lewis, George Lony, Arthur McDonald, Patrick McGee, John Mellon, William Mells, Robert Mitchell, Lawrence Moncaul, Thomas Parker, George Preston (aka James Young), James Pyper, Ebenezer Reed, James Robertson, Richard Rothwell, Philip Ryan, Robert Smith, William Storey, George Summers, William Symonds, John Tracey and George Whemys. Thirty-five only from 240, but deserving of memory.

---

61. The previous occasion it had been rung in this manner was to mark the loss of her sister ship, the 227,000-ton *Berge Istra,* in the Pacific on 19 January 1976.

62. Apart from the Muster Lists and Pay Books cited above, some of *Lutine*'s crew names can be found by examining records showing payments against wages and prize money paid out to their close relatives and kin in 1800, subsequent to their deaths. See *Navy Board, Navy Pay Office, and Admiralty Account General's Department: Registers of Remittances, 1795–1851,* ADM26/4 & 5, National Archives, Kew, London.

Chapter 6

Unlucky Horseshoe

The *Astraea*, 23 May 1808

The introduction of names from Greek and Latin mythology into the Royal Navy largely began at the latter end of the eighteenth century and reflected the classical tastes of the age, at least according to two of the members of the much later four-man Names Committee, Captain Thomas Davys Manning and Commander Charles Frederick Walker.[1] The much-touted originator of this trend is frequently claimed to have been John Montagu, 4th Earl of Sandwich, who served in the capacity of First Lord of the Admiralty on no fewer than three occasions between 1748 and 1782. He, it was alleged, kept a copy of John Lemprière's *Bibliotheca Classica*[2] on his desk for this task, but this particular allegation was dismissed as pure hyperbole by Manning and Walker, for the simple reason that this book was not composed until many years later, in November 1788 to be precise. Be that as it may, mythological gods, kings, heroes and monsters became the norm for battleship names, while goddesses, nymphs and princesses were selected for frigates, a most pleasing adaptation.

Astraea (Greek *Ἀστραῖα*) was described in the second volume of the 1911 edition of the *Encyclopædia Britannica*[3] as the daughter of Zeus and Themis[4] and a celestial virgin who embodied the essence of innocence, purity and virginity, and was also associated with the Greek goddess of Justice, Dike (Greek *Δίκη*). According to the poet Publius Ovidius Naso (Ovid) in his epic work *Metamorphoses*,[5] she was the last immortal to flee from the wickedness of Earth during the Iron Age, ascending to the heavens to become the constellation Virgo. When she returns once more she will bring again the new 'Golden Age', but, looking around our planet in the year of grace 2015, her return, though certainly highly desirable, does not appear imminent!

---

1. Manning, Captain Thomas Davys RNVR, and Walker, Commander Charles Frederick RN, *British Warship Names*, 1959, London, Putnam.
2. Lemprière, John DD, *Bibliotheca Classica* or *Classical Dictionary containing a Copious Account of all the Proper Names mentioned in Ancient Authors*, 1788, Reading.
3. Chisholm, Hugh (editor), *Encyclopædia Britannica* (11th edition), 1911, Cambridge, Cambridge University Press.
4. Alternatively she is defined as the daughter of Astræus and Eos.
5. Ovid, *Metamorphoses*, 1.149–1.150, org AD 8, Rome, as in Miller, Frank Justus, translator, p.6, 1916, New York, Barnes & Noble, Classics.

Mythology apart, the second Royal Navy vessel to carry the name *Astraea* was a unit of the *Active* class of eight 32-gun frigates of around 700 tons (716232kg) burden apiece,[6] which were 5th-rates. *Astraea*'s sister ships were the *Active, Cerberus, Ceres, Daedalus, Fox, Mermaid* and *Quebec*. The dimensions of these little vessels were 140 feet (42.672m) overall, 126 feet (38.405m) lower deck, 35.5 feet (10.820m) beam with a draught of 17.5 feet (5.3340m). *Astraea* herself was constructed in the shipyard of Robert Fabian at East Cowes on the Isle of Wight, being laid down on the stocks in September 1779, launched from there on 24 July 1781 and completed the same year, commissioning for active service at Portsmouth on 1 October. She had a crew of 220 officers and men, commanded by Captain Matthew Squires, and sailed for service off North America on the 7th.

Astraea had a particularly busy naval career up to the end of 1807. Her first notable action occurred when, under the command of Captain Squires, she took part in the closing stages of the American War of Independence. On 20 December 1782, in company with her sister ship *Quebec* (Captain Christopher Mason) and the 4th-rate *Diomede* (Captain Thomas Frederick), she sighted a rebel squadron that included the 40-gun frigate *South Carolina* (Captain Joss Joyner)[7] along with the schooner *Seagrove* (Captain Benjamin Broadhurst), the brig *Constance* (Master Jesse Harding) laden with a cargo of tobacco and the merchant vessel *Hope* (Master John Prole) off the mouth of the Delaware. A long stern chase followed which lasted for eighteen hours but, once within range, the American vessels were taken under heavy and accurate fire and within two hours all save the *Seagrove*, which escaped, were forced to strike their colours. The captured vessels were sailed to New York.[8] Further success followed on 15 March, when, assisted by the 6th-rate *Vestal* (Commander Robert Murray) and *Inverness*,[9] *Astrae* also captured the Massachusetts privateer *Julius Cæsar* (Commander Thomas Benson). These French privateers were continuing irritants for the British authorities and required constant culling.[10]

The *Astraea* was then de-commissioned from January 1786 until September 1786 when she was again brought into service under the command of Captain Peter Rainier, who took her out to the West Indies for a normal three-year commission. There followed almost a decade of inactivity before hostilities again broke out with France in

---

6. *Astraea* was of 703 tons (716,4280 kg) burden, see Lecky, Lieutenant Halton Sterling, *The King's Ships*, Volume 1, 1913, London, Horace Muirhead.

7. This vessel, the former *L'Indien*, was of French design and built in Holland. She had been chartered to the Navy of South Carolina by the Duke of Luxembourg in 1780.

8. The British distained adding *South Carolina* to their fleet, as was customary for prizes, as she was considered inadequately constructed; she ended her days carrying troops and stores to the Indian Ocean area.

9. This was a prize ship, the former French 32-gun privateer *Duc de Chartes* (Captain Jean Baptiste Louis L'Ecolier), taken on 19 December 1745.

10. Privateers (or Corsairs), were government-authorised 'unofficial' commerce raiders, differing little from pirates other than a rather loose legitimacy. They were popular among European nations who could not match the Royal Navy in strength as they forced the British to dissipate a high proportion of her naval strength as escorts for merchant ship convoys.

April 1793. Captain Robert Moorsom was appointed to the command of *Astraea* and again re-commissioned her from March 1793, and when that worthy was moved on to command the 4th-rate *Hindostan* he was succeeded by Captain Lord Henry Paulet, and she joined the Channel Fleet. Here she soon saw more action, being involved in the re-capturing of the merchantman *Caldicott Castle* on 28 March and assisting the 5th-rate *Cerberus* (Captain James Drew) and the 36-gun 5th-rate *Santa Margarita* (Captain Thomas Byam Martin).[11]

In April 1795 the blockading British Inshore Squadron, comprising the 2nd-rate *London* (Captain Edward Griffith), the 3rd-rates *Colossus* (Commander John Monkton), *Hannibal* (Captain John Markham) and *Robust* (Captain Edward Thornbrough) with the frigates *Astraea* and *Thalia* (Captain Richard Grindall) under Rear-Admiral John Colpoys, were off Brest. A French squadron composed of the frigates *La Fratenité* (*Citizen Lieutenant de Vaisseau* Jacob de Florinville), *La Gentille* and *La Gloire* (*Citizen Captaine de Vaisseau* Francis Louis Beens) was sighted on the 10th and the British set chase, forcing the enemy to split up. Under the command of Captain Lord Henry Paulet, and manned by a crew of 212 officers and men, *Astraea* undertook a long chase and finally fell in with the larger French frigate *La Gloire*, with a crew of 280. Battle was joined around sunset and continued long into the night, the enemy finally surrendering just before midnight.[12] The larger French vessel outgunned the British ship's thirty-six 12-pounder guns (plus six smaller pieces) to thirty-two and inflicted heavy damage on the British vessel's masts and rigging but caused no losses to her crew other than one man who later died of his wounds. In response the *Astraea*'s broadsides had killed or wounded forty Frenchmen including *Captaine* Beens.[13] This time the prize *was* taken into service and continued to serve as HMS *La Gloire* (there already being an HMS *Glory*, a 2nd-rate battleship, built in 1788, in service until 1825) until she was sold in 1802.

The *Astraea* was soon involved in action once more, this time under Captain Richard Lane, being part of Admiral Alexander Hood, First Viscount Bridport's, Channel Fleet of twenty-five ships which were bound for Quiberon Bay when they encountered the French Atlantic Fleet under Vice-Admiral Villaret de Joyeuse. On 22 June 1795 while some forty-two nautical miles (78km) off the Ole de Groix, an island off the Biscay coast of Brittany, the frigates *Astraea* and *Nymphe* (Captain George Murray) made the initial sighting contacts at 0330. The British chased the French for most of the day and through that night until battle was joined at dawn on the 23rd and the French battleships,

---

11. This former Spanish warship had herself been taken as a prize by the 6th-rate *Tartar* (Captain Alex Graeme) in 1779 and served in the Royal Navy under her old name until 1836. In the same year *Astraea* assisted in the taking of the French privateer *Le Jean Bart* (*Lieutenant de Vaisseau* Louis-Balthasa Néel) as a prize. This vessel was taken into Royal Navy service as the *Arab*.
12. Clowes, Sir William Laird & Markham, Clements Robert, *The Royal Navy: A History from the Earliest Times to the death of Queen Victoria*, Volume IV, 1903, London, Sampson Low, Marston & Co.
13. Duncan, Archibald, *The British Trident: or Register of Naval Actions*, Vol. III, 1805, London, James Cundee.

Alexander (*Capitane de Vaisseau* François Charles Guillemet)[14] and *Tigre* (*Capitane de Vaisseau* Jacques Bedout)[15] were captured while the rest were scattered and sought refuge in Lorient, where Hood decided to leave them, being much criticised for lack of endeavour for so holding off. After initially locating the enemy and leading the British fleet to them, the *Astraea* did not herself become engaged.

The following year *Astraea*, commanded by Captain Richard Lane, was part of a large force sent out to the West Indies. After two abortive attempts to cross the Atlantic by this large invasion fleet, which were thwarted by severe gales which inflicted much damage and some losses, they finally made it at the third attempt. On 10 March *Astraea* arrived at Jamaica. She embarked soldiers and reinforced the British Naval Squadron on 27 April. Here she was present, with the sloop *Bulldog* (Lieutenant Henry George Fownes), at the taking of the French island of St Lucie (St Lucia) on 26 May in which both ships' captains participated, but she and her crew were in such a poor state of repair that Rear Admiral Sir Hugh Cloberry Christian sent her back home with despatches of this success, which was accomplished at high cost in British lives. It was all in vain as those at home lost the stomach for the enterprise and, despite the capture of further French garrisons, the fleet was withdrawn, again resulting in all that had been gained soon being lost once more.

The *Astraea* was refitted and with a new crew commanded by Captain Richard Dacres returned to duty in 1797 in home waters. She avoided becoming involved in the mutiny of the fleet at The Nore and was in company with the sloop *Plover* (Commander John Cheshyre) on 16 February when they fell in with the French privateer *Le Tartare* (*Capitaine de Vaissseau* Henri de la Conté), which was duly captured. The prize money, shared between those 'Actually aboard' at that time, was later distributed at 'No. 7 Beaufort Buildings, London by Chris [topher] Cooke and J P Maxwell, Agents to the *Astrea* (*sic*)'.[16] Further such captures followed, the 10-gun Dutch privateer *Stuiver* on 1 June 1797 off the Skaw, the 5-gun French privateer schooner *La Renommée* off the Dogger Bank on 22 April 1798, in company with the 5th-rate *Apollo* (Captain John Manley) and the sloop *Inspector* (Commander Charles Locke), she captured the Dutch Greenlandsman *Frederick* and *Waachzamghheer* on 30 July, and the Dutch Greenlandsman *Liefde* on 6 August, all from Greenland. Dacres continued patrolling into the following year and, on 29 March, in company with the 5th-rate *Latona* (Captain Frank Sotheron), captured the Danish 12-gun *Neptunus*, a Galliot.[17] On 10 April a three-hour chase off the Texel resulted in the capture of the

---

14. A former British 3rd-rate battleship that had been captured earlier and was thus re-taken at this time, the 2nd-rate *Formidable* (*Capitane de Vaisseau* Charles Linois) was incorporated into the Royal Navy and renamed *Belleisle*.
15. Again, the former British 3rd-rate *Ardent*, re-taken but not re-incorporated due to her poor condition; quickly sold out the following year.
16. *The London Gazette*, No. 14077, p.1233, 14 October 1797.
17. A Danish two-masted coasting vessel. A neutral vessel, she had been just been warned that the port of l'Havre was under blockade, but still proceeded to run her cargo there, so was taken into custody. A lengthy legal battle duly followed her impounding.

14-gun French lugger and privateer *Le Marsouin*. The haul continued and *Astraea* assisted in the taking of both the French privateers *Aeolus* and the *Sex Soskendi* on the 15th of the same month and, again with the *Latona* as well as the armed cutter *Courier* (Lieutenant Thomas Searle) and the brig-sloop *Cruizer* (Commander Charles Wollason) in company, the Prussian hoy the *Seehandlung Dolphin* (Master Colundt).[18] Off Jamaica on 20 May *Astraea* took the French 6-gun three-decker Privateer *La Vengeance*.

The *Astraea* was consistently busy on such work and very successful at her job. In the North Sea she was part of a squadron led by the *Latona* working off the Dutch coast and, between March and 7 May, among the many other ships she assisted in taking were the privateers *Vrow Alyda*, the Dutch *Verwagting* (Master Jean Louis Le Riche), the Dutch *Vinnern*, *Almindeligheden*, *Sen Soskende*, *Bornholm*, the French *Fabius*, Dutch *Zee Star* and Dutch *Frou Eaagle* and the *Jonge Picter*. Along with the 4th-rate *Glatton* (Captain Charles Cobb) and the sloops *Scorpion* (Commander John Tremayne Rodd) and *Hazard* (Commander Alexander Ruddach), she eliminated the French privateer *Harmenie* (Master M. Naskell) on 21 April.[19] While serving with Admiral Sir John Borlase Warren's squadron on 30 August 1800, the ships' boats assisted in cutting out the 18-gun French privateer *La Guêpe*.[20]

Under the command of Captain Peter Ribouleau *Astraea*, armed *en flute*,[21] was part of a small British squadron which sailed from Portsmouth on 5 August 1800. This squadron's units included the former 3rd-rate *Dictator* (Captain John Oakes Hardy), converted to a troopship, the *Delft* (64), also acting as a troopship, the bomb vessel *Fury* (Lieutenant John Roberts), the East Indiaman *Sir Edward Hughes* (given the temporary Royal Navy name HMS *Tortoise*,[22] the sloop *Termagant* (Captain William Skidsey) and the former 4th-rate *Trusty* (Captain Alexander Wilson), also converted to a troopship. These small vessels became part of the 70-strong combined British and Turkish fleet despatched to convey a British army under command of General Sir Ralph Abercromby to oust the French from Egypt. *Astraea* and some of her companions formed the inshore covering and bombarding force that arrived on 1 March 1801 and, a week later, anchored close to the invasion beach and bombarded enemy positions to assist the successful landing of the Allied army at Abu Qir (Aboukir) Bay in the face of defending French fire. She remained off Egypt until the fall of Alexandria on 2 September before returning home.

In April 1805 Captain James Carthew took command of *Astraea* and, after a refit at Deptford on the Thames, she sailed for service in the Downs. Here she scored another success, assisting the taking of the Danish *Anna Wilhelmine* (Master Leider

18. Hoy, a two-masted sloop-rigged coasting ship of *circa* 60 tons.
19. She was taken in to British mercantile service as the *Grenada*.
20. She was taken into the Royal Navy as the brig-sloop *Wasp*.
21. *En flute* – lacking many of her cannon and not fully armed, sent to war with all, or some, of her cannon still missing due to the urgency and secrecy of the mission.
22. Journals, Ledgers, Paybooks & Imprest Book of *Sir Edward Hughes*, L/MAR/3/35/4, British Library, St Pancras, London.

Lyeman) on 21 October that year. When Carthew moved on in February 1806 he was succeeded by Captain James Dunbar. The *Astraea* continued her long service in the North Sea and her reputation as a 'lucky' ship continued to hold, even when, while conveying the diplomat Lord Hutchinson to St Petersburg, Russia, along with his retinue, she encountered a storm which put her on the shoals and reefs off Anholt Island in the Kattegat, running aground close to the Skaws.[23] One eyewitness recalled that they:

> had the shore upon the larboard hand, a good breeze of wind and were going at the rate of ten knots; when, on a sudden, without the smallest indication whatever that such an evil was impending, one of the most terrible of gales of wind broke upon us.

They were soon hard and fast on the reef known as the 'New Dangers'. The vessel appeared doomed as she was fast aground and in danger of foundering. The local inhabitants and several passing vessels all totally ignored their predicament and signals, and they were left to their own devices. All hands were put to the pumps, including his lordship. Finally, her captain ordered her masts cut off, and the crew ditched both guns and stores to lighten the ship. These emergency measures worked and she came free. A mizzen-jury mast was set up and, under this reduced sail, *Astraea* managed to make the twenty-five mile journey to Elsinore (Elsineur), Denmark, where she arrived, in the words of one crew member 'almost a total wreck'.[24] She duly delivered Hutchinson to Copenhagen to recuperate and at that port was sufficiently patched up and refurbished for her to make the voyage home, arriving at Sheerness at the end of February. Despatched to Denmark once more, and despite her earlier ordeal, she proved as good as ever at her job and was soon busy rounding up prizes as before. On 19 August 1807 she was instrumental in the seizing of the Danish ships *Three Brothers* (Master Holm) and *Two Sisters* (Master Andersen), while on the 26th, in company with the sloop *Comus* (Captain Richard Le Gallais) and the 5th-rate *Surveillante* (Captain John Bligh),[25] another quartet of Danes, the *Fama* (Master Thielsen), the *Anna Dorothea*, the *Anne and Catherine* and the *Anne and Margaret*, were all taken as prizes.

By November she was back to re-store and re-victual and, following a full refit at The Nore in November 1807, she received fresh orders to sail again to the West Indies. On this occasion her new commanding office was Captain Edmund Heywood. After a call at Barbados in February she was based respectively at Montego Bay and Port Royal, Jamaica. Quick off the mark *Astraea*, along with the brig-sloop *Royalist* (Commander

---

23. The Skaws (Skagen) rocks off the north-eastern coast of Denmark, between the islands of Læso and Arnholt.

24. *The Naval Chronicle for 1807*, Volume 17, January- June, *Dangers of the Astrea Frigate*, pp.42–4, 1807, London, Joyce Gold, Shoe Lane.

25. Herself a French prize which had run aground and was captured intact in the West Indies.

John Maxwell), pursued and captured the French privateer *La Providence* (Master Gullaume le Feuvre), a 14–gun lugger, on 14 December.[26]

Astraea was by now an elderly lady, who had already almost been lost twice to gale and wreck, but which had survived both and was still deemed a fully-fledged fighting ship. As such, she was assigned a new task as escort against the many privateers operating with relative immunity among the small islands of the Caribbean. In late March 1808 Heywood was duly charged with the protection of the *Prince Ernest*, a mail packet vessel, plying the Falmouth and Lisbon, Halifax, New York, the West Indies and Gibraltar route.[27] This little vessel, carrying important Government despatches, was to be given armed escort from the anchorage at Watlings Island, Bahamas,[28] from 9 May by *Astraea* to a point far out in the Atlantic where, it was hoped, her charge would be safely beyond the reach of the Caribbean corsairs.

The voyage out lasted about a week and the packet was duly released about 550 miles (885.14km) north–north-west of the island of Puerto Rico to continue to make her own way from that point while *Astraea* hauled about and started the return journey to base, taking a course that would lead her to the Mona Passage between Hispaniola.[29] For several days *Astraea* sailed back south toward the strait in good weather.

The unpredictability of the weather in this area was well-known and it remains so to this day. Contemporary sailors and yachtsmen still regard it as 'one of the most difficult and dangerous passage in the world', containing as it does

high North Atlantic seas, untenable rocky shore, great variation in depths, unpredictable currents and fast forming storm cells across the Mona Passage and the Puerto Rican trench, the deepest hole in the Atlantic Ocean.

Nowadays fairly reliable weather forecasts are available, using the latest satellite links, but still the uncertainty persists; one modern guide states unequivocally that 'If you should draw a sure 2-day forecast of flat seas and no winds, then you should drive straight across the Mona and damn the tactics ...' but the author warns to be very certain and, above all, 'don't listen to your friends!' Another bit of advice from the same source was 'Stay clear of the shoals in the Mona Passage'.[30] Maybe both pieces of

26. Records of the High Court of Admiralty – Captured ship: *La Providence*. HCA 32/52/43/5, National Archives, Kew, London.
27. See The *Prince Ernest* Packet Boat Ship's Log for voyages between 1800 and 1820,POST43/105-114, British Postal Museum and Archive, The Royal Mail Archive, Freeling House, London WC1X 0DL.
28. Reputed to be the landing place of Christopher Columbus on 12 October 1492 and named after the English buccaneer John (or George) Watlings. Sadly, the island was re-named San Salvador Island in 1925.
29. From the Isle of Mona in its centre and the passage is still the main shipping link between the Atlantic and Caribbean. Hispaniola is nowadays shared between the Dominican Republic and Haiti, while Puerto Rico is a United States dependency.
30. Van Sand, Bruce, *The Gentlemen's Guide to Passages South: The Traveller's Guide to Windward*, 2006, St Ives, Cambs., Imray Laurie & Wilson.

advice would have been followed back in 1808 as the *Astraea* approached what she took to be the entrance to the Caribbean on Monday 23 May pushed on by a brisk trade wind from the north-east. But it was *not* the Mona Passage that she was heading for.

At midday the four ship's officers conferred and agreed their noon position was 19° 00′ North, 65° 50′ West, which placed the *Astraea* some thirty miles north of the eastern tip of Puerto Rico. On that western coast of the island is Aguadilla with Mona Island itself just to the west, while the actual passage, the *Canal de la Mona*, is beyond the island, to the west again. Thrusting out from the island are the innumerable rocks, reefs and shoals that almost close the eastern side of the strait at this point. This was all known to them and, on checking again some two hours later, Heywood and Lieutenant Allan McLean, the ship's master, could clearly make out land to the south-west, although the visibility had worsened. They duly agreed that this must be Puerto Rico, averring that 'it could be no other',[31] and so they continued south-west with the intention of closing to within a safe distance of fifteen miles from shore and not attempting the Mona Passage until dawn and maximum visibility.

Alas for their calculations and hopes, far from being to the north-west of Puerto Rico, they were approaching the low-lying Anegada Island, the most northerly of the British Virgin Islands and the Anegada Passage between Virgin Gorda and Somrero Island. Framing Anegada in a huge arc is one of the largest coral barriers in the world, the notorious Horseshoe Reef. The island of Anegada is, of itself, low-lying. Along its nine miles length and two miles width the highest point is a mere twenty-eight feet (8.5m) and the translation of the Spanish name means 'drowned island'. The island becomes visible from an approaching sailing vessel at a maximum distance of eight miles. But it is not what little part of the land mass that can be seen from the deck of any vessel approaching the island, as the *Astraea* was doing, that is important; rather it is the *reef* itself that was the danger, and that reef was invisible. This hidden hazard is extensive, almost totally enclosing the island, save to the west, and extending as far as eleven miles out to sea in places. It is even more treacherous than the Mona in that large parts of it, rocks and coral projections, remain just below the waves.[32]

Still secure in the expectation that it was the Puerto Rico coast, and that they were at a safe distance, the *Astraea*'s officers continued with their planned approach and, at around 1930, Heywood, McLean and Maxwell were all assembled on the quarterdeck from where they gauged that the trade wind was increasing and might drive them farther close inshore than was safe. The order was duly given for the ship to heave to on the starboard tack and *Astraea* came round on a westerly course and then turned into the wind and away from the lee shore as the sails were rove down. At 1955 the ship's gunner, one George Lovet, appeared on the fo'c'sle to take his turn at watch-keeping

31. Courts Martial Papers, 1808 May–June, ADM 1/5387, National Archives, Kew, London.
32. There have been hundreds of ships wrecked on Horseshoe Reef down the centuries, including several Spanish treasure ships, the Portuguese slaver *Donna Paula* with a cargo of 235 African captives in 1819 and the 'Bone Wreck', the Greek freighter *Rokus* with a cargo of cattle bones *en route* from Trinidad to Baltimore in 1929. Ships continue to go aground there on a regular basis even today.

and, from that vantage point toward the prow of the ship, he almost immediately saw the white horses of breaking waves immediately ahead. He cried out a warning and Heywood shouted for the ship's helm to be put hard over to port.[33]

The *Astraea* still had considerable weigh on and the order came too late to save her. Within a trice she struck hard on the reef and her planking was pierced and opened. The sea began flooding into her hull. She was held fast but, despite the increasing force of the wind, the men worked valiantly at the pumps to stem the inflow. Others of the crew managed, with a considerable struggle, to lay out her kedge anchor, with the hope that, should she remain relatively intact and the weather ease, she could be refloated and saved as she had been once before.[34] But with the severity of her damage, which increased steadily as the stiffening breeze and swell kept her pounding on the rocks, this did not prove to be any sort of viable option. Several small local boats were briefly sighted inshore but they did not approach the *Astraea* due to indifference or the condition of the sea; both options were later mooted. Nor did any of her cannon shots, fired as distress signals, engender any aid from the island itself. Unfortunately one of the cannon so utilised burst during a firing, killing two of the gunners. The *Astraea* had grounded off the island's east end, which tapers down south–eastward to Pelican Point. There were no roads from the main centre of population, The Settlement, that lead to that end of the island, and one lone track peters out at Budrock Salt Pond, well short of the shore.

The heel of the ship on occasions caused the gravest concerns, and Heywood ordered that both the main and the mizzen masts be cut away. When this failed to remedy things sufficiently, the crew began to heave overboard many of the ship's cannon to further lighten the vessel. This proved to be unfortunate as the ship rose higher and the wind forced her further into the rocks and coral protrusions and worsened her condition. Soon the ship's carpenter reported to Captain Heywood that the keel had broken in half and it was obvious that *Astraea* herself was doomed. It was clearly suicidal to try and risk the unknown hazards that night and Heywood kept his crew aboard during the hours of darkness. Thankfully the ship held together and conditions eased a little. *Astraea* proved as sturdy as ever in her final *extremis*. Meanwhile rafts were cobbled together by the crew from her damaged structure in readiness for the abandoning of the wreck come the morning.

At dawn, while Mr McLean and some volunteers remained with the vessel to afford the salvage of what they could, the majority of the crew took to the water. Captain Heywood and the bulk of the officers and men managed to reach the coast of Anegada Island itself, one mile distant in boats or on the rafts, although unfortunately two of the

---

33. Courts Martial Papers, 1808 May–June, ADM 1/5387, National Archives, Kew, London.

34. Kedging – a secondary (warp) anchor was carried in addition to the main (bower) anchor, and this would be embarked on a ship's boat and taken as far out as the cable would allow and let go. Once conditions allowed, the chain would be wound in by muscle-power, using measured stages, on the ship's capstan, which would have the effect of winching the vessel up toward the anchor and thus hopefully lever her off the obstruction on which she was lodged. See Admiralty *Manual of Seamanship*, Vols. 1 & 2, 1908, London, HMSO.

exhausted crew members drowned in the attempt. One officer and seventy crewmen managed to embark in one of the ship's boats and they eventually made it safely to Virgin Gorda[35] Island some miles away to the south.

It was here that the brig-sloop HMS *St Christopher* (Captain Andrew Hodge)[36] arrived on Tuesday the 24th and the following day she anchored off Anegada and embarked the bulk of the survivors.

Apart from four of her crew who were lost in the accident, a further incident marred an otherwise successful evacuation. One of the crew, George Wright, resolutely refused to re-embark. He had apparently been among the first men off the *Astraea* and, before doing so, helped himself to Captain Heywood's coat, apparently deeming it legitimate booty! Once ashore he lost no time in selling this garment to one of the local inhabitants, receiving for it the sum of 'two guineas'.[37] He compounded the theft and the refusal to go aboard *St Christopher* (perhaps anticipating his fate once aboard) by accusing Captain Heywood of being a 'damned rascal'. Moreover, apparently adopting the maxim 'in for a penny, in for a pound', or 'here goes nothing', he also extended his vitriol to the rest of the officers who, he claimed, had run *Astraea* ashore through neglect of their duties. Finally, whether he was drunk, deranged or just totally abandoned, he stated that, had it not been for the loyal members of the crew, he would have also taken the captain's personal sword 'and given him the contents of it!' He would possibly have continued raving but at that point he was overpowered by a Royal Marine sergeant and the purser's steward, dragged through the surf and heaved into one of the *St Christopher*'s boats; he was duly embarked to face his fate. Nowadays, Wright would no doubt have received 'counselling', and also had his 'human rights' aired, and would probably have been discharged and received considerable damages to boot but, in 1808, while they were equally fair, and intended to give him a full hearing, they were far more forthright and direct. Wright duly received his comeuppance when Captain Heywood charged him with 'riotous and mutinous conduct and language'. His case was dealt with at the same court martial as Heywood and his officers. Wright was adjudged guilty on all counts and was subsequently hanged from the yardarm for 'mutinous conduct'.[38]

Meanwhile three more British warships arrived to conduct the salvage of the *Astraea*, these being the two 5th-rates *Galatea* (Captain George Sayer) and *Jason* (Lieutenant George Pringle) and the sloop *Fawn* (Commander Michael de Courcy). But, despite their attentions, *Astraea* proved too far gone to save, being fully submerged and, on 24 June, the little squadron gave up the attempt although *Galatea* remained on the scene until 2 July and again from 12 to 24 July, to salvage what little could be retrieved,

35. 'The Fat Virgin' as named by Christopher Columbus.
36. The former French privateer *Mohawk*, taken as a prize in 1807. See Master's Log 20 March 1807 to 25 June 1811, ADM 52/4224, National Archives, Kew, London.
37. A guinea was an English gold coin minted from gold obtained from Guinea and at the time of *Astraea*'s loss worth 21 shillings (s) – in 2015 terms approximately £1.5p or €1.35.
38. Courts Martial Papers, 1808 May-June, ADM 1/5387, National Archives, Kew, London.

which proved precious little.[39] Many of *Astraea*'s former crew were re-drafted to the brig-sloop *Gorée* (Commander Joseph Spear).[40]

Captain Heywood, the ship's officers and many of the crew of *Astraea*, were subsequently given passage aboard *Jason* to Barbados for the enquiry into her loss and Heywood wrote out his detailed report while on passage there. The *Astraea*'s ship's log, some charts and the captain's personal log survived the foundering and were all also produced as evidence.

A court martial was held for Captain Heywood and his officers and this took place aboard the flagship of Rear-Admiral Alexander Cochrane, the 3rd-rate battleship *Ramillies* (74), on 11 June 1808 while that ship was anchored in Carlisle Bay.[41] On hearing separate evidence from all the officers, who all gave much the same version of events, each claiming that the they had carefully and separately given the 'strictest attention' to the ships' reckoning on that fateful day, the verdict of the court was that:

having heard the narrative thereof by Captain Edmund Heywood, together with explanations given by himself and also by Mr Allan McLean, the master of the said ship, and having fully completed the inquiry, and maturely and deliberately weighed and considered the whole thereof, the court is of the opinion that the loss was occasioned by an extraordinary weather current having set the ship nearly two degrees to the eastwards of the reckoning of all the officers on board.

The court found that 'no blame is attributable to Captain Heywood, or his officers'.[42] In other words, total and compete exoneration.[43] However, more than a century of US Navy records since that trial indicate that, if anything, the prevailing drift, which is very small, is a westerly rather than an easterly one!

The wreck was later re-located by Captain Bert Kilbride, His Majesty's Receiver of Wrecks, based on Mosquito Island (Drake's Anchorage) in the British Virgin Islands in 1967. He headed up a diving team that located *Astraea* after detailed research by the Blythmann brothers, Finn and Tage, in London and St Thomas, had narrowed

---

39. Apart from some ship's boats, a single anchor and cable, just one carronade, and the fore and main topsail yards, little of value was retrieved. Had it been left to Anegada's populace themselves much more might have been recovered, though not to the Admiralty's benefit, those inhabitants, like most small islanders worldwide, having earned down the centuries a dubious reputation for stripping bare such wrecked vessels with enormous speed, efficiency and fervour!
40. She was the former HMS *Favourite*, captured by the French but re-taken in 1807 and renamed *Gorée* on re-entering Royal Navy service to commemorate the capture of the Île de Gorée, Dakar, Senegal, by the British in 1758.
41. Cochrane's fleet had captured the Danish West Indian islands of Sankt Croix, Sankt Jan and Sankt Thomas on 17 April 1807 and these remained occupied by the British until the end of the Napoleonic Wars in 1815. Just over 100 years later they were sold by Denmark to the United States, thus becoming the US Virgin Islands.
42. The two other ship's officers were Second-Lieutenant George B. Maxwell and Third-Lieutenant Richard Pawle.
43. Courts Martial Papers, 1808 May–June, ADM 1/5387, National Archives, Kew, London.

the possibilities down to a searchable area off Pelican Point. As always conditions on the reef remained as dangerous as when she went aground almost 160 years before but, despite that, the team was to find many artefacts that they were able to identify from Admiralty markings and some of the smaller items were salvaged. Their finds included four anchors, a few more cannon, cannon and musket balls, ballast bars and copper sheathing. It appears that only five of her heavy cannon could be raised due to working conditions.

To commemorate this find the *Astraea* was featured on both a $1.00 and a 25-cent stamp issued by the British Virgin Islands.

Chapter 7

The *Birkenhead* Drill

The *Birkenhead*, 26 February 1852

To take your chance in the thick of a rush, with firing all about,
Is nothing so bad when you've cover to 'and, an' leave an' likin' to shout;
But to stand an' be still to the *Birken'ead* drill is a damn tough bullet to chew,
An' they done it, the Jollies—'Er Majesty's Jollies—soldier an' sailor too!
Their work was done when it 'adn't begun; they was younger nor me an' you;
Their choice it was plain between drownin' in 'eaps an' bein' mopped by the
    screw,
So they stood an' was still to the *Birken'ead* drill, soldier an' sailor too!

(Verse from *Soldier an' Sailor*, Rudyard Kipling's
affectionate tribute to the Corps of Royal Marines.)

Women and Children First? In more recent times this British tradition, which had spread worldwide, appears to have been more honoured by lapse than observance as two prominent cases illustrate. On 13 January 2012 the 114,147-GT cruise liner *Costa Concordia*, owned by Costa Crocchiere, part of the giant Carnival group of companies, capsized on being run aground on the Isola del Giglio, off Tuscany, after touching rocks earlier. Of her 4,252 passengers, thirty-two lost their lives. The captain of the vessel, Capitano Francesco Schettino, who had his friend, dancer Dominica Cemortan, on the bridge at the time, claimed he 'fell into a lifeboat' and, despite being repeatedly urged by a Coastguard officer to go back on board, failed to do so. Innocent or guilty, his trial currently drags on interminably into the future. In the second incident, which took place on 16 April 2014, the South Korean ferry ship, *Sewol*, 6,825 GT, built in 1994 and owned by the Chonghaejin Marine Co. Ltd, capsized south of the islet of Donggeochado while on a journey from Incheon to Jeju Island with 476 passengers aboard, most of them students from the Danwon High School. At the time of the incident the ship was under control of the third mate. The captain, Captain Lee Joon-Seok, 69, instructed the passengers to stay where they were, and while he and his fourteen crew were all saved by rescue boats only 174 of the young passengers survived.[1] Joon-Seok, for whom the death sentence was called for, received rather faster justice – a long jail term.

---

1. On 10 February 2015 he was convicted of manslaughter and loss of the ship and sentenced to sixteen years and one month in jail, roughly six months for each life lost.

The *Birkenhead* herself was built as a steam frigate by John Laird & Company, of Birkenhead, being launched as the *Vulcan* by Lady Elizabeth Mary Leveson-Gower, Marchioness of Westminster, on 30 December 1845,[2] but was renamed as *Birkenhead* shortly afterward, she being the first warship so named. She had a length of 210 feet (64m), a beam of 37 feet 6 inches (11.4m), a draught of 15 feet 9 inches (5m) and a designed displacement of 1,918 tons, with a full load displacement of 2,000 tons. She was one of the first iron-hulled ships to be constructed for the Royal Navy but also one of the last paddle-steamers to be built for the service as the new triple-expansion steam engines were being introduced into the fleet. The 20 feet (6m) diameter paddle wheels were driven by two 564hp (421kW) Forrester & Co. side-lever steam engines which gave her a top speed of thirteen knots (24 km/h). To supplement steam power, she was additionally fitted out as a two-masted brig but was later re-rigged as a barquentine with three masts. As a frigate she had been designed to carry an armament of two single 96-pounder pivot guns mounted fore and aft and four 68-pounder broadside guns. She had a crew of 125 officers and men.

The *Birkenhead* undertook her maiden voyage from Birkenhead to Plymouth in 1846, but was not immediately put into active service. Instead, she was left idle, pending deployment, because of doubts over the effectiveness of her paddle propulsion, coupled with concerns about the strength and vulnerability of iron-hulled warships against cannon shot. [3]

When HMS *Birkenhead* was eventually utilised it was for limited service in home waters and one of her first employments was on 27 August 1847 when she was used by naval engineer James Bremnet to refloat Isambard Kingdom Brunel's mighty vessel *Great Britain* off the sandbar at Dundrum Bay, County Down, where she had run ashore the previous November.

Eventually Their Lordships decided that she was unsuitable for combat duties and she was converted and re-classified as a troopship in 1851.[4] As well as adding a third mast, a fo'c'sle and a poop deck were added fore and aft respectively, thus increasing cabin accommodation and her innards were re-modelled somewhat to accommodate

---

2. She was built with Vulcan, Lord of Fire and armourer-forger for the Gods, as her figurehead, with a hammer in one hand and the lightning bolts of Jove in the other.

3. The early brittle iron was battle-tested on the hull of the Laird-built paddle frigate *Guadeloupe*, a speculative build which was rejected by the Royal Navy but which subsequently served with the Mexican Navy with British officers and a Mexican crew. At the Battles of Campeche against the Republic of Texas Navy in April and May 1843, the effects of enemy shot piercing and tearing open her iron plating caused a large number of horrific casualties among her crew, and this was instrumental in convincing Their Lordships of the unsoundness of such construction, at least at that stage of its development.

4. Troopships have, at various dates in our naval history, been given the prefix HMS as warships or have been classified as merchant vessels in Admiralty service. The *Birkenhead* has been listed as both but, as my old friend, the late James Joseph Colledge ('JJ' to the founder members of the old Warships Record Club we formed in the 1960s) has always seen fit to list her as 'HMS' in his scholarly publications, I see no reason at all not to follow his excellent example. Furthermore, she is included in the 1851 Navy List as a full Royal Navy vessel (rated as a 4-gun transport), which would seem to be decisive. She was also listed as HMSV.

troops. These major alterations necessitated landing most of her guns ashore.[5] She conducted several trooping voyages to garrisons which varied from the Channel Islands to Lisbon and longer-range trooping runs to Halifax, Nova Scotia, with a detachment of artillery, and also runs to the Cape and back, one of the latter, in October 1850, being accomplished within thirty-seven days.

In January 1852 the latest of a series of conflicts known collectively as the Xhosa Wars[6] occurred and the eighth such conflict was being waged in the Eastern Cape. The rabid preachings of a rabble-rouser named The Prophet Mlanjeni (Riverman) had stirred up the Xhosa yet again and, as usual with such fanatics, he promised them immunity from British bullets and that white man's guns would only fire water! On Christmas Eve a detachment of British troops was ambushed in the Boomah Pass and suffered casualties, but the tinder was really ignited when Xhosa tribesmen, having been invited into the homes of settlers on Christmas Day as a gesture of reconciliation, turned on their hosts and slaughtered them without mercy. Other tribes rose in conjunction, native police deserted *en masse* and Fort Cox was besieged, with the Governor Lieutenant General Sir Henry George Wakelyn 'Harry' Smith having to find fight his way out to safety while Forts Hare and White were similarly surrounded.

As always in Britain's long history, there were insufficient soldiers on the spot for a quick containment of the problem before it got out of hand. Reinforcements from ten different regiments had therefore to be rushed out from home. The 2nd Battalion of the Queen's Own Royal Regiment was trained from Rochester to London and then from Nine Elms station down to Portsmouth and embarked aboard the *Birkenhead* on 1 January. *Birkenhead* then sailed from Portsmouth to Cork with contingents of troops from ten assorted Army units calling at Queenstown (now Cobh) where she took further cadres on board, including some officers' wives and families, before leaving for the Cape on 17 January 1852. The *Birkenhead* reached Simonstown, near Cape Town, Cape Colony, on 23 February, having touched at Madeira, Sierra Leone and St Helena *en route*, after a passage of forty-seven days, much of it in stormy conditions.[7] Here

---

5. Contrary to what was stated by Laird himself in his letter to *The Times* (12 April 1849), she *had* embarked her designed armament for the first years of her career (from 5 November 1846 to 14 January 1848) under Captain Augustus Henry Ingham. See *The Annual Register, or A View of the History and Politics of the Year 1852*, p.470 (1853, London, Francis & John Rivington) where it is clearly stated that 'her guns were taken out' during her conversion. Indeed she still carried four broadside guns at the time of her loss, as attested to by her gunner at the time, John Archbold, in *Gilley's Narrative*, and confirmed by Corporal William Smith of the 12th Regiment.

6. Known at the time as the nine Kaffir Wars. *Kafir (Caffre)* was originally an Arabic term used by Muslims to describe those who, having read the Koran, did not subsequently subscribe to its teachings. It is nowadays taken by some to be a term of abuse against native South Africans.

7. It is on record that during this voyage three of the women passengers died while giving birth and a fourth expired from consumption. Four babies were born aboard the *Birkenhead* before she arrived at the Cape, but how many survived is not recorded; see 'Women and Children First: Commemorating the 150th Anniversary of the Sinking of the *Birkenhead*', article in *Military History Journal*, Vol 12, No. 4, 2002, Capetown, *Die Suid-Afrikaanse Krygshistoriese Vereninging* (The South African Military History Society.)

Lieutenant Samuel Fairclough of the 12th Regiment of Foot,[8] eighteen soldiers, mainly sick men, along with the ship's clerk, John Freshfield, who was also indisposed, and the majority of the women and children were disembarked,[9] while in return three colonial troopers, three soldiers from the 91st Regiment, re-joining their unit from garrison duty on Robben Island, nine cavalry horses, the respective mounts of Cornet John Rolt, Sergeant John Abraham Straw, Privates Charles Colbey, John Englison, John Took and George Hutchins, along with the horses' fodder and accoutrements, were loaded aboard, as well as embarking some civilian passengers including Mrs Elizabeth Nesbitt, wife of Quartermaster-General Alexander Nesbit who was already on the Frontier, along with her four children, Richard Athol, Henry, Mary Anne and Elizabeth, and also Andrew White, the servant of Colonel Abraham Josias Cloete,[10] and thirty-five tons of coal. A few of the twenty-five women and twenty-nine children, who had originally been aboard, stayed with the ship for the last part of the journey. Thus laden, *Birkenhead* set sail at 1800 on 25 February for the final leg of her journey, the 425-mile (683km) section to Algoa Bay, near Port Elizabeth. This area had first been settled by the British in 1820 and was on the frontier with the Xhosa nation.

On 26 February 1852, while transporting these reinforcements,[11] from Simon's Bay to lgoa Bay, near Port Elizabeth, she was wrecked some six and a half miles (10.5 km) from what is today Gansbaai harbour, Western Cape, just eighty-six miles (140 km) out from Cape Town.

Most of the troops and their families were in their cabins and hammocks below deck. Her commanding officer, Captain Robert Salmond RN, had been ordered to rush the reinforcements across as quickly as possible (with 'utmost haste') and had decided that this would best be achieved by adopting a course eastward from her anchorage in False Bay (*Valsbaai*), just across the flats from Table Bay, and around Robben Island (*Robbeneiland* or Seal Island), onward, which meant cutting things fine by hugging

---

8. Fairclough recovered and later rejoined his regiment and subsequently saw action at Cawood's Post, in the Trappes Mountains near Albany, later going on to become a lieutenant colonel.
9. Article 'Loss of the *Birkenhead* Steam-Frigate', in *The Spectator*, 10 April 1852, p.8.
10. Who ultimately became a lieutenant general and a Victoria Cross holder.
11. The Army units involved were the 12th (The Prince of Wales's Royal) Lancers – Cornets Ralph MacGeough Bond-Shelton, and Rolt and nine other ranks; 2nd (The Queen's Own Royal Regiment) – Ensign Boylan and fifty-three other ranks; 6th (Royal Warwickshire) Regiment of Foot – Ensign Lawrence Growden Nickleson Metford and sixty-one other ranks; 12th (East Suffolk) Regiment –Lieutenant Fairclough and seventy-one other ranks; 43rd (Monmouthshire) Light Infantry – Lieutenant John Francis Girardot and forty-one other ranks; 45th (1st Nottinghamshire) Regiment – seventeen other ranks; 60th The King's Royal Rifle Corps – forty-one other ranks under temporary attachment to the 91st (Argyllshire) Regiment; 73rd (Perthshire) Regiment of Foot – Lieutenants Booth and Robinson, Ensign Lucas and seventy-one other ranks; 74th (Highlanders) Regiment – Lieutenant-Colonel Seton, Ensign Russell and sixty-two other ranks; and 91st (Argyllshire) Regiment – Captain Wright and sixty-one other ranks, as well as Staff Surgeon Philip Laing, Staff Assistant Surgeons Robert Bowen and Frederick Robinson. There was also the *Birkenhead*'s naval surgeon Dr William Culhane and a twenty-strong Royal Marine contingent.

the Agulhas coastline some three miles (4.8 km) offshore. This was a riskier route than normal but, by adopting it, an average speed of 8.5 knots (15.7 km/h) could be maintained. He consulted with his sailing master, William Brodie, telling him 'once clear of the blinders surrounding the harbour in Simon's Bay, to sail south by east until clear of Cape Hangklip and a good departure from Cape Point lighthouse. And from there to sail SSE by half east'. Brodie was instructed to give Cape Hangklip a wide berth, [four-and-a-half miles (6.4 km] and likewise keep clear of Danger Point by seven miles (11.2 km).

The *Birkenhead* had left Simon's Bay at 1800 and adopted a speed of seven knots. Both Salmond and Brodie were present when the changes of course were carried out sometime between 2030 and 2100, and then, some time subsequent to 2200, both men retired to bed, satisfied the ship was safely on course. Able Seaman John Haynes, who was at the wheel from 2200 to midnight, later recorded that he steered a course SSEE and giving Cape Hangklip, a wide berth of about four miles 'with directions not to go the Eastward of it'. Lookouts were posted and a leadsman positioned on one of the paddle boxes to take soundings. It was a fine night, with starlight, and the land was clearly visible all night from three to four points on the port bow and all seemed serene. However, it was later speculated that some small errors in the ship's magnetic compasses, coupled with a strong south-easterly current toward Walker Bay, located between False Bay and Cape Agulhas, may have edged the *Birkenhead* closer to danger than was realised. Several of the crew reported seeing a light ashore, and this was later assumed to be a fire burning, but which might have possibly been confused with the light from the lighthouse on Cape Agolha. The helmsman reported that the compass had appeared to be acting in a sluggish manner at the time when the ship struck. [12]

At 0150 the *Birkenhead* was steaming at the slightly reduced speed of 8 knots (15 km/h) on a south-easterly course through a calm sea, with only a light swell and under the clear night sky. The *Birkenhead*'s leadsman, Ordinary Seaman Abel Stone, took a sounding of 12 fathoms (22m) which he reported to Second Master Jeremiah O'Dwyer Davis, the officer of the watch. He was about to make a second sounding when she struck a hidden rock at 34° 38' 42" S, 19° 17' 92E just off the sandstone reef,

---

12. The *Birkenhead* had been supplied with a new standard compass by the Portsmouth Dockyard which had been checked at Greenhithe on the Thames on 15 April 1851. The compass should have been swung at Simon's Bay but due to the haste to get the reinforcements out to the fighting zone, time constraints forced this check to be abandoned and she was hurried to sea. A serving admiral of the time wrote to the press complaining about the manner in which Captain Edward John Johnson, Superintendent of the Admiralty's Compass Department since 1848, had gone about his duties at Greenhithe for the adjustment of the compasses before they proceeded on sea service. This was raised in Parliament by Rear Admiral Sir George Brooke Pechell, the MP for Brighton Ward and spokesman on naval matters, on 17 June 1852. However, in response, Mr Augustus Stafford, First Secretary to the Admiralty, stated that Their Lordships retained full confidence in Captain Johnson and that they had statements 'both from Captain Salmond, after his experimental cruise, and from Commander Robert Wylie, after the destruction of the *Birkenhead*, stating that Captain Salmond was perfectly satisfied with the compasses of the *Birkenhead*'. (*Hansard*, 17 June 1852, Vol. 122, cc866–7.)

known as Point Danger, some fifty miles out from Simon's Bay. At the time of striking Stone had the presence of mind to take further soundings alongside and she had two fathoms (3.7m) under her bow with eleven fathoms (20m) under her stern.

Helmsman Coffin related, 'Never shall I forget that morning! I was at the wheel, and well remember the sentry calling out to the officer of the watch, "Four bells, sir." The officer replied, "Strike them, sentry," which he did not do, for at that very moment she struck the rock and the sentry went rolling on the deck.'

The very placidity of the sea was the ship's undoing, for the rock on which she was impaled can be clearly seen at intervals when the waves pitch and toss and throw up clearly visible white foam in rough weather, but is almost invisible when the water is calm, especially at night. A few feet to either port or starboard and she would have been safe. The initial strike tore open the forward watertight compartment located between the fore-peak and the engine room. This sudden impact ruptured her hull and sea poured in.[13]

Captain Salmond was awakened by the impact and arrived on deck half-dressed; he immediately asked what the time was and what course was being steered. On being told it was SSEE he confirmed that that this was 'quite correct'.[14] Salmond at once began to organise the standard emergency drill. The quarter boats were lowered and told to lie at a safe distance off. The bower anchor was ordered to be lowered and all the women and children were brought up from below. In the case of two of the children their salvation was quite accidental. Captain Bond-Shelton, of the 12th Lancers, was to recall in a letter dated 14 April 1902 that he went below to search for some paperwork but stumbled by chance on something quite different, 'two little girls that I found on the floor of the saloon cabin, quite alone'. He picked them both up and took them up on deck, handing them over to the men loading the ship's cutter. One of these was apparently Marian Darkin, and Bond-Shelton recalled, 'I think that the other little girl I carried up must have been a bandmaster's daughter, who I heard, was married a few years ago'.[15] Miss Darkin and Miss Zwyker owe their lives to this officer, though how they came to be abandoned in the first panic is unclear. Another account relates how one baby was tragically lost during the transfer by its father aboard the *Birkenhead* to its mother in the 'quarter-boat'. The boat and its passengers were in the care of Master's Assistant Roland Bevan Richards.[16]

Gunner Archibold recalled that Salmond ordered him 'to fire some [of the] guns – but, on getting the key of the magazine out of the cabin, I found the lower deck full of

13. Addison, Albert Christopher & Matthews, William Henry, *A Deathless Story, Or, the Birkenhead and its Heroes: being the only full and authentic account of the famous shipwreck Extant, founded on Collected Official Documents, and Personal Evidence, and Containing the Narratives and Lives of Actors in the most glorious ocean tragedy in history*, 1906, London, Hutchinson & Co., and see also 'Loss of H.M. Troop Ship *Birkenhead* off Point Danger about sixty miles from Simon's Bay', article in *United Services Gazette*.

14. Report of Commodore Wyvill.

15. Bond-Shelton, cited in *A Deathless Story, op. cit.*, pp.203 & 254.

16. See O'Byrne, Sheilagh, 'Ensign Gould Lucas's account of the wreck of the *Birkenhead*', article in *Africana Notes & News*, Vol. 17, No. 6, pp.255–6, 1967, Johannesburg. Africana Society, Africana Museum, Johannesburg, RSA.

water'. As the guns could not be fired, some Congreve rockets were fired off and young Benjamin Turner, a second-class ship's boy and servant to Mr Archibold, recalled that:

> When the ship struck the rock I was in my hammock asleep forward in the eyes of the ship under the topgallant forecastle, and was thrown out on to the deck by the concussion of the ship striking the rock at the same time the boatswain's mate rushing under the forecastle piping 'Hands to save ship!' I then made my way aft to the quarter-deck, where I saw my master, Mr Archibold, in the act of sending up rockets and burning blue lights as signals of distress, and I held the staffs for him while he fixed them on.

These efforts were all in vain – there was no one ashore to observe either the light or the rockets and none afloat either to render any immediate assistance. The soldiers were told off to assist with muscle power, with sixty men sent to work the chain pumps, while an equal number were told off to the lifeboat tackles. The remainder were marshalled on the ship's poop deck aft in an attempt to lift the forward part of the vessel and stem the inrush of the sea.

The senior regimental officer aboard was requested by Captain Salmond 'to be kind enough to preserve order and silence among the men' and await further orders.

Salmond considered the only chance was to back his ship off from the reef and hope there was sufficient buoyancy left in her to keep her afloat until help came. This proved a fatal decision. As the paddles turned astern, the ship struck a second time, and a huge gash was torn in the hull under the engine-room. The sea rushed in flooding the furnaces, but not before the engineer on duty, Charles Kerr Renwick, and his team of stokers, had fled to the upper deck to escape.

Renwick described events in this way:

> I was awoke by the vessel going ashore and water rushing from the main deck into the fore cockpit. I ran into the engine-room in my shirt only, and found there Mr Whyham, Mr Kitchingham and Mr Barber. The engines were stopped, and water pouring from the main deck through the door over the starboard cylinder. I shut the door, and about a minute afterwards orders were given to go astern. The engines, after a making from sixteen to twenty revolutions, stopped, the water rising so high as to extinguish the fires. While opening the starboard injection cock I observed a large portion of the starboard bilge buckled upwards, plates and ribs both started and water rushing in. Mr Whyham having reported to the Commander that the water had risen above the level of the air-pump lids, ordered all hands out of the engine-room. I then went aft and remained on the poop until she broke in two.[17]

---

17. Charles Kerr Renwick, Chief Assistant Engineer *Birkenhead*, Report to Commodore Wyvill from aboard the 4-gun Store Ship *Rhadamanthus* (Master Commander Frederick Rannie Sturdee), dated 1 March.

It was thought that more than one hundred soldiers asleep below in this area were drowned in their hammocks instantly.[18] This second surge opened up the *Birkenhead*'s bilge in the engine room and tore apart the bulkheads, thus ruining the integrity of the two largest watertight compartments in the ship and dooming her.[19] In an instant the deck tilted, the stern rose, one of her masts collapsed and her single tall funnel crashed to the deck, killing the men who were trying to free another lifeboat, while her tow rope was dropped and drifted free of the ship. Meanwhile efforts to launch the larger paddle-box boats had proved difficult, it being found that, shamefully, they had had their winches painted over and that therefore they would not easily move, or were rusted in place. Thus two of the largest boats, each of which could have accommodated 150 men, were instantly found to be of no use. One boat was finally lowered overboard but was immediately swamped alongside; the second one, on the starboard side, could not be freed and was first crushed and then carried away by the falling funnel.

Private John Smith of the 91st Regiment recalled:

I was asleep below when I was aroused by a tremendous crash. I at once realised that something serious was amiss, and calling to my mate, a Romford man, I told him I thought we must be ashore. We ran up on deck with the rest, and afterwards I stood at the gangway and assisted to hand the women and children into the boat. The men all stood back until they had been got safely away; but there was no 'falling in' on the deck. When the vessel went down I was in the long-boat. There were about a hundred of us in it altogether, but when the ship broke in two the falling funnel caught our boat and smashed it, throwing us into the water.

Another large boat in the centre of the ship was also found to have been jammed in her stowage.[20] As a result the few boats that *were* got into the water proved totally inadequate for the number of persons still on board, these boats only having a total capacity for seventy-eight persons when several hundred required them. It therefore became very quickly obvious that not every passenger would be saved. The soldiers were ordered to 'Stand Firm' and, to their eternal credit, almost every man did so,

---

18. *The Annual Register, or, A View of the History and Politics of the Year 1852*, pp.470–3, 1853, London, Francis & John Rivington.

19. *Birkenhead* had been constructed with athwart-ships bulkheads which divided her main hull into eight watertight compartments, and, additionally, her engine-room was split by a pair of longitudinal bulkheads into four separate compartments, for a total of twelve. See Percy, Sholto & Perry, Fairfax, 'The Steam Frigate *Birkenhead* – Iron v. Wood', article in *The Mechanics' Magazine, Register, Museum, Journal and Gazette*, Vol. LVI, pp.327–9, 1856, London. William A. Robertson & Co.

20. *Report* by Captain Edward Wiliiam Carlile Wright, 91st Regiment to Commander, Cape Town, dated 1 March 1852, published in *The Southport Visiter*, 9 April 1852.

thus permitting the women and children to find safety. Of the 643 people aboard her,[21] only 193 survived.

A distant sail had been seen which gave some hope. This was the 58-ton London-registered coasting schooner *Lioness* (Master Thomas Emmanuel Ramsden). She was *en route* from England to Melbourne with Ramsden, his wife, Mary Ann, his 8-year-old daughter Christiana, and a crew comprising a mate and six seamen, but she was some distance away and, at first, those on watch failed to notice that *Birkenhead* was in trouble and she continued on her way.

All the troops not engaged in rescue work were ordered to muster into ranks, regiment by regiment. The captain meanwhile gave the order to abandon ship.

With only two small cutters (with coxswains George Till and Thomas Coffin respectively at their tillers) and the ship's gig safely put into the water, there was a question of priorities. The women and children, who had assembled under the poop awning, were lowered into one cutter in charge of Master's Assistant Rowland Bevan Richards, and her crew rowed 150 yards (137.16m) away from the sinking ship.[22] As the deck tilted and the water rose the troops remained standing fast, but then the *Birkenhead* broke her back crosswise, just abaft the engine-room. The forward section sank almost at once, while the after part, crowded with Royal Marines and the troops in serried ranks, remained afloat for just a few minutes longer before submerging.

Those in the bowels of the ship manning the pumps under the command of Lieutenant Audley Henry Booth died instantly. The men on deck must have known what would happen, yet still they did not budge until the order was given by the captain for all those who could swim to go over the side and attempt to reach the boats. This order, if carried out by every man, might easily have resulted in swamping the cutters. Lieutenant-Colonel Alexander Seton of the 74th Highlanders therefore raised his hand above his head and told his men to 'Stand fast' where they stood. 'The cutter with the women and children will be swamped, I implore you not to do this thing and I ask you stand fast.' Other officers took up the cry, urging the men to remain where they were for the sake of the women and children. And, to their eternal credit, and considering that many were just young recruits, merely boys in fact, that is exactly what every man, save three who panicked, did.

Meanwhile the cavalry horses were led blindfold from their stalls and then released unhampered and driven over the ship's side from the port gangway in the hope that

21. The exact number of personages embarked has never been established and remains subject to acrimonious dispute, *The Times*, for example, reporting a tally of 638, but more comprehensive analysis upped this total to 643; however, as all the muster rolls and ship's books went down with the ship, this still today remains mainly conjecture.

22. Report of Captain Wright to Lieutenant-Colonel William Bates Ingilby, Royal Artillery, Commandant, Cape Town, dated 1 March 1852. COS53/10, National Archives, Kew, London. The latter became General Sir William Bates Ingilby KCB. The rest of the crew of the first cutter were Able Seamen Thomas Daly and Thomas Drackford, engineer Alexander Russell and 2nd-Class boy Charles Matthews.

they might stand a reasonable chance of swimming to the beach, an estimated two miles (3.2km) distant.[23]

Cornet Bond of the 12th (Prince of Wales's Royal) Lancers, owner of the only lifebelt on the vessel, a Mackintosh life-preserver, his own private property, gave a graphic portrayal of the *Birkenhead*'s final agonies.

All the officers were then employed with gangs of men at the pumps; and a number of soldiers under the command of William Brodie, the Acting Master, were endeavouring to haul out the paddle-box boat on the port side; which was nearly hoisted out when the tackle broke, and it remained fixed in the air. The fore-part of the ship now broke off at the foremast, and soon after she cracked in the middle and filled with water. The poop immediately afterwards, owing to the force of the water rushing up, went down, drawing all those who were on it, as well as myself, under water. I rose to the surface almost immediately.

He continued:

The sea at this time was covered with struggling forms, while cries, piercing shrieks, and shouts for the boat, were awful. I swam astern in hopes of being picked up by one of them. I hailed one sixty yards off, but could not reach it, as they pulled away, I suppose for fear of too many attempting to get in. I then turned round and made for the shore, about two miles distant; which I finally succeeded in reaching, at a little after five a.m. by swimming only. Two men, who were swimming close to me, I saw disappear with a shriek, most probably bitten by sharks. I fortunately hit on the landing-place; but owing to the great quantity of seaweed I had to struggle through, and being quite exhausted, I almost failed in reaching it.

---

23. Incredibly, eight of the nine made it safely; the unlucky ninth mount had its legs broken while being manhandled over the side of the ship. Cornet Ralph Shelton-Bond was one of the eleven officers to make it ashore. Here, to his astonishment, he found his faithful steed standing on the beach, as if waiting for him! Private Joseph Edwarde of the 12th Lancers recounted that Bond, '...discovered his horse up to the knees in the water and secured him safe.' Later the five surviving horses, which were the mounts of Ingilby himself, Bond, Major Seton, Dr Laing and Lieutenant Booth of the 73rd, were all caught and Ingleby handed them over to William Mackintosh Mackay, the Civil Commissioner of Caledon, 'who is to send them on to me here, so that they may be sold, and that I may account for the proceeds'. However, 20-year-old Ensign Gould Arthur Lucas, in a letter to his father written in Cape Town while he was recuperating, and dated 20 March, recorded that another horse, that of Cornet Rolf, was found two days later standing patiently 'outside his stable in Cape Town, having traversed the 125 miles from Cape Danger unaided'. Lucas later settled in Natal and became Chief Magistrate of Durban. His letter was discovered many years later in Hilton College, Kwa-ZuluNatal, RSA, and transcribed by Major Antony George Drumearn Gordon. Local legend would have it that some of these surviving horses became feral and established a small herd which foraged on the eastern plains near Gans Bay (*Gansbaai*) and that this group's descendants survived there for over a century; but it would be appear from the above report that this simply could not have been the case, and that the herd must have owed its origins elsewhere.

I then walked up a sort of beaten track from the beach, in hopes of finding some habitation. In doing so I perceived my horse at a short distance, standing in the water on the beach. I got him out, and then returned to the place at which I landed; when I saw a raft, with about nine men on it, endeavouring to land; but they did not succeed in doing so until they saw me on the rocks standing opposite to the proper spot; they then steered straight for me, and finally landed at seven a.m. Lieutenant Giradot, of the Forty-third Light Infantry, was one of them. At the same time, two or three other men were thrown on the rocks off a spar, and landed, very much cut and bruised and entirely naked. We all then proceeded up this track; and, after two hours' march, we saw a wagon along the shore, to which we went and obtained some bread and water. The driver directed us further up the beach, and at five miles' distance we should find some fishing cottages belonging to Captain Smales; where we arrived, very much fatigued, at noon....

They later encountered other survivors and heard their stories.

One of the ship's quartermasters told me that there were seven others in the boat with him, which was full of water. They, however, all died from cold, having been many hours in the boat and quite naked. He had his clothes on. We also met Captain Wright, Ninety-first, who had landed on the sponson; he had been along the shore and had picked up several men. Some rafts reached the shore with bodies lashed on them quite dead, other bodies washed up, some of them dreadfully mangled by sharks.

Within twenty minutes it was all over and the *Birkenhead*'s broken hull slid beneath the waves. As she went down the soldiers finally took to the water, a fortunate few even managing to swim to the shore, the long journey made more difficult by the dense masses of weed that stretched out to sea from this part of the coast. As it was, between thirty and forty made the beach, but many subsequently expired from their exertions.

It was a hope, however remote, that the cutters might reach land, deposit their passengers, and then return to the ship for others, but this was not to be due to the speed with which she went down. Of those who could not swim some, a few, gained precarious handholds on the main topmast and topsail yard, the only parts of the *Birkenhead* still remaining above the waves; others grasped wreckage and eventually floated to safety, but these were very few.

The greater majority were drowned, sliced by the still turning ship's screws or taken by Blacktip sharks.[24]

---

24. *Carcharhinus limbatus* are normally wary of humans but when roused by blood in the water become extremely aggressive. And not just sharks; both the living and the floating bodies were reported as being attacked and eaten by huge Copper *steenbras* (*Petrus rupesiris*), especially closer in to the shore. These 'voracious predators' once inhabited the coastal waters from Cape Town to north of Durban in large numbers and could reach a length of 6.7 feet (200cm) and a weight of 114lb (52kg). A few of this, now 'Red Listed' and highly-endangered, species still survive and a huge specimen was caught off the mouth of the Kei River, Eastern Cape, on 27 November 2011.

Benjamin Turner recalled how:

I swam about for some time, resting on pieces of the wreckage, until I came across a part of the ship's bridge, which I lay on top of, and thank God, it enabled me to keep clear of the sharks.... I saw many poor fellows during the day who were hanging with their arms over a spar and their legs in the water, taken down by the sharks. A shark would come up, seize them by the leg, and drag them down.

Captain Salmond was seen clinging to one spar for a while, but was struck on the head by another, concussed and drowned.[25] Among other casualties among the *Birkenhead*'s crew were Master Brodie, 2nd Lieutenant Robert David Speer, 3rd Lieutenant Davies, Chief Engineer Whyam, Assistant Engineers Deeley and James McClaymont, Boatswain Thomas Harris and James Roberts the ship's carpenter. Of the Army personnel who left Queenstown for the Cape, who numbered thirteen officers, nine sergeants and 446 men, those lost included Major Seton himself and Ensign Alexander Cumming Russell also of the 74th; Lieutenants Audley Henry Booth and Charles William Robinson of the 73rd Highlanders; Ensign Boyland of the 2nd, Ensign Lawrence Growdon Nicholson Metford of the 6th and Cornet Rolt of the 14th Regiments.[26]

Master's assistant Rowland Bevan Richards, who commanded one boat, recalled in a letter dated 1 March, that:

At the time the vessel struck I was in my hammock in the fore cockpit. I immediately ran on deck in my shirt, and on looking down the fore hatchway I saw the cockpit was half-full of water. It was rising very fast. I went aft and heard the Captain give orders to rig the chain-pumps. I went below in the after cockpit, and with the purser's steward and carpenter shipped the pump-handles. I then went on deck and assisted in clearing away the first cutter and starboard paddle-box boat falls. The vessel was rolling heavily, and settling down by the head very fast. The Captain ordered the soldiers on the poop, which was done in a quiet manner. He then called me and ordered me to get the women and children into the second cutter and save them if possible. The boat was lowered with a quantity of water in her, and nearly swamped alongside. The women and children were

25. Another eyewitness, Assistant-Surgeon Culhane, however, attested that Salmond was later seen still alive in the mizzenmast rigging, which stretched above the water after the vessel had finally settled down at the bottom. Cornet Bond stated, 'Young Mr Rolt of the Lancers, asked the Sergeant of Marines to try and save him: he did try, and got him on the raft; but as it surged against the rocks, it parted, and he sank.'

26. While both Davis and Harris are on record as having died on 26 February, Speer is recorded as having died 'Before 31 May' and Roberts 'Before 23 June'. See Officers, Pensioners' and Civilians' Register – Claims, ADM45/29/154 (Claimant Octavius Ommanney, Contracts Corporation for The Crown Agents), ADM45/29/137 (Widow Eliza Ann Harris), ADM 45/29/175 (Claimant Duncan Frank Herbert for The Crown Agents) and ADM 45/20/174 (Widow Mrs Elizabeth Roberts) respectively, National Archives, Kew, London.

then passed into her, and some of the soldiers also jumped in off the gangway, in all thirty-five persons. I got clear of the vessel which immediately parted in tow just before the paddle-boxes. I then heard the Captain calling for a boat to save Mr Brodie, the master. I pulled to the wreck, but could not see him. I was obliged to get clear of the wreck again almost immediately, as the boat was nearly swamped and a great number of men swimming towards her. I then saw the first cutter and second gig astern of the wreck. I hailed and asked if they were full, and told them to take in as many as they could carry with safety. I heard Mr Renwick call to me to pick him up. I told him we were nearly sinking and full of people, and to go on a little further to the gig, which picked him up shortly afterwards.

Lieutenant John Francis Girardot, of the 43rd Light Infantry, in a letter also dated 1 March 1852, described to his father how:

the suction took me down some way, and a man got hold of my leg, but I managed to kick him off and came up and struck out for some pieces of wood that were on the water and started for land, about two miles off. I was in the water about five hours, as the shore was so rocky and the surf ran so high that a great many were lost trying to land. Nearly all those that took to the water without their clothes on were taken by sharks: hundreds of them were all round us, and I saw men taken by them close to me, but as I was dressed (having on a flannel shirt and trousers) they preferred the others.[27]

Mr George William Samuel Hire had been appointed as Freshfield's assistant clerk[28] and took over his duties when he had gone ashore at the Cape. He recounted his experience thus:

I slept in the fore cockpit, and between two and three in the morning ... I was awake by the ship striking against something. I got on deck and went aft to the Commander, who told me to get the books ready to go in the boat, as he did not think there was any immediate danger. I did so, and went again on the poop. I had hardly got there when she went in halves amidships. I stopped by the Commander and Mr Speer, the second master, at the wheel until the poop went down, taking us with it. I came up again close to the main-yard, and went thence

27. Dickens, Charles, *The Household Narrative of Current Events (for the Year 1852), being a monthly supplement to Household Words*, p.89, 1852, London, Bradbury & Hyans.
28. ADM 196/75/350, National Archives, Kew, London. The Royal Naval Rate, Captain's Clerk, was responsible for the captain's accounts, correspondence and record-keeping who worked with the ship's purser (later in 1852 Paymaster) and worked on up to twenty-five different documents that each captain had to have authorised by the Admiralty during a ship's commission. A 'passed clerk' was a young apprentice clerk who had successfully passed all his examinations and ranked with a ship's mate in status. In 1855 such worthies became Assistant Paymasters as the rates were replaced.

to the topsail-yard as she settled down, where I remained. I did not see any officer or the boats. There were, I think, about fifty men on the yard with me; some of whom dropped off during the rest of the night, and at daylight some went on shore on parts of the wreck.

Second Surgeon Dr Robert Bowen, was rescued and got aboard the second cutter. He reported on 1 March that:

I remained in the vessel 'till she parted in two just before the paddle-boxes, as it seemed to me, and then seeing no hope of the ship floating, and Mr Salmond saying that those who could swim had better try and save their lives, I lowered myself from the poop and swam. The ship went down in three or four minutes after I left her, so far as I can judge. I was picked up by the first cutter. During the time I was on deck the officers and men, both Naval and Military, displayed the greatest coolness and the perfection of discipline. Mr Salmond's orders were given, answered, and carried into effect with as much quietness as if it had been only an ordinary occasion. I spoke to Mr Salmond only a short time before the ship parted, and he was as cool and self-possessed as possible.

After I got into the cutter we took in as many men as she could with safety carry, and the crew behaved with the greatest courage and propriety with the exception of one Marine, whose conduct was disrespectful to Mr Renwick, and who appeared to grumble rather than assist. The first and second cutters and gig pulled in company for Cape Hanglip (sic), under the orders of Mr Richards, as when we neared the shore we found the surf breaking heavily.

Captain Wright recorded how he managed to get on a large piece of floating wood with five other men, and that they managed to pluck nine or ten more from the water to join them. The swell carried them toward Point Danger and they got ashore at Stanford's Cove, many of the men being naked or unshod. They pushed inland seeking shelter. Some sixty-eight survivors, Army, Royal Marine personnel and eighteen sailors, were eventually assembled under Lieutenant Girardot of the 43rd and Cornet Bond. A whaleboat from Dyer's Island was commandeered and taken outside the seaweed belt where they plucked two more from the sea and found another pair ashore and exhausted. Wright reported that eighteen were bruised and eight were 'burnt by the sun'. Some eighty-six hours after the wreck, Captain Wright joined the rest and obtained clothes for them.

The ship's gig, with a crew of nine, managed to get around Cape Hangklip and got aground in a small cove at the mouth of the River Bot at what is now Fischerhaven. After being succoured by local fishermen, they despatched one of their number, the ship's assistant surgeon Dr William Culhane, on horseback thirty-seven miles (60km) overland to Simon's Bay which he reached at 1500 with the dreadful news. The rest walked through Strandveld to Stanford's Cove, where, at Kleine Rivier, they found refuge at a homestead owned by former dragoon guard Paymaster, retired Captain Thomas Smales.

On arrival of the surgeon at his headquarters, the local commander, Captain and Commodore Christopher Wyvill, Commander-in-Chief, Cape Station, immediately despatched the 1,086-ton Navy transport HMS *Rhadamanthus* (Captain John Belam) to see what rescue could be achieved.[29]

The *Rhadamanthus* had been converted for use as a transport and had arrived on station earlier with stores and a large sum of specie, three tons worth if a letter written by Paymaster Sergeant Bernard Kilberry of the 73rd Regiment on 8 April 1902 to the War Office is to be believed, the manifests alleging £15,000 cash in gold and silver, even at that time hardly a fortune, it being the pay for the army ashore and stacked in the ship's powder room. However, Kilberry did also admit that 'I cannot say what cash each or all the boxes contained'. This was sufficient, however, for whatever sum was really in those mysterious boxes aboard the *Birkenhead* to assume mind-blowing proportions and prompt, as so often before, yet more endless vain searches for 'treasure-trove' among her wreckage.[30]

Around 0300 the schooner *Lioness*, which had been close at hand, finally realised something was amiss, turned back and made contact with one of the cutters,[31] taking in all aboard; the women and children were cared for by Mrs Ramsden 'who emptied her wardrobe to clad the scantily clad survivors, cutting up even her best silk gowns and leaving herself only with the clothes she was wearing'.[32] Captain Ramsden later wrote a letter to Wyvill dated 27 February in which he described events thus:

I beg to report to you that when the *Lioness* was off Walker's Bay I observed a boat inshore pulling towards me on the morning of the 26th inst. at about ten o'clock, which we picked up, and found her to contain 37 survivors from the wreck of the *Birkenhead*. On hearing that there were two other boats I proceeded in search of them, and three-quarters of an hour afterwards I succeeded in picking up the other cutter with the women and children; but after cruising about for the third boat I made for the wreck, which I reached about two o'clock in the afternoon of the same day, and sent the cutters away to pick up the men hanging to the spars, by which we rescued 35 soldiers and sailors in a nearly naked state. The wreck had disappeared all but a piece of the main topmast and topsail-yard, to which were men were clinging. Nothing else could be saved.

---

29. The *Rhadamanthus* had been built as a 2nd-class 5-gun paddle-sloop two decades earlier, and had originally achieved fame as the first Royal Navy vessel to cross the Atlantic *with the assistance* of steam power when she sailed from Plymouth to Port Royal, Barbados in 1833. Contrary to what the *Guinness Book of Records* sources tell us, this was *not* the first steam-power crossing, simply because the last part of her journey was conducted under sail.

30. In passing, it should be noted that Commodore Wyvill's broad pennant was normally flown in the old wooden 5th-rate *Castor*.

31. Survivors in the women's cutter included Bernard Kilkeary of the 73rd Regiment of Foot, who went on to take part in the Battle of Berea as well as the Indian Mutiny. He survived all of these dangers to become a colour sergeant.

32. See Lennox Kerr, James, *The Unfortunate Ship: The Story of H.M. Troopship Birkenhead*, 1960, London, George Godrey Harrap.

Ramsden's young daughter had received strict orders to remain below when the men, many naked, were brought aboard, but nonetheless sneaked up on deck, for which she duly received a walloping with a silver hairbrush from her mother! These fortunate few were freely fed and clothed likewise by Ramsden's crew before later being taken to Mussel Bay.[33] They were later transferred to the *Rhadamanthus*, which then towed the *Lioness* back the nine miles to port.[34]

Dr Robert Bowen was to confirm Ramsden's excellent work in his own account.

Nothing could exceed the kindness and attention of Mr Ramsden and his wife on board the *Lioness:* nothing was too good for us, and he made every effort to save as many souls as possible. He deserves the highest praise.

This commendation appeared to cut little ice with the commodore however. All that the crew of the *Lioness* subsequently received to make good their losses was a single cask of salt beef and another of salt pork, plus three bags of ships' biscuits, this to the Navy's shame. After her great work in rescuing and feeding so many *Birkenhead* survivors, the Nova Scotia-built *Lioness* later resumed her voyage toward Australia once more. (Alas, she herself was to be wrecked on 21 March 1854 on Moriarty's Bank, off Clarke Island in the Forneaux Group (Tayaritja) in the Bass Strait off north-eastern Tasmania. The mate, two of the crew and one male passenger were all drowned, but Ramsden and his family, with four other crew members, were fortunately saved.) A total of 193 were eventually accounted for. All the women and children survived. The final tally was seven women, seventeen children, six Royal Marines, fifty-four crew members, and 113 Army personnel of all ranks, plus at least one civilian. One soldier who was rescued, Private Boyden (also later a colour sergeant), stated that during the time that Major Seton's orders were being carried out one could have heard a pin drop. Major Seton walked about the deck giving his orders with as much coolness and presence of mind as if he were on parade, entirely forgetful of self. A list of those who survived was subsequently presented to the Royal Family.

Captain Wright, of the 91st, was to recall:

The order and regularity that prevailed on board, from the time the ship struck until she totally disappeared, far exceeded anything that I thought could be effected by the best discipline; and it the more to be wondered at, seeing that most of the soldiers were but a short time in the Service. Everyone did as he

---

33. Smith, Corporal William, *Recollections of a Rambling Life*, incorporated in *A Deathless Story*, *op. cit.*, p.299.
34. For which charitable work Ramsden received scant thanks from Wyvill. Ramsden had stated in his letter, 'I am desirous of prosecuting my voyage to the West Coast of Africa without delay. I beg you will be pleased to order the provisions to be replaced and the defects of the ship made good, my boat and gunwale being injured by getting in the cutters. The unfortunate people have been put on board the *Castor* at nine o'clock.' Wyvill's totally crass response was that he hoped Ramsden had not just been motivated by reward!

was directed, and there was not a murmur or a cry amongst them until the ship made her final plunge. I could not name any individual officer who did more than another. All received their orders and had them carried out as if the men were embarking instead of going to the bottom; there was only this difference, that I never saw any embarkation conducted with so little noise or confusion.

The resulting enquiry was hampered by the fact that so few of the ship's officers had survived. Commodore Wyvill summed up in this manner:

There is no doubt but the course of the ship was shaped to hug the land too closely; and, as it does not appear that either Mr Salmond or the master had attended on deck from ten o'clock in the first watch until the accident occurred, it would infer much inattention and extreme neglect of duty on their parts; and when soundings were first struck, had the helm been put to port, this ill-fated ship might have escaped the danger. It is much to be lamented that not an officer has been saved who can give any satisfactory information upon these points.

The Commodore added:

It is also to be deeply deplored that a young officer, Mr Richards, Master's assistant, should have been the only executive in command of the boats; as, from the circumstances of their leaving the scene of the wreck before daylight, the landing-place discovered on Point Danger by those who reached the shore on rafts would have shown itself, and the hapless individuals who were clinging to pieces of wreck and spars might have been picked off and carried to the shore by the boats, and thus many more lives would have been saved. Also, when the schooner visited the wreck, had the cutters examined the coast in the locality, it is probable they might have found a few others. I can only attribute this fatal error to want of judgment, and to the excited state of the people in the boats under such appalling circumstances.

However, Commander William King-Hall, commanding the 6-gun paddle-sloop *Styx* on the Cape Station was to write in his diary for 7 March, that:

A look out on the part of the Officer of the Watch of the *Birkenhead* was I hear wanting. Various reports are abroad all speaking very much against the discipline of the Ship – and I have been told it was the common remark, that if they arrived at their destination safely, it would be a miracle. It is said, the Birth night of the unhappy Officer of the Watch had been kept up the same night. There are two things which present themselves to my mind on this melancholy occasion. The Troopships are not efficient when commanded by Masters, from the paucity of responsible Officers, and that all Troopships should have more Boats hanging outside. It is said she struck off Point Danger, but I forbear writing any more until our arrival at Simons Bay. Thank God for so mercifully preserving us in our voyages, for 10 or 12 times have we passed this dangerous place at Night, and the last time on Friday it was a dense fog. The time previous I pointed out to Ellis rocks breaking apparently ½ a mile farther out than we had seen it, and said let it be a warning.[35]

The bulk of the crew's survivors, fifty-eight men and boys, were eventually brought home aboard the 24-gun 6th-rate corvette *Amazon* (Captain Charles Barker), which came very close to being lost herself.[36] These survivors had been preceded home by the clerk, Mr John Freshfield, who arrived aboard the General Screw Steam Shipping Company's Mail Steamer *Propontis* (Captain Thomas William Glover) which had just delivered a cargo of mail, Government despatches and ordnance stores to the army.[37] She arrived back at Plymouth on 6 April and Freshfield was able to break the news of the tragedy. The *Propontis* then proceeded up-Channel to Gravesend, where she duly arrived on the 8th, having run down the Dutch brig *Ann Rebecca* during her passage.

Significantly, at some point during Captain's Glover's stay between April and May, he was summoned to the Admiralty and testified before the Lords of the Admiralty his experience in reference to the extraordinary magnetic affection of the needle experienced occasionally at the Cape 'to which the wreck of the *Birkenhead* has been in some measure attributed'. Captain Glover was able to inform them that he had on previous voyages often observed a peculiarity in the compasses in that region, 'but not to so great an extent as on the 25th February, when the ill-fated *Birkenhead* struck the rocks'.

Captain Glover explained how:

Some days before making the Cape land, on board the *Propontis*, in February, we found there was nearly six points difference between our standard and binnacle compasses, the standard having nearly three points west variation, and the binnacle nearly three points easterly variation. On approaching the land, on the night of the 25th February, we found the binnacle compass so unsteady, and oscillating so much, at times taking nearly a round turn, that we could not steer by it, but coursed the ship by the standard, which remained steady.[38]

---

35. King-Hall Connections. See also HMS *Styx* Ship's Book (2 Volumes), ADM 135/453, National Archives, Kew, London.
36. She became becalmed north of Ascension Island on 30 March. Without warning a sudden blast caught her with her all her sails still set, and she was heeled over by the gust to, it was claimed, an incredible 23 degrees, before somehow managing to right herself.
37. Her outward-bound cargo had included the first consignment of 450 Colt revolvers for use by British Army officers.
38. Long after the loss of the *Birkenhead* the extent of magnetic fields on iron-built ship's compasses exercised naval minds. See, for example, Evans, Captain Frederick John Owen, 'Reduction and Discussion of the Deviations of the Compass Observed on Board of All the Iron-Built Ships, and a Selection of the Wood-Built Steam-Ships in Her Majesty's Navy, and the Iron Steam-Ship Great Eastern: Being a Report to the Hydrographer of the Admiralty', *Philosophical Transactions of the Royal Society of London*, Vol. 150 (1860), pp.337–8.

None of this evidence appeared at the Naval court martial, which was held aboard HMS *Victory* moored in Portsmouth harbour, and which was held under the Presidency of Rear-Admiral Henry Prescott CB, Second-in-Command Spithead and Portsmouth. The court comprised eleven captains: Henry Ducie Chads CB (*Excellent*), Robert Harris (*Prince Regent*), William Henderson CB (*Blenheim*), Lewis Tobias Jones (unallocated, formerly of the *Sampson*), Granville Loch CB (*Winchester*), George Bohun Martin CB (*Victory*), Henry Matson (*Highflyer*), Robert Robinson (*Arrogant*), Edward Hinton Scott (*Neptune*), Frederick Warden (*Retribution*), Thomas Matthew Symonds (*Arethusa*) and Charles Wise (unallocated, formerly of the *Queen*), with Sir George Lambum Greetham, Deputy Judge Advocate of the Fleet. These same gentlemen sat on what was, in effect, two courts of enquiry, the first commencing on 5 May and lasting two days. Those before the inquisition were Master's Assistant Rowland Bevan Richards and Stoker John Ashbolt, Seamen John Bowen and Thomas Dunn and Ordinary Seaman Abel Stone, while the witnesses called were Surgeon Dr William Culhane, Assistant Engineer Charles Renwick, Gunner John Archbold, Royal Marine Colour-Sergeant John Drake, Able Seamen John Lewis and George Till and Ordinary Seamen Thomas Coffin and Thomas Deely.

From Coffin the court elicited the fact that he had been at the ship's wheel on the poop deck at the time the ship struck, and had been steering by the binnacle. He had then been relieved by quartermaster James Heming. He had got aboard the second cutter with John Lewis as coxswain and ten oarsmen. He also confirmed that the port and starboard lookouts had been Thomas Daly and John Butcher, the latter also lost while the lead was swung from atop the after part of the paddle-box. He also confirmed that the Officer of the Watch, Mr Davis, had continually checked his compass prior to the grounding. Daly related how he had observed lights ashore prior to the striking, initially 'off the beam' and later 'a long way off the quarter' and that they had shone 'very brightly'. He confirmed that there had been thirty-six persons in the first cutter including 'seven women, four soldiers and several children' and that the coxswain had been George Till.

John Drake had not seen the lights at all while the Gunner, Archbold, and he related how he had been in water for several hours before dawn broke, when he located Captain Wright and ten soldiers on a large piece of wreckage. They also pulled out of the sea Mr Barber, an engineer, and a boatswain's mate and then paddled ashore. Dr Culhane re-iterated at great length the story that his report had already detailed. He had been in the four-oared gig with about ten others, including Mr Renwick and three or four soldiers. Renwick and four volunteer oarsmen later transferred to the cutter in an attempt to try and catch up with the *Lioness* which was pulling away from them in a stiff breeze, to bring her back and affect a rescue. The court then adjourned for the day.

Boatswain's Mate Wilson was the first to be called the next morning. He stated he had relieved the starboard watch at midnight, and had observed a light ashore, but had not taken any special notice of it. He was asked whether Abel Stone was capable of obtaining accurate soundings at twelve fathoms or more at the speed the ship was travelling, and replied, 'It would take a good man'. On being questioned on how he got ashore he stressed the difficulties of landing because of sunken rocks and dense masses of kelp.[39] Till was then called and explained he was selected to man the women's boat because he was the regular coxswain.

John Lewis told again how he had been ordered to the cutter as coxswain and that they saved thirty-two men, but that 'there were so many hanging on the gunwale that I could not take them all in', although later they threw overboard the boat slings and other heavy gear and got more men inboard as a result. Then Assistant Engineer Renwick was called. He again related the sequence of events and expressed the view that reversing the engines had 'hastened the crisis of the wreck' and that had this not been done the ship would have held together long enough to get some of the other boats into the water. He also expressed the view that the four separated watertight engine compartments had 'made common' by 'the bilge being buckled up the whole extent of the foremost division, or nearly so'.

The question of the magnetic compasses being faulty was then considered and expert witnesses and documentation produced to confirm that *Birkenhead*'s compass had been swung both at Spithead, twice, and also once in the Thames at Greenhithe, and not been found wanting on any of these occasions, a fact attested to by Captain Salmond himself to the Secretary of the Admiralty, dated 7 April 1851.

The Court then deliberated and their decision was read out on 6 May. They commented that they had been hampered by:

> the unfortunate circumstances of the master commanding, and the principal officers of the ship, having perished, they feel that it was in the highest degree difficult, and that it might be unjust to pass censure upon the deceased, whose motives for keeping so near the shore cannot be explained.[40]

The Court continued, however, that:

> they must record their opinion, that this fatal loss was owing to the course having been calculated to keep the land in close proximity. If such be the case, they still trusted that they were not precluded from speaking with praise of the departed, for the coolness displayed in the moment of extreme peril, and for the laudable anxiety shown for the safety of the women and children to the exclusion of all selfish consideration.

The Court's verdict was that 'the said Mr Rowland Bevan Richards, John Bowen, Thomas Dunn, John Ashbolt and Abel Stone, to be fully acquitted'.

---

39. Ensign Lucas related that this weed was known locally as 'Sea Bamboo' so thick did it grow and it attained lengths of up to fifteen feet. Another common name for it was 'Bottle Weed'.

40. Such considerations of feelings naturally carry no weight in the modern world where all kinds of motives, from robbery to conspiracy, are freely attributed to the deceased with little or no evidence.

On 7 May the rest of the survivors, Dr Culhane and forty-seven men had their turn, with Ashbolt, Brown, Dunn, Richards and Stone being called as witnesses. Although there were a great many men called, the hearing only lasted one day and was a bit of a formality. Each of the witnesses, on being formally asked whether they knew of any instance of misconduct by any of the prisoners then on trial, in respect to the loss of the ship, or subsequent thereto, replied that they did not. Dr Culhane was then allowed to ask certain questions but they brought nothing fresh to light and the Court's decision was the expected one, that 'no blame was imputable to Mr John Archbold, or the other surviving officers and crew of the said ship'. The Court stated quite the opposite, that they 'saw reason to admire and applaud the steadiness shown by all in most trying circumstances, and the conduct of those who were first in the boats, and who, to the best of their judgement, made every exertion for the rescue of that portion of the crew and passengers who remained upon the wreck'.[41]

The fact that the iron-built *Birkenhead*'s hull fractured so quickly and that Laird's watertight sub-divisions had failed to hinder her sinking very much, briefly re-opened the 'timber versus iron' debate in the contemporary press, with advocates of both materials duly piling in for or against. A more sober and detached (in terms of both distance in time from the event and professional analysis using the latest scientific understanding) consideration of the case was given by Kenneth Barnaby OBE BSc ACGI, Honorary Vice-President of the Royal Institution of Naval Architects, both a Froude Medallist and a Parsons' Medallist.[42]

At home the population in general was inspired by the heroism and stoicism of the troops and a pride in 'Britishness' and what was seen as our true values developed, a feeling which lasted for over a century before being replaced by wholesale cynicism in the 1960s and the rise of the 'anti-hero' culture ever since, while feminists, of course, regard the whole *Birkenhead* ethos of self-sacrifice with contempt and detestation. At the time, however, the bravery of the men gave rise to the 'Women and Children First' philosophy being adopted as automatic accepted procedure during the abandoning of British ships, while on a more abstract level Kipling's poem established the principal of courage and selflessness in the face of hopeless circumstances. Nor was this confined to Great Britain and the Empire. King Frederick William of Prussia had the description of what had occurred read out at the head of every one of his many regiments to inspire them in a similar manner.[43]

---

41. Sessional Papers of The House of Commons, British Parliamentary Paper (426) – Courts Martial on the loss of ship *Birkenhead*, 3 June 1852. See also British Parliamentary Papers, 1800–1900, Vols 9–27, South Africa, Irish University Press. Some of these volumes are currently held by The Library of New South Wales, Sydney, NSW. It is noteworthy that the sentiments that some had done all they could possibly have done to save more lives, was adverse to the opinion expressed by Commodore Wyvill in his own report on the matter, as we have noted. See also *A Chronological List of Trials by Courts Martial from AD 1812–(Cases 2436 & 2437)*, ADM 13/104, National Archives, Kew, London.
42. Barnaby, Kenneth C., *Some Ship Disasters and Their Causes*, 1968, London, Hutchinson's Scientific and Technical.
43. No such praise or commendation was *officially* adopted in Great Britain, however, a fact bitterly commented upon by the then Colonel Girardot.

One estimated number of survivors and lost in this disaster was as the table below:

Ship's Company, Regiment or Passengers	Drowned	Saved	Total
Royal Navy	65*	53	118
Royal Marines	14	6	20
12th Lancers	6	2	8
2nd Regiment of Foot	36	17	53
6th Regiment of Foot	48	14	62
12th Regiment of Foot	55	15	70
43rd Regiment (Light Infantry)	27	14	41
45th Regiment of Foot	3	1	4
60th Regiment (Rifles)	31	11	42
73rd Highlanders	56	16	72
74th Highlanders	50	16	66
91st Highlanders	45	17	62
Army Surgeons	2	1	3
Women passengers	0	10	10**
Children passengers	0	17	17***
Civilian servants and passengers.	1	2	3****
TOTAL (Estimated)	439	212	651

* This total includes nine crew members known to have died but whose names have still to be discovered and recorded.
** Mrs Honoria Kelly, wife of Timothy Kelly of the 73rd Regiment, along with her two sons, James and Thomas, were embarked but had been omitted from the 'Official' List. Timothy's last recorded words to his family were said to have been, 'Cheer up – we shall meet in the next world'. Major Colin Innes recorded that Ensign Lawrence Metford, who had only got married just a few days before he and his bride, Maria, embarked at Cork, was drowned but that his wife was saved because when the ship stopped off at the Cape she was disembarked and was not allowed to accompany her husband any further.[44]
*** The number of children has been underestimated in most previous histories; this is as close an estimate as I have been able to glean, but it remains, to my regret, still only an estimate. Several children were born during the voyage out to the Cape and many were landed there.
**** Those who joined the ship during her brief stop at Cape Town were not properly recorded and this can only be an estimate. One such claimant was Wilhelm Maris who is alleged to be a civilian survivor from the *Birkenhead*, but no records have yet been traced that he was aboard.

Captain Wright's initial report gave the first list of casualties which, over the decades has been refined by deeper historical research and diligent work in the various Regimental archives, and, although still somewhat speculative, currently stands thus:

Ship's crew – Master Commanding Robert Salmond, Acting Master William Brodie, Second Master Robert David Speer, Second Master Jeremiah O'Dwyer Davis, Chief Engineer William Whyham, Master's Assistant Charles William Hare, Assistant

Engineer 1st Class Edward Deeley, Assistant Engineers 2nd Class George Kitchingham and James McClymont, Boatswain 3rd Class Thomas Harris, Carpenter 3rd Class James Roberts, Quartermasters James G. Heming and Roger Reed; Able Seamen Francis Aldridge, John Alterton, Richard Blake, John Butcher, Henry Gilbert, Joseph Hall, Joshua Harrison, Peter Thomas and John Wallace; Ordinary Seamen James Burton, William M. Butler, Charles Carter, Charles Lane, John Patterson, Charles Pratt; Leading Stokers John Kinsdale, Samuel Stoodley and James Tapscott; Stokers Daniel Brien, John Robert Darkinman, Isaac Dibble, John Dopson, William Fiford, Thomas George, Alfred Hawkins, James Hobbs, John Jarvis, William Lovell, John J. Mayers, William Monck, Charles Scott and James Wilkins; Captain's Cook Benjamin Gerrard; Gun Room Cook John Richards Howard; Ship's Cook James White; Boys 1st Class Charles Dortnell, John Duffy, Joshua Hodgskin, Henry Lowry and James Watts; Boys 2nd Class John Haylock, John Kelly and Samuel Stone.[45]

12th (The Prince of Wales's Royal) Lancers – Cornet John Rolt, Sergeant John Abraham Straw, Troopers William Butler, Charles Colbey, John Englison, John Took and George Hutchins.

2nd (The Queen's Own Royal) Regiment of Foot – Ensign George Augustus Boylan, Corporal Peter McManus, Privates Joseph Edward Burke, Richard Cileman, William Clay, James Coe, Richard Coleman, Charles Cornell, Henry Cull, William Day, William Forbes, William Green, John Greenleaf, John Howard, George Knight, Patrick Lavery, George Marsh, James Rowley, John Martin, George Marsh, Thomas McKenzie, John A. Mills, Charles Mooney, Christopher Morny, James Nason, Michael O'Connell, James Oxley, George Price, John Quinn, James Rowley, Francis G. Shaughnessey, Thomas Simmons, Nathaniel Thomas, Samuel Vesse, George Walker, William Way, Benjamin Webster, George Waller, William Henry Wheeler, Thomas Woodfall and German Bandmaster Private (assumed or courtesy rank) Zwyker.[46]

---

45. Even today it is estimated that a further nine crew members remain unidentified due to incomplete muster-book registrations. Annabel Venning asserts that 643 people were embarked, of whom 436 died. She also states six women were pregnant, of whom three died in childbirth before reaching the Cape, but does not name them- see Venning, Annabel, *Following the Drum: The Lives of Army Wives and Daughters, Past and Present*, p.47, 2005, London, Headline Book Publishing. See also Edwarde, Corporal Joseph, *Reminiscences of the wreck of the Troopship Birkenhead*, MS Text dated 25 February 1952, Royal Hospital Chelsea. Authorisation of Prize Money (£37.10.0) for Services at Banda and Kirrwee 8 March 1869. Archives of Army Museum, London, 2000-01-27. Edwarde wrote that, 'The total number on board the ill fated ship is aid to have been 631, of whom 193 were saved. The number perished was 438.' He added that he was, '... in the Kaffir War with my regiment 12th Lancers and we had a large draft of men on board under Cornet Bond, amongst them was several old comrades that I knew well; my old drill sergeant was also among the victims. Only Cornet Bond and Private Took survived.'

46. Also recorded as Zwicker. Note that it was certainly quite common for regimental bands to have German band-leaders at this period. See also Jooste, Professor Fanie, *Experts and anecdotes of cultural-historical interest from the history of wind music in South Africa (c. 1770–1900)*, article in *South African Journal of Cultural History*, Vol. 19, No. 2, November 2005, pp. 99–110. Sabinet. The Anglicisation of German bandmasters' names was also quite common at this time. However,

6th (Royal Warwickshire) Regiment of Foot – Ensign Lawrence Nickleson Growden Metford, Sergeant Isiah Terbe, Corporal Thomas Smith, Privates Abraham Bark, Michael Beckett, Joseph Bromley, William Brown, John Bryan, Patrick Bryan, Joseph Bryan, William Bryan, Dennis Caulfield, Alfred Clifford, John Colrenshaw, Patrick Carrigan, John Wilson Crocker, Hugh Dickson, Richard Thomas Finn, William Fletcher, James Goldin, John Grady, James Handley, Joseph Harris, Joseph Hudson, R. Hunt, Henry Jacob, Henry Keane, Michael Kelly, William Kitching, Henry Lambrest, John Lewis, Patrick McCann, John Mayn, Hugh Meara, James Milham, Cornelius Maloney, Patrick Maloney, Thomas Maloney, Michael Morgan, John Olorenshaw, Charles Prince, John Rennington, John Rider, Patrick Ryan, James Smith, Thomas Spicer, Michael Starr, Mark Summerton, John Tierney, Edward Torpy, George Tully, James West, Thomas White and George Worth.

12th (The East Suffolk) Regiment of Foot – Corporal William Smith, Privates Thomas Archer, James Armstrong, Charles Barrett, Thomas Bellingham, William Boswell, George Bradley, James Byrne, Moses Carrington, Michael Cellars, Mathias Clince, Bernard Cummins, John Costello, John Cragg, William Demmack, Joseph Durkin, John England, John Thomas Field, Thomas Fitzgerald, Patrick Flanagan, Thomas Flanley, Owen Freeman, William Fynn, Ambrose Grimshaw, Francis Hart, Samuel Hayward, Samuel Johnstone, Thomas Kelcher, John Kelly, Charles Lambden, Michael Lawler, Edward Lee, John McDermott, James McDonnell, Timothy McMorrow, William Maltravis, Austin Meally, John Mullany, John Moran, Robert Morrison, Robert Munns, Dennis O'Connor, Jeremiah Owen, William Palmer, John Pettifer, Thomas Purcell, George C. Reynolds, John Roche, Robert Shephard, William Springs, John Thompson, William Tigne, Thomas Wales, William Wilson and Joseph Wootton.

---

there is no record of Zwyker in the 2nd Regiment's Regimental Musters for 1849 through to 1852 (WO 12/2056, WO 12/2057 & WO 12/2058, National Archives, Kew London). The closest are entries for Private Charles Whicher (Regimental number 1046), but he was at the front and later became a corporal. See also a letter to M. Alleande Bernard from M. Hartung in *Cork Examiner* Issue dated 14 November 1851. What is known is that recorded by Lieutenant Francis Lionel Octavius Attye of the 2nd Queen's Own Royal Regiment, in a letter to his sisters (the Misses Hannah-Lucy, Margaretta-Ellen, Harriett-Carolina and Augusta-Jeans Attye, residing at Ingon Grange, Snitterfield, near Stratford-on-Avon. Warwickshire County Archives, CR. 2812.) written from Fort Cox, Amatola dated 15 March 1852, recorded that Bandmaster Zwyker, 'had gone to Capetown to fetch his wife' and that she had survived the loss of the *Birkenhead* while he had not. He also noted, 'Poor 'Twickers' loss is irreparable. He was a very clever musician and took great interest in the Regiment, having been with us the whole time we were at home. He had several capital offers of regiments to remain at home, but would not.' See Scott, John Burridge, *The British soldier on the Eastern Cape Frontier, 1800–1850*, p.28 & c. 1973. University of Port Elizabeth, Cape of Good Hope, RSA. It is felt regrettable that such a loyal man should apparently not have his Christian names, let alone those of his wife and children, held in the recorded memory of the regiment to which he was so true to the end, and at such a price. Bandmasters earned an additional £55 per annum (WO 143/32 – National Archives, Kew, London).

43rd (The Monmouthshire) Regiment of Foot (Light Infantry) – Sergeant William Hicks, Corporals Benjamin Cozens and Joseph Harrison, Privates John Anderson, Daniel Brennan, William Bullen, John Butler, John Byrne, Thomas Cave, John Cosgrave, William Debank, Thomas Dews, William Donnell, George Gillham, Francis Ginn, J. Houghton, Lackey McPartlan, Edward Quin, John McQuaid, Edward Outing, Joseph Penning, Michael M. Parklin, Charles Ranshaw, John Riddleston, Daniel Riordan, Timothy George Sheppard, Timothy Sullivan, Henry William Tucker, Edward Vickery and Maurice Welch.

45th (The Nottinghamshire) Regiment of Foot – Privates George Cocker, William Connell and Martin Dockery.

Royal Marines – At this period in history the Royal Marines took precedence in the Army after the 49th Regiment. Corporal Jonathan Luff, Privates William Allen, William Cinnamond, Robert Doble, James Major, John Martin, Henry Miner, John Miner, Isaac Payne, Sidney Piper, William Stone, James Wittock, John Woods and Fifer Thomas Saxton.

60th or King's Royal Rifle Corps – Corporal Francis Curtis, Privates James Brookland, James William Brown, James Callaghan, Henry Chapman, Daniel Conlan, Eli Elliott, Thomas Frost, Arthur Hamilton, Simon Jacobs, Michael Thomas Kelleher, William Kelley, Joseph Ladd, Charles Edward Lucas, Michael John McAcy, James Maher, David McQuade, James Moore, Patrick O'Brien, Thomas Peacock, John Rees, William Russell, Horace Thomas Scutts, Patrick Stokes, James Storey, James Thompson, John William James Wallis, William Wilkins, Samuel Wilkinsen, John Wilson and William Woodward.

73rd Regiment of Foot – Lieutenants Audley Henry Booth and William Charles Robinson, Privates James Bernard, James Biggam, Henry Thomas Bermingham, Edward Brennan, Edward Bryan, Daniel Buckley, William Buckley, William Burton, William Bushe, John Byrne, Michael Caffery, John Clements, Mathew Collins, Patrick Cooney, George Darsey, Charles Dawson, Hugh Deegan, Patrick Doyle, John William Dudley, Hugh Feeley, Matthew Fitzpatrick, Michael Flanagan, William Flynn, William Frank, Michael French, Michael Gavin, Maleck Gavin, Lawrence Giles, John Grant, John Haher, William H. Hall, Patrick Hanley, John Hannen, Henry Holmes, Robert Houchen, Michael Hurley, William Kearns, Timothy Kelly, Thomas Larkin, George Lawrence, John Maher, Michael Maher, James McMurray, John Murphy, Thomas Murray, William O'Connell, George Randall, Philip Scott, Daniel Shea, Timothy Sheehan, Robert Shepherd, George Smith, James Sullivan, Michael Tonen, Charles Wells and James Wilson.

74th (Highlanders) Regiment – Lieutenant-Colonel Alexander Seton, Ensign Alexander Russell, Sergeant John Harold, Corporals William Laird and Murdoch Matheson, Privates George Anderson, Archibald Baxter, John Bennie, Robert Blackie, Walter Bruce, John Cattaneech, David Cousin, John Cowan, William Donald, David Donaldson, James Gibson, David R. Gorman, Charles Gowan, James Henry

Graham, Peter Hamilton, Thomas Harrison, Alexander Hendry, David Hunter, James Kirkwood, John Lowrie, Alexander Matheson, Thomas Maxwell, William McAnley, John McElarney, James McKinnon, Edward McLeod, Alexander Miller, David Miller, George Miller, James Morton, Alexander Donald Murdock, John Neilson, Thomas Pride, Thomas Robertson, Ebenezer Rutherford, Duncan Shaw, Robert Smith, William Smith, Robert Stewart, William Stewart, Adam Thomson, John Thomson, Francis Turner, Robert S. Walker and George Watson.

<u>91st (Argyllshire) Regiment of Foot</u> – Captain Edward William Carlile, Sergeant William Butler, Corporal Arthur Alexander Webber, Privates Joseph Birt, James Bryan, James Buckingham, Thomas Cavanagh, William Clark, Daniel Dailey, James Delaney, James Drury, James Evans, Hugh Ford, William Foster, Patrick Gaffey, Joseph Grant, Francis Hackenley, Patrick Haggan, Stephen Haggan, John Harpey, Henry Hayward, Patrick Hussey, Thomas Jays, George Justier, Patrick Kelly, George Kemp, Alexander Ledgwood, Francis Mackenly, William Matheson, Alexander McFadden, John McGuyre, William Measure, Alexander Montgomery, James Moon, John Moore, David Pratt, William Sedgewood, John Smith, Luke Smith, Patrick Smith, William S. Smith, John Sweeny, James Tarney, James T. Walsh, Alexander Winnington, William Woodman, William Weybrow and Christopher Wyer.
Staff Surgeon Philip Laing and Staff Assistant Surgeon Frederick Robinson.

<u>Passenger</u> – Andrew White, Civil Servant.

Those who survived were listed as:

<u>Ship's Crew</u> – Assistant Surgeon Dr William Culhane,[47] Assistant Engineers Charles Kerr Renwick, Benjamin Barber, Master's Assistant Roland Bevan Richards, Gunner John Archbold, Clerk George William Samuel Hire, Quartermaster Henry Maxwell, Able Seamen John Bowen, George Till, John Smith, Thomas Dunn, Charles Noble, Thomas Daley, Thomas Langmaid, Edward Croker, Samuel Harris, Richard Tiggle, Henry Cheeseman, Martin Ruth, Robert Finn, George Windon, Thomas Harris, John Lewis, John Phalan, John Dyke, John McCarthy and Thomas Forbes, Ordinary Seaman Abel Stone, Seamen Henry Bewhill, William Woodward, Thomas Driackford and Thomas Coffin, Stokers John Ashbolt, George Randall, John King, Thomas Drew, Thomas Handrain, Edward Gardner, John Hoskins, John McCabe, William Chuse, George Kelley and John Woods, Boys 1st Class William Gale, John Richards Howard[48] Benjamin Turner and George Wyndham; Boy 2nd Class Charles Mathews; Boatswain's

---

47. Despite aspersions cast upon his character, Culhane later served as surgeon aboard the troopship (former iron screw frigate) *Vulcan* (Commander Edward Pelham Brenton von Donop), the sloop *Scourge* (Commodore John Adams) and steam frigate *Chesapeake* (Commodore Harry Edmund Edgell) on the East Indies and China Station, in which ship he again found himself in company with Chief Engineer Renwick. He died in 1860.

48. Son of Cook Richard Howard who was lost. As an orphan he was educated by the Navy at the Royal Hospital Greenwich. (See AD 73/260, School Report Papers, Greenwich, London.) He went to sea but later emigrated to Salt Lake City and became a prominent Mormon.

Mate Edward Wilson, Captain Maintop James Lacey, Sailmaker's Mate James Messum, Captain's Mate William Neale and paymaster and Purser's Stewart James Jeffrey.[49]

12th (The Prince of Wales Royal) Lancers – Troopers John Dodd, M. Schofield and John Yule.

2nd Queen's Own Royal Regiment – Privates Andrew Anthers, John Banden, James Boyden, William Budd, Thomas Chadwick, Henry Double, James Gildea, Terence Gleeson, Samuel Hales, Michael Malay, Patrick McCleary, John Moore, Robert Page, John Peters, Patrick Peters, William Rabb, John Smith, Henry Vernon, John White and Benjamin Worill.

6th (Royal Warwickshire) Regiment – Sergeant Isiah Terbe, Privates William Bushe, William Clarke, Thomas Con, Patrick Gleeson, James Goldin, James Michael Hortly, John Herrick, Thomas Hodby, Richard Hunt, John Kitchen, James Wade, Edward Walshe and William Welch.

12th (East Suffolk) Regiment – Sergeant George Walker, Privates George Bridges, Robert Doolan, Robert Firman, Michael Hearty, Thomas Higgins, John Irvin, James Johnson, Charles Kerrigan, Thomas Langan, John McDonald, William Smith, John Simon, Patrick Ward, Daniel Waters and George Wells.

43rd (The Monmouthshire) Regiment of Foot (Light Infantry) – Lieutenant John Francis Giradot, Privates Peter Allen, Edward Ambrose, George Brackley, Love Daniel Bunker, Thomas Ginn, Michael Horhet, George Harrison, Michael Healey, John Herin, George Lyons, George Peters, William Sharp, James West and James Woodward.

45th (The Nottinghamshire) Regiment of Foot – Adam Keating

Royal Marines – Colour Sergeant John Drake, Privates John Northoven, Thomas Daniels, John Cooper, William Tuck and Thomas Keans.

60th or King's Royal Rifle Corps – Sergeant David Andrews, Privates William Burlon, Henry Foss, Jerome Hanlon, Alexander Lackie, Michael Laffey, Henry Mather, Thomas Nutall, Thomas Smith, William Sooter and John Stanfield.

73rd Regiment of Foot – Sergeant Bernard Kilberry, Privates William Burke, Thomas Cash, William Dobson, James Fitzpatrick, Patrick Green, William Halfpenny, Patrick

---

49. Jeffrey had a remarkable series of escapes while acting in this capacity – he was already a survivor from the Paddle Sloop *Thunderbolt* which had been wrecked, also at Algoa Bay, on 3 February 1847; after the *Birkenhead* episode he joined the Paddle Sloop *Tiger* in the Baltic and Black Sea during the Crimean War, and survived again when she grounded off Odessa and was destroyed by Russian artillery fire in 1854. Nothing daunted, Jeffrey continued service, first at Malta aboard the 3rd-rate *Cornwallis*, which was converted to a screw ship, and then another iron-built screw-propelled troopship, the *Urgent*, in the China Wars, finally retiring from the battleship *Royal Oak* in 1897. For these experiences Jeffrey was awarded three Long Service and Good Conduct Medals (LS & GC), finally passing away, (peacefully!) in 1903. One feels his parents might have been wiser to have named him Jonah rather than James.

Lynch, Daniel Maloney, James Maloney, Patrick May, Michael O'Brien, John O'Reilly, Daniel Sullivan, John Sullivan, Patrick Taylor and William Wood.

74th (Highlanders) Regiment – Sergeant John Harold, Privates William Boyce, Charles Ferguson, Richard Hartley, James Henderson, John Kriffe, D. Kirkford, James McGregor, John McKee, Thomas McMullin, Donald Munro, Archibald Nathaniel, Daniel Shaw, John Sharpe, George Taylor and Charles Walker.

91st (Argyllshire) Regiment – Corporal John O'Neil, Privates David Carey, John Codie, John Congham, Patrick Cunnyngham, Patrick Flinn, John Haggart, John Holden, Mark Hudson, John Lamb, John Lancey, Allem McMay, Patrick Mullins, John Stanley, John Walmsely and Frederick Winterbottom.

Women – Mrs Anne Darkin, Mrs Sarah Hudson (wife of Mark of the 91st Regiment) and her son, David[50] Mrs Honoria Kelly, Mrs Anne Mullins, Mrs S. W. Montgomery (wife of Alexander Montgomery of the 91st Regiment), Mrs Elizabeth Nesbitt, Mrs Jane Spruce, wife of Sergeant Charles Spruce, 12th Regiment, already at the front, Mrs G. Wicher, wife of Corporal Charles Wicher, 2nd Regiment, Mrs Zwyker and also, according to Roger Webster, Mrs Anne Chapman, pregnant wife of Private William Chapman of the 60th Regiment[51] and sixteen or seventeen children, these apparently being James Kelly and Thomas Kelly, sons of Timothy Kelly, 73rd Regiment; Marian Darkin and Master Darkin, children of Drum Major John Robert Darkin; Richard Athol Nesbitt, Henry Nesbitt, Mary Anne Nesbitt and Elizabeth Nesbitt, on their way to join their father, Quartermaster Alexander Nesbitt, 12th Regiment of Foot, who was already at the front; Jean Montgomery and Isobel Montgomery, the daughters of Alexander Montgomery; Master and Miss Zwyker; the two Miss Fosters, daughters of William Foster; Master David Hudson and the two Mullins girls, Bridget and Mary.[52] Anne Mullins gave birth to a third daughter, Lawry, seven months later.

---

50. The boy was born in harbour aboard the *Birkenhead* very early on in the ship's passage out to Queenstown. Sarah died aged 83, at Hawe, Colac, west of Melbourne, Australia in 1909 and was believed to have been the last survivor. See *The Colac Herald*, 28 May 1909. Mrs Honoria Kelly died in County Kildare in 1889.

51. Webster, Roger, *The Illustrated at the Fireside: True South African Stories*, p.34 *et seq.*, 2003, Claremon, Spearhead, New African Books Pty.

52. Lieutenant Francis Attye of the 2nd Battalion recorded how an officer was sent to fetch Mrs Zwyker and other women from Cape Town after the disaster off Gansbaai. Scott, *op. cit.*, p.328a. I have been unable to verify the names of the two Montgomery girls, which were listed on an American web site and are therefore to be treated with grave reservations on both counts. The Army wives and children were initially taken to Lea Army Camp, King William Town, Caffraria (see WO 12/2058 & WO 97/699, National Archives, Kew, London). Many of the women and children were given lodgings and help by the sympathetic Cape population, and later sailed home aboard HMS *Castor* (Commodore Christopher Wyville), and she left Simons Bay on 7 December 1852 and reached Chatham on 4 February 1853. Unfortunately, despite my best efforts, current South African sources all seem unable to verify their names. It should also be noted that Richard Nesbitt, aged fifteen at the time, was considered too old to join the women and children's cutter. He took to the water and swam for it, reaching the other cutter and grasping her gunnels. However, as later recalled, a seaman sliced the tips of his fingers with

Another recorded incident concerned Mrs Anne Mullins, the wife of Patrick Mullins of the 91st Regiment. The story was that both survived but neither realised the other had; they were said to have met, quite by chance, some seven years later, and made up for lost time by having a further four children!

<u>Staff Surgeon</u> – Mr Robert Bowen

<u>Civilian Passengers</u> – Charles Daly, an adventurer who took passage by boarding at Cape Town on a whim and who got ashore safely, and William Henry McCluskey, a volunteer for the Cape Mounted Rifles at the front and on his way to join his unit, which he later joined.[53] In the immediate aftermath, the Admiralty continued to investigate possible reasons for the disaster. Between 28 and 29 April 1852, the Survey Paddle-sloop HMS *Hydra* (Commander Thomas Belgrove) retraced the *Birkenhead*'s passage from Simons Bay across to Danger Point. On 23 December of the same year, the Admiralty again ordered the *Hydra* (by this time commanded by Acting-Commander William Everard Alphonso Gordon after the illness of Commander Belgrove) to

---

a cutlass forcing him to relinquish his hold. Later, this same sailor relented and hauled him inboard. On reaching the shore he was later reunited with his mother. Twenty-nine years after this event the marks of the cutlass cuts were still discernable. See anonymous article *Reminiscence of the loss of the Birkenhead*, published in *The Singapore Free Press and Mercantile Advertiser*, issue dated 8 March 1897, page 2, citing *The Westminster Gazette*. According to The Black Watch Museum, the (unnamed) wife of a corporal removed two Regimental claret jugs from where they were stored aboard the *Birkenhead* and hid them under her skirts. Some years after the disaster, these trophies were discovered in a London sales room and were purchased and restored to the Regiment. They are still on display today. Only twelve wives per infantry regiment were permitted to accompany their husbands overseas at this time. See Henderson, Diana, *A Social and Domestic History of the Kilted and Highland Regiments of Foot, 1820–1920*, Vol. 2, University of Edinburgh, 1986.

53. Among the animal survivors, other than the officers' horses, was the *Birkenhead*'s ship's dog. It is not known whether it was transferred into the women and children's boat, or swam ashore and evaded the sharks, the rocks and the seaweed snares, but survive it apparently did! Even more incredible was the fact that the dog was subsequently taken aboard the 464-ton Barque *Eglinton* which had sailed from Gravesend for Swan River Colony in April 1852. On the way she anchored at Simon's Bay, Cape, where the dog was taken aboard, presumably by Mrs Walcott who, with her daughter, two sons and two servants, joined the ship there. Off the Australian coast later the ship's master, Captain Robert Bennett, ignored warnings from his crew and particularly First Mate George Carphin, as a result of which the *Eglinton* herself was wrecked on the Wanneroo Coast, about fifty miles north of the Swan River on 3 September with the loss of two lives. The dog was recorded as being swept off the ship's deck by 'mountainous seas' but again somehow survived that experience and once more reached land. Adopted by a Fremantle family, this animal, either the luckiest pooch ever or the unluckiest, depending on your point of view, lived out its remaining years to its appointed time with no further mishaps, earning the epithet 'the most famous canine in the Colony'. Letter from Mrs James Walcott to her children at the Cape, 4 December 1852, Henderson Papers, Reel 133/1, (This microfiche has been withdrawn from Norfolk Record Office); *Eglinton* details from Nicholson, Ian, *Log of Logs: A Catalogue of Logs, Journals, Shipboard Diaries, Letters, and all forms of Voyage Narratives 1788 to 1988 for Australia and New Zealand, and surrounding Oceans*, The Australian Association for Maritime History Inc. Publication No. 41, 1990, Brisbane, Roebuck Books.

conduct a fresh survey of the scene of *Birkenhead*'s loss.[54] However, Their Lordships appeared very little wiser than before after these surveys.

Today of course, this being the twenty-first century, there is the inevitable 'conspiracy theory' that is now invariably associated with any significant event, historical or current, in order to start and then continually feed a media frenzy. Thus we have constantly postulated to us the spectre of some fervid hidden plot to anchor and 'secretly' offload 120 boxes of gold currency (presumably doing all this without arousing the attention of the crew, passengers or troops) ashore as accounting for the route taken by the ill-fated vessel. Such bullion cargo is mooted by journalists like Pauline Bevan, and given prominence in books on the subject such as that by novelist David Bevan[55] and continually acted upon by ever-hopeful hunters from diving teams down the years.[56]

In 1952, for example, an Irish-based salvage company, Risdon Archibald Beazley Marine, mounted an expedition from Southampton with the newly-constructed recovery vessel *Twyford*. The *Twyford* sailed on 29 November 1952 and maintained strict silence over her subsequent activities but it was reported in the Canadian press that the *Birkenhead* wreck was among her expected targets. However, nothing seems to have been discovered on that occasion. The attempts continued down the years. The full four-year salvage operation that followed was conducted by the Depth Recovery Unit (Pty) Ltd, a Johannesburg consortium led by Doctor Allan Kayle, aided by a team of divers from Aqua Explorations. The work was overseen by the National Maritime Museum and South African Cultural History Museum. Work continued from 1986 from the MV *Reunion* for several seasons in bad conditions, but no huge treasure trove was located. The most interesting thing to come out of the three expeditions was that they were able to reconstruct the disaster itself with reasonable accuracy.[57]

The pinnacle, on which *Birkenhead* fatally struck south-west of the reef, is still known as the 'Birkenhead Rock'. The wreckage lies about eighty-six feet (26.21m) down on a mainly white sandy bottom. The engines of the *Birkenhead* still remain in fairly intact condition but the rest of the wreckage is now scattered, with the boiler, both the paddle hubs and the engine strewn separately across the seabed. In 1895 a fifty-nine feet (18m) high lighthouse was built on Danger Point, with a light

54. Logbook of HMS *Hydra*, 14 January 1852 to 30 June 1852, ADM 53/4982, and 1 July 1852 to 8 February 1853, ADM 52/4983, National Archives, Kew, London.

55. Bevan, David, FRGS, *Drums of the Birkenhead*, 1972, Burdett NY, Larsen Publications. Republished in 1998 as *Stand Fast: 'Women and Children First'. The True Story of the Birkenhead Troopship Disaster of 1852*, p.161,1998, New Malden, Traditional Publishing.

56. After much discussion an agreement was reached between the Republic of South Africa Government, who wanted to open the wreck up for salvage, and the United Kingdom Government, who regarded the wreck as a war grave. See *Background Materials on the Protection of the Underwater Cultural Heritage*, Vol. 2, *II- Bilateral Agreements*. UNESCO/ Ministère de la Culture et de la Communication (France), 2000, Paris, UNESCO. Also United Kingdom Treaty Series, No. 31. 1990 and *Salvage Wrecks – 1989*, FO 93/189/12, National Archives, Kew, London.

57. Martin, Roy Victor & Craigie-Halkett, Lyle, *Risdon Beazley, Marine Salvor*, 2005: Southampton, self-published, for background on this company; and Kayle See Kayle, Dr Allan, *Salvage of the Birkenhead*, 1990, Johannesburg, Southern Book Publishers, pp.113–15.

visible for twenty-five nautical miles (46km). At the base of this structure is affixed a remembrance plate for the *Birkenhead* and those who did not return and it points to *Birkenhead* pinnacle. At home, as just one example, there is a Memorial Tablet to the victims of the 12th (East Suffolk) Regiment at a churchyard in Bury St Edmunds.

Again, on the fiftieth anniversary of the disaster, a nationwide publicity hunt revealed nineteen survivors of the wreck still alive and well. A roll call of these was prepared on a parchment scroll by Messrs Wing & Son, Boston, which was sent to King Edward VII in May 1902 together with an explanatory letter. Another century passed and, on the sesquicentenary of the sinking, a ceremony in 2002 of remembrance was held at the Simons Town's Garden of Remembrance and at Gansbaai, where many of the corpses that came ashore lie buried. There also remain various regimental memorials in both the UK and South Africa.[58]

---

58. See, for example, the memorial located at St Mary's Interior Cemetery, Bury St Edmunds, Suffolk, which lists all fifty-four members of the 12th Regiment lost that night. It should be noted that the *Birkenhead* was *not* the first troopship to be wrecked off the Cape, nor was this the 91st Regiment's first example of extraordinary discipline. Some fifty officers and men of the 91st were embarked aboard the 1,331-ton troopship *Abercrombie Robinson* (Captain Joseph Gordon) along with detachments of the 27th (Inniskilling) Regiment and the Cape Mounted Rifles, when a fierce storm drove her ashore on the Salt River Beach, Table Bay, on 28 August 1842. There were 509 passengers aboard but, again thanks to discipline and lack of panic, not a single soul was lost. The bravery of the *Abercrombie Robinson* (owned by Joseph Soames, a director of the East India Company) is almost totally unknown while the loss of the *Birkenhead* is fabled. Such are the weird vagaries of history.

In the case of the *Birkenhead*, however, the public response was enormous. Queen Victoria herself personally contributed £200 to a trust fund for the survivors. Other donations included £100 from Prince Albert and £50 each from Prime Minister Edward Smith-Stanley, the 14th Earl of Derby, Spencer Horatio Walpole QD LLD, Home Secretary, James Browne William, 2nd Marquess of Salisbury, Lord Privy Seal, Admiral Algernon Percy, the Duke of Northumberland, First Lord of the Admiralty and Benjamin Disraeli, Chancellor of the Exchequer, among other leading figures of the day. See *Manuscript List of Subscriptions in aid of fund for the relief of the survivors and the widows and children of the sinking of the ship* Birkenhead, dated 22 April 1852, National Army Museum, Chelsea, NAM 1964-09-21-1. See also Surrey History Centre, QRWS/1/18/4/2, 1852–2002, Documents relating to loss of troopship *Birkenhead*.

Another mystery concerns Mrs Elor Harrison, widow of the late Corporal Joseph Harrison, 43rd Regiment. A letter from Lieutenant-Colonel John Clarke, the Commandant of the Royal Military Asylum, Chelsea, to the Secretary of the *Birkenhead* Subscription, at Gosport, dated 29 March 1853, stated that this lady was 'still in this Institution, and that any relief afforded her will be duly administered as directed'. See WO 143/32, p.333, National Archives, Kew, London. Ironically, having survived the shipwreck itself, Trooper John Took of the 12th Lancers was killed the same year at the Battle of Berea in Basutoland. Took was one of thirty-eight British soldiers to die in that encounter during Major-General George Cathcart's ill-organised first expedition. Took (and also, incidently, Cornet Bond-Shelton) were part of two squadrons of the 12th Lancers, commanded by Major William Heathcot Tottenham, under Lieutenant-Colonel George Conolly Napier CB, who apparently concentrated more on rounding up the Chief Moshoe's tribal cattle than fighting the battle, and who were ambushed in the process by a far larger Sotho force, with dire results. Trooper Joseph Edwarde (*op cit*) recalled that 'At the Battle of Berea ... one of the first to be killed was Trooper John Took who had survived the *Birkenhead*.'

Chapter 8

Violating *Tapu*

The *Orpheus*, 17 February 1863

In the middle of the nineteenth century the ships of the Royal Navy were reflecting the momentous changes of the age and, while Their Lordships at the Admiralty were later to be accused of being hidebound and backward-thinking, everywhere in the fleet evidence of the new ideas could be seen. Although masts and rigging were to continue for many years, the principal propulsion was increasingly steam. However, not all far-flung ports could be relied upon, in case of deployment to such remote regions, to have available a sufficient supply of coal and so, for this practical reason if no other, masts and sails were still deemed essential for warships serving in such places. Funnels were made telescopic for ease of raising or lowering, and the screws themselves could also be raised or lowered when the sails were brought into play. Thus, when the wind dropped, 'Up funnel, down screw' became the evolution of the hour and so these ships, regarded, in retrospect, as nostalgic throwbacks, were, in fact, versatile. Not until machinery became far more reliable, and supply of fuel equally so, did masts and sails finally fade from the scene.

Paddle steamers, so dominant in the Crimean War period, were being replaced by the new screw propulsion and no more paddle warships were launched after 1858. Although steam had eclipsed the frigate's original role as the eyes of the fleet, heavily armoured 'ironclad' battleships being equally as speedy, they still had a role as a seaworthy traditionally wooden-hulled projector of British power beyond the main fleets and on distant stations of the ever-growing Empire. However, due to their size, cost and manpower demands, the frigate was phased out and its role taken over by the smaller, faster and, above all, cheaper screw corvette. Breech-loading (BL) heavy guns were ordered to replace the old smooth-bore (SB) muzzle-loaders (ML) but, following the failure of the Armstrong BLR (R = rifled) gun in combat, the MLR was introduced and held sway for a further twenty years. The old broadside layout continued but modified by guns on slide-mountings whose positioning thereby became more flexible, they being manoeuvred around on iron slides let into the deck. While battleship guns mushroomed into 12-inch, and larger, monsters, slow-firing and mounted in barbettes and in turrets, again, being more lightly constructed, the new corvettes retained the lighter weapons of the period, 6-inch and 7-inch guns.

At the time of this period of flux and the transition of the fleet, a new class of wooden screw corvettes was commissioned by the Admiralty which encompassed most of these features. They were designed by Admiral Sir Baldwin Wake Walker, then Controller of the Navy. Six such ships of the *Jason* class were laid down, *Barossa*, *Jason*, *Orestes*, *Orpheus*, *Rattlesnake* and *Wolverine*. Built as fully-rigged ships, with three masts, they had telescopic funnels and a single hoisting screw. Initially the main armament comprised twenty of the Armstrong 8-inch ML (68-pounder/65cwt) guns mounted on the broadside, plus a single pivot-mounted 7-inch (110-pounder/82cwt) Armstrong BL gun.[1] They had a crew of 259 officers and men and were all constructed in Admiralty Dockyards at Chatham, Devonport, Sheerness and Woolwich, with one laid down at Sheerness, which was ordered on 1 April 1857 and laid down there on 12 May that same year. She was constructed by the team under Mr Oliver William Lang, Master-Shipbuilder at Chatham, and formerly at Woolwich.

This last-mentioned vessel was launched on 23 June 1860 and was named *Orpheus*, becoming the fourth Royal Navy vessel to bear this title. Orpheus was the mythological son of Œagrus and Calliope and became King of the Cicones (*Kikoveç*), a tribe of south-west Thracia. He was presented with a gold lyre by Apollo who taught him to use it and his playing became so sublime that it had the power to enchant the wild animals of Olympus itself, its trees and even the very rocks on which it was built. He was a famed poet and prophet who, when his wife, Eurydice, was killed by snakes sought to soften the hearts of those in Hades so that she might return to him.

The *Orpheus* was completed and commissioned for service at Portsmouth on 24 October 1861.[2] *Orpheus* had dimensions of 225 feet (68.58m) length, a breadth of 40 feet 8in (12.39m) and a draught of 18 feet (5.5m) forward and 19.75 feet (6m) aft, with an overall displacement of 2,365 tons or 1,702 ton burden (bm). Her two 400hp (298.279kW) 2-cylinder horizontal single-expansion engines were constructed by Humphreys & Tennant, of Deptford Pier, in south-east London,[3] and these developed 1,333 ihp (994kW)[4] which gave her a best speed of just 11.15 knots (20.6 km/h). She had four boilers and four furnaces.

In December 1861, under the command of Captain Robert Heron Burton, and flying the broad pennant of Commodore William Farquharson Burnett CB, Senior Naval Officer of the Australian and New Zealand Stations, to which she was assigned for duty, *Orpheus* was ready for duty. However, the first leg of her planned maiden voyage, to Sydney, New South Wales, was put on hold and *Orpheus* was, on 7 December, instead sent across the North Atlantic escorting a troopship to Canada. This re-scheduling was due to what became known as 'The *Trent* Crisis' which almost led to all-out war by

---

1. cwt = hundredweight, which is 112lbs (50 kilo, 802.34 grams).
2. A Friday and to the superstitious sailors a most inauspicious day; whatever their feelings on the matter she was quickly to earn a reputation as an 'ill-fated' vessel.
3. The company had been founded in 1852 by Edward Humphreys and Charles Tennant; Edward's son Robert developed the engine side until the site was closed down in 1908.
4. Indicated horse power, which is the horse-power (hp) of a reciprocating engine as detailed on an indicator record. The power output is calculated from the mean effective pressure in the cylinder, derived from the indicator diagram and the speed of the engine in revolutions per minute (rpm) which in *Orpheus* was a nominal 400.

the United Kingdom against the Federal American Government, which at the time was engaged in the American Civil War against the Confederate States.

On 8 November 1861 the Federal steam frigate USS *San Jacinto*, at the instigation of her hot-headed and Anglophobic commanding officer, Union Captain Charles Wilkes, fired upon and then boarded the British Government Royal Mail Steam Packet *Trent* in the Bahamas Channel in the Caribbean. The American warship then sent a boarding party aboard this neutral vessel,[5] despite having gone to war in 1812 for the British doing just this very self-same thing to American ships! The American ship forcibly removed two passengers and their entourage from the *Trent*, ignoring the protests of her captain and International Law. These two personages were Confederate commissioners James Murray Mason and John Sidall, on the way to the UK via Havana, Cuba, and France to try and convince their governments to abandon neutrality – something which neither, in fact, was intending to do.[6]

News of this unprovoked aggression arrived in London on 27 November and a Special War Cabinet was convened two days later. In Government circles there was much sympathy for the Confederate cause but such unprovoked action concentrated British minds totally and it was decided to send an ultimatum to the Federal Government on 30 November. A full mobilisation for war was ordered on 4 December and five days later an initial Army contingent of 25,000 men was ordered to Canada, which Federal Secretary of State William Henry Seward had previously threatened to invade and annex, something which the usually vociferous American press campaign originating in New York and Chicago was agitating for. These reinforcements for Canada comprised 1 Guards Brigade which included the Coldstream Guards, while the Mediterranean Fleet began despatching all available warships to North America and at home parts of the reserve fleet were mobilised.[7] Sir George Lewis, Secretary of State for War, promised to commandeer a Cunard liner and send out a regiment of infantry and a battery of artillery immediately.

Pending the despatch of these forces, emergency measures were put in place and the steam transport *Melbourne* was loaded at Woolwich Royal Arsenal Pier with an advance force of reinforcements under General Sir Richard Dacres and his staff, along with Commodore Sir Frederick Nicolson and a large quantity of munitions, and hurried to sea on 7 December, bound for the St Lawrence river. The intention was that the troopship should be protected by the screw steam frigate *Emerald* (Captain Arthur Cumming) which awaited her at Plymouth to act as her escort against interception by Federal warships. Unfortunately, *Emerald* had earlier encountered a severe storm which had so damaged her that she had to be docked, and, being thus unavailable and the matter urgent, her place was taken hastily by the *Orpheus*, and it was she

5. Lord Palmerston, British Prime Minister, had long before declared that Britain would remain neutral in the Civil War and had not officially recognised the Confederacy. The hothead Wilkes chose to ignore this fact.

6. Mason and Sidall were taken back to America and incarcerated in Fort Warren, Boston.

7. See Bourne, Kenneth, 'British Preparations for War with the North 1861–2', article in *English Historical Review*, Vol. 76, pp.600–32, 1961, Oxford, Oxford University Press.

that accordingly sailed from Plymouth Sound in company with the *Melbourne* on 10 December.

Rushed to sea with a largely inexperienced crew, *Orpheus* soon found herself in trouble. Caught by a typical North Atlantic gale she was given a severe battering and almost foundered on her maiden voyage. During the storm all contact with *Melbourne* was lost and when *Orpheus* finally arrived at Halifax, Nova Scotia, on 8 January 1862 *Melbourne* had already arrived. The *Orpheus* took departure from Halifax again on 15 January and rendezvoused with the large wooden screw frigate *Orlando* (Captain Francis Scott)[8] from Great Britain and the two ships reached St John's, New Brunswick, on 18 January 1862, but *Orpheus* again suffered the misfortune of running aground there, although she was soon refloated.

Despite these difficulties the troops were put ashore to stiffen the largely neglected Canadian border defences. In the end the Federal Government agreed to release the detainees, stating that Wilkes had acted 'unofficially', but they never apologised for their high-handed action. Until that had been done, however, Britain continued to organise for a possible war, and further naval and troop movements took place throughout 1862, until the situation calmed down. *Orpheus* and *Orlando* left New Brunswick for St John's, Newfoundland, which they reached on 5 February 1862, but only remained there a short while before sailing on 7 February for Halifax once more, arriving there two days later.

The arrival of yet further warship reinforcements from home, including the sloop *Hydra* (Captain George Frederick Cottam) with the barque-rigged screw steamship *Calcutta* (Captain Samuel Harry Wright RNR), meant that *Orpheus* could be released and, on 16 February 1862, she left Halifax once more and resumed her original assignment to New Zealand, reaching Bermuda on 28 February. *Orpheus* subsequently called at Simon's Bay at the Cape of Good Hope, 14 May, and arrived at Sydney, New South Wales, on 18 July 1862.[9] Due to the fact that many veterans were still required to man the ships on the North American station at this time many of her ship's complement were young lads, some as young as twelve, first-time boy sailors sent to gain sea experience. By the time they arrived at Sydney they had certainly gained that. *Orpheus* was docked at Sydney to undergo a refit to replace parts of her copper bottom, which had been torn off by ice while in Canadian waters. Once repaired, between 7 November and 25 January 1863, her crew gained further sea time when *Orpheus* made a visit to Hobart, Tasmania. However, after the briefest of respites, for they were behind schedule, they sailed again for Auckland on 31 January 1863 with ammunition and stores for New Zealand.

Two British wooden screw sloops of war, the *Harrier* (Captain Sir Malcolm MacGregor) and the *Miranda* (Captain Robert Jenkins), had been in action providing

---

8. *Orlando* was one of six enlarged frigates designed in direct response to America's such vessels by Sir Baldwin Walker, and known as 'Walker's Big Frigates'.
9. Fairburn, Taylor, *The Orpheus Disaster*, monograph for the Whatatane & District Historical Society, 1987, Whatatane.

naval supplies and troop reinforcements to aid the campaign being undertaken against the Māori tribes in what was later termed the First Taranaki War[10] and were now in the beautiful, but dangerous and shallow, Manukau Harbour, near Auckland. Some 100 miles in circumference, its western entrance is made difficult by a three-mile bar, inshore of which are large, and ever-shifting, sandbanks. The bar itself had several Māori names, including the ominous *Te Kupenga o Tara-mai-nuka* ('Tara's fishing net), and the sandbanks once formed the land known as Paorae.[11] The *Orpheus* sailed from Sydney on 31 January 1863 in order for Commodore Burnett to oversee the withdrawal of these two vessels and was due to rendezvous with them at the more-favoured Waitemata Harbour to the north-east of this isthmus. Course was therefore re-set for Onehunga and, after an uneventful passage of eight days out from Sydney in fine weather, during the forenoon watch, the entrance to Manukau was sighted at a distance of eight miles on 7 February.

Lieutenant Charles Hill later recalled:

Steam was got up in two boilers; we had been condensing. The ship proceeded at 1230 under all plain sail, with starboard foretopmast studsail set, towards Manukau, steering east till 1 o'clock, then N.E.E., being the courses laid down – so the Master told me – in Captain Drury's sailing directions, keeping the Ninepin on with the end of Paratūtai. The hands were on deck, the ropes manned for shortening sail, the commodore, commander and master on the bridge; leadsmen in both chains; spare tiller shipped, with relieving tackles hooked, and six men stationed; gratings and hatchway covers were placed ready for battening down.

The wind S.W. to S.S.W., force 5 to 6, with occasional slight squalls; high water at 1230. As we approached the bar there was nothing more to see, in the shape of rollers or sea on, than I had been led to expect. The signal from the pilot station had been flying since 1130 am 'Take the bar'; the commodore and master were very attentive with the chart on the bridge, and very particular in the steerage of the ship, and in their orders to the engine-room, to keep the steam at command, the signal officer and signalman on the lookout.[12]

All reasonable preparations for the passage therefore appeared to have been taken.

There is a notoriously fast tidal flow over the bar at the mouth of the bay between Manukau Heads off Whatipu beach and it was long known that the approach was dangerous, with ever-shifting sands.[13] *Orpheus* by this date had an estimated fully-

10. Day, Kelvin (editor), *Contested Ground: the Taranaki Wars 1860–1881, (Te whenua I tohea)*, 2010, Wellington, NZ, Huia.
11. Supplement to *The Illustrated London News*, 14 April 1863, pp.437–8.
12. *Narrative* to Secretary of the Admiralty by Charles Hill, Lieutenant Her Majesty's Ship *Orpheus*, written aboard Her Majesty's Ship *Miranda*, Auckland, 10 Feb.1863.
13. Even today it is decidedly dangerous, the Auckland Council Directional Pilotage, 2–14, issued by Harbourmaster Andre Hayton, describes the waters bounded to seaward by the arc of a circle radius four miles centred on Paratutae Island (37° 2.9′ S; 174° 30.6′ E) and notes that pilotage

laden deep draught of between 20 feet and 23 feet (6.096m to 7.0104m) and, because of this, it was originally planned to reach Waitemata by way of the North Cape and along North Island's eastern coast.[14] but Burnett decided to press on via the more direct, if risky, route.

Earlier surveys of these waters had been conducted, one in 1836 by Captain Thomas Wing, which remained in use for the next two decades, and two more by the Royal Navy had followed, one in 1853 by Commander Byron Drury in the brig *Pandora*,[15] and another in 1856,[16] but these latter surveys, detailed though they undoubtedly had been, were considered out of date following another survey conducted in 1861. This updated survey had indicated that the sandbar in the middle of the channel had by that date increased in size and presumably it had continued to do so since, as well as shifting to the north.[17]

The 1861 survey work in the channel had been conducted by Captain Peter Cracroft in the screw corvette HMS *Niger*, and her master, Mr Alfred James Veich, had noted in that ship's Remark Book that since the Drury report the main channel had shifted and he also noted that New Zealand Pilot had accordingly been altered and improved. He therefore had advised:

The north side of the middle banks forming the southern boundary of the main channel to Manukau, has extended to the northward since Captain Drury's survey in 1853; vessels, therefore, in crossing the bar of this harbour should bring Nine Pinrock twice its base open to the southward of Paratūtai, N. E. by E ½ E, which will lead about a cable northward of the breakers.

---

is 'compulsory', ref. Harbourmaster, Auckland Council, 10 July 2014. It is estimated that at least eighteen ships have come to grief in these waters from 1848 to the present day. Ironically one of these was the Royal Navy brig-sloop *Osprey*, commanded by Captain Frederick Patten, which was wrecked not far away at Herekino (known as 'False Hokianga') on 11 March 1846. She had been told, 'Take the bar, there is no danger'.

14. Stone, Russell Cyril James, *Logan Campbell's Auckland: Tales from the Early Years*, 2007, Auckland, Auckland University Press.

15. Richards, Captain George Henry and Evans, Frederick John, *The New Zealand Pilot – from surveys made in H.M. Ships Acheron and Pandora, Captain John Lort Stokes and Commander Byron Drury*, 1856, London, Hydrographic Office, Admiralty.

16. See HM sloop *Harrier* Logbook kept during Coastal Patrol Duties by Master's Assistant John Harding, 1856–59, GB/NOVAE/C 28342, London, National Maritime Museum, The Caird Library, Manuscripts Section.

17. Again the shifting sands in this notorious area had been known well before the arrival of Europeans. The local tribes had an alternative name for this entrance, which was *Te Manukanuka ā Hotuiroa*. (The anxiety of Hoturoa, a reference to the High Priest and captain of the legendary ancestral *Tainui* canoe (*waka*) when preparing to sail through the Strait on his way to Kāwhia.) The Māori also were well aware, even then, that the coastline was in a continuous state of flux due to the movement of the dark 'iron sand' along the coast. The early settlers learned of it from the tradition of the vanished shape-changing *Paorae*. See Murdoch, Graeme, Monograph No. 04, *Whatipu – Our History*, p.8, 2010, Auckland, Auckland Regional Council.

Veich himself vouched for the fact that this notification was sent to Portsmouth on 13 November, and placed in No. 5 Australia chart box. This box was drawn from store by *Orpheus* at Portsmouth on 23 November and, as required, she had left a signed receipt for it.

The *Orpheus* was therefore provided with this new guidance and her sailing master, William Strong, naturally expected to use this for the dangerous passage and had it in his hand during the approach. For some reason Burnett decided not to follow his advice and instead the 1856 chart, known generally as 'Drury's Chart', was employed.[18] The weather was clear and the sun was shining brightly on the sparkling waters as *Orpheus* approached under full sail and steam, making a good 12 knots (22.224 km/h), but these outward appearances were very deceptive.

The *Orpheus* was given several further opportunities to evade her doom. As she steered through the passage she was signalled by Thomas Wing's eldest son Edward, from Paratūtae Island Pilot Station Semaphore Signal Mast, located atop the central high point of this rocky little outcrop on the north side of the entrance, south of Wing Head and west of Wonga Wonga Bay. The signal set by Wing Junior at 1000 was two squares hoisted on the mast's yardarm which stood for 'Take the Bar'. Edward later stated that the sea was at half-flood and the bar was 'clear of brake'[19] whereas the South Spit had 'heavy rolling'. By this, he later claimed, he had indicated that *Orpheus* should immediately veer north as it was safe there.[20] When no apparent action was taken by 1300 and Edward observed that the *Orpheus* was still steering south of the entrance he set up a second signal, with the north arm of the semaphore raised, which indicated 'Stand out to sea'. According to some local newspaper reports, the *Orpheus* apparently made no response to these signals.[21] Edward stated that this signal was set 'to keep the ship in that direction,[22] but that no notice appeared to be taken of it'. However, it was later claimed that she did, in fact, acknowledge both signals each time by hauling down her ensign flying at the peak and raising it again, which in the Royal Navy indicated 'message received and understood'. Finally, just before 1330 according to Edward, the ship was obviously 'drawing near danger' and signal was changed to 'Keep the vessel more off shore'. Edward's statement continued:

---

18. It was also a relevant fact that, whereas the *Niger*'s draught in 1861 had been 14 feet 9 inches (449.58cm) forward and 17 feet 1 inch (520.70cm) aft, the *Orpheus* on her final voyage was drawing 17 feet 8 inches (538.48cm) forward and 20 feet 1 inch (612.14cm) aft.

19. Edward was a 21-year-old who was standing in for the usual signalman, Hugh Evans, who was on leave of absence due to a dispute over pay. By 'clear of brake' he meant that he could see no breaking waves there and that he therefore assumed that there was sufficient water covering the bar at that point.

20. Fairburn, Taylor, *The Orpheus Disaster*, monograph for the Whatatane & District Historical Society, 1987, Whatatane.

21. Report in *Otago Witness*, 7 March 1863, p.7.

22. i.e. north.

This they did not obey, but continued under sail and steam and about 1400 the ship was observed to hang and roll heavily on the South Bank, and shifting afterwards, took the ground on the South Spit, broaching-to with head northward near deep water and then all the sails were clewed up.

On board the ship only two of her crew had ever sailed through this entrance before, one of whom was the Paymaster Edward Albert Amphlett and the other was Quartermaster Frederic Butler, a native of Alvestoke, Gosport, and a former midshipman aboard the *Harrier*, who had twice in recent times crossed the bar but not by the current route. He observed the approach through the bow ports and, increasingly agitated, told his shipmates the ship was not sufficiently far north to make it. They insisted he immediately inform an officer, which he was reluctant to do, being only an AB, but, on being coerced, he did approach First Lieutenant William Tertius Fitzwilliam Mudge and told him that the *Orpheus* was 'going wrong'. Mudge asked why he had not mentioned this before and, while apologising, Butler saw the danger was increasing quickly and, fearing the worst, he took a further risk, approached the ship's master (of whom it was later said 'a more efficient mariner did not hold a commission under Her Majesty') and also warned him of the danger the *Orpheus* was in should they continue on her existing course. Only then was remedial action taken.[23]

When, finally, some inkling of their danger was felt, the helm was put hard over to avoid the bar, but too late, and, around 1320 on the afternoon of 7 February, the *Orpheus* first struck the middle sandbar in position 37° 04′ S; 174° 28.3 E and then shortly afterward grounded again, more severely. It later transpired that *Orpheus* had 'struck on what was subsequently discovered to be the extreme northern edge of the middle bank, and at about fifty feet from the deep water'.[24] The order had already been given to shorten the sails, but when the engine was ordered to reverse to get her off it was found that it was inoperable, due either to the shaft having been damaged or the screw having broken off. The surf pounding Whatipu beach was so fierce that the *Orpheus* was swirled around and her port side was quickly inundated by the heavy seas which broke over her as she broached at once, heeling her over so that the cabin windows were smashed and the seas burst open the ship's hatches. Many heavy guns were knocked off their carriages, killing one man outright and crippling several more. The stern part of the vessel was cut off from the rest of the ship.

Lieutenant Hill's description of events continued:

---

23. Butler, whose advice was not acted upon until too late, had earlier deserted from *Harrier* in Sydney, but had been arrested and was being taken to rejoin his ship to face court martial for desertion. He survived the wreck, gave evidence at the coroner's hearing, but then apparently deserted again and was lost to history. Incredibly, in the light of what had just happened, a few weeks later, on 24 April 1863, the *Harrier* was also to strike the sandbar, being so damaged that she required repairs in dock!

24. Supplement to *Illustrated London News*, 14 April 1863, pp.437–8.

At about 1.30 she touched slightly in the after part, when the Commodore gave the order, 'Give her all the steam you can.' At about 1.40 the ship struck forward; order given, 'Astern full speed;' but the engine or screw never moved. At the same time the commodore ordered 'Hands shorten sail,' The ship broached-to, with her head to the northward, lurching heavily to port, the rollers coming in from the westward, which immediately made a clean sweep of the upper deck, taking away port quarter boats (second cutter and jolly boat), netting and bulwarks. Sail was shortened as far as possible, the men not being able to keep the deck; immediately the ship took the ground the hatchways were battened down, which, however, proved perfectly useless, as the fastenings were thrown up by the bumping of the ship.

The order was given to throw the port guns overboard and four guns were indeed levered overboard with considerable difficulty, as well as some shot, to lighten the ship, but this had little effect. Some officers and men were swept away into oblivion by the seas which now continually broke over her.[25] The vessel quickly began to founder and her back broke. As the deck became impassable many of the crew took to her masting and rigging, including Commodore Burnett who was seen clinging to the mizzen mast aft. Others abandoned ship in the ship's pinnace,[26] launch and cutter. Commander Burton ordered Midshipman Bernal Whitley Fielding to save the ship's papers and documents, which he succeeded in doing and got away in the starboard cutter, but she was swamped several times and lost five of her men. Commander Burton ordered Lieutenant Hill into the pinnace to go and help the cutter but the latter assured him the cutter was all right, so Burton ordered Paymaster Amphlett, who knew the shoreline well, to join him with the stated aim of getting assistance quickly and at 1430 they shoved with considerable difficulty due to the ebb and cleared the ship. After two hours' hard pulling they met the Pilot Boat near the Ninepin and observed that a steamboat was in view.

In the interim, however, about thirty men had embarked aboard the ship's launch, commanded by Lieutenant Arthur John Jekyll, which had been lowered alongside in an attempt to lay out anchors. The launch was made fast by bow and stern but, in the huge seas, the tether was twice accidently let go aft as eight more men jumped in seeking safety. Released the second time around 1700 the launch careered ahead but almost immediately a heavy sea drove her into the bower anchor of the *Orpheus*, which was hanging over the bow, and this capsized her with all save three aboard her either being crushed between the boat and ship or swept away and lost.[27] Others who had taken refuge in the bows of the ship were washed overboard, being quickly swept away to be dashed ashore and some gradually lost their tenuous holds and also went into the sea. The captain of the foretop, John Davey, had an equally horrendous end for, 'while

25. *Daily Southern Cross*, Auckland, 9 February 1863.
26. Pinnace – a ship's tender which could be either sail or oar propelled.
27. *Otago Witness*, 21 February 1863, p.8.

descending from the maintop to the foretop, the stay was carried away, and the coil caught him round the neck and strangled him'.

Great gallantry was shown by some; one of the captains of the mizzen-top, William Johnson, a member of a boat's crew, went over the side of the cutter with a rope no less than three times, on each occasion managing to haul back a drowning man. Some incredible pieces of fortune were recorded, for example Commodore's Servant John Horrigan survived in the water all alone for eight hours and was not picked up off Poponga Point until 1300 on the 8th by the schooner *Matilda*. A shard of copper sheathing attached to the spar had gradually sliced into his chest during all this time and he required urgent hospital treatment.

Burnett himself, who refused to board any of the boats, was struck by a falling spar and killed, Burton was crushed to death by the falling mast itself. Those men in the forward part of the ship stood the best chance of survival as both the foremast and the mizzen followed the mainmast overboard. Some of the crew clawed their way up the bowsprit and dropped down into boats or the sea, but many failed to make it. Both pinnace and the cutter managed to land their men. About 190 of her complement of 259 were drowned.[28] Some twenty-six miles up-harbour at Onehunga, nothing was known of the tragedy taking place in broad daylight across the bay. There were three vessels present that afternoon, the *Harrier*, which was moored at the Bluff along with the *Moa*, a small Admiralty tender, and the armed colonial paddle steamer *Avon* (Lieutenant Frederick John Easther) at the Onehunga wharf; this last-named was temporarily out of commission awaiting machinery parts from Auckland. The Port Pilot Station was unmanned as the pilot was already afloat aboard the Wellington Steam Navigation Company's 103-ton (93,440kg) inter-provincial mail steamship *Wonga Wonga*.[29] The *Wonga Wonga*, under Captain Frederick Renner, had started a routine voyage to Taranaki, and had embarked Thomas Wing and members of the Manukau Harbour pilotage team and was towing their whale boat astern[30] and thus, being already at sea, was actually the first rescue ship on the scene. The *Wonga Wonga* was small and slow, with only a 30hp (22.37kW) engine and took a couple of hours to reach the scene of the disaster. She arrived at the bar around 1400 and it was noticed that a man-of-war was in the offing, but not until clear of the channel and Captain Renner climbed the rigging for a better view, did it become clear to him that this vessel was labouring very heavily and apparently aground.

Captain Renner proceeded to the entrance of the North Channel and hailed her, asking if he could be of any assistance but, receiving no reply, returned to the pilot's station by the South channel. Here at about 1500, they found the pinnace and the cutter

---

28. These figures vary from source to source.
29. Which vessel should not be confused with the much larger Australian Steam Navigation Company's 1,002 GRT (908,999kg), Glasgow-built, iron-hulled coastal steamer of the same name also in service at this time. Plowman, Peter, *Across the Pacific: Liners from Australia and New Zealand to North America*, 2010, Dural, NSW, Rosenberg Publishing Pty Ltd.
30. Wing's father, Thomas, had been Harbourmaster in his day, and, coincidently, had been the originator of the 1836 chart.

among the breakers off the Orwell Shoal with survivors from the *Orpheus* in charge of
Second Lieutenant Hill and Midshipman Fielding respectively, also Paymaster Ankett
along with their crews totalling twenty-one men who had brought ashore the mail,
ship's money and papers. Amphlett, two fit seamen, two sick hands and two boys were
then sent off in the whaler to notify the *Harrier,* while Wing and the four-man Māori
patrol team joined Hill's cutter, which, along with Fielding's boat, were taken in tow
as the *Wonga Wonga* hoped to use them to effect a rescue. But when they finally got
close to the *Orpheus* around 1800 she was lying hard over to port and the seas proved
too rough and it was impossible for *Wonga Wonga* to get alongside. The two small boats
were therefore manned and manoeuvred as close as possible to the wreck's jib boom
and the survivors told by the officers to jump into the water where the boats would
try and pick them up. Many of them made the leap and fourteen were indeed hauled
out of the water, but other unfortunates were 'drowned in the surf by the drawback'.
The survivors were taken to the *Wonga Wonga* while the second lieutenant took his
boat again and rescued a few more. Around 2030 the guns that remained aboard and
secured began breaking loose and adding to the damage while the deck itself began
to splinter and break apart. By 1900 the jib boom had broken off at the cap and this
means of egress, dangerous as it was, was cut off for good.

The *Wonga Wonga* herself was being tossed around like a cork and had to withdraw
to a distance of about three cables (556m) and, as night fell, she burnt blue lights and
awaited a better opportunity, but the boats continued in their attempts to save further
lives until midnight. Among those so rescued was Midshipman Henry Barkly, son of
Sir Henry Barkly, Governor of Victoria, who, along with six or eight others, had clung
to a ship's spar and other wreckage for two hours and were carried in by the flood.
These were landed at the pilot station by the boats as they could not get alongside the
Wonga Wonga. The mainmast of the *Orpheus* went overboard at around 2100 taking
the foretopmast down and with it Burton, Mudge, Strong, Midshipman Thomas
Broughton and about fifty men. By 2200 the mizzen masts had also gone, taking the
bulk of those surviving exhausted men still clinging to them into the swirling and now
darkening waters. Included in these latter from the mizzen was Commodore Burnett
who, although it would appear he must bear a large measure of culpability for the
tragedy itself, nonetheless was inspirational in his final hours, refusing to board any
boat and any offer of aid, vowing to stay with his men to the end. He was wedged
between the top and futtock rigging of the mast whose top fell directly onto him,
knocking him overboard unconscious.

The *Wonga Wonga,* joined by a small Māori boat from the Whatipu Pilot Station,
stayed in the vicinity of the wreck all through what Hill described as 'a beautiful clear
moonlight night', but by dawn there was little left to do but search the sand dunes
ashore for bodies, of which there were a great number. Lieutenant Hill recorded, 'At
daylight nothing could be seen of the ill-fated *Orpheus* but a stump of one mast and a
few ribs.'

Many bodies were subsequently interred near the Kakamatura Inlet, Titirangi. The
Harrier had not been alerted until the arrival of the Paymaster aboard the Pilot Boat at

2000 that evening, and then it was found that the tide was too low for her to turn around in order to sail and she grounded on the harbour silt. She did not finally get underway until noon on the Sunday. Those rescued by the *Wonga Wonga* were later transferred to the little 40-ton (36287.4kg), former-GPO wooden paddle package steamer *Avon*, which was used for inshore survey work and which had finally got herself under way with Captain Robert Jenkins of the *Miranda* embarked. She transferred them back to the port of Onehunga, in Hillsborough Bay, now an Auckland suburb.[31]

In total only eight officers and sixty-two men remained accounted for and were finally taken aboard the *Miranda*; of these all the officers and ten of the crew took passage to Portsmouth where they were to appear before a Board of Inquiry court martial. Of the remaining fifty-two, twenty-seven joined the crew of the *Miranda* and twenty-five were sent to make up the *Harrier*'s complement. Meanwhile, Commodore William Burnett's place as Senior Officer, Australia Station, was taken by Captain Sir William Saltonstall Wiseman, aboard the screw frigate *Curaçoa*.

The Duke of Newcastle received a despatch from Sir George Grey, Governor of New Zealand, on 18 April which gave the situation appertaining to the positioning of the *Orpheus* thus:

> Running thus from the southward, she was intending to make the passage across the bar as laid down in the chart of 1853. Since that time the bar has shifted about three-quarters of a mile to the northward. She was thus rather more than that distance too far to the southward, and touched first on a small shoal off the middle banks, and in a few minutes ran directly on to them, where there is always a very heavy sea, and where her position (about four miles out at sea) was hopeless.[32]

This led to an exchange in Parliament on April 20 between Edward Law, The Earl of Ellenborough (who stated that merchant seamen knew the bar had shifted so why had the Admiralty not made this fact known) and Edward Seymour, The Duke of Somerset, who was able to confirm that not only had the fact been distributed, but that *Orpheus* had drawn a copy of it before she sailed and that surviving eyewitnesses had already stated that her master actually had a copy on the fateful day!

The court martial was finally conducted aboard HMS *Victory* at Portsmouth on 27 April 1863. The court itself was held under the Presidency of Captain Francis Scott (*Victory*) and comprised Captains William Charles Chamberlain (*Asia*), Arthur Cumming (*Emerald*), Augustus Phillimore (*Defence*), John Seccombe (*Hannibal*) and James Francis Ballard Wainwright (*Shannon*).

---

31. The little *Wonga Wonga* herself was to suffer a similar demise in her turn, for, three years after this event, she was wrecked on the bar of the Grey River attempting to make the port of Greymouth.
32. Sir George Grey, Governor of New Zealand to The Duke of Newcastle (Henry Pelham Fiennes Pelham-Clinton, Secretary-of-State for the Colonies.) Despatch No. 10. Government House, Auckland, dated February 9 1863.

Paymaster Amphlett gave evidence that Commodore Burnett had spoken to him and said, 'You see, Mr Amphlett that the correct bearings are on'. Amphlett also revealed that when walking on the quarterdeck with the ship's master he had enquired of him whether he had the new chart. The answer he had received was, he stated, 'Oh, yes. I have got Veich's Sailing Directions', to which Amphlett replied, 'Oh, that's all right'.

Lieutenant Duke Doughton Yonge was examined about the signals from the pilot station and he said, 'I saw the Commodore and the Master on the bridge, evidently steering by signal as being made from the shore'. When asked specifically 'Were they apparently steering by signal from the Pilot Station at the time?' he replied 'Yes'.

Signalman William Oliert (apparently also known as Alexander Hills) was very forthcoming on this matter. He was asked, 'Did you receive any signals from the Pilot Station?' to which his reply was 'Yes – Take the Bar'. When asked what he then did, he replied that he reported to Midshipman Arthur R. Mallock, the Signals Officer. 'And did Mallock reply?' 'Yes, he did'. 'Were there any other signals?', 'Yes. North Arm of the Semaphore raised.' 'What action was taken?', 'Starboard the helm.' He added that the Ship's Master was all the time consulting the book. 'Any further signals from ashore?' 'Yes. Both arms on Semaphore raised which meant "Dangerous – Stand Off".' Orders were given to get the starboard topmast studding sail and the top-gallant sails and royals in, but, as he was making his way aft, within two minutes the ship had struck. Lieutenant Charles Cracnell Hill put the blame on the tardiness that this last signal was set, He felt they had been let down and that the signal 'was not made in time'.

One would have expected those in command of *Orpheus* to have been held at least partly responsible, even though they had died, but, as often before, Admiralty officials tended to close ranks in the face of criticism. The final report stated that 'After a lengthy deliberation, the Court found that the loss of the *Orpheus* was occasioned by the shifting nature of the Manukau bar, and which rendered navigation particularly difficult.'[33]

Criticism of the verdict was widespread. *Examiner*, writing in *The Times*, was scathing. 'This is an astounding verdict ...' he wrote.[34]

The conclusion is that no one was to blame for the loss of a fine ship in broad day and moderate weather. It was all right that she should attempt to enter the Manukau when she had no particular business there; it was all right that she

---

33. Lieutenant Charles Hill, having survived the wreck and the court martial, had his sword ceremoniously returned to him and he returned to New Zealand, being appointed to the *Curaçoa*. He served ashore during the Waikato campaigns and was killed in action at the Gate Pah Tauranga battle on 29 April 1864 along with another *Orpheus* survivor, Ordinary Seaman James Harris. Another survivor, Midshipman Bernal Whitely Fielding, also lost his life in a separate incident on 3 November 1864 while serving aboard the *Orlando* (Captain George Granville Randolph) when her ship's cutter was suddenly upturned by a squall in Tunis harbour. All the occupants save one were lost and only Fielding's jacket was ever recovered – ADM 196/15/512, National Archives, Kew, London.

34. Anon, 'No One to Blame!', article in *The Times*, 4 May 1863.

should make the attempt at the wrong tide-time; in short, it was right that she should be lost, for, if there was no wrong in the case, all was right and as it ought to be.

While acknowledging that the officers to whom blame may have attached were not living to defend themselves, the writer said that, if for no other reason than to prevent it happening again, and with direct censure, the court might have 'adverted to the causes of the disaster with regret'.

Examiner was knowledgeable and his analysis brutally detailed.

The Court found that the ship was lost by striking on the bar when going over it in the absence of pilot boats. The bar is only a cable's length in breadth. The ship first touched according to Lieutenant Hill's statement, at 1.30 and 10 minutes afterwards struck, where she went to pieces. Was she, then, with all plain sail set, a fair wind and steam power in aid, 10 minutes in traversing the distance of a cable's length? If not, she was clearly not lost on the bar, the passage over which could not have taken her two minutes, allowing for a strong adverse tide. As we have before explained, the ship was lost on the Middle-bank, inside the bar, and not at all in the position of a bar.... The Court find that the ship struck in the absence of pilot boats. Does it pretend that pilot boats could be expected? Is it not well known that the pilot boats do not go beyond the Heads, and in the Admiralty Sailing Directions is it not notified that 'It is seldom possible for the pilot boat to board outside the bar?' But if, notwithstanding information to the contrary, the ship expected a pilot and was disappointed, why did she not then give up the attempt and proceed to Auckland, with a leading wind round the north cape?

Examiner concluded that:

It is quite clear that the disaster was referable to the culpable error of attempting the entrance at the wrong tide-time. The signal for water was made at 11.30, 50 minutes before high water, and if there was only water enough in the 50 minutes before high water, there would certainly not be more in the 50 minutes after high water; for whenever there is a great inlet like the Manukau the first ebb runs off quicker than the last of the flood runs in. But with only 50 minutes of tide time to be depended on the *Orpheus* did not even approach the bar 'til that time had expired, and might have passed it about an hour and ten minutes after high water, when the tide had fallen full half a fathom, and a rougher weather-tide had increased the same, and by so much diminished the depth of water necessary to float the long-legged ship over the shoals. But there is nothing to blame in all this according to the view of the naval Court, and officers are free to follow the example of Commodore Burnett without fear of censure, living or dead.

The writer added, 'Certain we are that the unfortunate officer himself must in his last moments bitterly have reproached himself for the rash error by which he had thrown away the lives of so many brave men.' He concluded:

> Perhaps it never occurred to the Court to inquire what the ship was doing from daybreak, when she made the land, to midday, when she ran her head against the shore, for the answer might give some clue to the cause of the disaster, and might not be reconcilable with the forgone conclusion that no one was to blame.

In actuality much of the blame was instead attributed to Edward Wing, who, it was alleged, failed to pilot the *Orpheus* in and failed to maintain the navigation marks on Puketutu Island up to par.[35] Nonetheless, Wing and his family continued to operate the pilotage for many years after the tragedy.[36]

In the immediate aftermath of the tragedy the widows and dependants of those lost were paid from the relief fund set up at the Royal Naval College, Portsmouth, through the offices of Admiral Sir Michael Seymour GCB, in monthly instalments. Queen Victoria herself again donated a considerable sum to the trust fund, as did other notables of the day. A plaque was placed on the site of the wreck in 2005 to replace the memorial bolted to the side of Paratutae Island in 1976, which had been stolen.[37] It was noted that the total number of fatalities remains unknown, recorded as 189 sailors and soldiers, and is really still uncertain because many of those that did survive fled the scene as deserters to avoid further sea duty.[38] The wreck site is preserved under the Auckland Regional Plan: Coastal, with the 'Orpheus Track' leading to Cornwallis where are the graves of many who perished. However, the only apparent current artefact of any size at all apparently appears to be part of a mast on display at the Huia Museum. In 1914 it was reported that the ship's figurehead was discovered two years after the wreck by the Reverend John Charles Eccles,[39] it apparently being seen by him floating on the sea from a beach several miles south of Manukau entrance. It was in good condition and preserved at Woodville where it was damaged by fire. In

35. Hetherington, Roy Marshall, *New Zealand's worst sea disaster: the Wreck of HMS Orpheus*, 1968, Auckland, Institute Printing & Publishing Society.
36. Byrne, Timothy Brian, *Wing of the Manukau: Capt. Thomas Wing: his life and harbour 1810–1888*, 1991, Auckland, Byrne, self-published.
37. See *Western Leader*, Auckland, NZ, 6 May 2005, p.3. On 20 November 1976, more than a century after the event, the NZ Historic Places Trust had attached a small bronze memorial plaque to Paratutai Rock on the northern Manukau Heads, close to where the signal flagstaff had stood in 1863. This read: 'On 7 February 1863 the steam-corvette HMS Orpheus was wrecked entering the Manukau Harbour. Of the 259 officers and men, there were 70 known survivors.' Some years later, the plaque was stolen by mindless vandals. Some years later it was recovered by a Park Ranger and, after a period in storage, was placed in the Huia Settlers' Museum. It remains on display there with other *Orpheus* memorabilia today. The Paratutai site has not been forgotten and a memorial service was held there in 2013.
38. See article in *Western Leader*, 6 May 2005, p.3. Henderson, NZ.
39. Irish-born Canon Eccles of Woodville, 1893–1918, buried at Waipawa 1926.

1914 Eccles was said to have had it restored and presented to Auckland Museum.[40] However, in 2000 it was reported that the New Zealand National Maritime Museum was hunting for the figurehead and that its existence was considered 'remote'.[41]

In 1887 the island of Goolboddi, off the Northern Queensland Coast, some fifty miles (80 km) off Townsville, Australia,[42] was named Orpheus by Lieutenant Geoffrey Edward Richard, a Royal Navy hydrographer commanding the survey vessel HMQS[43] *Paluma,* to honour the memory of the *Orpheus* and her crew. Despite taking no part in any of the fighting, *Orpheus* was for some reason awarded the battle honour 'New Zealand', perhaps as a gesture to those who died in what is the worst maritime tragedy in the history of New Zealand.

The Māori tribesmen of the area had a different take on the cause of the loss of the *Orpheus.* According to them a sacred *Pūriri* tree,[44] which they deemed *tapu,*[45] was growing on Puketutu Island. On the day before *Orpheus* went aground this holy object was violated when the tree was cut down by a *Pakeha* (Caucasian – European) settler, who required timber for fencing posts. The resulting vengeance was the loss of the *white-pigs'* ship the next day. The Paratūtai signal mast itself was actually chopped down by the Waikato Māori that same year.[46]

Some of the crew of *Orpheus* survived. Among these were Lieutenants Charles C. Hill and Lieutenant Duke D. Yonge, (who was taking passage to join the *Miranda);* Paymaster Edward A. Amphlett; Midshipmen Henry Barkly, Bernal W. Fielding and Charles George Hunt; Boatswain William Mason; Boatswain's Mate Henry Stupple; Carpenter James Beer; Quartermaster Henry Brown, Henry Corps; Painter William E. Bayliss, captain[47] of the Fo'c'sle John Morley; captains of the Foretop John Quinton, James Wilson; captain of the Hold John Finnis; Boatswain's Mate Henry Stupple; Signalman William Oliert (aka Alexander Hills); captains of the Mast Charles Weir and James Kennedy; captain's coxswain Arthur Haggis; Cutter coxswain Robert Carpenter; captain of Mizzentop William Johnson; Commodore's Servant John Horrigan; Carpenters Edward Briggs and John Nicolson; Able Seamen Samuel Bannister, James J. Brown, Frederick Butler (belonging to the *Harrier),* Patrick Daley, William Fisher, Charles Fox, Thomas Geary, Thomas Herbert, John Higham, John Hill, Henry Holmes, William Mayes, William Palin, Henry Portbury, Thomas Russell, Thomas Smedden, Henry J. Walker, George Ward and George Young; Ordinary

---

40. *Evening Post,* 27 January 1914, p.2, Auckland.
41. *Otago Daily Times,* 27 April 2000.
42. Orpheus Island is now a popular National Park and Tourist Resort.
43. HMQS = Her Majesty's Queensland Ship.
44. An evergreen tree (*Vitex Lucen*) of the *Lamiaceae* family. It produces very hard wood and also leaves, which, when boiled up and infused by the Māori people, produced a remedy for rheumatics and a preservative of the body for the 'afterlife'.
45. *Tapu* in Polynesian culture means taboo or sacrosanct.
46. Murdoch, Graeme, Monograph No. 04, *Whatipu -Our History,* 2010, Auckland Regional Council.
47. The word 'captain', with a small 'c', denotes a rôle rather than a rank as such.

Seamen Alfred Ankelt, William Ball, Henry Bentell, James Boland, John George Cochrane, Henry J. Graham, James Henry Graham, James Hall, John Hall, Charles George Hurlestone, Joseph Jordan, William Langush, John Morby, Henry Newman, John Nicholson (carpenter), James Parsons, Alfred Pilbeam, George Roberts, Thomas Rusgel, William Russell, John George Seale, Thomas Snudden, William James Sparshott, James Summers, Arthur S. Tilley, George Turtle, Henry Walker, Edward Walsh, George Ward and Noah Wells; Stokers Alfred Brown, William Clews,[48] James Taylor; Royal Marine Drummer Joseph Crouson; Royal Marine Private Richard Roe; Boys Henry Bentlett, Thomas H. Burton, William Herbert, George Hurlstone and Boy 2nd Class John D. Ideson; while one Edward John 'Jack' Lofley also survived and later joined the New Zealand Armed Constabulary and resided at Taupo.

Many more had been lost, most people would say totally needlessly. Among those known to have drowned, beside Burnett and Burton, were Lieutenants Arthur John Jekyll and William Tertius Fitzwilliam Mudge; Master William D. Strong; Assistant 2nd Master William J. Taylor; Master's Assistant John J. Tozer; Chaplain Revd Charles Baker Haselwood; Chief Engineer Samuel Stephens; First Lieutenant Edward E. Hill, Royal Marine Artillery; Assistant Surgeon James Clarkson; Assistant Paymasters William Henry Patey Morgan Gillham and A. D. Johnston; Midshipmen Thomas H. Broughton, Arthur R. Mallock and George H. Verner; Clerk Henry Nelson Aylen; Engineer John H. Adams; Assistant Engineers William Adamson and George Frederick Gossage (on loan from *Miranda*), Edward J. Miller and John H. Vickery; Gunner William Hudson, Ship's Steward George Townsend; Ship's Cook George Drew; Master-at-Arms John E. Ernest; Gunner's Mates John Hutching and William Shephard; Ship's Corporal Thomas Osborne; Leading Stokers Frederick Allen, Jesse Bignell, Frederick Kemp and Thomas Lane; Ropemaker Michael Mahoney; Blacksmith John Bosworthick; Carpenter's Mate John Trautman; Caulker David Norris; Quartermasters Henry Corps and George Warn; captain Maintop Thomas Ambrose; Coxswain Launch, Abraham Voice; Captain's Coxswain Arthur Haggis; Boatswain's mates William Milliard and John Pascoe; captain Hold Joseph W. Wilson; Captains After Guard Edwin Lloyd and John Plowman; Caulker's Mate George Vincent; captain Mizzen-top John Davey; Armourer George Redman; Musician Samuel Mardon; Cooper Henry Baker; Sick Berth Attendant Henry Redman; Stokers Alfred Brown, Charles Davis, Andrew Dorey, James Healey, Felix Kelley, David Lee, John H. Maud, John Moore and William Swain; Sailmaker Thomas Smith; Painter William E. Bayliss; Leading Seamen George Hill and Thomas Kelly; Carpenters John Pay, Charles E. Rowe and Henry Thomas; Shipwright John Wealords; Tailor John Woodrow; Leading Seaman George Hill; Able Seamen George Anderson, William Cooper, William Cowen, John Hewitt, John Higham, William M. Hutton, Edward Jenner, George Mark, Harry Mark, James McCloud, Joseph Northover, Thomas Parke, Edwin Pelham, Robert Randall, Joseph James Rockett, Henry Sheargold, Edward

---

48. Clews had deserted on 14 September 1862 and there were no records of whether he was returned to the ship or not.

Springer, William Stephenson, Charles Whetham and John Young; Ordinary Seamen Herbert Adams, John Bennett, William H. Bickle, William Blackwill, John Cleary, Samuel Cole, Alfred Crow, James Ellis, Edward Finn, William Gannaway, John Hall, William Halson, William Hillier, Daniel Hines, Noah Jones, Peter Newman, William Palmer, William Rowland, Henry Weatherstone and Henry Welstead; Captain's Steward C. Goldshmidt; Captain's Cook Augustus Holdgate; Wardroom Steward William H. Cookney; Wardroom Cook Thomas Stoneham; Gunroom Steward John Hyde; Gunroom Cook George Mitchell; Engineer's Servant Samuel Scutt; Engineer's Cook John Phillips; Boys 1st Class John T. Broadway, William J. Bridle, George Bunce, Denis Donoghue, George Duffett, James Goodwin, William F. Hunt, William Jenkins, John Kingston, Jeremiah Murphy, William Thomas Orchard, John Searle, John Simmonds, Samuel F. Spencer, Charles Theobald, Isaiah Thompson, Edward M. Warner and Richard White; Boys 2nd Class John H. Avis, Thomas Callaghan, John Cronin, William Davis, Albert Early, William Hartfield, John Knowlden, Robert H. Veal; First Lieutenant Royal Marine Artillery Edward E. Hill; Royal Marine Sergeant William Tranter; Royal Marine Corporals George Gordon and John Howard; Royal Marine Gunners Thomas Brady, William Burge, John Broadwood, Henry Crabb, Lewis Cramp, Charles Henth, William Hobbs, Samuel Johnson, John Kave, George King, Thomas Letheby, Bradley Starkay and John Vince, RMA; Royal Marine Privates James Andrews, Henry Baylam, Charles Binfield, John Budge, Thomas Collins, Daniel Davis, Thomas Doren, John Durkin, Michael Flanaghan, Stephen Foyle, Henry Gardner, Thomas Gould, George Gray, John Greenwood, John Heard, David Horsfield, Sidney Hoyle, Thomas Ladbroke, Thomas Littlefield, John P. Masters, Peter Pafford, Henry Pearin, John Shorthouse, Francis Starrs, George Trott, Thomas Tucker, John Williams and Richard Williams. In addition some of the missing turned out to have been left in Sydney, including Royal Marines Sergeant Thomas Carter, Private Stephen Hodge, and Gunner George Monday; Able-seaman Thomas Rees and Boys 1st Class James Ashwood and William Barnes and Boy 2nd Class John H. Davis.

Honour to their memories.

Chapter 9

Ashore on Lundy

The *Montagu*, 29 May 1906

HMS *Montagu* was a pre-*Dreadnought* battleship of the *Duncan* class and was built in 1901 by Devonport Naval Dockyard near Plymouth. She was ordered as part of the 1899–1900 programme, being laid down on 23 November 1899, launched on 5 March 1901 and christened by Lady Ada Mary Scott, wife of Admiral Lord Charles Montagu Douglas Scott, Commander-in-Chief, Plymouth, who was also in attendance, as was Rear-Admiral Thomas Sturges Jackson, Admiral Superintendent of Devonport Dockyard. She was named as the *Montague* but was officially re-named *Montagu* later the same year. The six battleships of this class were *Albemarle, Duncan, Cornwallis, Exmouth, Montagu* and *Russell*, named after famous admirals; *Montagu* was named to honour Ralph Montagu, 3rd Baron Montagu of Boughton, 1st Earl of Montagu. She cost £1,046,992. This class of battleships was laid down as responses to a group of fast Russian battleships, *Osliabia, Peresviet* and *Pobieda*, following the then customary (and sensible) practice of building two ships to each potential foe's one and making our ships bigger, faster and more powerful ship for ship.

The *Montagu* had a load draught of 13,420 (1363kg) and a deep load draught of 14,950 tons (1519kg) and her dimensions were 432 feet (131.7m) overall, 405 feet (123.44m) pp x 75 feet 6 inches (23.01m) x 25.9 inches (7.85m). She had a 7-inch (178mm) thick Krupp's Cemented (KC) armoured belt along her waterline, fourteen feet deep, with 11-inch (279mm) thick maximum bulkheads and 11-inch (279.40mm) thick maximum armour atop her two main barbettes with 10-inch (254mm) maximum on their shields and 12-inch (356mm) maximum on her conning tower. Her armour decks were 2-inch (51mm) low, 1-inch (25.4mm) middle and 2-inch (50.80mm)main, while casemate armour was 6-inches (152mm), giving her a total armour protection of 3,655tons (3713kg).

Her power plant, built by Lairds, developed 18,285ihp, (13,000kW) which gave her a top speed of 18.8 knots (35.km/h). Her engines were two 4-cylinder, vertical inverted triple-expansion steam engines, with twenty-four Belleville boilers with economizers, at 300lb (136.078 kg) pressure which consumed fifteen tons of coal per hour, all driving twin screws. This gave her a range of 7,000 nautical miles (12,964km) and an economical speed of 10 knots (18.5 km/h). They were the first British battleships to achieve a maximum speed of 19 knots (35.188 km/h) and were the last ever to be painted black, white and buff.

She was armed with four 12-inch (304.8mm) 40 calibre Mk IX BL guns in two twin turrets, one forward and one aft, with twelve 6-inch (152.4mm) 45 calibre Mk VII QF single guns, six either side in casements, and had ten 12-pounder single QF guns and two more 12-pounders (5.443kg) in her boat, with six 3-pounder single QF guns plus two Maxim machine guns for close-in defence. She was also equipped with four 18-inch (457.20mm) submerged torpedo tubes; she carried eighteen 18-inch and six 14-inch (355.60mm) torpedoes. She had a complement of 720 officers and men.[1]

Montagu was completed in November and was commissioned at Devonport on Monday 27 July 1903 under the command of Captain John Dennison[2] and went out to the Mediterranean. While up the Straits, Captain Dennison was relieved by Captain Thomas Benjamin Stratton Adair in September. Coming from a naval and military family[3] Adair had soon made his mark, earning the Goodenough Gunnery Medal and later specialising in the subject under Admiral John Arbuthnot Fisher at the Royal Navy Gunnery Establishment HMS *Excellent* and subsequently serving at the Naval Ordnance Department. He was also to serve on the Navy Ordnance Committee as he rose steadily through the ranks.[4] Adair was a stickler for detail and, on being appointed captain of the *Montagu* from command of the protected cruiser *Gladiator*, had enhanced that reputation. It was his submissions on the dangers of relying on candle-boxes for illuminating the ship's magazines in the event of the failure of electrical supply, and the dangerous practice of having the magazine doors themselves being left slightly ajar in such circumstances to permit an oxygen flow, that led to their abolition on the grounds of safety.[5] The *Montagu* also took part in an exercise competition with other battleships to see how rapidly submerged torpedo tubes could be fired four times in succession; starting with the tube loaded and the bar out, *Montagu* achieved speeds of 11 minutes and 8 minutes 17 seconds in two trials.[6]

HMS *Montagu* remained in the Mediterranean until January 1905 when she came home and joined the Channel Fleet. On the afternoon of 29 May 1906, the still fairly-recent battleship was anchored off Lundy with the fleet conducting exercises as part of the 'Blue' Fleet of fifty-seven ships operating from Portland. The *Montagu* herself had been fitted with, and was utilising, the still new form of radio communication, the wireless telegraphic signalling apparatus which the Admiralty was trialling in the Bristol Channel as part of the exercise. Accordingly the *Montagu* anchored off Lundy

1. Parkes, Oscar OBE Ass INA, *British Battleships: Warrior to Vanguard: A History of Design, Construction and Armament*, 1960, London, Seeley Service & Co.
2. *Naval & Military Intelligence* (Official Appointments and Notices), *The Times*, No.37146, Thursday 30 July 1903, p.6, column B.
3. His great-uncle Captain Charles William, a Royal Marine officer, had died aboard the *Victory* alongside Vice-Admiral Horatio Lord Nelson at Trafalgar; his father General Sir Charles William Adair had commanded the Royal Marines and his brother General Sir William had been Adjutant General of that same corps, while another became Admiral Sir Charles Adair.
4. Service Records (Series III) in ADM196/87/82; ADM198/27/42, National Archives, Kew, London.
5. *Principal Questions Dealt with by the Director of Naval Ordnance, 1905*, pp.429–30.
6. *Annual Report of the Torpedo School, 1904*, pp.45–7.

Island and began work. At that time the island was privately owned by the Reverend Hudson Grosett Heaven, who had inherited it from his father, Mr William Hudson Heaven, a Bristol man who had purchased it in 1834. The Royal Navy had a semaphore station ashore there. Lundy itself lies at the entrance of the Bristol Channel which lies twelve miles north-west of Hartland Point and the north Devon coast, directly in the path of major shipping routes into Bristol and the coal ports of south Wales.

It was hoped *Montagu*'s wireless equipment would be able to contact the Isles of Scilly from her anchorage point but this proved beyond the range of the experimental gear and, after requesting permission from the Commander-in-Chief Portland to move ten miles south and receiving no reply, Adair upped anchor and moved away from Lundy to a point closer to her target. Three cross bearings at 1900 fixed her position at that time as South 40.5, West 4.8 miles from Lundy South light. Approval was received from the C-in-C and *Montagu* proceeded on course S 58 W. The wireless equipment was tested at various points to see whether *Montagu* was within range. On the third occasion, some sixty-five miles from Scilly, satisfactory contact was achieved; the ship was stopped, turned and, to facilitate the experiments, was again turned and stopped again and again. All the time the murk was morphing into fog which thickened and became denser as the evening wore on. Here the seeds for the tragedy were sewn for these constant shifts of position in dense weather, coupled with the strong set of the tide and the wind, caused a certain amount of drift each time the ship was stopped. This uncertain movement meant that the navigation team somehow miscalculated their final position; unfortunately they themselves remained supremely confident in their assumptions that they did know *exactly* where they were. Alas not.

Captain Adair's attention to detail had not slackened any, and it was attested by Lieutenant John Douglas Harvey that 'Captain Adair was very frequently in the wireless room, especially during the latter part of the programme. He was there almost entirely from 8 p.m. to about quarter to 11 o'clock'. This commendable zeal with regard to the wireless experiments that he had been entrusted with could unfortunately only have been undertaken by some necessary neglect of the navigation. This devotion to the one task at the expense of another ultimately proved the undoing of Adair and his command.

While in her position way out to sea she clearly presented a considerable hazard to other shipping in the Bristol Channel while the thick weather persisted, and so, and also to comply with his Channel Fleet C-in-C's orders, Adair decided to move his command back to the original anchorage close in to Lundy, despite the risks. However, in his report Adair had written that he had 'decided to return to Lundy Island to obtain any message that might be at the signal-station relating to his movement'.

A great many ships have been wrecked on Lundy down the years, which is not surprising considering that at one time many ships per annum passed by the island. These losses had, decades earlier, stirred a generation of Bristol merchants into erecting a lighthouse on the island which was built and maintained at their own expense. Due to the fact that he was under orders to return in order to achieve the expected rendezvous with the fleet, Captain Adair considered it of prime importance to arrive at his rendezvous at the appointed time and, although the fog was by now very thick, he scorned waiting for clearer conditions and continued under way despite the dense fog. The fog siren on Lundy Point sounded its warning in a sequence – Low-High-Low-High – every two minutes and Adair later testified that he expected that sound to give him some warning. He stated that he had heard 'two high and two low' notes as he approached, but that this was thought to be a steamer.[7]

Continuous depth soundings were taken every thirty minutes as the *Montagu* edged closer and extra lookouts were mounted. The Navigation Officer, Lieutenant James Hartley Dathan, however, was given permission by Adair shortly before 2330 to retire to his quarters due to lack of sleep, he having been continually on the bridge for twenty-four hours. He left orders to be called should any sounding less than twenty-five fathoms be taken or at the last by 0150. He lay down but fully dressed save his sea-boots. At 0107 on the 30th a depth of seventy fathoms was recorded. Called by Midshipman Herbert Court Osborne at 0150 he was just putting on his sea-boots when the 'Middie' returned again in a rush and reported 'twenty fathoms, Sir'.[8] He immediately ran on deck where the boatswain's mate was preparing another sounding. Realising they were in shoal water he ran for the fore-bridge, but felt the ship bump before he arrived there.

At 0200 the battleship was found by wire to be in nineteen fathoms of water when, according to all calculations, she should have been sounding thirty fathoms. The officer of the watch:

came to the conclusion that with the set of the tide to eastward they could not have got so far north as to get that depth off Lundy. He ordered another sounding to be taken at once. While that was being done his attention was caught by the sound of a siren, and almost immediately he heard a grating on the port bow. He immediately gave orders to have the ship put hard to starboard, when the man on the lookout in the bows reported through the megaphone 'Land ahead!

At 0212 she bumped gently on. The second sounding had just shown seventeen fathoms but the *Montagu* was considered to be still some miles from Lundy, but nonetheless she had suddenly run hard aground on the bar of Shutters, a three-mile ledge of granite rocks running out from the south-west corner of the island.[9] Adair recorded that her speed at the time was just three knots, but, even so, the impact was so strong that the foremast was canted forward over her bridge. The hull was ripped

---

7. Davis, Gill (Jill) M. & Roger C., *Trial of Error (The Court Martial arising from the Loss of HMS Montagu, Lundy 1906)*, 1983, Atworth, Davis.
8. Midshipman Osborne testified that he cried 'We have sounded nineteen fathoms, Sir' and that Dathan, fully dressed, 'jumped up suddenly, exclaiming, "My God!"' and immediately went up on deck.
9. According to his granddaughter, Mrs Mary Tudge, Mr Tudge, Captain Adair's valet aboard the *Montagu*, always stated she went aground at 0200, it being his birthday.

open with a 91-feet (28m) gash opened up on her starboard side and she suffered many smaller holes in her hull.

Commissioned-Engineer John George Lightfoot Baker investigated. The first thing reported was that the water was leaking into the starboard side bunker of No. 1 boiler-room. He immediately proceeded there and found that a seam was leaking about 18-inches (2.54cm) long. He had the plates removed. He examined the bilge and found the door leaking. They tried to tighten it but could not succeed. They then tried to shore it down. While they were doing this work there was a rush of water, evidently from a large hole. He added that when the sudden rush of water occurred in No. 4 boiler-room it was such 'that the circulating pumps were absolutely powerless to cope with it. Had they been used the engine-rooms would have been flooded'.[10]

Immediately her massive engines were put to hard astern but all that this achieved was the ripping off of one of her propellers and she remained hard and fast, with water pouring in through leaks in her hull. She had grounded at full flood tide and the stern was swung around, ending up a mere 15 feet (4.572m) from the vertical cliff face. The grinding of the hull with the tidal flow steadily accentuated this damage and soon the lower compartments were all flooded to a depth of between fifteen and twenty feet (6.096m). The force of the strike had thrown several crew members down and some suffered fractures and severe bruising. Fortunately there was no loss of life.

At high water the boiler rooms, steering compartment, starboard engine room and forward capstan engine room, with other compartments, had flooded. The *Montagu* took on a starboard list. This led to the deliberate flooding of the port engine room to even her up but this just made her settle more firmly.

Artificer-Engineer Ernest Jacob William Marchant later gave evidence of the assumed seriousness of her position.

> The engines worked so erratically as to cause him to come to the conclusion that the starboard propeller had either broken off or that the shaft was fractured. He had just come away from the voice pipe when he received a message from the port engine-room to say that the port propeller had gone too.[11]

In fact the port propeller had gone, but the starboard propeller had not sheared off. Midshipman Nelson Clover recorded in his personal log the following terse entries:

> 2.5, stopped – hard a starboard. 2.10, full speed astern. 2.12, grounded by the bows. When the telegraphs were put over again the engines raced round as the propellers were broken. As soon as we ground closed W. T.[12] doors and so people had only time to put on very scanty clothing. As soon as possible we hoisted out the pulling boom boats and three steam boats; the steam boat being very

10. Court martial as reported in *The Times*, Friday 17 August 1906.
11. *Ibid*.
12. W.T. = water-tight.

When HMS *Winchester*, with her sick and dying crew, was bottomed-out on the Carysfort Reef off the Florida Keys, many artefacts went down with her as the seas broke her up. Numerous relics have been recovered down the years, the most important of which were some of the ships cannons, whose identification helped confirm the location of the ship's watery grave. Five of these salvaged cannon now stand at the Lignum Vitae Key Botanical State Park near Tavernier Key. (*Courtesy Florida State Parks*).

The Great Storm of November 26, 1703, wherein Admiral Beaumont was lost on the Goodwin Sands. Beumont's Squadron of Observation off Dunkerque. No. 25.

A contemporary engraving depicting a warship being driven ashore during the Great Storm o November 1703.

An eighteenth century engraving, representing the loss of Admiral Sir Cloudesley Shovell's flagship HMS *Association*, on the rocks off the Isles of Scilly in 1707.

Admiral Sir Cloudesley Shovell.
An oil on canvas created between
March 1702 and January 1705 by the
England-domiciled Swedish painter
Michael Dahl (1659-1743).

HMS *Lutine* leaving Yarmouth Roads on her final voyage, October 9 1799. From the painting by
Frank Mason, R.A, hanging in the Committee Room of Lloyds, London. (*Courtesy Lloyds of London*)

A Lloyd's Waiter, in traditional robes, rings the *Lutine Bell* under the Rostrum. The bell was run[g] twice to herald the birth of HRH Prince George of Cambridge on 22nd July 2013. (*Courtesy Lloyd[s] of London*)

HMS *Bedford* in 1909, on joining the China Squadron at Hong Kong.

When completed in 1916, the destroyer HMS *Narborough* (F11), part of the War Emergency Programme and ordered from John Brown Shipbuilders in February 1915, joined the Grand Fleet and fought at the Battle of Jutland in the same year. She later transferred to the 12th Destroyer Flotilla and continued to operate with the Grand Fleet, based at Scapa Flow. Pendant numbers were frequently changed to confuse the enemy and, at the time of her loss in 1918, she carried F02.

Able Seaman William Sissons, the 'sole survivor' from the HMS *Opal* after she and the *Narboroug* ran into the Cletts of Clura, Wind Wick, South Ronaldsay in a blinding snowstorm during Januar 1918.

HM destroyer *Opal*, being fitted out at the William Doxford & Sons Company at Sunderland shipyard on the River Ware. She had been ordered in November 1914 and had fought at the Battle of Jutland in 1916. She carried the Pendant Number G41 when she was wrecked in January 1918.

The cruiser HMS *Raleigh* aground at Point Amour, Labrador, in August 1922.

Waves breaking over the cruiser HMS *Raleigh* shortly after she had been evacuated after running aground. Note her White Ensign is still flying.

The cruiser HMS *Effingham* at the review of the Reserve Fleet in August 1939, during which she was visited by HM King George VI. Her original 7.5-inch guns had been replaced by single 6-inch guns and she had had some AA weapons added.

The cruiser HMS *Effingham* at anchor in a Norwegian fiord just prior to her final voyage.

The final configuration of the cruiser HMS *Effingham* after being torpedoed by the destroyer HMS *Echo*. She did not sink but the Germans ignored her during hostilities, dismissing her as being unworthy of salving, and she was broken up by Norwegian salvage teams after the war. (*Australian Government Collection, Canberra ACT*)

Aerial photograph of the wreck of HMS *Effingham* in 67°, 22' N, 14° 10' E, taken by Douglas SBD-dive-bomber from the American carrier *Ranger* (CV-4) on 4 October 1943. (*US Navy*)

The destroyer HSM *Sturdy* was not completed until well after the end of World War I, and spen many of the inter-war years as an unarmed trials vessel.

The destroyer *Sturdy* living up to her name! For a time she was based at Portsmouth pre-war and utilised for 'Rough Weather' trials, deliberately seeking out bad conditions. However, even these experiences failed to prepare her for the extremes she encountered on the night of 29/30 October 1940, which led to her loss.

The destroyer HMS *Nottingham* being 'piggy-backed' home to the UK for repairs after suffering severe damage by striking Wolf Rock off Lord Howe Island in the Tasman Sea, north-east of Sydney. Thanks to the prompt reaction of her crew, there was no loss of life. (*MoD*)

The 3,500-ton destroyer HSM *Nottingham* at speed. Completed in 1983, she carried a mass of 'sta[t]
of the art' navigation electronics but, in the event, was almost lost on an isolated but well-chartere[d]
rock, just off Lord Howe Island. (*MoD*)

dangerous as the ship was rolling heavily, both the picket boats had their bows stove in.....

He added that 'the fog was so heavy that although the rocks and cliff were less than eighty yards away yet we could hardly make anything of them at all'.

The ship fired off distress signals and fired minute guns continually, until all six cases of ammunition had been expended, but without response from ashore. The officers continued to assume that they had gone ashore on the north Devon coast, and a landing party led by Lieutenant Somerville Peregrine Brownlow Russell was hastily disembarked in the ship's gig to fetch help and request assistance. In the dense fog the party turned right, away from the nearby South Light lighthouse, and proceeded right across the length of Lundy before reaching the cottage of John Lakey Ellis, the North Light keeper. When roused Ellis was requested to contact the local authorities and to tell them *Montagu* was aground at Hartland Point but eventually, after some acrimonious exchanges, he managed to persuade them that he was *indeed* a Trinity House light-keeper but of the North Lundy Light and *not* the Hartland Point Lighthouse keeper, and had been for several years![13]

The *Montagu* herself sent divers over the side to assess the damage and it was found that it was very bad indeed. The ledge of rock had dished the hull inward to a depth of 10 feet (3m). Assistance finally arrived on the scene when the fog lifted but by then the ship had settled more firmly and the tides were washing in and out of the holes on her bottom. The cable-laying ship *Monarch* arrived on the scene early in the morning and provided fresh water for the *Montagu*'s crew.[14]

When contact was finally made with the Naval authorities it was found that they had no suitable heavy equipment for such a task and they contacted the Liverpool Salvage Company, who sent their most experienced operative, Captain Frederick William Young. Born in 1872, he had spent some of his earlier years as a gunnery lieutenant in the Argentine navy and was an accomplished diver to boot, but in 1886 he had become an apprentice with the Liverpool Salvage Association, which had originally been formed as far back as 1857, and he later became their principal salvage engineer. He had studied the salvaging of heavy ships in such conditions, based in part on observations of the six Russian battleships sunk at their moorings at Port Arthur during the war with Japan, which were all raised by use of cofferdams, and he had earlier advised the Admiralty to be prepared for similar emergencies. However, when Young arrived aboard the Association's principal little salvage vessel, *Ranger,* he found that Admiral Sir Arthur Knyvet Wilson VC GCVO KCB, commander of the

---

13. Ellis served for Trinity House on Lundy from 1903 to 1910. The original old single lighthouse had by this date been replaced by two, the North and the South lights, in 1897 because the original was considered inadequate due to the frequent fogs that enshrouded the island.
14. On 23 June the fleet auxiliary repair and distilling vessel *Aquarius* (Lieutenant-Commander John E. Edwards RNR) arrived from Milford Haven and secured a wire hawser from her port quarter to *Montagu*'s bow, along which a water hose was run which pumped across 1,600 tons of fresh water. She also acted as a store ship for those working aboard the battleship.

Channel Fleet, had arrived with the battleships *Albemarle* (Captain Edward Stafford Fitzherbert), *Duncan* (Captain John Casement) and *Exmouth* (Captain Edward Eden Bradford), the protected cruiser *Dido* (Captain Stuart Nicholson) and later the armoured cruiser *Euryalus* (Captain George Alexander Ballard) and had assumed control of the operation while Young, despite his expertise, had been relegated to the role of assistant and advisor.

Norfolk-born Wilson had the heart of a lion. He won his Victoria Cross fighting the Dervishes ashore near Suakin in the Sudan campaign at the Battle of El Teb and was a brilliant seaman, but, besides being 'incoherent and opinionated', had little or no knowledge of salvage matters and proved totally out of his depth. He immediately initiated a series of operations, which Young considered 'wrong, impractical or both'. Despite the presence of the fully-equipped *Ranger*,[15] Wilson ordered up a large number of vessels laden with all manner of gear and each put aboard the battleship their own teams without any proper co-ordination of effort or purpose – the result was chaos and all the while the *Montagu* sank lower and the damage increased.

More practically the ship's papers and pay books were taken ashore and secured at the Reverend Heaven's abode of Millcombe House, with an armed guard posted. The crew's personal effects, hammocks etc., were brought up on deck. The Island Agent, Frederick William Allday, sent off the first reports of the stranding to Lloyd's of London, followed by another, later, to the Admiralty.[16] The bulk of the *Montagu*'s crew were quickly transferred to the *Duncan*, *Exmouth* and *Dido*. Despite long and costly efforts to refloat her, she therefore steadily deteriorated into a total wreck. The mishaps continued apace; four of her 6-inch (15.24cm) guns were hoisted out and lowered into a lighter along with her anti-torpedo nets, on Friday 1 June, but the lighter promptly 'carried away the tow-rope and passed over the Sutter rocks and sank'. Although two more of her 6-inch guns were got out of her on 3 June, followed later by the ship's torpedoes, it did not lessen the feeling of general incompetence. This feeling was reinforced when Admiral Wilson was swept overboard from his launch by a heavy sea at one time, and only retrieved with difficulty, and by the behaviour of some of the men who broke into a liquor store on the island, got paralytic and fell over a cliff, happily without any terminal effects.

Increasing acrimonious divergences of views between the Admiral and Young ended in shouting matches and Young being further side-lined. The *Duncan* herself briefly

---

15. The *Ranger* was a former Royal Navy gun vessel built in 1880. She had been sold out of the service in 1892 and had been converted for salvage work. She had an enormously long career, commencing with the salvage of the White Star Liner *Suevic* which went full speed onto Stag Rock on the Maeheere Reef off the Lizard in March 1901; among *Ranger*'s many other achievements was the raising of the submarine *Thetis* from Liverpool Bay in 1939 and the work on the SS *Politician*, of *Whisky Galore* fame, when she went aground at Eriskay, South Uist, in 1941.

16. His choice of priorities, although no doubt well-intentioned, did not win him the affection of Their Lordships; the very public humiliation of the *Montagu* was to bring them constant embarrassment as the weeks went on and more details emerged.

went aground on a rock on 23 July while trying unsuccessfully to haul the *Montagu* off; she was herself got off but suffered considerable damage and required repairs and had to withdraw from the scene; the battleships *Cornwallis* (Captain Charles Henry Coke) and *Mars* (Captain Henry Loftus Tottenham) arrived as replacements but could do little. Efforts were made to pump the water out, to no avail as there were too many openings. Among those involved at this time, Petty Officer John Henry Palmer, an RNR reservist from Devonport called up for the exercise, took a whole series of photographs of the efforts on board which provide an invaluable record of events.[17] An effort was made to physically blow the water out of her engine rooms with compressed air, but this also failed for the same reason. The final brainwave that the Admiral put forward was to fill the *Montagu*'s compartments with cork with the hope that she would 'float off at high tide'! The battleship *Venerable* (Captain Henry Bertram Pelly) loaded a cargo of this commodity at Berehaven and brought it over on 27 July. It was stacked on the main deck ready to be crammed into various departments. Young, despairing, predicted that this would merely block the pumps. He concluded that the ship herself was lost.

By summer's end work was suspended without any progress and the Admiralty made a detailed inspection of the ship. This revealed that all the efforts to date had been fruitless and that *Montagu* was being pounded and lifted steadily inshore with resultant pressure on her hull which warped and bent under the strain. Her boat davits collapsed and other visible signs of her breaking up were that her deck planks began coming apart while, although invisible, her seams were springing open. Armed guards were placed aboard her to prevent civilian looting of the ship.

Finally, and far too late, the Navy resigned itself to the loss of the battleship and, seeing sense, requested Young and Liverpool Salvage to try and resolve something worthwhile from the fiasco. His initial suggestion was to lighten the ship by removing the four 12-inch wire-wound guns, each of which were 40 feet (12.192m) in length and had a weight of forty-six tons (41730.5kg).[18] Reserve stocks of these weapons, the standard Royal Navy battleship armament of the day, were always insufficient, and the guns themselves were very costly to manufacture, having a monetary value of £9,049 apiece. The Navy, naturally, was to be responsible for these weapons once saved, and Captain Arthur Wartensleben Ewart arrived aboard the *Eclipse*-class protected cruiser *Doris* to oversee their safe removal to Pembroke Dockyard should Young succeed. Ewart was later to provide us with a detailed account of how the work was carried out, which Rear-Admiral 'Kit' Craddock included in his book.[19]

Young arrived back at the scene on 20 August aboard the *Ranger* with, finally, *carte blanche* to assess and carry out the operation. He actually achieved the first part within

---

17. These photographs are contained in an Album held by Plymouth City Museum at Armada Way, Plymouth.
18. Ordnance College, Woolwich, *Text Book of Gunnery*, Table XII, p.336, 1902, London, HMSO.
19. Craddock, Rear-Admiral Sir Christopher George Francis Maurice, *Whispers from the Fleet – Saving the 12 inch Guns and Mountings of H.M.S. Montague (sic), Aug to Oct. 1906*, pp.366–71, 1908, Portsmouth, Gieves & Co.

five weeks, even though bad weather frequently intervened. Young had a team that comprised his assistant, Lieutenant John Richard Williams RNR,[20] thirty-four riggers, three divers, three carpenters, two engineers and four firemen, while nine shipwrights were lent from Pembroke Dockyard itself. Young's team had cleared away all the superfluous shipping and left just his own team on station to commence the work in a logical manner. The salvage vessel *Plover* arrived on 27 August with a Government lighter in tow which had embarked aboard Young's requirements for the job, viz. two pairs of sheer legs, two boilers, two steam winches, one air compressor, coils of wire and manila ropes, blocks and tackles.

The lighter was towed into position on *Montagu*'s starboard (inshore) side by a small tug on 28 August, brought into position to commence operations. Using *Montagu*'s derrick, which was still fully operational, and aided by volunteers from the *Doris*, the boilers, winches and air compressor required for pneumatic cutting and drilling tools were all hoisted inboard and secured.

The two guns of the forward turret were tackled initially, commencing the following day. The turret's top plates were removed to reveal the two barrels in the barbette. The guns could not be lifted until this armoured plate was removed as it was tied to the adjoining plates by dove-tailed taper keys which could only be removed by forcing them up from below. This entailed cutting away the foundation plate upon which the armour sat and it took a week to do this. Young had planned to lift the guns from the turret while it was trained fore and aft which was described as 'place each gun on chocks on top of the turret, parbuckle[21] each gun down on an inclined plane to the ship's side, and then pick it up with sheers stepped fore and aft'. On further consideration Young decided instead to train the turret on the starboard beam:

so that the sheers on the ship's side would be stepped across the muzzles of the guns; each gun being first lifted out of the turret by another pair of sheers stepped across the ship, transported down an inclined plane, muzzle foremost, until far enough outboard, and then lifted in to the lighter by the ship's side sheers.

Difficulty was encountered in training the turret due to the 5-degree list the *Montagu* had by now adopted, and due to Wilson's earlier bodged efforts which had wedged and cemented the ammunition trunk to the fixed trunk, while the seawater had by now firmly rusted the rollers, roller paths and spindles. All the securing bolts were therefore removed, and a 3.5-inch (88.90mm) wire lashing was passed round the gun muzzles, fixed to a 6-inch (152.40mm) wire hawser. The tug then went ahead but the muzzles only moved nine inches (22.86cm) and then stuck, parting the tow rope. A tackle was substituted and on the second attempt the turret was hauled around to the desired position.

---

20. Williams later went on to pioneer replenishment in the Royal Navy, commanding the Royal Fleet Auxiliary oilers *Petroleum* in 1913 and *Reliance* in 1915.
21. *Parbuckling* – the righting of a sunken vessel using rotational leverage.

Over a twenty-one day period Young had part of the battleship's side blown out which enabled these barrels to fall down into the hull itself. A huge 60–feet (18.288m) tall centre sheer-legs was then positioned and the 50–feet (15.24m) long side set rigged with a 5–degree cant outboard. They had been floated alongside and then hoisted inboard by specially rigged derricks. A square hole was cut in the deck through the deck planking and steel plating and exposed the deck beams. No shoring was considered necessary to take the strain as the beams supporting the turret were considered strong enough not to buckle. Once lifted above the turret the barrel had to be run down an inclined plane (built of timber baulks bolted together), until the second set of sheers could be affixed for the final lift.

The operation proceeded well at first and the first barrel came clear to turret-roof level but then the rising swell of yet another storm imperilled the work team and operations were halted. All next day heavy seas broke over the *Montagu* and no work could be done, while anxious eyes watched the dangling barrel, which had been left hanging in the tackles. The operation was finally resumed the following day and the gun 'was skidded slowly down the inclined plane'. The gun was then eased very carefully over the port side of the ship and into the lighter alongside, where it rested on timber chocks. This was achieved by 1500 on 8 September and, without waiting for the second barrel to be lifted out, this was towed by the tug safely to Pembroke Dock on the 9th. The same procedure was adopted for the second barrel of the forward turret, once the lessons learnt earlier had been applied to the apparatus. With the return of the lighter on the 12th this barrel followed the same procedure without mishap the next day. Also removed was the after warhead magazine and the twelve-and-a-half-ton starboard propeller, which was blown off its shaft by 18–pounds (8.164kg) of gelignite. The port shaft had already become detached and, although located by divers off *Montagu*'s port quarter, was left *in situ*.[22]

The saving of the two barrels from the after barbette followed a similar procedure and the sheers were unrigged forward on 24 September and re-positioned aft by the 28th, work made more difficult by virtue of the fact that the quarterdeck was always awash at the high tides. Young had sought a larger, more suitable lighter for this lift, but was unable to secure one immediately and the third barrel followed the way of the first two. The new lighter appeared in time to transport the fourth and last gun, which was towed into Pembroke on 1 October.

Then the storms began again in earnest and work was halted for several days, during which time further severe damage was inflicted upon the stranded battleship. As they could not be retrieved, the Admiralty ordered that the submerged torpedo tubes be totally destroyed and this was done on 10 October with charges of gelignite. Further operations had been planned but the deterioration in the weather caused the Association to cease further work for the rest of the year. Admiralty proposals to

---

22. It was re-discovered by chance some time later when the salvage ship *Zephyr* had her anchor caught up in it and divers went down and reported what it was. It was recovered in two pieces as it was too large for her to lift in one go.

subject the wreck to target practice by the *Doris* were turned down after protests from the islanders as to the risks involved.

The court martial of Captain Adair, one of the Navy's most distinguished gunnery officers of the day, and Navigating Officer Lieutenant Dathan took place aboard HMS *Victory* at Portsmouth from 15 to 20 August, under the Presidency of Rear-Admiral Charles Henry Cross while this salvage work was still in progress.[23] The officers of the court were Captain Frederick Tower Hamilton (*Excellent*), Captain The Honourable Walter George Stopford (Commodore in Command, Royal Naval Barracks, Portsmouth), Captain Charles John Briggs (*Vernon*), Captain Francis Alban Arthur Gifford Tate (*Hindustan*), Captain John Casement (*Duncan*), Captain Herbert Augustus Warren (*Jupiter*), Captain Douglas Austin Gamble (*Canopus*), Captain Edward Eden Bradford (*Exmouth*) while Fleet Paymaster Edmund Frederick Estcourt Gipps, Secretary to the Commander-in-Chief, was Deputy Judge-Advocate. Adair was assisted by Captain Charles Henry Coke (*Cornwallis*) while Lieutenant Oswald Harcourt Davies (*Mars*) performed for Lieutenant Dathan.

Function for Dathan

Both accused officers had hitherto exhibited excellent records and the *Montagu* was acknowledged as having a high reputation for efficiency and discipline. Adair's principal argument was that he was obeying the orders of his superior. He had been so ordered the previous day, once the radio experiments were completed, to return to the anchorage off Lundy, and this he determined to do. Adair stated in his defence that he was very conscious of the importance of the wireless experiments he was entrusted with to the Navy and the nation and was aware that the very success of his mission relied totally on his precisely carrying out his orders.

The Court drew Adair's attention to Article 977 of King's Regulations,[24] which spelt out that:

> the captain is to exercise a very careful discretion before endeavouring to make unlighted or dangerous land, or to get into or close to difficult, unlighted ports during darkness. Except in case of emergency or other necessity, he should consider whether, instead, the service he is employed upon will not be more certainly performed by standing off until daylight.

Adair's response was that he *had* duly considered it and thought himself 'imperatively bound' to so proceed. The Court responded by quoting the Regulations at him once more, particularly Article 975, which spelt out that:

---

23. Captain Douglas Austin Gamble, of the battleship *Canopus*, had already held an enquiry into the loss of gear from the *Montagu* on 13 August.
24. *The King's Regulations and Admiralty Instructions for the Government of Her Majesty's Naval Service*, 1902, London, HMSO.

whenever the ship is approaching the land, or any shoals, the captain is to take care that the navigating officer keeps a good look-out upon deck, and that deep-sea soundings are always taken in good time and continued until the safely of the ship's position is ascertained and secured.

Here Adair was found wanting; he had not *ignored* this Regulation but, the Court pointed out, he had most certainly not *acted* on it. Why was this? Well, the Navigation Officer was *not* actually on the bridge at the time of impact; instead a fatigued Lieutenant Dathan had been allowed to go to his quarters to sleep. In mitigation, it was admitted that Dathan himself had been awake all the night before and had not had his clothes off all that time. Even if he had been on the bridge at 0200 he would probably not have been able to prevent, or even mitigate, the accident when the sounding came back at an unexpected and alarming nineteen fathoms. The defendants also pleaded mitigation due to 'the irregularities of the tides' in the region of Lundy, but to no avail.

Adair's case was not helped by the fact that he contradicted himself on occasion. When asked about why he had pressed on regardless, he stated:

The fog had become very thick, but after weighing the matter in my mind I decided to continue towards Lundy, hoping that the explosive fog signal would give me due warning of my approach ...

but the following day he was to state in response to a question from the Court he remarked that 'it is well-known at Lundy that there is an area of silence to the westward, and although close to the island the fog-signal is inaudible'.

On the question of miscalculation Adair told the Court:

There are two factors which I can mention in explanation of the actual discrepancy between the dead reckoning position and the ship's position when she struck. One is the 11 o'clock position being plotted too far south: and the other is, no drift, so far as I can know, being allowed. I did not make any provision for drift myself, when, for example, I said we would use 9¼ knots between 8 and 10. I think that possibly the ship was over-logged between 8 and 10, but not to the extent that is necessary to fill up the discrepancy.

Two local men attested to the unpredictability of the tides and currents, and the inaudibility of the fog sirens at Lundy. Master William Popham of the ketch *Kitty* stated that on 29 May he was about two-and-a-half miles west of Lundy: 'A dense fog prevailed, and the wind was light. During the whole of the night he heard no explosive signs whatever from the South Lundy lighthouse.' William P. M. Dark, master mariner of Padstow, had a lifelong experience of the Bristol Channel and the Lundy area, having carried mail to the island for forty years. He stated, from his own observations over that long period that the tides:

were very irregular in the set of the current, and ran at different angles at different states of the tide, circumstances which were not accounted for in the chart. He had, on different occasions, been approaching the island in thick weather from the southward, and had come close to the island, but had not heard the explosive fog signal or the siren of the north lighthouse, although he had satisfied himself afterwards that they were being let off.

He added that he:

had stood on the highest part of the west side of the island when there was a belt of fog below, and had seen vessels coming towards the island from the west-south-west, and narrowly escaping the rocks. Apparently, they had not heard the signal until they were well up under the Rattles.

A further testament was read to the Court, not being allowed as evidence as it had not been sworn to. It was from Master Thomas Henry Blewitt, of Tywarath, Cornwall, who regularly operated the *Dashing Wave* out from Fowey.[25] He stated that two weeks before the stranding he was in the same position and:

had expected to hear the gun on Lundy Island. At 3 a.m. the lookout reported a sound under my lee, which he took to be a steamboat. When abreast north-west to this sound, suddenly the gun went off on Lundy. I had then to haul my ship about east south-east to avoid going on the Shutter Rocks. Had this fog signal been in use I should have heard it at least an hour previous, as there was only a light wind, and my vessel was going about four miles by the log. The sound which I took to be a steamboat was the sea breaking on the rocks, so that I was near being on shore.

Cross-examined by Captain Ommannery, Lieutenant Dathan stated that during the run southward he had calculated the speed of the ship by the revolutions; he did not use the distances given in the log.

He was on deck at 8 p.m. on the 29th and took a bearing. He was on deck until after the ship altered her course, and again when the ship was stopped at 9.17. Between the time the ship stopped and 10.50 p.m. he was on the bridge continuously. By that he meant that he only left it for a few minutes at a time. It was possible that he did make a mistake in estimating the distance the ship had run to the south-west. But he made careful calculations and did not consider at the time that he was mistaken.

---

25. Blewitt was later to be drowned off the West Cant Buoy at the entrance to the River Medway on the night of 22 February 1908.

He also admitted to the court that his 'dead-reckoning' position and the actual position of *Montagu* when she struck was out by 'About nine miles'. When asked to explain such a large discrepancy Dathan replied, 'I cannot say. I possibly calculated my run to the southward to be bigger than it was. But certainly could not account for this discrepancy', adding, 'my judgement of the currents possibly was out. But even that would only make a mile or so.'

The examining officers were very thorough in their examination of all the evidence but concluded that both men 'did negligently or by default hazard, strand, and lose' the ship. Their considered opinions were that the ship's officers had had 'implicit' reliance on their own 'dead-reckoning' computations and had paid the price.

The announced verdict was:

> The Court, having found the charges against both prisoners proved, adjudges Captain T. B. S. Adair to be severely reprimanded and dismissed HMS *Montagu*: and adjudges Lieutenant J. H. Dathan to be severely reprimanded, dismissed HMS *Montagu*, and to forfeit two years' seniority as lieutenant in His Majesty's Fleet.

Both were severely reprimanded. Adair was dismissed his ship, as was Dathan, the latter losing two years seniority, a setback to his naval career.

Adair's hitherto relentless naval progression was effectively terminated by this accident, one contemporary, Rear-Admiral Sir Christopher 'Kit' Craddock, later hinting at a common feeling in the fleet that the court's findings had been unduly harsh by stating that his account would 'never lessen the regret felt throughout the Navy for the one man who suffered – A victim of unexpected circumstances'.[26]

In March 1907 Adair was taken off the Active List and took official retirement on 2 December 1908, his length of service granting him the nominal promotion to the rank of Rear-Admiral. However, a new opportunity had already fallen into his lap, his gunnery expertise being instrumental in his appointment as Superintendent of the Gun Department at the private shipbuilding company of William Beardmore & Co., based at Parkland Steelworks, Glasgow, where he served most efficiently for the next twelve years, which included the whole Great War period. This firm built the mighty battleships *Benbow*, *Conqueror* and *Ramillies*, which so far outclassed the *Montagu* of only a few years earlier as to make her passing superfluous.[27] Beardmore were also

---

26. Craddock, Rear-Admiral Sir Christopher George Francis Maurice, KCVO CB SGM, *Whispers from the Fleet*, pp.365–78, 1908, Portsmouth. Gieves.

27. The very naïve view expressed that, had she survived, *Montagu* 'might have won great battle honours at Jutland or Zeebrugge – perhaps witnessing the final surrender of the German fleet at Scapa Flow' (Davis, Gill M., *The Loss of H.M.S. Montagu – Lundy 1906*, p.15, 1981, Atworth, G. M. & R. C. Davis.) are without any real foundation; the arrival of the all big-gun *Dreadnought* within months of her loss had made her and her many contemporary 'Four 12-inch -Ten-6-inch- 18 knots' type of capital ships that had previously been the standard the world over, totally obsolete almost instantaneously.

responsible for the appearance of the world's first aircraft-carrier, the *Argus*,[28] a type
of warship that was to make *all* battleships, no matter what their size, obsolete within
three decades. Under Adair the company diversified into the manufacture of heavy
naval guns to arm these monsters.

A third, if briefer, career followed for Adair, who stood as the Unionist representative
in the Shettleston Division of Glasgow in the General Election of December 1918,
which seat he won. He campaigned powerfully on naval issues, particularly for the
Navy to regain control of its own aircraft from the fledgling RAF (and that service
most shamefully neglected the Fleet Air Arm for the next twenty years); and also
campaigned hard on the payment of marriage allowances to naval officers. In both
cases his powerful advocacy failed to achieve their very laudable aims.

He also campaigned for affordable accommodation for working-class tenants, which
won the support of Lloyd George. His political downfall, as with so many others, was
the Irish Question, when he felt the Government had caved in to the Nationalists in the
creation of the Free State in December 1921 and he was de-selected soon afterward,
dying in 1928.

Portsmouth-born Lieutenant Dathan, also from a distinguished naval family, fared
rather less well. The court martial had brought out the fact that *Montagu*'s reciprocal
course back to Lundy was many miles off-track, which was hardly an endorsement of
his skills. However, the unpredictable tides may have contributed here. The fact that
he had a 'highly meritorious' naval record up to that point did not save him, nor the
fact that he was 'a staunch teetotaller'.

Public opinion was less kind to Dathan than to Adair and, more importantly, so was
expert opinion, for example the *Marine Engineer* was scathing in its criticism.

The cause of the loss of the ship was evidently the extreme reliance placed on
the *Montagu*'s navigators on dead reckoning, and the somewhat crude methods
by which that dead reckoning was reached. The patent log[29] was not in use, and
the speed of the ship through the water was arrived at by a calculation that three
revolutions meant half a knot's speed. This is a rule-of-thumb method which we
might have expected to have seen used by those who drove the early steam-boats,
but which does not commend itself to those who are accustomed to the exact
systems of modern science. For it must be apparent to everyone that, though at
certain speeds this may be fairly accurate, it cannot be considered that it could
be true at all possible speeds. For every engineer knows that slip is variable,
that at low speeds it decreases and at high it is intensified. Again, we have the
difficulties which the *Montagu*'s mission placed upon those who had to direct

---

28. Converted from the incomplete hull of the Lloyd Sabaudo Line's liner *Conte Rosso*, she appeared
    in September 1918, equipped with eighteen Sopwith Cuckoo torpedo-bombers, just before the
    end of the Great War two months later.
29. The Patent Log was a torpedo-shaped instrument with rotary fins, which was towed behind a
    warship to measure the true speed or the distance travelled from a given point. Alternate names
    were Taffrail Log or Screw Log.

her course. Her last departure was taken about seven and a quarter hours before her stranding. In that time she ran away down channel towards Scilly, stopping from time to time, and even slightly swinging, and then she was made to retrace her steps. All this time she was under the influence of the tidal streams – which in these waters are both strong and uncertain – and of such wind as there was. The difficulties of calculating all the factors that had to be considered are appreciable by any person who considers the matter, and it is clear that dead reckoning could not be relied on under the circumstances. The lead was, indeed, used as an aid to the navigation of the ship. But Admiralty directions – which the captain had not, apparently, read – point out that in this vicinity the lead is not reliable. Moreover, the half-hourly soundings which were taken were not sufficient for the purpose of checking the ship's position. The fog-signals of the Lundy Station were being listened for, and it is said were not heard. But this is not to be wondered at. For everyone who has experience of the sea is aware that fog has a strange effect upon sound signals. Sometimes they are not heard at all, sometimes their bearing is entirely altered. These things may have been difficulties in the way of the safe navigation of the ship; but the difficulties have generally been but an incentive to effort with the King's sailors. If it was imperative, as Captain Adair believed it to be, for him to keep on his way to Lundy in the dense fog in which he found himself, he should certainly have realised the condition, and especially the fact that his dead reckoning was not to be trusted, and so neglected no precaution. If the ship had been kept dead slow, and the lead kept going continuously, this casualty need never have happened. Even as it was, at the eleventh hour, the lead gave a distinct warning of what was coming, when it announced that the ship was in 19 fathoms, thirty being expected. Had the ship been stopped at once she would have been saved. But both the captain and the navigating lieutenant were below, and precious time was lost, whilst they were told of the warning. The court-martial could not, on the evidence, have come to any other decision than it did.[30]

The verdict of the court automatically placed 160 junior lieutenants above him in the ranking, a hard blow indeed. What is certainly to be counted to Dathan's subsequent credit was that he later became one of the very few Royal Navy officers who attained a Master's Certificate (No. 76752) in the Mercantile Marine, which he received at Liverpool on 3 December 1907.[31] He was put on the retired list on 30 June 1906 as a lieutenant-commander. But the Admiralty decided to re-employ him after a period of half-pay (NI 8457/06) from 27 September 1907 but not on navigation duties. He remained on half-pay until 20 August 1908, having retired at his own request on 22 July and applied for appointment to the Naval Salvage Service in September.

---

30. Article in *Marine & Naval Engineer & Architect*, Vol. XXIX, January 1907, London, Institute of Marine & Naval Engineers.
31. BT 124/23/0, National Archives, Kew, London.

He worked on ship salvage overseas and eventually reached the rank of commander (retired) on 12 October 1914. That did not prevent him playing a role in the naval war. He was at the Dardanelles operations in 1915 aboard the Special Service Vessel *Egmont* (the former 'broadside ironclad' battleship *Achilles* of 1863 and re-named in 1904) at Malta, salvaging vessels mined in the Straits, returning home in October, and served as Salvage Officer at the Admiralty on full naval pay and allowances. After a period as a 'Whitehall Limpet', he worked under Captain Cyril Asser RN, Superintendent of Torpedo Boat Destroyers building by Contract, helping speed this essential work; he also worked with Captain Christopher Powell Metcalf DSO (Rtd) at the Salvage Section of the Admiralty and was mentioned by Lord Jellicoe for his work.[32]

Frederic Young, however, went from strength to strength and followed up his work on *Montagu* with the salvage of Adair's old ship, the cruiser *Gladiator* at Yarmouth, Isle of Wight, in 1908, after she had been in collision with the American steamer *St Paul*, and also the American liner *Minnehaha* in 1909 and the Red Funnel Line's Belgian-flagged *Gothland* from the Isles of Scilly, once more, in 1914. He was appointed Head of the Salvage Section at the Admiralty during the Great War as a commodore, and among his achievements were the repair of the battleship *Conqueror* and the battle-cruiser *Lion* after battle damage.[33] In the immediate post-war period Young raised the blockship *Vindictive* at Ostend and those other old warships used to block Zeebrugge during the famous raids against the U-boat bases there. He was appointed Honorary Naval Salvage Adviser to the Admiralty and, as Sir Frederic KBE RNR, established the Sir F. W. Young & Co. consultancy and was managing director of the Young Accumulator Company. He died, aged 69, on 20 December 1927.

On conclusion of the legal side of things *Montagu* was officially 'paid off' and she passed from the service. The Admiralty put the wreck up for auction in January 1907, and the winning bid of a mere £4,250 was made by the Syndicate of South Wales Adventurers. Thus she became a mere commodity for salvage and was scrapped *in situ* in 1907. As part of their recuperation of outlay they constructed a 500-foot (152.40mm) long aerial footway from the top of the cliffs to the roof of the *Montagu*'s charthouse. They also constructed a pathway down the cliff face utilising granite steps with carved footholds into the rocks themselves, and these, 'The Montagu Steps' can still be made out today. Every ploy possible was used to make money from the wreck, one local timber merchant, James Ellis, even going to the extent of selling souvenir walking sticks made from the teak of the battleship's deck and inscribed 'Wood from H.M.S. *Montagu*'. Other enterprising traders, like cabinet-maker Thomas Strout of Ilfracombe, used the mahogany to make furniture items. Slightly more reverence was paid to the ship's ensign, which was originally consigned to the safe-keeping of Ilfracombe Museum

---

32. Jellicoe, John Rushworth, Admiral of the Fleet Viscount Jellicoe of Scapa GCB OM GCO, *The Crisis of the Naval War*, pp.279 & 287, 1920, London, Cassell and Co. Ltd. He reverted to the retired list on 1 August 1919 and died on 17 December 1941 (CW 42919/41).
33. Booth, Tony, *Admiralty Salvage in Peace and War: 1906–2006 –Grope, Grub and Tremble*, 2007, Barnsley, Pen & Sword Maritime.

along with four wooden panels from Adair's cabin. The Reverend Heaven noted on 5 June that the islanders had been much excited by the three battleships and a cruiser plus the fleet of salvage craft. Prophetically he noted: 'If the weather continues fine as at present, they may refloat her, but should it come in rough and stormy, I think it is very problematical.' Ten days later he was noting that the local pleasure steamers were making the most of it also. 'The Barry or "Red-funnelled" boats at present come here on Tuesdays and the Brighton on Fridays' and that 'We have been simply swarming with photographers and their Kodaks, snapshotting in all directions'.[34]

Six months of salvage work followed, made difficult as there was only a single readily-accessible landing place on the island. Work aboard the wreck was also hampered by the fact that it could only be carried out at low tide. The Adventurers brought lighters alongside at such times and began dissecting the armoured plate, along with the copper and brass fitments which had high commercial value. They used explosives to open up the hull and this weakened the already strained structure yet further, but they were successful in also extracting the ship's condensers, pumps, etc. Tons of non-ferrous metals were stripped out of her, her bow armour was levered off and even her propellers were removed following the fouling of one of the salvage ship's anchors during the work. Further work was planned but in October a series of ferocious gales broke over Lundy forcing the abandonment of the project. It was hoped that this was a temporary delay but, in the event, Mother Nature quickly reduced what remained of the *Montagu* to shreds and she vanished from sight and, with her, all hope of further profits, which had been considerable. Desultory work was continued on and off over the next fifteen years by the Western Marine Salvage Company from Penzance.

Today the island is National Trust property maintained by the Landmark Trust as a nature reserve and home to, most famously, a Puffin colony with other seabirds and seals. There are some visitors' chalets for guests and a pub. The island is serviced by the MV *Oldenburg* from Ilfracombe or Bideford. What remains of the salvaged wreck lies scattered over a wide area and is broken up with seventy-eight-inch (2m) high heaps of armour plate still lying among the kelp. There are warnings of still live 12-inch shells among the wreckage.

The words of a *Times'* correspondent commenting on Adair's unfortunate experience, were to have a distant resonance one hundred years later off the coast of Skye, under no less exacting difficulties involving cutting-edge technology. He wrote:

Is it wise, when you mean to put into the power of a single brain a million pounds' worth of steel and the lives of a thousand men, to risk even momentary desertion of the tried paths of seamanship for important scientific experiments?

He added:

---

34. Davis, Gill M., *The Loss of H.M.S. Montagu – Lundy 1906*, p.15, 1981, Atworth, G. M. & R. C. Davis.

it must be remembered, the responsibility of executive officers in modern naval work and warfare does not diminish, nor does it remain stationary. It increases with every ton added to the battleship and every mile added to the range of the gun. The officer in command of a battleship of the *Dreadnought* class of today has an infinitely greater responsibility than the officers who bombarded Alexandria. It was not possible twenty years ago for a single captain to lose a million and a half of the nation's money, perhaps to alter the balance of power in Europe. Today that possibility, unparalleled in any other profession, lies before every naval captain. The sense of that tremendous responsibility is emphasised by the knowledge, properly and rightly instilled into the youngest midshipman, that failure will be swiftly and terribly punished. But if the punishment is to remain unalterable, there comes a point when it could be unwise that the responsibility should be increased. A simple strain in one direction, however strong, can be met by strong strain in the other direction. But when the strain becomes complicated and more complicated still, the breaking-point may occur at an ever-increasing number of places. Though there is a danger of unduly complication the strain is the chief lesson to be learnt from the loss of the *Montagu*.[35]

35. Anon., 'The Loss of H.M.S. *Montagu*', article in *The Spectator*, 25 August 1906, p.5. Also reproduced in *Otago Daily Times*, 12 October 1906, and credited to 'our own correspondent'.

Chapter 10

'An Unreliable Fix'

The *Bedford*, 21 August 1910

HMS *Bedford* was a first-class armoured cruiser of the *Monmouth* class, ten of which were ordered at the turn of the twentieth-century under the Admiralty's 1899–1900 Programmes and which were cut-down versions of the *Drake* class in an effort to cut costs and get more ships.[1]

Bedford herself was built by Fairfield Shipbuilding and Engineering Company Ltd, at Govan on the Clyde,[2] one of Britain's leading shipbuilders at that period, and was later allocated the Admiralty pendant number D28. Her sister ships were *Berwick*, *Cornwall*, *Cumberland*, *Donegal*, *Essex*, *Kent*, *Lancaster*, *Monmouth* and *Suffolk*. The *Bedford* herself was named after the county town of Bedfordshire and was laid down on 19 February 1900, launched by Charlotte Mary Emily Burns, wife of James Cleland Burns, of the famed Cunard Line shipping dynasty, on 31 August 1901,[3] and finally completed for service on 11 November 1903.

The *Bedford* was steam propelled and had a displacement tonnage of 9,800 long tons (10,000 tons normal). Her dimensions were an overall length of 463 feet 6 inches (141.27m), a maximum beam of 66 feet (20.1m) and a deep draught of 25 feet (7.6m). She was propelled by two 4-cylinder triple-expansion engines, each of which drove a shaft, with thirty-one Belleville water-tube boilers giving 22,000 indicated horsepower (16,000kW), driving dual shafts giving her a maximum speed of 23.9 knots (26 mph or 43 km/h). She carried bunkers of 1,600 tons of coal.

She was armed with no fewer than fourteen 6-inch (152.4mm) Mk VII breech-loading (BL) guns in two twin mountings positioned ahead and astern, with ten further single mountings in two-storey casements on either side amidships, but three of these lower mountings on each side were situated on her main deck and, in service, proved frequently to be awash and therefore unusable in any sort of seaway. Each of these weapons fired a 100lb (45kg) shell to a distance of 12,200 yards (11,200m). HMS

---

1. They were to be much criticised as being under-armed and under-protected by contemporary observers when they first appeared. See McBride, Keith, 'The First *County* Class Cruisers of the Royal Navy, Part I: *The Monmouths*', article in *Warship* magazine No. 47, April 1998, London, Conway Maritime Press, pp.19–26.
2. Yard No. 414.
3. See 'Naval & Military Intelligence', article in *The Times*, Monday, 2 September 1901, p.5.

Bedford also carried ten 12-pounder (12cwt[4] (609kg) quick-firing (QF) guns mounted amidships on either side of her superstructure as defence against the menace of fast torpedo craft, plus three single 3-pounder (1.36078kg) Hotchkiss saluting guns. The *Bedford* also mounted two underwater 18-inch (450mm) torpedo tubes. These tubes had an extended bar from which the torpedo itself was launched. During trials in 1904 *Bedford* managed to fire these weapons four times in rapid succession in an overall time of 7 minutes 40 seconds.[5]

The *Bedford*'s armour protection comprised a belt along her waterline of between 2 inches to a maximum of 4 inches (51–102mm) thickness covering her vitals, with deck protection of between 0.75 inch to 2 inches (19–51mm), with 4-inch (127mm) barbettes and turrets and 5-inch (127mm) casemates, and an armoured conning tower with 10-inch (254mm) thick armour. Her inner citadel was sealed by traverse bulkheads which themselves were of 5-inch (127mm) thick steel. *Bedford* cost the nation £707,020 and was considered a fine bargain for such a state-of-the-art warship on her completion. She was manned by a crew of 678 officers and men.

On commissioning at the Nore, she was a Chatham-manned ship.[6] Under the command of famous naval gunnery expert Captain Frederick Charles Doveton Sturdee, who was appointed in command on 11 November 1903, *Bedford* worked up and then joined the 1st Cruiser Squadron with the Channel Fleet for a full term. Sturdee moved on to command the cruiser *Drake* a year later, being succeeded in command by Captain Richard Henry Peirse. In another twelve months Peirse was moved to command the battleship *Commonwealth* and was followed in turn aboard *Bedford* by Captain Herbert Lyon in December 1905 who commanded her until March 1906. The *Bedford* had meanwhile been relieved by the protected cruiser *Antrim* in July 1905 and joined the 2nd Cruiser Squadron but was subsequently paid off and reduced to reserve at The Nore, where she was under the command, initially, of Captain Henry Holland Torlesse who, when he moved on to command the armoured cruiser *Leviathan*, was succeeded aboard *Bedford* by Captain Drury St Aubyn Wake from 6 November. This latter was appointed to command the protected cruiser *Hawke* and command of *Bedford* became the responsibility, from 12 February 1907, of Captain Seymour Elphinstone Erskine when she was commissioned for service on the China Station, arriving at Hong Kong on 25 March 1909. This powerful squadron comprised the modern armoured cruiser *Minotaur* (Captain William Osbert Boothby), the *Kent* (Captain Gerald Charles Adolphe Marescaux) and the *Monmouth* (Captain George Walter Smith). When Captain Erskine moved on to command the battleship *Venerable*, Captain Edward Stafford Fitzherbert assumed command in December 1908. In the

---

4. cwt = hundredweight.
5. *Annual Report of the Torpedo School, 1904*, ADM 189/24, pp.45–7, National Archives, Kew, London.
6. The Royal Navy's three 'home' ports were Chatham (Nore), Portsmouth ('Pompey') and Plymouth (Devonport or 'Guz'). By reason of proximity Chatham crews comprised mainly – but by no means exclusively – Londoners, although one victim had been transferred from the Devonport Division.

Far East the *Bedford* quickly established an outstanding reputation and, in 1910, proved herself the superior gunnery vessel of all six of that squadron's warships. With an average score for the station of 56.628, Captain Fitzherbert's command achieved a remarkable 67.81.

Bedford's untimely end came quickly and quite unexpectedly when she was wrecked on Quelpart Island, off the southern coast of Korea, in the East China Sea on 21 August 1910. Eighteen of her crew were lost.

On Saturday 20 August 1910 these four vessels sailed from the fleet anchorage at the leased port of Wei-hai-Wei, in north-eastern China, bound for the southern Japanese port of Nagasaki where, it was announced, general leave was to be given to most of the ships' companies. Japan at this period was a firm and staunch ally of the United Kingdom. A typhoon had passed through the area just prior to their sailing, which had been delayed accordingly. Despite this, and the fact that the area was notorious for navigational hazards, it was nonetheless determined that the following day a speed trial would be held and in the early hours of Sunday morning the squadron was steaming hard, in fact full out, with the *Bedford* leading the line-ahead formation and about twenty miles ahead of her next astern, thus, in the words of one of her officers, 'beating all the fleet at steaming'.[7] However, despite the fact that a navigational 'fix' was obtained that the ships were somewhat off their planned route, it was dismissed, and the officer recorded that when he turned in from the middle watch at around 0430, there were no qualms; 'all was snug and secure'.

Just around 0420, while it was still dark, land was sighted on the port beam. This was assumed to be Lonely Bluff and would put the ship within three miles of the DR position. The trial itself had by then concluded and the ships subsequently eased down to about 19 knots by around 0800. Captain Fitzherbert was asleep in his cabin but ten minutes later he was awakened, as per routine instructions, by a ship's messenger who reported 'Quelpart Island on port beam'. This was expected and, having acknowledged the information, the Captain went back to sleep. Up on the bridge the *Bedford*'s officer of the watch, Lieutenant Albert Edward Dixie, entered the same information in the ship's log. He had earlier made a dead reckoning, based on the known course, time, speed of the vessel and last known position, and noted that the sighting was within three miles of his earlier estimate. All seemed well, but at 0443, on checking by means of a Pole Star observation by getting sights of Polaris (the Pole Star) and Aldebaran, Dixie was made uneasy because this sighting appeared to make the location of the *Bedford* actually some *twenty-eight* miles off the dead-reckoning.

Dixie considered that he had made a faulty observation, due to a poor horizon, and dismissed such a large variation as 'unreliable' but, at 0445, land was sighted once more and immediately ahead of the ship! Dixie was alarmed, and immediately ordered a change of course and duly sent the messenger back to notify Captain Fitzherbert of this. On receipt of this news, the Captain left his bed and began to make his way to the

---

7. A contemporary account published in the *Japan Weekly Chronicle* account quoted in *Poverty Bay Herald*, Volume XXXVII, No. 12269, 5 October 1910, p.7.

bridge to take control but, before he could reach it, events were taken out of his hands as the *Bedford* struck.

A routine change of watch had taken place a little earlier and the watch below were just turning into their hammocks and getting to sleep, when there came 'a grinding of plates' as *Bedford* ran at full tilt onto the Samarang rocks, off the south-eastern coast of Quelpart Island.[8] The area had been well charted and surveyed and there were lighthouses and navigation aids in place. Despite this, the Japanese Naval Attaché noted that the area was hazardous to shipping, along the line of tiny islets, shoals, and small rocks, and was particularly so due to the rough seas and treacherous unpredictable currents which often combined with the foggy weather which prevails at that time of year. In fact a Japanese merchantman, the *Tetenrei Maru*, had recently been wrecked in that area.[9]

'The shock was terrific,' reported the officer,

> but I did not realise at the moment what had happened until she struck the hidden rocks a second time. Then it was I was aware of floating through space, and I was stopped by the hard deck. When I got up I naturally made for the hatchway. Before I reached it a loud report with a hiss was heard. It was No. 1 boiler exploding and this is what killed the 18 men.

It was conjectured that, had the accident occurred during the working hours of the day, many of the men would doubtless have received severe injuries by being thrown down. As it was, although the messdecks were covered by escaping steam and soot, no additional casualties were sustained apart from the victims of the flooded stokehold.

Up on the bridge Dixie immediately ordered 'Stop all engines', while the Captain, having just reached the bottom of the ladder leading to the bridge, ordered 'Collision Stations'. A gash initially thought to be some thirty feet (9.1440m) long by fifteen feet (4.572m) deep had opened up. Four bulkheads had been badly damaged. The watertight doors were all closed to stem the inrush of water and the surviving ship's crew turned out promptly and mustered on the deck without panic and waited patiently for further orders. After an inspection below, the order was given 'Lash and stow hammocks' which indicated that the ship was in no immediate danger of foundering. After searching below the *Bedford*'s chief engineer reported that fifteen

---

8. Also known as 'Jeju' or 'Jejudo' or 'Cheju Island' and situated sixty miles south-east of Cape Providence, the most southerly tip of the Korean peninsula in the Straits of Korea which connect the Sea of Japan and the Yellow Sea. Korea at that date had just been annexed by Japan and the island initially became the *Jeju Myeon* under their rule. The Samarang rocks, far from being 'unknown' were well recognised, and had been so for many years, so much so that a British warship had been named after them, HMS *Samarang*, which, under the command of Captain (later Admiral) Edward Belcher, had conducted extensive surveys of the Korean coastline between 1843 and 1846.

9. Report of the wrecking of HMS *Bedford*, articles in *The Times* (London), 23 and 24 August 1910.

men working in No. 1 boiler room were missing, either killed outright or drowned by the inrush of water, and this loss tally was later increased to eighteen when the bodies of three seamen who had been working as coal trimmers were also found. Only one man, an unidentified engine room artificer, from the forward boiler room survived, being miraculously swept upward by the flood of water to the top of the chamber where he just managed to grab hold of a grating and then somehow pulled himself clear through a hatchway.

Fitzherbert ordered that a signal be immediately sent to the rest of the squadron astern by searchlight but only one signal was sent before all power failed. It was still dark as all lights had gone out when all the machinery abruptly ceased functioning and the ship's company awaited the coming of dawn to further assess their damage.

It was stated later that this loss of function was providential for, had the natural reaction of reversing the ship's engines to back off the rocks been attempted, with her bottom ripped out she would have probably sunk like a stone in deep water. It later transpired that *Bedford* had a rent 140 feet (42.672m) long in her hull with a pinnacle of rock in No. 1 engine room 18 feet (5.484m) high. As it was *Bedford* remained firmly pinned to the reef by this. Thus the ship bumped and ground on the rocks with the motion of the waves adding to the existing damage, and the ship's boats were lowered by hand in readiness for the wreck to be abandoned and valuable gear began to be salvaged. Meanwhile, fortunately, the rest of the squadron, in the order *Minotaur,* who was still astern of *Bedford, Kent* and *Monmouth* managed to avoid her fate. The *Minotaur* was alerted to the danger by arc lamp in time and avoided following *Bedford* aground, and the flagship led the rest of the squadron all out to sea and safety. It later transpired that the *Kent* had obtained a 'fix' as early as 0500 on the 21st and from it had discovered a northerly set, duly advising the other ships of this; but it would appear that little importance was attached to her warning.

At first light *Minotaur* and *Monmouth* returned and stood in as close as deemed safe to the reef to render assistance and the bulk of the *Bedford*'s crew were ferried aboard them. The *Kent* had meanwhile been sent on to Nagasaki to report to the Admiralty representative there and arrange for *Bedford*'s salvage. The bulk of the ship's officers and men were evacuated by the steamer *Nubia* and the E and A steamer *St Albans*, on Saturday and taken to Nagasaki.[10] Ashore the officers said very little, the local press reporting that they maintained 'a discreet silence pending the inevitable court-martial'.

The Monarch, a dying King Edward VII, was at Balmoral when the news came in and his equerry-in-waiting despatched a telegram in which the monarch stated he deeply regretted hearing of the loss of HMS *Bedford* and that he 'wishes to express his sincere sympathy with the relatives and friends of those who have perished. His Majesty desires to be kept informed of further particulars.' On 23 August the Lord Lieutenant of Bedfordshire despatched a telegram to the Admiralty which read:

10. A contemporary account published in the *Japan Weekly Chronicle* account quoted in *Manawatu Standard*, Volume XLI, No. 6 October 1910, p.2.

County of Bedford desires to express its deep regret at the accident to H.M.S. *Bedford* and also its sympathy with the relatives and friends of those whose lives have been lost. The Lord Lieutenant is anxious for further information.

On 23 August *The Times* recorded that Miss Agnes Weston, the well-known philanthropist who established the Royal Sailors' Rests[11] at Portsmouth and subsequently other naval bases, was on record as taking steps to afford 'early relief to the widows and other dependants'.[12] When all the victims' names became known they were also assisted by the Mayor of Portsmouth's special fund which had been set up in the wake of the loss of the protected cruiser *Gladiator* (Captain Walter Lumsden) and destroyer *Tiger* (Lieutenant Commander William Edmund Middleton) in separate collisions, both disasters having occurred in April 1908.[13]

The two armoured cruisers remained in the vicinity of the wreck until 25 August when an hour-long ceremony was held for the *Bedford*'s lost crew members. The *Monmouth* steamed slowly by the wreck before herself steaming to Nagasaki, with the surviving *Bedford* crew members assembled aft while their ship's chaplain, the Reverend William Herbert Maundrell, conducted the service, which included the singing of the hymns 'Rock of Ages' and 'Abide with Me'. Three volleys of rifle fire were discharged and Royal Marine buglers sounded 'The Last Post'.

After detailed inspection by the Commander-in-Chief, China Station, Vice-Admiral Alfred Leigh Winsloe, who had recently taken over that post from Vice-Admiral Sir Hedworth Meux, the *Bedford* herself was deemed beyond salvage or reclamation. Winsloe recorded that *Bedford* had 'an enormous gash' along her starboard side, about 30feet (9.1440m) wide and about 10 to 15feet (3.045 to 4.572m) wide, also another, smaller hole in the forward boiler room and with at least four of her bulkheads damaged 'very badly' and was lying heavily on her keel on the reef. While aboard the *Minotaur* the Admiral informed Their Lordships on 31 August that in his opinion the *Bedford*'s salvage would extend over many months and be at the mercy of the weather.[14] Vice-Admiral Winsloe singled out for special commendation the work of Gunner Fred J. Luscomb from the *Kent*, who was in charge of the diving parties, for

11. Universally and fondly known throughout the fleet as 'Aggie Weston's'.

12. Wintz, Sophie Gertrude, *Miss Weston's Life and Work among our Sailors*, London, *orig.* 1894, new edition HardPress Publishing, 2012.

13. The full alphabetical list of the *Bedford*'s casualties was: Andrews, Alfred Percy, Stoker First Class; Calam, James Henry, Stoker First Class; Cook, William, Stoker First Class; Crust, Henry James, Able Seaman; Eastwood, Arthur Richard Austin, Stoker First Class; Ferguson, Colin, Leading Stoker First Class; Fogarty, John Thomas, Stoker First Class; Fovargue, George, Stoker First Class; Goodall, George William, Stoker First Class; Hart, John, Chief Stoker; James, Allan, Engine Room Artificer; Lill, Walter, Stoker First Class; McDowell, Andrew, Stoker First Class, McElligott, William George, Stoker First Class; McKittrick, John, Stoker First Class; Taylor, William Horner, Stoker Petty Officer; White, Thomas, Able Seaman; Wilson, John, Leading Stoker.

14. Admiralty Report, The Grounding of HMS *Bedford*, ADM116/1118, National Archives, Kew, London.

his work during salvage attempts.[15] In the end, the Hong Kong steamer *Yunnan* and her crew were chartered to salvage what could be saved, but even that was costing £60 per day! Among the items salved were the *Bedford*'s two steam-boats. Overseeing the Chinese operation were six of *Bedford*'s crew, including the ship's carpenter, gunner and artificer engineer with three storekeepers.

The ship herself was, in truth, a total write-off, even with the full resources of the China Fleet and the willing help of the Japanese Dockyard at Sasebo under Admiral Dewa Shigeto aboard the armoured cruiser *Tokiwa* (Captain Mizumachi Hajime). In recognition of this fact, her wreck was sold, *in situ*, on 2 September to the Mitsubishi Company for demolition as salvage in the hope of raising about 20 per cent of its value. Work commenced on 10 October of the same year. All the armaments were taken out of the wreck, including two of the 6-inch guns taken aboard *Minotaur* as deck cargo and lashed to her decks. The rest of these main guns were embarked later by Japanese lighters. By far the majority of the ship's fittings were subsequently taken off by the Chinese and loaded aboard the China Steam Navigation Company steamer *Yunnan*, which sailed with them to Hong Kong with the remaining survivors of *Bedford*'s crew. The amount of equipment salvaged was enormous and included thirteen torpedoes and associated gear, range clocks, yards of cables, eight searchlights, all the wireless telegraphy (W/T) equipment and instruments, all the fire-control instruments, two range-finders, fifty-six coal trolleys, all eight 12-pounders and the three 3-pounder guns, plus two Maxim machine guns, gun sights, small arms – rifles, pistols, swords, bayonets and (in 1910) cutlasses! Locusts would have been hard-pressed after the Chinese had finished. In total almost 300 tons of stores and equipment were removed. The subsequent scrap value of *Bedford* amounted to a mere £3,000.

The *Bedford* was quickly replaced in the China Squadron by the brand-new 4,800 ton *Bristol*-class light cruiser *Newcastle* (Captain George Percy Edward Hunt) which arrived on station in February 1911. On 14 November, in a court martial held aboard the battleship *Bulwark* (Captain George Price Webley Hope) at Sheerness, both Fitzherbert and Dixie being examined on successive days, intensive questioning was made of the course selected and how the speeds of the ships had been calculated. During the examination of Dixie the same line was taken. Dixie's defence was that he and the Captain had agreed between them to pass twenty miles to the west of Ross Island, there being greater sea-room there and, with no light on the island itself, this course was considered the safer option. The eastern alternative was the more direct line, but deemed unsafe at night and at high speed. The speed of the *Bedford* he estimated from the engine revolutions but confessed he had difficulty assessing the currents.

The verdicts were delivered on the 16th. The conclusion drawn was that the *Bedford* was lost due to the failure to take account of the strong currents in the area, and the effect on speed of *Bedford*'s clean, barnacle-free hull. Captain Fitzherbert was found

---

15. McBride, Keith, 'The Wreck of HMS *Bedford*', article in *Warship*, Vol XII, No. 48, 1988, London, Conway Maritime Press.

guilty of negligence in that he had caused his command 'to be stranded'. He was severely reprimanded and dismissed his ship, HMS *Pembroke*, to which he had been seconded following his return to England.[16]

Lieutenant Dixie the court subsequently found 'not guilty' on the charge of negligence. He was, however, found 'guilty of default, whereby the ship was stranded' and on this Dixie was sentenced to be dismissed his ship.[17] Dixie went on to attain the rank of lieutenant-commander and became a navigational instructor, but died at an early age from an illness while aboard the harbour depot ship HMS *Crescent* (the former battleship *Glory*) at Rosyth on 16 May 1920. He was buried at Leith War Cemetery, Edinburgh.[18]

It later transpired that the courses selected were, in fact, sound, but that two different Admiralty publications gave different directions and rates for the currents to be encountered there. The south-easterly wind and strong current took them north-west into danger. Quite how Their Lordships squared the two sets of totally different information that their names were appended to has never been revealed.

The loss of the *Bedford* did not affect Captain Fitzherbert's career. He joined HMS *President* as Captain-Superintendent Ships Building by Contract, Clyde District, and commanded the battleship *Colossus* at the start of the First World War, later being made Commander-in-Chief of the Cape of Good Hope Station in May 1918, not finally retiring as a full Admiral until 1925. He was made 13th Baron Stafford in 1932 and died in 1941 at the age of 77.

There is a shield in the corner of the north clerestory of the Nore Memorial Chapel[19] as a memorial to those who lost their lives when HMS *Bedford* ran aground.

---

16. *Nelson Evening Mail*, Vol XLV, 17 November 1910, p.5.
17. Report in *Sydney Morning Herald*, datelined London 15 November 1910.
18. Articles in *The Times*, 15 to 19 November 1940. See also ADM 197.45/4, National Archives, Kew, London.
19. St George's Church, HMS *Pembroke*, had its chancel set aside as a memorial to the sailors of Chatham Port Division, and was named as the Nore Memorial Chapel on 12 February 1975.

Chapter 11

Sole Survivor

The *Narborough & Opal*, 12 January 1918

The last quarter of the nineteenth-century saw a whole new type of Navy emerge from almost fifty years of experimentation. At the Battle of Trafalgar in 1805 great four-decker ships of the line, with tier upon tier of trucked cannon, had exchanged close-range broadsides at point-blank range as they had done in the centuries before. The Navy was still building such wooden-walls as late as 1858 to 1860 when the 1st-rates *Howe*, *Prince of Wales*, *Victoria* and *Windsor Castle* were all put afloat. For all intents and purposes these were but bigger versions of Lord Nelson's flagship, *Victory*; of twice the tonnage certainly and with 130 guns but, with their black-and-white hulls, buff upperworks, multiple gun ports and full sets of masts and rigging, from a distance still pretty obvious descendants of forebears like the *Coronation* of 1690 and indeed even of King Henry's great ship the *Henry Grace à Dieu*[1] of 1514. In 1860 then, the fleet was composed of warships that were larger but essentially the same as before. Within thirty years all this had been swept away. Long before the new millennium arrived the ships that made up the Royal Navy would have been totally unrecognisable to Nelson and the men he led.

Engine-driven paddle-wheels supplemented sails, and steam became first a supplement, then the principal and finally the sole means of motive power. Iron sheathing gave way to hardened-steel construction for sides and decks. Guns became huge and more mobile, moving at first on inset iron traverses inlaid into the decks so they could fire from different ports, then becoming encased in armoured barbettes and being raised and lowered. The barbettes were given hoods or shields and became known as turrets. The range at which battleships now fired upon each other increased steadily from yards to miles. Scouting, hitherto the preserve of the fast frigate, became the role for the cruiser type of vessel. Torpedoes and mines became increasingly sophisticated underwater threats to the hitherto dominance of the battleship. To deliver mass torpedo attacks against fleets, a small carrying vessel, the torpedo-boat, was introduced by Britain's potential enemies, France and Russia. To counter this threat a new type of warship was introduced in the last decade of Victoria's reign, the torpedo-boat destroyer (TBD), a term that quickly became shortened to destroyer. They operated in

---

1. Affectionately dubbed by the sailors and his subjects alike, the *Great Harry*. Her other 'nicknames' included *Henry Imperial*, *Imperial Carrack* and *Great Carrack*.

flotillas of twenty led by a small cruiser and were larger and faster than their intended prey. As they grew in size, the destroyers also took over the torpedo-boat's function and added to it their own myriad uses, which grew into fleet escort, light strike forces, anti-submarine screening, minelaying and the like. They became ubiquitous and with the outbreak of the Great War huge numbers were required, and built.[2]

There were never sufficient destroyers for all the duties required of them but by far the elite were those attached to the Grand Fleet, more than a hundred at a time.[3] Unlike the German High Seas Fleet, which only sortied on rare occasions and scurried back to port at the earliest opportunity if challenged, the destroyers of the Grand Fleet were expected to screen their big sisters on almost weekly sweeps to dominate the North Sea, and in every type of weather. Based at Scapa Flow in the Orkney Islands, and then, later, the Firth of Forth, they encountered every type of bad weather possible. The seas off the North Cape were very unpredictable and the huge seas developed were so powerful that on one occasion a battleship's bridge was washed away by them.[4]

Not surprisingly there were some losses among such frail little craft as destroyers, operating in such terrible conditions. When the destroyer type had first appeared on the naval scene, one of the leading builders, John Isaac Thornycroft, pointed out the fact that destroyers were 'necessarily quick rollers from their small size'. He also pointed out that their:

---

2. Smith, Peter Charles Horstead, *Hard Lying: The Birth of the Destroyer 1893–1913*, 1971, London, William Kimber. In the Royal Navy the designation TBD was not officially abandoned until 1922.

3. Their zenith, and incidentally also that of the Royal Navy, was at the surrender of the German High Seas Fleet. On the afternoon of Thursday 21 November 1918, there was assembled a record number of 121 British destroyers to take the surrender of the dirty and unkempt Imperial German High Seas Fleet, with their self-appointed 'delegates' of the Workmen's and Soldiers' Council as a rotten core in their midst, that steamed across the North Sea to a rendezvous fifty miles east of May Island for the final time. This was the appropriately-named Operation Z.Z. Commodore Hugh Justin Tweedie, embarked in the light cruiser *Castor*, wrote that '*Castor* was eventually in the proud position of leading 170 Destroyers to an anchorage, and the fact that 49 surrendered Germans formed the centre of that great assembly is a record which will probably never be surpassed ...'. See -H.M.S. *Castor: Grand Fleet Destroyer Flotillas 1915–1918; Souvenir of a War Commission*, f/p 14. 1919: Glasgow. Private Circulation.

4. This was HMS *Albemarle* (Captain Raymond Andrew Nugent), a battleship of the *Duncan* class and a sister of the ill-fated *Montagu*. While serving with the Grand Fleet on 11 November 1915, and 'deeply-laden with ammunition', she encountered heavy seas in the Pentland Firth off Dunnet Head while steaming at sixteen knots. She was swamped by two successive waves which swept in to a height just below her lower top on her foremast, demolishing her charthouse and sweeping away her bridge structure and part of her conning tower while filling the fore-turret with water. Several officers, petty officers and men were drowned and Nugent was washed onto the upper deck, but survived, while many others were badly injured. See Scimgeour, Alexander, *Scimgeour's Small Scribling Diary: 1914–1916*, p.231, 2008, London, Conway Maritime, Anova Books Ltd.

righting moment, as shown from the stability curve, is a maximum at 46° and vanishes at 95°. There is a noticeable change in the stability conditions. At full speed the vessel appears to be more tender, and although this impression is, perhaps, chiefly due to the greater heeling effect of small movements of the helm at high speed, the stability is actually reduced, as compared with the normal still-water condition. The change in the water-line, which falls amidships and rises at the finer parts of the vessel, at the stem and stern, reduces the Metacentric height.[5]

So they were always 'tender' ships and prone to capsizing. When the extra equipment required by war was added to their slender hulls, already over-burdened with guns, torpedoes and other apparatus, great care was necessary.

Under the pen name 'Taffrail' Captain Henry Taprell Dorling, who commanded the destroyers *Murray* and *Telemachus*, devoted a whole chapter of his wonderful book *Endless Story* to how destroyers were affected by storms and tempests, in both peace and war.[6] Among the destroyers that succumbed to the weather rather than enemy action during the First World War were the *Success* (Lieutenant William Pennefather), wrecked off Fifeness in December 1914, *Erne* (Lieutenant-Commander John Palmer Landon), wrecked off Rattray Head in February 1915, *Goldfinch* (Lieutenant-Commander Reginald Guy Stone), wrecked off the Orkney Islands in February 1915, *Louis* (Lieutenant-Commander Harold Dallas Adair-Hall), wrecked in Suvla Bay in October 1915, *Racoon* (Lieutenant George Levack Mackay Napier) lost with all hands off Donegal in January 1918, and *Pincher* (Lieutenant Patrick Wylie Rose Weir) wrecked on the Seven Stones in July 1918.

But it was Sir Lewis Richie, writing as 'Bartimeus', who first told, in the guise of fiction, the story of the worst such disaster of the First World War.[7]

By the outbreak of the Great War in August 1914, British destroyer design had settled down to a standard pattern. The ships were around 900–1,000 tonners, oil-fired, with a design speed of 34 knots, three-funnelled and armed with three single QF 4-inch guns, forward, amidships and aft, a pair of 2-pounder guns and four 21-inch torpedo tubes in two pairs. In wartime they had crews of about 120 officers and men. There were improvements and variations on this theme but, generally, this was the basis of destroyer construction, from the L class of 1914 through the M Class (M, N,

5. Thornycroft, John Isaac FRS, 'On Torpedo-Boat Destroyers', Lecture delivered at The Royal United Services Institution, London, on Friday 17 May 1895 and printed in *The Journal*, Vol. XXXIX, No. 211, September 1895.

6. Dorling, Captain Henry Taprell, DSO RN ('Taffrail'), *Endless Story: Being an Account of the work of the Destroyers, Flotilla-Leaders, Torpedo-Boats and Patrol Boats in the Great War*, 1931, London, Hodder & Stoughton.

7. Ritchie, Captain Sir Lewis Anselmo, KCVO, *The Navy Eternal: Which is The Navy-that-floats, The Navy-that-flies and The Navy-under-the-sea*, 1918, London, Hodder & Stoughton. I included the relevant Chapter, entitled *The Survivor*, in my anthology *Destroyer Action*, 1974, London, William Kimber.

O & P names) to the S Class (S, T & U names) for the first three years of the war. Not until the arrival of the V–class Leaders of 1917, followed by the V and W classes that followed, did the pattern change.

Narborough and *Opal* were of the *Matchless* class, built under the War Emergency building programmes, of which there were five variants. They were built by John Brown at Clydebank and Doxford at Sunderland respectively, both being launched in 1915 and completed in 1916.

HMS *Narborough* was named to honour Sir John Narborough (1640 to 1686), who flew his flag afloat during the Second and Third Dutch Wars. She was the first ship to be so named. HMS *Opal* was the second ship to be so named.[8] Both these destroyers were 'chummy ships' that had fought at the Battle of Jutland in 1916 and had subsequently been transferred to the 12th Flotilla.

One current source, with all the inaccurate and shallow authority such sites seem to have, asserts that 'HMS *Opal* collided with another British destroyer, HMS *Narborough*, at Scapa Flow during a snow storm'.[9] This is incorrect on two counts: there was no 'collision', nor did the incident occur 'at Scapa Flow'. If it had there would not have been such a dreadful loss of life, nor would a prolonged search have been required. A rather more informed account had previously been offered up by Keith Donald McBride.[10]

Let us here examine in greater depth exactly what actually took place. On Saturday 12 January 1918 two destroyers of the 12th Destroyer Flotilla, *Opal* (Lieutenant-Commander Charles Caesar de Merindol Malan) and *Narborough* (Lieutenant Edmund Mansel Bowley), sailed from Scapa Flow to rendezvous with the scout cruiser *Boadicea* (Captain Edwin Harold Edwards) at sea, in order to conduct a Dark Night Patrol. Dark Night Patrols (DNPs) were a standard patrol procedure whose *modus operandi* was described by one veteran thus: 'No lights burning anywhere, steaming lights or anything. And you just went by, following a blue light on the ship ahead of you.'[11] Another veteran, British this time, described them thus: 'Every night when there was no moon a light cruiser and two destroyers left Rosyth two hours before sunset and cruised out to the eastward of the May Island, and returned to coal two hours after sunrise. This was to guard against mine–laying off the port.' He also stated that being selected to participate in these patrols as akin to being 'the sacrificial lamb'.[12] These patrols off Scapa at this time also had as their main purpose intercepting

---

8. The first Royal Navy ship of this name was a corvette of 1875, which had been sold out of service in 1891.

9. www.traffordwardead.co./uk

10. McBride, Keith Donald, *The Mariner's Mirror,* Vol. 85, No.2, pp.212–15, May 1999, London, The Society for Nautical Research, Portsmouth.

11. Oral History Recording, S01301, *Australian Veterans of The Great War History Project.* Interview of Mr Alistair Thomson, HMAS *Sydney*, by William Bridgeman on 1 May 1983, Williamstown, Melbourne.

12. See King-Hall, Commander Stephen Richard, *A Naval Lieutenant,* 1919, London, Methuen. (later republished as *A North Sea Diary: 1914–1918,* Newnes.

or deterring fast German minelayers from operating off the Grand Fleet's bases on moonless nights. The patrols were almost completely successful in that, although no enemy minelayers were encountered, the only successful mine-lay by the Germans had been conducted by the *Berlin* (*Kapitän zur See* Hans Pfundheller) north-west of the entrance to Lough Swilly in 1914. This converted liner had laid mines off Tory Island on 23 October into which a battle squadron on a gunnery exercise unwittingly sailed four days later. The battleship *Audacious* (Captain Cecil Frederick Dampier), while turning, struck a mine on her port side and began taking on water which the engine-room bulkheads failed to contain. After prolonged efforts at salvage, her crew were taken off, she capsized, B magazine eventually detonated and she sank. This loss took place despite the fact that two merchant ships had been mined and sunk in the same area the day before but the Admiralty had not been notified! The White Star Liner *Olympic* (Captain Herbert James Haddock RNR), packed full of Americans, was in the same area but managed to escape hitting any mines. This was a serious blow to the Grand Fleet's strength and exactly the type of attrition Germany had hoped for. This success was never repeated but made a deep impression, hence the maintaining of DNP patrols throughout the rest of hostilities.

Boadicea had sailed at 1430. When the two destroyers first put to sea conditions were very favourable, with the wind from the north-east, the sky clear and the barometer low but steady. There was little indication of what was in store. Malan had previous first-hand knowledge of torpedo-craft operations, having commanded the destroyers *Mallard* and *Waveney*, and Torpedo Boat *30*, as well as the patrol boat *P-29*, but had not much experience of the waters off the Orkney Islands and the vagaries of their treacherous currents and tidal shifts. He had commanded the *P-29* in southern waters, first at The Nore and then at Portsmouth Command, before handing her over to Lieutenant John Douglas Harvey on 17 August 1971. Bowley was also very new to command, having taken over the *Narborough* when her previous captain, Lieutenant-Commander Ralph Wilmot Wilkinson, had been appointed to the new destroyer *Verulam* on 21 November 1917.

The two destroyers met the *Boadicea*[13] at 1535 some 2.4 miles, 13 degrees from the Pentland Skerries, and the little squadron then steamed at 16 knots, on a course N76E,

---

13. *Boadicea* was the name ship of a class of small Scout cruisers that were designed specifically as leaders of the then existing destroyer flotillas by providing Captain (D) with a fast-enough command ship. At the time they were designed, the destroyers they were to lead were either rated as 27-knotters or 30-knotters, and the contemporary *River* class were even slower, but as these speeds were rarely reached in normal sea conditions, the design speed of the *Boadiceas* was, at 25-knots, considered to be sufficient. Later, newer and larger destroyers pushed speeds up by between ten to twelve knots and their place was taken by specifically enlarged destroyers, Flotilla Leaders, whereupon some, including *Boadicea* herself, were converted into minelaying cruisers, but, in January 1918, she was still performing patrol duties in her original capacity. At 3,400 tons displacement, however, the Scouts could keep to sea when their flock could not, as this incident highlighted.

with the destroyers screening while a zig-zag course was being steered. The weather was still fine with the barometer steady.

By 1628 the Copinsay Lighthouse bore N40W (Mag), with Burgh Head N19W (Mag) and Old Head S75" (Mag). By this time the weather was rapidly deteriorating with a rising south-easterly wind and a heavy easterly swell, which forced the ships to reduce speed to 15 knots and five minutes later they adopted a straight course. Even so, by 1705 the seas were such that they were breaking over the destroyers' forecastles and the speed of the squadron was again reduced to just 12 knots. A dead-reckoning position was taken indicating they were in 58° 55′N, 2° 17′ W and course was altered to S73E (Mag) in order to approach their allocated patrol position from the northern side. The destroyers were ordered to take up positions astern of *Boadicea*.

Soon the going became increasingly tough for the two little ships, with frequent blinding snow squalls that made keeping in touch almost impossible and, at 1805, another reduction in speed was ordered, down to just 10 knots. The wind increased in intensity to Force 5 with a rapidly rising sea. It became clear that the destroyers could not contribute much in such conditions and so, at 1822, Captain Edwards reported by W/T that he had decided to send them both back to base and to continue patrolling alone. The two destroyers were actually detached from *Boadicea* in position 58° 55′N, 1° 48 W, at 1830 and steered to the westward.

Back at Scapa the weather was still clear, but heavy snow began falling at 2000 although the wind itself was light in the anchorage until 0700 the following morning. However, farther east and out at sea there existed a very different picture. Heavy snow was reported in the neighbourhood of the Pentland Skerries at 1945 and the fog signal there was started up at 1953 and continued sounding throughout the whole night. The fog signal at Duncansby Head was also started up at 2015. At Copinsay the blizzard hit around 2010 and this fog signal was also started up; however, the pipes were frozen up and, after sounding but intermittently for a period, the system stopped totally at 2140 and was not got going again until 2235.

Ten minutes after parting company with *Boadicea*, Malan signalled by radio asking that shore lights of Group I be shown between 2020 until 2230 and those of Group II be shown from 2100 to 2300. At 1853 *Opal* signalled to her Captain (D) aboard the flotilla leader *Valhalla* (Commodore Theodore Evelyn Johnstone Bigg) that her position at 1830 was 58° 55′N, 1° 46′W, steering N88W and her speed was thirteen knots. At 1905 progress was such that she advised by radio that the destroyers' ETA was 2000. But visibility continued to worsen, and the frequent 'white-outs' were becoming almost continuous. In such conditions Malan realised that visual sightings were insufficient and, at 1955 he requested by radio that fog signals also be sounded in Groups I and II, citing as the reason 'blinding snow'. The *Opal* and *Narborough* were not alone in this respect; other patrols and convoy escorts were reporting terrible conditions as the storm continued to worsen. The *Ophelia* (Commander Hamilton Coclough Allen) radioed in that she was at the Switha boom, but could not actually see it, while the two convoys at sea in the area had to abandon their prescribed routes in order to also seek some respite. At 1955 *Opal* signalled to Rear-Admiral, Scapa, 'Acknowledge. Request lights in groups 1 and 2 until no longer required.'

The *Boadicea* herself stuck it out and continued her patrol to East magnetic in order to bring the sea broader on the bow. The patrol area had already been restricted in scope by the presence of two convoys, one northbound and one southbound, passing through the area. The scout continued to slow down to cope with worsening conditions, to just 8 knots at 1925, and at 1955 Edwards changed course to WSW. A signal timed at 1950 from SNOA[14] was received giving him discretion to return to base if the weather was unsuitable and at 2000 she did turn back, increasing speed to 12 knots at 2030 steering westward. *Boadicea* sighted the Copinsay light at 2210 and ten minutes later an approximate fix placed her in 58° 52′.30″N, 2° 29′.30″W, which was about five-and-a-half miles 333° from the dead-reckoning position. This was no mean difference and Edwards altered course to S56W and at 2250 was able to take her position by the Copinsay and Pentland Skerries lights in 58° 46′ 50″N, 2° 36′ 50″W, altering course to S78W for Pentland Skerries. This latter position was six-and-a-half miles 4 degrees from the dead reckoning position worked up to the same time. A force 7 wind still blew from the south-east with very heavy seas, while visibility varied between seven miles between blizzards. Meanwhile snatches of signals were received from the *Narborough* at 2108 and from the *Opal* at 2124. *Boadicea* passed the Pentland Skerries at 2335 meeting a very heavy snowstorm which persisted for more than three hours but she made it safely home.[15] A clue as to what had befallen the two destroyers was that Captain Edwards discovered that *Boadicea* had been set 330°, five-and-a-half miles, between 1628 and 2200.

Around this time a final signal from *Opal* to Longhope, Pass to Commodore (F) and Rear Admiral, Scapa, was taken in stating 'have run aground'; the time of origin seemed to be 2117 or 2127 or 2120, but there was only time for part of her position to be broadcast before all communication abruptly ceased. Several more fragmentary radio reports, in plain language, one apparently from the *Narborough*, were taken in but these were so garbled they could not be understood save possibly for the word 'Pentland'. After studying the signals her position appeared to be 58° 55′N, 2°.41W. Old Head directional station reported the last bearing for *Opal* was 195° at 2120, which read as the reciprocal 15°, which almost indicated her onshore position. Comparing these reports and the experience of *Boadicea*, it appears probable that *Opal* and *Narborough* had not accounted for the northerly set of the tide in their navigational calculations.

Once these signals were received at Scapa, both tugs and destroyers were put at instant notice to steam to render assistance, but no ships were actually despatched

---

14. SNOA =Senior Naval Office Afloat.
15. It is of interest to note that, on 15 December 1914, in the waters of the Pentland Firth, *Boadicea* herself, while serving with the 2nd Battle Squadron and under the command of Captain Louis Charles Stirling Woollcombe, had had her bridge swept away and several of her crew drowned after encountering severe weather and was so damaged that she had to return to harbour for repairs. Her sister ship *Blanche* (Captain Richard Hyde) was also damaged, although to a lesser degree, at the same time.

at this time because the heavy driving snow made it 'impossible to move any vessels until shortly after 0700 on Sunday'. By that time a heavy northerly gale had set in with thick snow squalls interspersed with moderately clear intervals. At 0700 the tug *Alliance* (Temporary-Engineer-Sub-Lieutenant (A) Charles John Crabbe RNR)[16] and the trawler *Diana* (Skipper Fred Savage RNR)[17] sailed to search in the vicinity of the Pentland Skerries, South Ronaldshay and Duncansby Head and, shortly after this, the Scapa minesweeping trawlers were sent to search in the Pentland Firth. The sea searches were to be supplemented by coast-watching patrols ashore on the Orkneys at first light, but deep snow drifts rendered these shore searches ineffective.

The two minesweeping flotillas, the 1st and 2nd, had anchored in Kirkwall by Saturday evening and they had orders to conduct their sweeping operations in the Eastern Channel on Sunday the 13th. On 0830 that morning they reported that minesweeping was 'impracticable' due to the 'Very heavy, south-easterly swell' and that they were returning to base. The senior officer on the flotillas was therefore ordered to join in the hunt by detaching four of his ships, two of which were to cover the area from Lowther Rock to Old Head and the eastern coast of Ronaldshay, while the other two covered the area from Duncansby Head to Ness Head. They could find no traces of wreckage along the coast but, at 1430, the *Myrtle* (Lieutenant Commander Basil Richard Brooke DSO)[18] fished out of the sea an officer's washstand, marked 'Sub Lieutenant HMS *Narborough*' about half a mile south of the Pentland Skerries.[19] By Monday the 14th the weather had turned fine and a much closer inspection of the eastern coastline of South Ronaldshay was possible and *Castor* and four destroyers were despatched. At around 0930 that morning the wreckage of both ships was located in Wind Wick Bay.

The subsequent signals say it all.[20]

AC.1 (Admiral Commanding 1st Battle Squadron) to C-in-C. 13/1/18. 0139.
Opal returning from Eastern patrol reported at 2127 today, Saturday, that she was ashore but gave no position. No further W/T communication has been obtained with her, nor any communication with *Narbrough* (sic)[21] which is presumably in company

---

16. A *Rover*-class Admiralty tug, built by Chatham Dockyard in 1910, of 615 tons, with an overall length of 153 feet, beam of 29 feet, draught of 12 feet and a speed of 11 knots. She was acting as tender to the *Cyclops* at this time.

17. A hired trawler used for minesweeping, of 311 GRT, built in 1906, armed with a single 12-pounder gun.

18. A 1,200-ton *Flower*-class minesweeping sloop, built by Lobitz, Sunderland in 1915, with an overall length of 262 feet, a beam of 33 feet and a draught of 11 feet, with a speed of 16.5 knots and two 4.7-inch guns. She was later lost when mined in the Gulf of Finland in July 1919.

19. This would have been the property of Sub-Lieutenant Eric Oloff De Wet DSC MiD.

20. ADM 137/3726, dated 3 March 1918. Admiralty E1260. 198/H.F.0021/76. Report of Court of Enquiry held into loss of HMS *Opal* and HMS *Narborough* on 12 January, 1918.

21. Throughout the signal exchanges the *Narborough* is cited as *Narbrough*. And not only here, but, oddly enough, in the records held at the National Maritime Museum and even some Navy Lists also.

with her. Thick snow prevents vessels going out to search at present. Tugs and destroyers ready to proceed directly weather clears. Flat calm inside Flow (2342)

AC.1st BS to C-in-C. 13/1/18. 0958.
Wind N.W., 5 to 7, snowy, visibility quarter to half mile. Tugs are searching for *Opal* and *Narbrough* (1930).

AC.1st BS to C-in-C. 1008.
PRIORITY. No news of *Opal* or *Narbrough*. Snow too thick throughout night for tugs or destroyers to go out, wind inside Flow N.W. 1 up to 0700. Now fresh from NNW, weather clearing, vessels going out.

AC.1st BS to C-in-C. 13/1/18. 1016.
PRIORITY. Two destroyers ashore near Pentland Skerries, request salvage vessel be sent.

AC.1st BS to C-in-C. 13/1/18. 1249.
No signs of *Opal* and *Narbrough* in vicinity of Pentland Skerries. Four sloops, available trawlers and tugs are search land to the North and South of Pentland Firth. Commodore (F) will remain at Base in *Castor* and use sloops to continue search.

Commodore (F)[22] to C-in-C. 13/1/18. 1525.
PRIORITY. *Opal* and *Narbrough* missing. Last signal received from *Opal* at 2121 on Saturday 12th Jan. as follows, begins: 'Have run aground'. No further communication from either ship. Search has been made in vicinity of Pentland Skerries, so far without success. Weather conditions very bad, heavy snow all night with Northerly gale.

AC.1 to C-in-C. 13/1/18. 1915–2030.
Following additional details in regard to disappearance of *Opal* and *Narbrough* are submitted. At 1830 on Saturday 12th January these two destroyers parted company from *Boadicea* in 50–55N 1–49 W to return to northern base owing to bad weather. Wind was SE strong. *Opal* gave this same position to *Valhalla*[23] at 1853 adding my course N 88 W 13 knots. At 2127 *Opal* reported have run aground. Nothing further that is intelligible was received from her. Endeavours are being made to make sense out of fragmentary signals that followed probably from *Narbrough*. *Boadicea* reports that she was set 5½ miles 333° between 1628 and 2220 when she made Copinshay. The destroyers must have experienced the same set and probably grounded between Old Head South Ronaldshay and Mull Head Deer Sound. The coast has been searched from Copinshay to Ness Head from the Sea and all coast Watches have been out. No wreckage has been seen on the coasts but dense snow squalls have prevented a close

22. Commodore commanding Grand Fleet Destroyer Flotillas.
23. Commander Theodore Evelyn Johnstone Bigg, Captain (D).

search from seaward and snowdrifts have hindered shore search. Floating wreckage was found this evening Sunday 1/2 mile to Southward of Pentland Skerries among it an Officer's washstand marked Sub-Lieutenant *Narbrough*.

A search seaward in Northern and Eastern Channel has been carried out by 1st and 2nd FSF with the destroyers *Mounsey*[24] and *Musketeer*[25] who arrived by eastern channel and *Peyton*[26] from Invergordon today Sunday and saw no wreckage. I fear there is no hope that either vessel is above water and little hope that there are any survivors. Search both afloat and ashore will be continued tomorrow Monday. The sound signals on Pentland Skerries and in Pentland Firth were working correctly from 2000 on Saturday 12th January, that on Copinshay was started at same time. At 2150 RA Scapa reported: Copinshay reports fog signal sounding but very erratic, stopping at times and has now stopped. It is possible it was stopped when the destroyers made the coast, this is being enquired into.

AC.1st BS to C-in-C. 13/1/18. 2200.

My 1000 and your 1306 and 1310, services of Commander Herbert Rivers Malet, RNR, and *Melita*[27] are not required as *Opal* and *Narbrough* must be presumed to have foundered.

ACO & S[28] to C-in-C. 13/1/18. 2240.

PRIORITY. Your 414 and 415. Pentland Skerries South and East side South Ronaldshay, Duncansby Hd. East side Stroma have been searched by AP Vessels and tugs. No sign of destroyers found. Search continuing south of Duncansby Head and East side of Orkneys, all lookouts and coast-watchers have been warned. Owing to heavy snow drifts little can be done from shore side.

---

24. Lieutenant Francis Worthington Craven.
25. Lieutenant John Mansel Porter.
26. Lieutenant-Commander Charles Lewis Maitland Makgill Crichton.
27. HMS *Melita* (Lieutenant John Edward Francis Gibney RNVR), was originally built as the 1st-class gunboat *Ringdove* in April 1889. Of 805 tons, with an overall length of 177 feet, beam of 31 feet and a draught of 11 feet, she had been armed with six 4-inch guns, and had a speed of 13 knots. At the end of her first service career she was handed over to the Coastguard Service in 1906 with just a single 4-inch gun retained. On outbreak of war she had served as an Examination Service vessel based at Queensferry in 1914–15. She was converted to a salvage vessel in November 1915 and renamed *Melita* the following month. After the war she was sold out of service and became the salvage ship *Telima*.
28. Admiral Commanding Orkney and Shetlands, Admiral Edward Errington Brook.

Admiral Rosyth[29] [to C-in-C 14/1/18. 0234
Melita has been recalled. Lieut. Gibney[30] has been directed to proceed to Aberdeen in connection with *Muskerry*[31] Admiralty has been informed.

AC.1 to C-in-C 14/1/18. 1103.
884. Wreckage of two destroyers reported in Windwick Bay 58 degrees 46 seconds N. 2°-0'-56" W.

AC.1. to C-in-C 14/1/18 1200.
Propose to assemble Court of Enquiry into loss of *Opal* and *Narbrough*. Rear Admiral William Nicholson President.[32] Do you approve? 1142.

C-in-C to A.C.I. 14/1/18. 1252.
Your 1142. Concur. 1252

AC.1 to C-in-C. 141/1/18. 1157. Eco.
885. Trawler has received one survivor from *Opal*.

1407. SNOAS to Com. F & ACO & S for information.
Search party cannot be sent overland. Land parties from the destroyers if sea permits. 1210.

1418. SNOA[33] to ACO & S
Following from Com.F. Consider that only men with local knowledge would be of any use for search parties. Men ashore were told to search. Dogs would probably be more useful than anything. Ends. What do you propose. 1415.

1617. ACO & S to SNOA

---

29. Admiral in Command Rosyth, Rear-Admiral Henry Harvey Bruce.
30. Lieutenant John Edward Francis Gibney RNVR, Assistant Salvage Officer. Gibney was discharged in 1919 but was recalled as a temporary lieutenant-commander on 27 November 1939 serving with the Admiralty Salvage Department in the Second World War assigned to HMS *President*.
31. *Muskerry* (Lieutenant-Commander Harold de Gallye Lamotte DSO) was a *Hunt*-class minesweeping sloop launched in November 1916 by Lobnitz & Co. at Renfrew. She was of 750 tons, had a length of 231 feet (70.40m), a beam of 28 feet (8.53m) and a draught of 7 feet (2.13m). She served with the 3rd Minesweeping Flotilla based at Granton on the Firth of Forth. She was scrapped in 1923.
32. Rear-Admiral William Coldingham Masters Nicholson, 1st Battle Squadron, with flag in the battleship *Emperor of India*.
33. Senior Naval Officer Afloat – Admiral Sir Frederick Charles Doveton Sturdee aboard the battleship *Resolution*, (Captain Brian Henry Fairbairn Barttelot) temporary flagship of 1st Battle Squadron.

Your 1415. Suggest that parties landed from ships endeavour to obtain local inhabitants as guides for searching operations. The ground is very rough and deep snow drifts make movements very difficult. 1506.

1640. RA *Cyclops*[34] to SNOAS

Following from APO. Both destroyers total wrecks awash at high water two 12pdr guns and two pom–poms and torpedo tubes of both wreck could be salved weather permitting. Search for survivors or bodies. None found. Nothing possible today owing to swell, returning to base 1400 ends. 1615.

1700. SNOAS to Com. F

Following received from RA Scapa. It is proposed to ask Procurator Fiscal to hold enquiries tomorrow Tuesday, at 1230 into the death of the two bodies brought to the base by HM Trawler *Michael Maloney* (Skipper James Calvert RNR).[35] Both bodies are being taken to *China*.[36] Submit that if this proposal is approved necessary warnings be given for attendance of witnesses. 1525 ends.

Request you will communicate with RA *Cyclops*[37] and arrange for necessary witnesses to attend. 1700.

1650. SNOAS to AC.4

Request you will arrange direct RA Douglas Nicholson, together with two Captains of 4th BS to hold Court of Enquiry into loss of destroyers *Opal* and *Narbrough* and will inform SNOAS names of Captains detailed. Papers will be forwarded as soon as possible probably tomorrow. 1630.

---

34. Surgeon Commander William Wallace Keir.
35. *Michael Maloney* was an Admiralty trawler of the standard *Castle* class (N. 3513). Built in May 1917 by Smiths Dock she was of 360 tons displacement, had a length of 125 feet (38.1m), a beam of 23 feet (7.01m) and a draught of 13 feet (3.96m) and had a speed of 10.5 knots, being armed with a single 12-pounder gun.
36. HMHS *China* was a former Peninsular & Orient Steam Navigation Company liner of 7,911 GRT, one of a class of five identical liners, which had been built by Harland & Wolff, Belfast, in 1896. She had a length of 500 feet (152m), a beam of 54 feet (16.56m) and a draught of 26 feet 9 inches (8.153m), and a speed of 18 knots. The SS *China* ran aground off Perim, Aden (now known as Mayyun, Yemen) in the Red Sea on 24 March 1898 and was later purchased by the Admiralty and re-modelled as a hospital ship (Hospital Ship No.6) by Messrs Lester & Perkins at the Royal Albert Dock in London. She served at Scapa Flow between August 1914 and February 1919.
37. *Cyclops* (Captain Charles Tibbits) was a liner laid down for the Indra Line Ltd as *Indrabarah*, but purchased while still on the stocks at Sir James Laing's at Sunderland in 1905 and launched as *Cyclops* in October the same year. She was commissioned into the Royal Navy as a Fleet Store ship on 5 November 1907 and was later converted into a submarine depot ship. She had an overall length of 476 feet (145m), a beam of 55 feet (16.8m) and a draught of 8 feet 3 inches (2.51m), being armed with two 4-inch guns and having a speed of 13 knots. She served with the Grand Fleet at Scapa from 1914 to 1919 and post-war served in the White Sea against the Bolsheviks and then right through the Second World War, being finally scrapped in July 1947.

1720. SNOAS to Comm. F

A Court of Enquiry will be held by RA Douglas Nicholson and two Captains of 4th BS on a date to be notified later into the loss of destroyers *Opal* and *Narbrough*. A report giving all information as to the duty on which these destroyers were employed with a copy of all signals bearing on the case and any remarks you may have to offer is to be sent to RA *Colossus* as early as practicable and copies forwarded to C .in C. and AC.1 BS 1715.

1750. SNOAS to AC.4

Request that Captain of *Boadicea* may be directed to report to RA *Colossus*[38] with copy to C.in.C and AC.1 BS (Admiral Commanding 1st Battle Squadron) all communications with which he is acquainted leading up to the loss of destroyers *Opal* and *Narbrough*. A copy of all signals bearing on the case should accompany the report. Also a chart showing track of *Boadicea* when on DNP on 12th and 13th January and any remarks that the Captain of *Boadicea* has to offer. Comm. F. has been directed to forward a report on the loss to RA *Colossus*. 1715. A *Submission* to that effect from Commander-in-Chief, Grand Fleet to Admiralty, dated 22 January 1918.

At 0920 on the morning of 14 January the destroyer *Peyton*, one of those searching for any signs, reported wreckage, and also a man ashore at the Clett of Crura, Winds of Wick, South Ronaldsay. Both destroyers had apparently run straight into the cliffs at Hesta Rock just north of Windwick Bay. Captain Crichton, Captain (D) of the 14th Destroyer Flotilla, reported that on sighting the man he closed to safe distance, lowered the ship's whaler and went to inspect the wreckage to firmly establish the identity of the ships. While doing so three trawlers arrived from the south and he gave them the position and the trawler *Michael Maloney* closed the position and sent a boat herself. The sea was calm but a heavy swell from the south east made any close examination 'difficult and dangerous'. The man ashore was seen to be sending a semaphore message to the ships and the trawler sent her boat in, which picked him up.[39] This survivor was of course Able Seaman William Sissons, (Po.J 16486) the second gunlayer on the midships 4–inch gun of the *Opal*. Sissons was subsequently transferred to the *Peyton* where he was given medical assistance for his exposure and his many cuts and bruises. The ship's surgeon also continually rubbed his feet and hands with snow in attempt to get circulation. Despite his severe condition Sissons proved quite capable enough to answer some questions and, in Crichton's words, he gave 'intelligent answers to all questions'. Crichton duly reported the gist of the interrogation as follows:

About 9.30 pm on Saturday, 12th January, HMS *Opal* and *Narbrough* were in company *Opal* leading. There was a thick blizzard on at the time and a heavy

---

38. Rear-Admiral Douglas Romilly Lothian Nicholson, 4th Battle Squadron, aboard the battleship *Colossus* (Captain Charles Pipton Beaty-Pownall) to which *Boadicea* was attached.
39. Signal from *Michael Maloney* to RA Scapa. 1615.

following sea. *Opal* struck heavily about three times and shortly after appeared to slide into deep water. Almost immediately after striking, *Opal* was pooped by the following sea which filled up her after part and carried away her funnels and mast. After apparently sliding into deeper water her fore part broke off at the break of the forecastle and the remainder foundered in about a quarter of an hour from striking.

Directly *Opal* who, Sissons states, had been sounding with sounding machine, struck, she blew three blasts on her siren which were answered by *Narbrough*. *Narbrough* appeared to pass *Opal* on the port quarter, strike heavily and heel over. Nothing more of *Narbrough* was seen by the survivor. He states that Captain and Sub-Lieutenant Henry Stavely Pilkington Shaw of *Opal* were on the bridge at the time of striking,[40] and that, after the ship striking, orders were given to abandon ship. He did not observe any boat manage to get away safely and states that the Carley floats were launched but owing to sea no one could remain on them. He swam ashore and reached a ledge, with crevices, well sheltered from the wind, with about 50 yards to walk about on. He kept himself alive with shellfish and snow, and at one time managed to scale the cliff to within a few feet of the top but fell back again.

He considers that men on deck before the midships gun-platform should have had some chance of saving themselves but can give no information as to anyone from *Narbrough*.

While this was being done Commodore Hugh Justin Tweedie had arrived on the scene aboard the *Castor* and had also assessed the situation. At 1045 Tweedie ordered *Peyton* to return to base and discharge Sissons to the Hospital Ship *China*. Sissons later recalled that once aboard the *China* he fell asleep for a solid thirty-six hours, the same period of time he had spent ashore. When he came round again, on 17 January, Sissons was again questioned 'under caution'. He gave clear, detailed answers to the questions put to him, much of which was as related to Crichton, but expanded on several points. Due to the bad conditions and cold the 'midships gun's crew were ordered to close up in the shelter around the sounding machine'. He described *Narborough*'s fate graphically:

When we ran up on the rocks we blew three blasts on the siren, the *Narbrough* repeated it coming up on our starboard quarter, in turning she appears to have heeled right over and seemed to crack like a piece of firewood, she went to pieces quicker than the *Opal* did. The *Opal*'s bows appeared to have broken off completely and the *Narbrough* was lying in two pieces on the starboard side.

---

40. Sissons later recorded that other officers, including, presumably, Lieutenant Robert Evan Lewis-Lloyd, the first lieutenant, were trapped in their cabins aft, as the ship was fully battened down and seas were running the full length of the vessel. See *Private Papers of W. Sissons*, IWM Document 17064, 2pp. Imperial War Museum, London.

He stated that the *Narborough*, had no time to turn, 'she was all over just alongside us', adding that the two ships had no chance to signal each other, it was all over too quickly, 'the only thing you could hear was the men yelling'.

Likewise his description of the fate of his companions left nothing to the imagination.

> The order was given to abandon ship, all boats and whalers and Carley rafts, which were still on board at time of grounding, were manned but the sea carried away the whalers davits, and the people in the boat were shot out, the same thing happened to the motor boat, and the men sat on the Carley rafts waiting to float off.

He added, 'Directly we ran aground we started making wireless [signals], but the sea washed everything away immediately, and the mast went over the side and the sea went down into the boilers.' Asked whether he saw anyone else try to swim ashore Sissons replied, 'I did not see anyone trying to swim ashore at all, I could see people in the water, but the sea came on top of them and they went down.'

His own escape was miraculous.

> I jumped up the midships funnel and stood on the grating and waited my turn, the sea was getting worse, the sea then washed the after and foremost funnels away, and then the midships funnel went over and I had to swim for it, the funnel tumbled over the side, the next thing I remember was that I was up on the beach.

He recounted how he fell from the cliff and built a little shelter which kept him alive for the following thirty-six hours. He confirmed that the sounding machine was run continually from the last dog watch onward and, when also quizzed about the soundings taken just prior to the grounding, asserted that the last one he heard was 33 fathoms without tube. The earlier soundings, with the tube, had been 35, 34, 33, 35 and 33 again. What also came out was that *Opal* was only making about 7 knots at the time she struck.

Sissons spent nine days aboard the *China* and was then sent to the Royal Hospital Haslar, at Gosport, where his severe frostbite and immersion were treated for a period of three months. He was finally discharged as fully fit and was assigned to a new ship.

A Board of Enquiry was convened on 16 January and duly met aboard the *Colossus* two days later with Rear-Admiral Douglas Nicholson assisted by Captain Edwin Veale Underhill from the battleship *Temeraire* and Captain Hugh Dudley Richards Watson of the battleship *Bellerophon*.

From aboard the battleship *Revenge* of the 1st Battle Squadron, Admiral Charles Edward Madden, Second-in-Command Grand Fleet, appended several incise comments to the findings of the Enquiry. He thought it 'hardly probable' that *Opal* might have been expected to see the Copinsay Light within one-and-a-half hours of leaving *Boadicea* because *Opal* had asked for Group 1 lights to be shown at 2030. 'By 2030 *Opal* had Copinsay well abaft the beam, and this points to the Commanding

Officer's intentions to make Pentland Skerries Light.' With regard to the depth soundings recorded by Sissons, Madden considered that these figures:

> probably refer to fathoms of sounding wire run out, and not to depths. If the speed of *Opal* was seven knots, she was inside the 30-fathom line for twenty minutes or more before taking the ground. Thirty-three fathoms of wire out at a 7-knot speed would give a depth of 22 fathoms, which was about that of the water in which *Opal* actually was ten minutes before going ashore.

With regard to opinion that a light on Lowther Rock would have helped matters he commented that 'the light formerly exhibited in that position was extinguished early in the war, because it was unwatched, and, once alight, always alight. It might therefore have been of great assistance to the enemy in making the entrance at night.' Only if the light was controlled was it of value, otherwise it was 'not recommended.' Madden summed up by suggesting 'that it be impressed upon destroyer officers that, when following a senior officer, an accurate reckoning is as essential as when detached...'.

Following this and the Sissons interrogation, the Commander-in-Chief,[41] in a submission to the Secretary of the Admiralty,[42] stated that a court martial had not been ordered 'as it does not appear that any further evidence throwing light on the losses would be elucidated'. He expressed the opinion that the two destroyers had been lost 'due to want of seamanlike caution in making the land' which, he considered, 'should not have been attempted in the weather conditions prevailing at the time'. He also considered that the showing of the light on the rock at Lowther Beacon was 'not germane to the accident' because 'such a light would have made no difference to the situation'. It was considered that the lights at the Pentland Skerries and Stroma were 'sufficient navigational aids for making the eastern entrance to the Firth, and if these lights cannot be seen no vessel should attempt to enter at night'. The displaying of an intermittent light on Lowther Rock, had it been attainable, would 'not be sufficient to counterbalance the assistance it would give to enemy submarines'.

It was pointed out that *Opal* had made no attempt to obtain a bearing from the Old Head direction-finding W/T station. In mitigation it was admitted that 'destroyers have not hitherto been able to transmit on R-wave'. It was noted that 'Arrangements are being made locally for this to be done, with special precautions as to limitation of power in order to avoid risk of damage to deck insulators'.[43]

The wreck sites (Nos. 002600791 & 002600808) are located at N 58° 146' 15", W 002° 55' 48", both remains being submerged and with one in about 26 feet (7.92m) depth of water on a rock ledge, and the other, more intact, in a slightly greater depth at around 36 feet (11m). The destroyers lie together, about 80 feet (24.38m) apart from

41. Acting Admiral David Richard Beatty, Commander-in-Chief, Grand Fleet, Flagship *Queen Elizabeth* (Captain Alfred Ernle Montacute Chatfield.)
42. Sir Oswyn Alexander Ruthaven Murray.
43. Signal No.480 dated 16.9.17.

each other, under the cliffs, still aligned roughly on their northern headings. After several attempts at private purchase had been rejected the MoD finally sold them to Messrs Sutherland and Mawat. A memorial to the two ships was erected which overlooks Wind Wick Bay in position ND 45734 86931. Surviving artefacts included a 4-inch gun which was restored by Willy Budge and which he donated to the Lyness Museum, which also holds a Kisbee ring[44] lifebelt donated by George Esson.

The full list of the men lost in this tragedy is a long one. *Opal*'s casualties included: Lieutenant-Commander Charles Caesar De Merindol Malan; Engineer Lieutenant-Commander Thomas Henry Fielder Dampier; Lieutenant Robert Evan Lewis-Lloyd, Sub-Lieutenants James Melhuish Gunning, Henry Staveley Pilkington Shaw; Gunner Edward Duggan; Surgeon Probationer Louis Percival St John Story; Chief Petty Officer Edwin George Gill; Petty Officers Henry George Cull, William Joseph Rush; Yeoman of Signals John Lund Gaffney; Leading Signalman Eric Joseph Mitchener; Leading Telegraphist Ronald Robert James; Telegraphists Frederick John Calton and Alexander Gordon Farquhar; Signalman Frank William Somers; Leading Seamen William Cook, Charles John Gill, George Ernest Merrick, Alfred Charles Young; Able Seamen Harry Lewis Bayton, Edward Bramwell, Eric Woodward Carver, James Connor, Francis Gill Cowing, James Lowrey Elliott, William John Garner, Albert Edward Green, Richard Thomas Griffiths, Albert George Harrison, Walter Stanley Harrison, Ernest Edward Hill, Victor Jolliffe, Ernest Le Gros, George Sidney Matthews, John James Murray, Henry Douglas Neep, Robert Liddell Nichol, John Joseph O'Connor, John Thomas Pack, Edmund Gordon Payne, Robert Edgar Pratley, James Robertson, Francis Joseph Rollinson, Sydney Shelmerdine, Albert Edward Smith, William Taylor and Christopher Wane; Ordinary Seamen Hilton Appleyard, Frederick Atkinson, Albert Percy Bartlett, George Beach, James Charles Chaffer, Alexander Frazer Grant, Frederick William Tubbs Holdstock, Edward Parsons, Frederick James Rotchell and John Russell; Wireman Albert Joseph Montague; Leading Stokers Jesse Ballam, John Herbert Hibbs and George Ernest Lethbridge; Chief Engine Room Artificer Robert Black DSM; Engine Room Artificers Owen Champion, Ernest Stanley Cubiss, Charles Mayes and Herbert Whalley; Petty Officer Stokers Albert Edwards, Frederick Charles Homburg, Francis Lee, Frederick Edward Loveless, John Quigley and Charles William Stovell; Chief Stoker Frederick George Irwin; Stokers 1st Class Henry Catford, Herbert Christie, Felix Harper, John Thomas Hore, Joseph Lunt, Thomas McMenemy, William McGregor, Henry Moody, Alexander McPhee, Joseph Murray, William Pratt, Samuel Richards, Charles Edward Terry, George Henry Tippett and John Watson; Stokers 2nd Class Fred Burgin, Alexander McKee and Leonard Albert Mortimer; Officers' Steward Jack Salmon; Officers' Cook John Ernest Denyer; Leading Cook's Mate Harold Douglas Randall.

Narborough lost her entire crew including Lieutenant Edmond Mansel Bowly; Lieutenant John Gould Nicolas DSC; Sub-Lieutenant Eric Oloff de Wet DSC

---

44. So-called after Captain Thomas Kisbee (1792–1877) who also invented the Breeches Buoy. He circumnavigated the globe in the steam-paddle sloop *Driver* between 1842 and 1845.

MiD; Midshipmen Cecil Gordon Kennedy and Harry Adrian Venables; Chief Petty Officer Walter Edward Cobb; Petty Officers John Alexander Blues, Arthur George Gaffee, Philip John Marett Jordan CM, and Edward William Sheppard; Leading Telegraphist Francis William Brockway DSM; Boy Telegraphist Alfred George Potts; Leading Signalman Jacob Lee; Signalman Herbert William Clear and Cecil John Carter; Officers' Stewards Albert Thomas Deacon, William Frederick George Fowler and Frederick Jeram; Leading Cook's Mate Samuel Martin Julians; Leading Seamen Albert James Grant, William Henry Hodge and Frank Arthur Strange; Able Seamen George Ellis Barber, Albert William Beckensall, George Edward Boynton, Alfred Bunn, John William Dunbar, Reginald Foreman, George William Francis, George Gingall, Horace Richard Hibling, Albert Howe, George Frederick John Kenney, Robert Lawson, Charles Mason, Robert Mingles, Hector Redvers Nicks, Percy Orange, James Thomas Pegg, William Edward Price, William Stephen Pink, Norman Scott, Alfred George Thomas Southam, James Charles Stone, George Toms, Frederick William Walker, John Albert Walsh, Alfred Charles Winkworth, Victor William Woobey and Frederick Reynolds Woodhouse; Ordinary Seamen Harold Percy Archer, John Metcalfe Brown, Sidney Button, Thomas Foley, Francis Wallace McCheyne, Thomas Abraham Richards, Henry Percival Ritter, Ernest Trimmer and Herbert Thomas Whitby; Mechanician Walter Brennan Padley; Engine Room Artificers Wesley Bramwell Bennett, Harry Howard Parkes, Sidney George Powney and James Till; Petty Officer Stokers George Henry Beames, William Henry Barrett, Thomas Hayes, Samuel Howard, Charles James Langridge and Richard Morris; Chief Stoker John Marshall; Leading Stokers Samson David Hibbert, Arthur Albert Loose and John Charles Rogers; Stokers 1st Class Charles Herbert Ashen, James George Bull, George Creech, David Crutchlow, Andrew Ford, George Alfred Green, Robert Green, Alexander Lawrie, John Lillico, Walter Mellows, George Bagnall Reid and Charles Frederick Taylor; Stokers 2nd Class John Askew, Robert Bullerwell Farbridge, Lawrence Edward Nicholson and Harry Edward Parker; and Wireman Frederick William Brooke.

What of the indefatigable William Sissons? He had been born in December 1895 and became a boy seaman in March 1912, his first ship being the battleship *King George V* before he joined the *Opal*. His naval career continued for some time after these traumatic events – they built 'em tough in his day. There was no trauma counselling but straight back to the job. In January he joined the destroyer *Vancouver* at Queensferry and later moved to a sister ship, the *Vivacious*, until 1922. After periods at the *Vernon* and *Excellent* shore bases he joined another destroyer, the *Vanessa*, at Malta in 1925 and was finally discharged on 31 December 1928. In civvy street he became a coachbuilder.

Chapter 12

The Wrecking of *Raleigh*

The *Raleigh*, 8 August 1922

It would seem as if some classes of warships are almost fated to repeat the mistakes of others. To take just one example, the Royal Navy developed an aversion to naming ships after snakes after a string of misfortunes when the gun-brig *Adder* (Lieutenant Molyneux Shuldham – in 1832), the brig-sloop *Snake* (Captain Thomas Brown – in 1847), the destroyers *Cobra* (Lieutenant Bosworth Smith – in 1901) and *Viper* (Lieutenant William Speke – in 1901) and the torpedo-cruiser *Serpent* (Commander Harry Leith Ross – in 1890), were all wrecked with heavy loss of life. The destroyer *Python* was re-named as the *Velox* (Lieutenant Frank Pattinson) in 1914, but that failed to save her and she was sunk by a mine in October 1915. But other groupings also seemed fated for disaster and thus we shall see in these pages, not just one, but two cruisers of the same class suffering similar fates, albeit some eighteen years apart.

HMS *Raleigh* was a *Cavendish*-class cruiser, her four sister ships being the *Cavendish*, *Effingham*, *Frobisher* and *Hawkins*, all being named after prominent Elizabethan naval commanders. *Raleigh* was of course named in honour of Sir Walter Raleigh and was the sixth Royal Navy warship to bear the name.

These cruisers (known initially as 'Improved Birminghams' although bearing no resemblance to those vessels) were designed by the Director of Naval Construction, Sir Eustace Tennyson D'Eyncourt, in response to an Admiralty requirement for a type that could hunt down German raiders in distant waters. For this a higher speed, greater endurance and heavier armament were considered essential. These requirements were met by including mixed-fired boilers as part of their engine arrangement, but by the time they were nearing completion this was no longer thought necessary and only the first pair, *Cavendish* and *Hawkins*, carried this set-up for a while. Both the *Effingham* and *Frobisher* were converted to an all oil-fired arrangement before completion while *Raleigh* had an entirely unique power-plant of four Brown Curtiss turbines and twelve Yarrow boilers which produced 70,000shp (52,000kW) driving four shafts for a designed speed of 31 knots (57km/h). Given a similar hull form to the battle-cruiser *Furious* with 10-degree inboard-sloping sides, she had 5 foot (1.524m) bulges over her machinery spaces and had a 25 feet (7.620m) freeboard which made them excellent sea-going ships.

To provide long-range fire it was decided to adopt the tried-and-tested 7.5-inch (190mm) 45-calibre breech-loading gun as used on the *Devonshire*-, *Warrior*- and

Minotaur-classes of armoured cruisers, but with the elevation increased to 28 degrees, which fired the 200lb (91kg) projectile to a maximum range of 22,000 yards (12 miles or 18km) with a muzzle velocity of 2,770 fps (844 m/s) and an impact velocity of 1071 feet per second (fps) (326 m/s). This became the Mk VI single mounting, utilising the Asbury hand-loading system, and it was later provided with electrical training and elevation. They carried seven single guns on CP Mk V open-backed mounts, two forward, one each side abreast the after funnel, and three aft. This weapon was powerful enough to cause considerable envy among other powers post-war, particularly the United States, and led to the imposition of a maximum gun size of 8-inch (20.320cm) for cruisers in the subsequent Washington Treaty extensions on future cruiser construction, with which the British delegates limply complied. The secondary armament comprised four 3-inch (76mm) 20-cwt (1016.04 kilo) Mk1 QF HA single guns for AA defence and eight 12-pounder (76mm) QF single guns; six 21-inch (53.3cm) torpedo-tubes, four fixed surface-mounted and two submerged tubes.

Armour protection was provided by a 1.5-inch (3.8cm) to 2.5-inch (6.3cm) belt increasing to 3 inches (7.6cm) amidships to cover the machinery spaces with 1.5-inch (3.8m) deck protection over the boilers. The turrets had 2-inch (5.1cm) armoured faces with 1-inch (2.5cm) crowns and sides.

In the end only *Cavendish* was completed during the war for which these ships had been designed, and even she had been totally re-designed and completed as an aircraft-carrier, being renamed *Vindictive* in 1918. The other four were all completed postwar at a very leisurely pace.

The *Raleigh*[1] was built by William Beardmore & Co., Dalmuir, Glasgow, being ordered in December 1915, laid down on 9 December 1915, launched on 28 August 1919 and completed on 23 July 1921. Her dimensions were an overall length of 605 feet (184m), a beam of 65 feet (19.812m) and a draught of 19 feet 3 inches (5.8674m). Her standard displacement was 9,700 tons (9,900 tonnes), and her fully loaded displacement was 12,000 tons (12,000 tonnes). She had a complement of 700 officers and men. On trials off the Isle of Arran between 7 and 9 September 1930, she reached 31 knots (57 km/h) at 71,350shp (53,210kW) and could still make 28 knots (52 km/h) at half power (35,000shp (26,000kW). *Raleigh* was commissioned for service at Devonport on 19 April 1921.

The *Raleigh* sailed from Plymouth Sound bound for Bermuda on 26 July to take her place as flagship. She spent time at Grassy Bay and Murray's Anchorage in company with the light cruisers *Calcutta* (Captain Walter Burge Compton), *Cambrian* (Captain James Denham) and *Constance* (Captain Arthur Charles Strutt). Vice Admiral Sir William Christopher Pakenham embarked on 12 August, several members of his staff embarking on the 24th. *Raleigh* sailed for Montreal on 1 September, arriving a week later, where she joined the cruiser *Aurora* (Captain Henry George Horner Adams CBE) and destroyers *Patrician* (Lieutenant George Clarence Jones RCN) and *Patriot* (Lieutenant Charles Tachereau Beard RCN) which the Royal Navy had handed over

---

1. Yard number 555, Pendant Number 96 in September 1920.

to the Royal Canadian Navy. She returned to Bermuda in November and visited Kingston, Jamaica. She sailed from Kingston to San Pedro, Panama, between 11 and 14 February 1922, passing through the Panama Canal and arriving at San Francisco on 21 January, where she saluted the American battleships *Arizona* (Captain George Ralph Marvell), *Mississippi* (Captain Orton Porter Jackson) and *Nevada* (Captain Douglas Eugene Dismukes).

Raleigh returned to Balboa, Panama, on 16 February, saluting and being visited by the President of the Panama Republic, the American Minister, the French *Chargé d'Affairs*, the US General in Command and the Governor of the Canal Zone, requiring a total salute of seventy-nine guns! *Raleigh* then sailed back through the canal to Bermuda. In 1922 Pakenham's tour continued with the arrival of the *Raleigh* at Washington DC on 29 May 1922. She anchored in the Potomac River and was also engaged in a pulling race on the Potomac against the crew of President Warren Gamaliel Harding's Presidential Yacht *Mayflower* (Lieutenant-Commander Carl Townsend Osburn) whom they diplomatically allowed to win.[2]

In June *Raleigh* left for Hampton Roads and Bar Harbour before sailing to Sydney, Cape Breton, Charlottetown and Montreal. She subsequently visited Quebec from 11 July and then called at Murray, Dalhousie, anchoring in the Bay of Island on 1 August. At each of these ports of call the ship was opened to formal visitors and the general public alike, with children's parties and the like. Finally, in Hawke Bay, on 3 August 1922, Admiral Pakenham and his staff transferred across to the light cruiser *Calcutta* and he hoisted his flag aboard her, the *Raleigh* thus becoming a 'private' ship once more.

The ship's officers aboard *Raleigh* at this date were now headed by the commanding officer, Captain Arthur Bromley CMG. He had entered the Royal Navy in 1890 in the cadet training ship *Britannia* (Captain Noel Stephen Fox Digby) at Dartmouth and served in the protected cruiser *Blake* (Captain Eardley Wilmott) on the North America and West Indies Station in 1892. In 1895 he joined the screw-corvette *Ruby* (Captain John Ferris) in Spithead Portsmouth Training Squadron and then to the *Cleopatra* (Captain Robert Kyle McAlpine). After service aboard the Royal Yacht *Victoria and Albert* the Great War found him a captain in command of the AMC *Columbella* (Captain Hugh Lindsay Patrick Heard), 10th Cruiser Squadron. He relieved Captain Sidney Robert Drury-Lowe as captain of the light cruiser *Chatham* on 1 May 1916 and from 8 September he then stood by the new battle-cruiser *Courageous*, briefly commanded the armoured cruiser *Bacchante*, and returned to *Courageous*. He was commended by Their Lordships for that ship's 'consistently good gunnery' while in command, and was still in command at the end of the war, being present at the surrender of the High Seas Fleet. He then moved to command the light cruiser *Cardiff*, taking over from Captain Claude Hamilton Sinclair on 18 February 1919 until August 1919. He

---

2. A servile British government also allowed Harding to win a very much bigger game by imposing United States' limitations on the strength of the Royal Navy at the Washington Naval Conference the same year – what the Americans call 'a win-win' situation.

served as Flag Captain to the Vice-Admiral, Light Cruiser Force.[3] He was appointed in command of *Raleigh* on 14 February 1920, due to act as Flagship of Vice-Admiral Napier, the C-in-C North American and West Indies Station, but Napier died on 30 July and was succeeded by Vice-Admiral Sir William Christopher Pakenham KCB KCVG KCVO.

The Navigator was Commander (N) Leslie Charles Bott, who had been navigating officer aboard the aircraft-carrier *Furious* (Captain Wilmot Stuart Nicholson) during the war, for which he earned his OBE on 10 June 1918; the ship's Gunnery Officer was Lieutenant-Commander Edward William Herford Blake; the Director Gunner was William Bailey,[4] while the Torpedo Officer was Lieutenant-Commander Gaisford St Lawrence. Other officers were Lieutenant-Commander Massey Goolden DSC; Surgeon Lieutenant-Commander Herbert Richard Barnes Hull,[5] with Lieutenants John Annesley Grindle, Humphrey Greenwood Hopper, Denys Patrick O'Callaghan and David Orr-Ewing and Sub-Lieutenant Charles Edward Lambe. *Raleigh*'s gunroom was full of young midshipmen going to join the various ships of the North Atlantic Squadron and the 'middies' included William Leslie Graham Adams, Stephen Hope Carlill, John William Forrest, Richard Pennington Garnett, the twins Geoffrey and Langton Gowlland, William Edmund Halsey, Peter Coats Hutton, Herbert Lovegrove, Ian Mackenzie Martineau, Robin Charles Todhunter and William Henry Wood BEM, with William R. Gould as a very busy gunroom messman.

Raleigh had cleaned ship while anchored in Hawke Bay and weighed anchor at 1029, plotting a course for Forteau at an economical 12 knots (22.24 km/h) as requested by the Admiralty. At 1052 she rounded Robinson Island and at 1112 Keppel Island bore 075° when she altered course to 315° and at 1142 altered course again to 025° sighting Rich Point, 1.9 miles distant, two minutes later. By 1220 she had Twin Islands bearing 038°. Her estimated time of arrival (ETA) at Forteau was 1615.

---

3. This was Vice-Admiral Sir Trevylyan Dacres Willes Napier ('Long Napier') and his command comprised the 1st, 2nd, 3rd, 4th and 6th Light Cruiser Squadrons.

4. A survivor of the armoured cruiser *Aboukir* (Captain John Edmund Drummond) sunk, along with her sisters *Cressy* (Captain Robert Warren Johnson) and *Hogue* (Captain Wilmot Stuart Nicholson), by the German submarine *U-9* (*Kapitänleutnant* Otto Weddigen) on 22 September 1914.

5. Hull had joined the Navy in 1911 and between June 1912 and December 1914 served aboard the battleship *Caesar* (Captain Edward George Lowther-Crofton) based at Devonport. He then joined the sloop *Fantome* (Captain Lewis Tobias Jones) and then the Devonport shore base HMS *Vivid* until 1915 when he joined the seaplane carrier *Ben-my-Chree* (Commander Cecil L'Estrange Malone) at Gallipoli and Palestine. He was seconded to the RAF's embryo college at Cranwell for a month, returning to *Vivid* as a surgeon and served with the RAF again as a surgeon lieutenant between May and November 1918 before returning to naval duties. Hull later went on to serve at the Royal Navy Hospital, Chatham as a surgeon commander in April 1941 and later became surgeon rear-admiral in charge of the Royal Naval Hospital, Haslar, an MRCS and LRCP. He attended His Majesty King George V. ADM 104/50 – *Medical Director General's Notes Promotions and Appointments*, National Archives, Kew, London.

The precise sequence of events that followed can be traced from HMS *Raleigh*'s log entries for 8 August.

1457 – Iceberg 001°.

1510 – Sighted land on port bow.

1524 – a/c to 300°. Ran into fog. Commenced sounding.

1537 – Land ahead and to port. Reduced speed to 8 knots [14.816 km/h].

1538 – Sighted breakers on star[board] bow. Full Speed astern. Hard a starboard. Collision stations.

1539 – Grounded.

1540 – Stopped engines. Ship bumping heavily.

1541 – Hard a port. Ship's stern swinging to E[ast]ward. Full astern starboard.

1543 – Stop Star[board]. Full ahead port. Engines as required to stop to prevent stern swinging on rocks.

1549 – Finally stopped engines. Position 262° – 4.8 cables [889.52m] from Amour Point. Heading 292°.

Hard aground f[ro]m Star[board] bilge and bumping heavily.

1607 – Let go Port ↓ Cutter and crew washed ashore on rocks.

1615 – Two lines ashore by Coston Gun[6] Command abandoning ship by lines and Carley Floats.

2000 – Ship abandoned.

The most graphic account of the grounding was recorded by the late Vice-Admiral Sir Stephen Carlill, a young midshipman aboard *Raleigh* at the time. 'Engines were going full astern', Skipper, from starboard side, 'Put the helm over.' Lambe, 'Hard a-starboard.' From the Skipper again, 'Good God, Bott, where are we?' He suddenly looked ninety, and old Nuts [Bott] looked cold and blue. Massey[7] from the other end of the bridge, and through a megaphone: 'Hands to collision stations!' Never did I expect to hear that 'pipe' in any actual circumstances outside evolutions.'

A more contemporary account was given by one of the officers in an article written a mere six months after the event. The author complained that 'Much inaccurate and misguiding information has been written about the wreck ... and the subsequent proceedings of her crew while on shore on the Labrador coast'. What was written in

---

6. This was a line-throwing gun, named after Martha Jane Coston, widow of US Navy Pyrotechnic Laboratory Chief Benjamin Franklin Coston, and manufactured by her company, Coston Supply Co., New York. They used a 45/70 blank cartridge to fire a rope to another ship or ashore and the gun came in a wooden case with ten rope rods, three canisters of rope and two boxes of cartridges.

7. Lieutenant-Commander Massey-Goolden Carlill; see Vice-Admiral Sir Stephen KBE CB DSO, 'The Wreck of HMS *Raleigh*', article in *The Naval Review*, Volume 70, No. 3, July 1982, pp.165–73, 1982, London.

the press at the time 'created in the Service, an entirely false impression of what actually happened'. If nothing else, it proves that media reporting has not improved in ninety or more years. Among the totally false stories printed at the time, the author lists 'that the sea-boat was manned by a volunteer crew of stokers; that the officer in charge alone was able to reach the shore; that the ship's company were three days without food or shelter; and that the coast in the region of the wreck is uninhabited'. We shall see that even today even more false allegations continue to be made in the Canadian media.[8]

The strong wind from the south-west soon swung the *Raleigh* beam-on to the heavy sea despite the engines going full ahead port in attempt to keep her stern off the rock.

> The ship struck the shore practically at right-angles at a speed of perhaps six knots, and her bottom was torn open to a point somewhere in the vicinity of the chain lockers. The shock on the fore-bridge was not as violent as might have been expected and no damage was done to the masts, funnels, upperworks or boats, the latter being turned in and secured in their crutches, with the exception of the two sea boats.

Once aground she began to pound and grind herself against the rocks. She shook so much that the wireless aerials came down in a heap although the topmasts survived. Captain Bromley ordered the steam anchor to be got out and went aft to supervise, but the pinnace, when lowered, proved impossible to operate and had to be abandoned, so Lieutenant Orr-Ewing let go the port anchor. One boiler began to blow and a small fire broke out in the ship's galley. 'Abandon ship' was ordered although the port-side boats could not be lowered. Meanwhile, the main steam pipes in the after engine-room had buckled from the continual thumping she was receiving as big seas continually swept in over her quarterdeck, so steam was turned off and the men brought up on deck. The fog continued to thicken and the darkness was intense which did not aid the evacuation of the ship.

The *Raleigh* had a list to port of about 8 degrees and consideration was given to flooding the starboard tanks to stop her going any further over. Despite this the list had increased slightly, to 9 degrees, by dawn. Those ashore got fires lit in an effort to dry off and keep warm while others made their way to the lighthouse some three-quarters of a mile distant, to seek refuge for what remained of the night; others slept in a hayloft nearby.

The place where the *Raleigh* had gone aground was L'Anse Amour, Strait of Belle Isle, Labrador, Newfoundland.[9] This had been the original site of the first Marconi radio station opened in 1904 near the lighthouse, one of the largest and tallest on that coast. The area already had a reputation of ill-repute for mariners and especially so for the Royal Navy. Some thirty-three years earlier, at almost the very same spot on 16 (or

---

8. Anonymous – 'The Wreck of the *Raleigh*', article in *The Naval Review*, Volume XI, No. 2, May 1923, pp.319–23, 1923, London.
9. The name corrupted from 'L'Anse aux Mort' – 'Cove of the Dead', due to its notoriety for shipwrecks.

20 – sources disagree) September 1889, HMS *Lily* (Captain Gerald Walter Russell) had been wrecked.[10]

Seven of the crew of the *Lily* died that day and this was also due to the capsize of a lifeboat. These two losses were eerily alike in so many ways that, not surprisingly, superstitious locals still believe that *Raleigh* came to grief 'on the bones of the *Lily*'.

Twelve of the crew of the *Raleigh* were lost in the wreck, half of whom were from a lifeboat commanded by Midshipman Peter Hutton, which was manned by a mixed crew of seamen and stokers and which was being lowered in the raging sea in a gallant attempt to get a line ashore. The boat's crew, in their haste, did not fend her off the side of the ship sufficiently and, as the ship lurched with the swell, she swung into the hull. Several planks were stove in by the collision and when she reached the sea she was immediately washed straight onto a protruding rock ledge. Most of those aboard panicked and jumped overboard at this point and then the boat was swept away from them onto a second ledge further in where she became jammed while many of the crew in the water were simply swept away and drowned. Hutton and some others managed to struggle ashore but one man, AB Herbert R. Reynolds, was carried back into deep water and was seen to be *in extremis* and about to share the fate of the others. Midshipman Hutton, still fully clothed, plunged back into the surging surf once more and swam out pushing an empty wave-breaker ahead of him. He managed to reach the by now unconscious Reynolds despite the strong wind and heavy swell. He pulled him back to the *Raleigh*'s starboard side and both men were hoisted back aboard, where Reynolds was successfully resuscitated. For this brave deed the Royal Humane Society later awarded Hutton the Gold Medal for 1922.[11]

Another act of bravery was also recorded that day. Lieutenant-Commander Humphrey Hopper went over the side of the *Raleigh* and swam to shore through the dangerously breaking seas with a line.[12]

An eyewitness recorded that the men probably died of hypothermia almost instantly, the water being so very cold, with blocks of ice on the beach. All had life-belts on

---

10. The *Lily* was an *Arab*-class barque-rigged composite gunboat, built by Napier, Govan, Clydeside, and launched in 1874. She was of 620 tons, with a length of 150 feet (45.72m), a beam of 28 feet 6 inch (8.686m) and a draught of 10 feet 6 inches (3.2004m). She was powered by a single shaft, 2-cylinder CR engine developing 570ihp which gave her 10.5 knots (19.446 km/h) top speed. She was armed with a single 7-inch (17.78cm) muzzle-loading rifled (MLR) gun and had a crew of ninety. The wreck was sold in 1890.

11. Royal Humane Society, Case 46560A. A sketchy account of this included in Fevyer, William H., *Acts of Gallantry*, Volume 2, p.17, 1996, Uckfield, The Naval and Military Press.

12. Hopper was no stranger to dangerous deeds. Having left the 19,180-tonne (19,487 tons) light battle-cruiser *Glorious* (Captain Charles Blois Miller) as a sub-lieutenant in 1916–17, he joined the 1,200-ton (1,219 tonnes) minesweeping sloop *Mallow* (Lieutenant-Commander Charles William Augustus Baldwin) between June 1917 to December 1918. When the 3,716-ton (3,775 tonnes) French troopship *Djemnah* (*Capitaine* Charles Méric) was sunk in the Mediterranean on the night of 14 July 1918 by the German U-boat *UB-105* (*Leutnant* Wilhelm Marschall) south of Crete, Hopper had gone over the side and rescued several exhausted French soldiers. For this he was awarded the Royal Humane Society Medal in Silver. His work with *Raleigh* earned him a Bar to this medal.

them, except Hutton himself, who was in his shirtsleeves, but the men in the water 'seemed helpless'.

The full casualty list included, from the engine-room staff, Stoker Petty Officers Edward Effard and John E. Lloyd; Leading Stokers William J. Sowden and Sydney George Tripp; Stokers 1st Class Herbert Bashford, Silas Field, George Fisher, George Mafeking Thornhill and Reuben Tyler; along with Able Seamen Pat Pettet, James Weaver and William Raynor Whitton. They were buried in a small local cemetery on the way to Forteau itself along with their forebears lost from the *Lily*. Each year, during a local re-enactment of the disaster, they are remembered.

Dawn revealed the true extent of the damage. The gash down the side was 260 feet (79.248m) long, almost a third of her total length. At dawn many re-boarded the ship in two groups to see what might be salvaged. They found the port-side cabins flooded with 'thick brown oil' and most personal belongings lost. 'Nothing whatsoever was saved,' according to the *New York Times*, which also sneered that the *Raleigh* was a 'White Elephant',[13] and noting she was the first British warship to visit Washington since Royal Marines landed in 1814, a fact that they still did not appear to have forgiven. In neither case was this true, and neither was their report that Vice Admiral Pakenham was on board at the time. Meanwhile the cruisers *Capetown* (Captain Edward Roynon Jones) and *Calcutta* (Captain Walter Burdge Compton) were *en route* to the scene. On their arrival they provided one hot meal for all hands.

Lieutenant-Commander Goolden announced that the bulk of the crew would assemble at 0430 and march to embark aboard the liner *Empress of France* at 0730 to sail for home. These refugees included a couple of 'guests', Lieutenant Reginald William Armytage of *Capetown* and Lieutenant William Frederick Eyre Hussey of *Calcutta,* who had had the misfortune to be aboard at the wrong time.

Another group of about 150 officers and men were kept back. These consisted of those who were on the bridge of the ship at the time she had struck or who had any relevant information as an enquiry into the grounding was to be held on the spot. Others, mainly a vigilant party of fully-armed Royal Marines, were required to guard the ship as a large party of Newfoundlanders ('an extraordinary rough and fierce crowd') had crossed over the Belle Isle Strait sensing easy pickings on the assumption it was yet another merchant vessel gone ashore and ripe for looting. They claimed they had come to 'inspect' the wreck! The Marine guard aboard the *Raleigh* was supplemented by a similar guard ashore where a salvage dump had been established, with an officer, a petty officer and eight seamen on twenty-four-hour watch. The rest of those retained formed a salvage party of about one hundred petty officers and hand-picked skilled crew members. The salvage part was left at L'Anse Amour to await better weather before commencing work.

---

13. Presumably out of pique because there was absolutely nothing to match her and her sisters in the United States Navy at the time.

An interim Board of Enquiry was held aboard the cruiser *Constance* in Forteau Bay on Thursday 17 August with Captain Arthur Charles Strutt (CO of *Constance*) as President.

The next day, and on the following morning, most of the men duly marched in a long straggling line the bleak six miles to Forteau to board the Canadian Pacific's 18,481 GRT liner *Empress of France* (Captain Eric Griffiths RNR) for passage home, but when the authorities of that ship realised the number of survivors involved they flatly refused to take them due to inadequate provisions on board and they had to wait a few more days for the brand-new 16,402 GRT Canadian Pacific liner SS *Montrose* (Captain Henry Parry) to do the job, Bromley and Bott sailing with them. Many of these midshipmen were re-united at RN College Greenwich as acting sub-lieutenants in autumn 1923. However, others of the midshipmen aboard went instead to other cruisers of the squadron, the *Cambrian*, *Capetown* (Captain Kenneth Gilbert Balmain Dewar), *Calcutta* and *Constance*, and returned, much later, across the North Atlantic aboard them.

Others took a little longer to get back; for instance, on 19 August, Lovegrove and Carlill joined *Constance* at Bermuda, not finally returning home for a further two years aboard HMS *Dartmouth* (Captain John Even Cameron MVO).[14]

On their return to England the full court martial of Commander Bott was held at Royal Naval Barracks, Portsmouth, on 26 October 1922 with the captain of HMS *Dryad*,[15] Captain Harold Owen Reinhold, as President. As a result *Raleigh*'s Navigating Officer was dismissed his ship and severely reprimanded and he later retired at his own request on 25 October 1922. Bott returned to duty during the Second World War and served on the staff of Rear-Admiral Richard James Rodney Scott AM CB MD, Commander of Dockyard and Assistant King's Harbourmaster aboard the parent ship *Boscawen*[16] at Portland.

---

14. The *Dartmouth* was a cruiser of the *Weymouth* class built by Vickers and launched in December 1910. Of 5,250 tons, she had an overall length of 453 feet (135.588m), was armed with eight 6-inch (15.240cm) guns, a 3-inch (7.620cm) AA gun and two 21-inch (53.340cm) torpedo-tubes. She was powered by turbines producing 22,000hp which gave her a speed of 25 knots (46.30 km/h). She had a 2-inch (5.080cm) thick armoured deck, and a complement of 375 officers and men. She served in the Grand Fleet to 1915 and then went out to the Mediterranean. Post-war she served on the South American station until 1921 when she was part of the Reserve Fleet at Dartmouth. In 1925–26 she was converted for trooping duties at Devonport Dockyard, in which role she served until 1929. She was a 715-ton (726.5kg) vessel, 165 feet (50.29m) long, with a beam of 29 feet from 1924 to 1927. She was sold and scrapped in December 1930.

15. This was the former Victorian composite screw gunboat *Rattler*, of the *Bramble* class built by Elswick. Of 715 tons displacement, she had a length of 165 feet, a beam of 29 feet (8.84m) and a draught of 11 feet (3.35m). She had a speed of 13 knots and was armed with six 4-inch quick-firing (QF) guns, with a crew of seventy-six. She spent her final service life as a navigation training ship at Portsmouth and was renamed *Dryad*.

16. The former Motor Boat *3632*.

The captain of *Raleigh* was tried on 27 October, with Rear-Admiral Hugh Francis Paget Sinclair KCB, Rear-Admiral (S) Submarine Service, as President,[17] charged with negligently or by default stranding and losing his ship. In his defence he argued that had the charts he had been supplied with been accurate then his ship would not have stranded.[18] The Court found the charge proved, and he was summarily dismissed his ship and severely reprimanded.[19] Bromley retired at his own request on 7 November 1922.[20] With regard to his subsequent life, Bromley was advanced to the rank of rear-admiral on the Retired List in 1926. He thus retired as Rear-Admiral Sir Arthur Bromley, Eighth Baronet, KCMG KCVO RN. He held the office of Gentleman Usher-in-Ordinary to HM King George V in 1927 and was Ceremonial and Reception Secretary for the Dominion and Colonial Office between 1931 and 1952. He was invested as a Commander, Royal Victorian Order (CVO) in 1935. He then held the office of Gentleman Usher to HM King Edward VIII in 1936 and, after the abdication, held the office of Gentleman Usher to HM King George VI between 1937 and 1952. He was invested as a Knight Commander, Order of St Michael and St George (KCMG) in 1941. He later held the office of Gentleman Usher-in-Ordinary to HM Queen Elizabeth II between 1952 and 1961. Bromley was invested as a Knight Commander, Royal Victorian Order (KCVO) in 1953 in the Coronation Honours List. He succeeded to the title of 8th Baronet Smith, of East Stoke, Nottingham, his place of birth, on 7 November 1957 and died on 12 January 1961.

There have been several descriptions of this affair, including a large number of web sites of various degrees of inaccuracy. Indeed, these exceed in fiction a novel based on the event published in Canada. Ignoring these, hitherto the most responsible account of her loss in print is that written by a former Chief of Reserves Canadian Armed Forces.[21]

The young officers the *Raleigh* were alleged to have been so ashamed of their experience that they pretended that they had never been aboard her, according to the words of one Canadian writer.[22] In actuality, nothing could be further from the truth and most of these young officers went on to have highly distinguished naval careers with many taking prominent roles during the Second World War. A few passed away

---

17. Sinclair had served as Director of Naval Intelligence 1919–20 and later succeeded Sir Mansfield Smith-Cumming as Head of the Secret Service and Head of the Government Code & Cypher School, retiring as vice-admiral in 1926. He died as an admiral in October 1940.

18. This seems to be confirmed by Midshipman Carlill's diary which contains the following entry made while the ship was in Hawke Bay, and which was, he wrote at the time: 'entirely devoid of any buoys or leading marks, and the chart is from a somewhat old survey. The part around Robinson Island is very tricky too, and there are several tide rips.' Carlill Diary, *op. cit.*

19. Court Martial, Loss of vessel. Captain A. Bromley CMG RN and Cdr (N) L. C. Bott OBE, HMS *Raleigh*. ADM 156/57/ ADM1/8631, 25 October 1922, National Archives, Kew, London.

20. *The London Gazette*, No.32767, p.8034, 14 November 1922.

21. Rohmer, Major-General Richard, *Raleigh on the Rocks: The Canada Shipwreck of HMS Raleigh*, St John's, 2003, St John's, Creative Publishing.

22. This fictional account is contained as the story-line of the novel *One Single Hour* by Harvey Sawler, 1954, Renfrew, Ontario, General Store Publishing.

earlier; as an example Lieutenant-Commander Denys O'Callaghan was killed in an accident while serving aboard the light cruiser *Constance* on 16 September 1924; R. P. Garnett had attained the rank of lieutenant by December 1925 and served a two-year stint as a flying officer with the RAF between 1931 and 1933, but was placed on the retired list on 1 September 1934 at his own request; sixty-five-year-old Surgeon Lieutenant-Commander Henry W. Hull, who had served aboard the scout *Pathfinder* (Commander Francis Gerald St John) in 1908 and the Armed Merchant Cruiser *Orotava* (Commander Godfrey Edwin Corbett) during the Great War, also retired and died pre-war at HMS *Watchful* (Surgeon-Captain Charles Malcolm Russell Thatcher MC ChB), the Royal Navy Hospital at Great Yarmouth, Norfolk, on 15 September 1936, aged 65; he is buried at nearby Caister-on-Sea; Martineau became a lieutenant and also had a two-year detachment to the RAF between 1930 and 1932 as a flying officer, on termination of which he joined the battleship *Valiant* (Captain Bertram Chalmers Watson) and later served aboard the aircraft carrier *Eagle* (Captain Arthur Robin Moore Bridge) in the Mediterranean as a lieutenant-commander; another early loss was Lieutenant William H. Wood who died of an illness aboard the battle-cruiser *Hood* (Captain Sir Irvine Gordon Glennie) on 29 June 1939. Tragically, also, the *Raleigh*'s gunnery officer, Lieutenant-Commander Blake, was killed aboard the *Victory* (Captain Sir Atwell Henry Lake Bt OBE) in Portsmouth harbour when she was bombed on 11 March 1941, being her sole casualty;[23] another casualty of the war was Peter Hutton, who previously served aboard the battleship *Revenge* (Captain Roderick Bruce Tremayne Miles) in peacetime and the cruiser *Frobisher* (Captain Markham Henry Evelegh) at the beginning of the war. He joined the experimental tank landing craft organisation being set up in the eastern Mediterranean in 1941 to carry out some of Churchill's wild and impractical invasion schemes of the time, like the proposed occupation of Pantellaria (Operation WORKSHOP) and equally unrealistic adventures against Rhodes and other islands. Hutton was involved with the first such amphibious vessels, which, built by Scotts Shipbuilding & Engineering in great secrecy, were given the cover name of A-lighters.[24] They found more useful work in supplying the besieged Tobruk garrison, but suffered heavy losses from the Luftwaffe's Ju87 Stuka dive-bomber units during their attempts. Unfortunately, Hutton was reported missing in action after his command, *LCT-15*, was sunk in one such attack on 27 April 1941; Humphrey Hopper, was appointed to command the 2,326-ton minesweeper depot ship *St Tudno* at Sheerness, and was later awarded the DSO for his work with minesweepers opening up the Scheldt, and clearing a route to Rotterdam and Ijmuiden, Operation FIREBALL, enabling Belgium to be freed from German occupation. Post-war he retired as a commodore with a DSO and MiD, as well as the Belgian Order of

---

23. *Reports and Studies Relating to War Damage and Protection of Ships*, RG.19 – Item S-14 – 27 Boxes. Box 16. ARC ID 1104997. National Archives and Research Administration (NARA) College Park, MD.

24. They were of 226 tons (229.6 tonnes) and 46 feet (14.021m) long, with petrol engines developing 1,000bhp (745.699kW) for a speed of 10 knots (18.52 km/h) and were armed with two single 2-pounder (0.907kg) pom-poms.

Leopold and the Croix de Guerre, on 25 November 1948; Lieutenant-Commander Massey Goolden later became SNO Halifax, Nova Scotia, and retired as a captain in 1928. He founded the Massey Goolden Squash Trophy. Recalled to service during the Second World War, he became SNO Esquimalt in 1942, retired for the second time in March 1944 and settled in Canada; John Forrest was a lieutenant-commander at Devonport in 1935–36 and later achieved a different sort of fame as secretary of the Royal Navy Rugby Union team between 1946 and 1948; William Adams who went on the cruiser *Cambrian* and then the sloop *Valerian* (Commander William Arthur Usher)[25] had an exciting time. He became a destroyer man, serving in the *Seawolf* (Commander Geoffrey Schomberg CB DSC), *Vendetta* (Lieutenant-Commander Hugh Evelyn Raymond), *Codrington* (Commander Noel Marcus Francis Corbett), the *Sepoy* (Lieutenant-Commander William Leslie Graham Adams),[26] *Wolfhound* (Lieutenant-Commander Edward William Boyd Sim) and *Foxhound* (Lieutenant-Commander Stuart Austin Buss). He moved to Naval Intelligence Division and then became Executive Officer (XO) of the light cruiser *Perth* (Captain Harold Bruce Farncomb RAN) in 1939. During the war he was in the Persian Gulf in 1941 as commander of the Armed Merchant Cruiser *Kanimbla* when she stormed the port of Bandar Shapuron at the head of the Gulf on 25 August with her flotilla, and captured the German ships *Weisenfels*, *Wildenfels*, *Sturnfels* and *Hohenfels*, the Italian *Caboto*, *Barbara* and *Bronto*, and the Persian gunboats *Karkas* and *Shabaaz*. He later survived the sinking of the *Prince of Wales* (Captain John Catterall Leach) and *Repulse* (Captain Sir William George Tennant), and was Director of Coastal Forces in 1944–45 and, later, as a Rear-Admiral and an OBE, was aboard the carrier *Implacable* (Captain Cecil Aubrey Lawson Mansergh KBE CB) post-war, commanding the training squadron which also included the carrier *Indefatigable* (Captain John Annesley Grindle). After leaving *Raleigh*, Robert (Robin) Todhunter served aboard the battle-cruiser *Repulse* (Captain Herbert Wiles Webley Hope) during the Duke of York's round the world cruise, and was aboard the aircraft-carrier *Furious* (Captain Thomas Hope Troubridge) during the Norwegian campaign in 1940. Later he worked with Combined Operations where, as a captain, he became Director of Landing Craft procurement and, in the USA, helped develop the landing craft personnel (large) LCP (L). By 1944 Todhunter was a Director (DCoM) at Royal Navy College, Dartmouth, in 1951 and retired soon afterward, but not to rest for, in 1987 at the age of eighty-three, he became the oldest man to compete on the Cresta Run. He died in 1999. Lieutenant John A. Grindle became the Executive Officer of the famous battleship *Warspite* (Captain Douglas Blake Fisher OBE) in 1940 and later performed the same role for the battleship *Rodney* (Captain James William Rivett-Carnac DSC) in 1941; he organised the landing craft

---

25. See Diary of Rear-Admiral W. L. G. Adams, (NMM JOD/118) National Maritime Museum, Greenwich. The *Valerian* was caught in a huge hurricane off Bermuda in October 1926 and sank with most of her crew.

26. The *Sepoy* was badly damaged at Hong Kong, and several men killed, by the premature explosion of a depth charge aboard her and was paid off, brought home and scrapped.

flotillas used in the successful invasion of Sicily – Operation HUSKY – in 1943 and later took command of the fast minelayer *Apollo* later in the war. Post-war he commanded the aircraft carrier *Indefatigable* in the training squadron from March 1950. Lieutenant Hopper went on to Combined Operations and earned high praise for the clearing of the River Scheldt in 1945, enabling the First Canadian Army advancing into north Germany on the 'long left flank' of the British Army, to be supplied. Lieutenant Orr-Ewing served aboard the battle-cruiser *Hood* (Captain Ralph Kerr), leaving just before her final sortie in May 1941, then took command of the light cruiser *Diomede* and, subsequently, the fast minelayer *Abdiel*, in which he was sunk in Taranto harbour when she was herself mined; post-war he commanded the battleship *Anson* in the training squadron in 1947. Midshipman Adams later earned fame with Coastal Forces during the war, gaining a CB and an OBE, and post-war became Flag Officer, Training Squadron, at Portland where he was relieved by Stephen Carlill. Herbert Lovegrove had an eventful enough career; a commander by 1938, as a captain during the war he became Deputy Naval Assistant to the Second Sea Lord by 1944, and post-war saw service with the Royal New Zealand Navy. He finally retired in 1956 with a KCB and CBE. Midshipman Geoffrey Gowlland's pre-war career embraced the extremes of the submarine *L-56* (Lieutenant-Commander John Reginald Hughes D'Aeth) in the 2nd Submarine Flotilla at Malta, and then a dizzy succession of aircraft-carrier appointments, *Eagle, Furious, Vindictive, Argus, Glorious, Eagle* again and *Glorious* once more; his twin, Langton Gowlland, served aboard the aircraft carrier *Ark Royal* (Captain Arthur John Power) and the cruiser *Frobisher* (Captain Peveril Barton Reibey Wallop William-Powlett), later commanding the light cruiser *Birmingham* when she was torpedoed in the eastern Mediterranean in 1943 while conveying a cargo of gold to the Egyptian Government.

To expand this theme of success rather than alleged failure, Carlill became Vice-Admiral Sir Stephen, a KBE and CB with a well-merited DSO. His pre-war ships included the battleship *Ramillies* (Captain Ronald Wolseley Oldham), the minelayer *Adventure* (Captain Robert Gordon Duke), the heavy cruiser *Norfolk* (Captain Alexander Guy Berners Wilson), the New Zealand-manned light cruiser *Dunedin* (Captain Martin John Coucher de Meric MVO), battle-cruiser *Hood* (Captain Arthur Francis Pridham) and light cruiser *Galatea* (Captain Edward Gerald Hyslop Bellars). His war was mainly spent in destroyers, commanding the *Hunt*-class ships *Hambledon* and *Farndale* between 1940 and 1942, then the new fleet destroyer *Quilliam*. Post-war he served in the Admiralty and with the British Pacific Fleet at Hong Kong aboard the heavy cruiser *London* (Captain Peter Grenville Lyon Cazalet) during the Yangtse Incident, and the aircraft-carrier *Illustrious* (Captain Ralph Alan Bevan Edwards), before becoming Flag Officer Training Squadron aboard the light fleet carrier *Theseus* (Captain Anthony Cecil Capel Miers), 1954–55. Stephen Carlill in fact relieved Adams as Flag Officer, Training Squadron, Portland Harbour, in 1954, thirty-two years after *Raleigh*'s stranding. His last appointment was as the final British Chief-of-Staff of the Indian Navy to 1958. As a last example, Charles Lambe joined the battleship *Benbow* (Captain James Fownes Somerville) in the Mediterranean in 1923 as a lieutenant and, after torpedo training, was appointed to the flotilla leader *Stuart* (Captain Charles Albert Freemantle). By 1930 he was a lieutenant-commander aboard the cruiser *Hawkins* (Captain Lancelot Ernest Holland) in the East Indies and then rejoined destroyers before becoming equerry to the king in 1936. His first command was the light cruiser *Dunedin* and further Admiralty appointments followed before he became captain of the aircraft-carrier *Illustrious* with the British Pacific Fleet in 1945. Post-war he was Flag officer, Training, and then Commander the 3rd Aircraft Carrier Squadron, Home Fleet. A vice-admiral in 1950, C-in-C Far East in 1953 and admiral in 1954, he became Second Sea Lord, C-in-C Mediterranean Fleet and NATO Commander, Allied Forces Mediterranean in 1957. He ended his career as First Sea Lord and Chief of Naval Staff in 1959, the apex of anyone's naval career – *Raleigh* or not.

Allegations of some baneful *Raleigh* influence on her survivors' careers can thus be seen to be spectacularly and totally groundless. Other myths, unfounded allegations and downright misinterpretations surrounding this incident, which are still widely promulgated in Canada without any substantiation or relationship to the facts right up to the present day, can be similarly dismissed; they are:

1: *Raleigh* certainly did *sight* an iceberg but most certainly did *not* strike an iceberg, nor did she suddenly see an iceberg and 'swerve to miss it', thus running aground. Between sighting the iceberg, at a distance at 1457, and changing course at 1524, twenty-seven minutes had elapsed; and between sighting the berg and running aground at 1539 forty-two minutes had passed. Contrary to this being the major contributory factor, Vice-Admiral Carlill recorded at the time that he had ample time to study it from afar at his leisure. 'Lambe was the OOW, and sent a messenger down to say that there was an iceberg about six miles on the port beam. I went up to have a look at it. Immensely massive and motionless – I remember it struck me what an awkward thing it would be to bump into in a fog or at night.' This was before the fog came down and Carlill was having a cup of tea later when the start of the ship's siren 'was the first intimation that we had run into a fog'.[27] Another eyewitness recalled that 'icebergs were in the vicinity and one was in sight during the afternoon watch distant about three miles on the port side of the ship'.[28]

2: The *Raleigh* was *not* proceeding 'full steam ahead' when she struck. Her log clearly shows she had reduced speed from the economical 12 knots at which she had been instructed to steam, to just 8 knots at 1537.

3: The *Raleigh* had reverted to the status of private ship and was therefore *not* a 'Flagship' at the time of her loss.

---

27. Carlill Diary, *op. cit.*
28. *The Naval Review*, May 1923, *op. cit.*

4: Reports in the *New York Times* and other newspapers at the time, and allegations since, that Vice-Admiral William Pakenham was on board when she stranded are totally false.

It was impossible to refloat the *Raleigh* and so she was stripped of everything worthwhile and then abandoned on the rocks. Four years later, in 1926, despite the fact that she had become a tourist attraction with the passing ocean liners of the Canadian Pacific Railway who used to divert and pass close to her during the summer months for the benefit of their passengers, the Admiralty considered her to be a hazard to shipping and ordered her to be recovered. Further surveys resulted in the conclusion that this was just impracticable, if not impossible, and so it was decided to dynamite her to pieces.

Four years after the original calamitous event, the *Capetown* (now commanded by Captain Oswald Henry Dawson) and *Calcutta* (now under the command of Captain Andrew Browne Cunningham) returned to the wreck site to carry out Vice-Admiral John Ian Edward Drummond's[29] orders from the Admiralty to remove as much of the wreck as possible and render what remained unrecognisable.[30] A party from the *Capetown* conducted a preliminary survey of the wreck and removed the main top section of her masting. This was followed by a team from the *Capetown* which removed the gunshields of the 7.5-inch main armament, what remained of the other mast and other items.[31] Finally, on 23 September, *Calcutta* returned to carry out the final demolitions, which took five days to complete.

While much earnest debate has recently been conducted on an internet site concerning the alleged shelling of the wreck by the Royal Navy, with 'experts' giving their detailed analysis of what effects certain types of shells had on the *Raleigh*'s structure, many continue to speculate on just how it was done. All could have saved themselves much heartache by consulting the memoirs of the man who oversaw the operation, Britain's most famous and successful wartime naval commander, Admiral of the Fleet Viscount Cunningham. Here he explains both why this work was done and precisely how he did it.

The cruiser *Raleigh* had gone ashore on Point Amour, on the Labrador side of the Strait of Belle Isle, in August 1922, and had become a total loss. The ship was fast on the rocks, and a Canadian professor who often made the voyage through the Straits had written to the Admiralty suggesting that the wreck should be blown up, as the sight of it lying there apparently undamaged caused much derision

---

29. Drummond died on 15 November 1926 at the early age of 53, so these were among his last official decisions.
30. It has been alleged in Canada that negotiations with the Halifax salvage company of James Augustus Farquhar & Co. had failed due to the possibility of live ammunition remaining *in situ*.
31. However, contrary to these reports, again, it is claimed by dive groups that her 'gun turrets' are still clearly visible on the seabed. In truth *Raleigh*'s big guns were carried in open mountings and *not* in enclosed turrets.

among his American fellow passengers at the expense of the Royal Navy.[32] So we had been ordered to destroy her, and were given an unlimited allowance of depth-charges to do so.

We anchored in Forteau Bay, Labrador, our first sight of the *Raleigh* having shown us how right the professor was. Except for the absence of guns and a rusty side the ship looked quite undamaged. The winter ice had pressed her hard up on the rocky shore; but on surveying her I found 2 fathoms (3.675m) of water on the landward side and no less than 5 fathoms (9.144m) to seaward. One supposes that the distance from a port with the necessary appliances, or the lateness of the season, prevented any effort to salve her at the time. Her destruction proved a tough proposition. She was very strongly built; but by blowing our way down to the magazines and putting the charges there we finally made a complete job of it.[33] When we left her, the bow and stern were off[34] and the port side blown right out. She looked like a wrecked tank, quite unrecognizable as once having been a ship.[35]

Despite this work much wreckage still remains. In a more concerned and conscious age the Royal Canadian Navy was forced to return again to the wreck site in 2003 and 2005 when dive teams from the Department of National Defence were involved clearing ordnance from the seabed and removed a large number of still (allegedly) 'live' 7.9-inch rounds and other ammunition. The work was probably done in response to lobbying by the Ordnance Controls and Remediation Services Decommissioning Consulting Services Ltd., which still continues. It is claimed that four locals have

---

32. These Americans ought to have first examined the motes in their own eyes. A year after *Raleigh* went ashore in thick fog, on the other side of the North American continent, a squadron of fourteen US Navy 1,190-ton (1,209 tonnes) *Clemson*-class destroyers encountered similar conditions at Devil's Jaws, a notorious danger spot off Point Arguello at Honda Point, on the north edge of the Santa Barbara Channel, California. No fewer than nine of the destroyers, *Delphy* (DD-261, Captain Edward Howe Watson), with the Squadron Navigator, Lieutenant-Commander Donald Taylor Hunter, embarked, *Chauncey* (DD-296, Lieutenant-Commander Richard Henry Booth), *Farragut* (DD-300, Lieutenant-Commander John Franklin McCain), *Fuller* (DD-297, Lieutenant-Commander Walter Dudley Seed Jr.), *Nichols* (DD-311, Lieutenant-Commander Herbert Otto Roesch), *Somers* (DD-301, Commander William Peace Gaddis), *S. P. Lee* (DD-310, Commander Howard Hartwell James Benson), *Young* (DD-312, Commander William Lowndes Calhoun) and *Woodbury* (DD-309, Commander Louis Poisson Davis) ran aground and only the *Farragut* and *Somers* managed to get themselves off again, the rest being lost with twenty-three men killed. Whereas *Raleigh* was demolished in 1926, the seven American destroyer wrecks were still in evidence as late as August 1929 and were not broken up for several years after that.
33. The resulting spectacular detonation blew a large chunk of *Raleigh*'s superstructure right atop the cliff, a good 250 yards (228.60m) distant where it remains.
34. The size of the bow section demolished was 90 feet (27.423m) in length and the stern section was a chunk some 30 feet (9.144m) long. The ship's upperworks were also pulverised.
35. Cunningham of Hyndhope, Admiral of the Fleet Viscount Kt GCB OM DSP, *A Sailor's Odyssey*, p.129, 1951, London, Hutchinson.

been killed by the detonation of munitions from the *Raleigh* in the nine decades since she was wrecked.[36] However, ten years on, amateur dive teams are still reporting the odd shell being discovered in the vicinity, as when the Navy Island Dive Company's owner, Mark Sprague, dived on the wreck to commemorate the ninetieth anniversary of the loss.

Neither the *Raleigh*, nor the unfortunate *Lily* before her, were the first nor by any means the last ships to come to grief in the Cove of the Dead. During the Second World War the *Raleigh*'s wreck site was witness to extraordinary scenes when a panic broke out among the ships of convoy SC46 on 26 September 1941. Fearing they were under U-boat attack the convoy scattered, resulting in one collision and many near misses. The 4,957 GRT *Empire Mallard* (ex-*Anacortes*, Master J. C. McLaren) collided with the Latvian *Everoja* (Master Aldred Kirshfelots) and also the *Empire Moon*. While the latter two were damaged but survived, the former went ashore and was a total write-off. The 3,044 GRT *Culebra* (ex- *Riposto*, Master George Douglas Bonner) was another victim, also running aground the far side of Forteau Bay, her captain being killed, but she was subsequently salvaged and repaired. Both the 6,262 GRT *Empire Kudu* (Master C. A. Beacham) and the 5,619 GRT *South Wales* (Master F. Sydney H. Grice) also ran aground, almost atop the *Raleigh* and *Lily*'s remains. *Empire Kudu* (the former *Duquesne*) was reported to be 'Aground Point Amour 26/9. Abandoned', with the loss of Second Engineer George Keig. But it was later noted 'Vessel may be salved'.[37] In fact the ship was a write-off but David Ballantyne Caswell, a salvage expert, managed to get 6,300 tons of steel, copper and aluminium scrap, plus 900 tons of phosphates, off the wreck to feed Canada's war-starved economy.[38]

A year later a U-boat really *was* present in the strait and found a victim here; the 1,781GRT Great Lakes steamer *Donald Stewart* (Master Daniel Percy Nolan), from convoy LN-7, was torpedoed by the *U-517* (*Kapitänleutnant* Paul Hartwig) and sank very close to *Raleigh*'s last resting place on 3 September 1942. Ships continue to find their nemesis here and probably will do as long as men venture out in such waters.

---

36. See Long, Terrance P., Manager OCRSDCS, 'Introduction to Sea Dumped Munitions and Hazardous Wrecks', address to the Canada-Nova Scotia Offshore Petroleum Board, 14 July 2005.
37. BT/389/11, Movements Card, National Archives, Kew, London. See also Voyage Records Cards (VRCs) at Guildhall Library, Aldermanbury, London. South Wales details in Gwent Archives, Ebbw Vale, West Wales Steamship Company, GB0218. D3856.
38. Pritchard, Professor James S., *A Bridge of Ships: Canadian Shipbuilding during the Second World War*, 2011, McGill-Queen's University Press. *Empire Mallard*, also written off, was described as a 'Marine Casualty' (BT 385/60); *Empire Kudu* was a 'Total Loss' (BT 385/59), both National Archives, Kew, London.

Chapter 13

Short-cut to Nowhere

The *Effingham*, 18 May 1940

The big cruisers of the 'Improved *Birmingham*-class' were, despite the unfortunate loss of the *Raleigh*, considered to be excellent sea-boats, being designed with distant-water operations in mind. They had high freeboards and long-range; their conversion, while building, to oil propulsion increased their shp by 10,000 and, instead of their intended anti-aircraft armament of twelve 4-inch, six of them being HA guns capable of engaging aircraft, they mounted three 4-inch weapons. They were strongly-constructed and had generous crew accommodation for their day. They were well-aired and ventilated, which made them ideal flagships for hot-weather stations around the world, which, on their leisurely peacetime completion, they spent the greater part of their lives. Many consider them to be the first 'heavy' cruisers as the term later became to be known, and their existence caused much heartache and envy in other nations, particularly in the United States.

The *Effingham* was ordered in December 1915 and laid down on the slipway at the Royal Dockyard, Portsmouth, on 6 April 1917, but construction was not pressed forward and she still lay there in an incomplete state three years later. In fact, so slow was her progress that it provoked questions in the House of Commons, with the usual evasion and procrastination from the Government benches.

Sir Thomas Bramsdon (Liberal) asked[1] Sir James Craig (Unionist), the Parliamentary Secretary to the Admiralty, whether he would reveal

> when the cruiser *Effingham* was first laid down in Portsmouth Dockyard, her tonnage, estimated cost, and when was it expected at that time that she would be completed; what is her present state; how many men are now engaged in her construction and is it intended to finish her, and by what date; what is the value of the work already done upon her and will the delay in her construction render her obsolescent; in view of the Admiralty's intention to allow merchant ships to be constructed when will the slip now occupied by the *Effingham* be vacant so that a new mercantile keel can be put down?

Sir James responded that:

---

1. *Hansard*, Volume 131, cc 420–1, dated 30 June 1920.

Effingham was first laid down on 2nd April, 1917. Her tonnage is 9,750 tons. The estimated cost cannot at present be given, as this matter is still under consideration. She was originally laid down as part of the War programme without definite date for completion, but to be accelerated as required. So far as the dockyard work is concerned, the condition is about 35 per cent complete. The machinery, however, which is being obtained by contract, is about 97 per cent complete, and the gun mountings are ready. The average number of men engaged in her construction during the last four weeks is about 890. It is the intention to finish her, but the date cannot at present be given. The value of the work already done is £953,249. Any delay in her construction will not render her obsolescent. So far as can be foreseen at present, with the men available and the work in prospect, the slip now occupied by the *Effingham* will be vacant about May, 1921.

This reply did not satisfy and Bramsdon pressed the matter further. 'Do I understand that it is now the intention of the Admiralty to proceed with the completion of this ship, and is it not a fact that it is occupying the principal slip in the dockyard where mercantile ships could be put down?' A bland 'politician's reply' was received: 'There are great difficulties at the moment. It is not intended to proceed with it as rapidly as possible, but as rapidly as the circumstances permit.' This moved an intervention by the well-known pacifist and anti-war politician Richard Cornthwaite Lambert (Liberal): 'Is it not an uneconomical proceeding to lay down a ship three years ago and only have reached this stage of completion?', to which Sir John gave another urbane, and equally unrevealing reply: 'As my right Honourable Friend knows, a good deal has happened in the last three years.'

Even with this spur the work dragged on and she was not launched by Lady Salisbury[2] until 8 June 1921, being named in honour of Lord Howard of Effingham (1536–1624), who had been Lord High Admiral of the English Fleet in the destruction of the Spanish Armada. *Effingham*, strangely-enough, was the first Royal Navy vessel to carry this name.[3] Even when finally afloat, construction continued at a snail's pace and she was not commissioned under the command of Captain Cecil Nugent Reyne until 2 July 1925, finally entering service on 25 July, an incredibly slow rate of construction, even for the Royal Dockyards, and an eight-year process that reflected only too accurately the parsimony of the immediate post-Great War era. This pushed her total cost well over the £2 million mark which made her an expensive proposition.

The *Effingham* spent most of her time in the Far East and, as Flagship of the Far Eastern Squadron, from May 1925 to September 1925 under Captain Reyne. He was followed by a succession of commanding officers over the following decade: Captain Roger Mowbray Bellairs from October 1925 to October 1927; Captain Patrick Macnamara between October 1927 and September 1929; Captain Bruce Austin Fraser

---

2. Cicely, *née* Gore, wife of the Marquis of Salisbury.
3. After her loss the name was perpetuated in the Royal Navy as a shore base, being a Combined Operations Base at Dartmouth (the former *Dartmouth III* at Eaton House) from 19 July 1943.

from September 1929 to October 1932. On 30 October 1930 *Effingham* arrived at the port of Berbera, British Somaliland, at the southern mouth of the Gulf of Aden and, on 2 November, representatives of the ship, having transferred across the border to Addis Ababa, attended the coronation of His Imperial Majesty Haile Selassie of Ethiopia, (who went by the modest title of 'King of Kings, Lord of Lords, Conquering Lion of Judah'). The *Effingham* herself received a mention in Arthur Evelyn St John Waugh's short satirical account of the event, which he saw as an elaborate façade to cover the barbarous manner in which Haile Selassie had come to power.[4] *Effingham* featured because, as well as transporting some celebrity guests, she had provided her Royal Marine Band to play for the event.

Having spent most of her early years in the exotic regions of the East Indies, *Effingham* was briefly reduced to the role of Flagship to the Reserve Fleet in 1932 before, on 14 June, she hoisted the flag of Rear-Admiral Martin Eric Dunbar-Smith. On 1 October Captain Bruce Austin Fraser OBE became her commanding officer and she was once more allocated to the 4th Cruiser Squadron, East Indies. From March 1933 the *Effingham* commenced a Bay of Bengal cruise which was completed in April whereupon she returned home. On 29 July she left Rosyth for Portsmouth, arriving the next day. In April 1934 a new commanding officer was appointed, Captain Cuthbert Coppinger, and he took her over on the 24th. She also was flagship to a succession of Cs-in-C, including Vice-Admiral William Munro Kerr, then, from June 1934, Vice-Admiral Edward Astley Astley-Rushton, and, from 28 June 1936, Vice-Admiral Gerald Charles Dickens, serving in Home Waters, including attendance of the Silver Jubilee Review. Captain Wilfred Rupert Patterson commanded between March and September 1936 and on 29 September the *Effingham* ceased to be the Flagship of Vice-Admiral Dickens and entered Devonport Dockyard for a major re-construction.

Under the terms of the London Naval Treaty the three surviving cruisers of this class, *Effingham*, *Frobisher* and *Hawkins*, were supposed to be scrapped because the thirteen *County*-class cruisers and the two further 8-inch gun armed units (which had been reduced in size and power due to Labour government reductions of defence expenditure), *Exeter* and *York*, would by then have totalled the fifteen such units the Royal Navy was permitted to operate. However, due to their size, speed and acknowledged usefulness, plans were put forward to re-build and re-arm the three 'Improved Birminghams' as 6-inch cruisers to fill an expected gap until the new *Town*-class ships could be completed, utilising spare 6-inch single guns that were becoming spare mountings due to the modernising of the smaller C-class cruisers *Coventry* and *Curlew* and their conversion into AA ships. All three were scheduled to be taken in hand and various alternate plans were put forward based on designs promulgated by the Directors of Naval Construction at the time, Sir Arthur William Johns KCB CBE and then Sir Stanley Vernon Goodall.

---

4. Waugh, Evelyn, *The Coronation of Emperor Haile Selassie of Abyssinia*, 1935, London, Allen Lane, The Penguin Press.

The *Effingham*, the last of the trio to have been completed, was selected to be the lead ship in this re-building programme and was taken in hand in 1937 with the work extending for over two years. Her old armament was stripped out and the forward superstructure re-modelled; nine 6-inch BL Mk XIII guns with 30-degree elevation in open-backed shields were added, three super-firing forward and three aft, with a fourth on her after quarterdeck, plus two mounted on either beam amidships, just abaft the new single massive flat-sided and unraked funnel which had trunked access from the boilers, two of the old ones being removed and the remaining ten Yarrow-type being replaced by more efficient types. The shp was reduced to 56,000 which, driving four shafts, gave her a best speed of 29.75 knots at deep load. She now had a range of 5,400 nautical miles (10,000km) at an economical speed of 14 knots (26 km/h).[5] The raised superstructure was split into two, with a gap between, with an aircraft-handling crane of the type later mounted aboard most cruiser classes in the 1930s but, in the event, the planned Supermarine Walrus amphibians, to be perched on a newly-designed rotating launch catapult, were never actually carried. On the forward superstructure a new bridge was built around a stump tripod fighting-top for AA control which housed two directors and a rangefinder, with a pole mast abaft it. On the after superstructure was a second pole mast. The initial 'fix' saw her mount four single 4-inch guns as a temporary armament but these were later replaced by four twin 4-inch QF Mk XVI HA guns which were added on each side both fore and aft for a total of eight barrels, while close-range weaponry comprised a pair of quadruple 2-pounder pom-poms either side of the bridge, and three quadruple 0.5-inch machine guns were carried on the after superstructure. The underwater torpedo-tubes were taken out, but the fixed above-deck torpedo-tubes were retained. Oil-fuel capacity increased to 2,620 tons. These alterations (which were done in two stages) left her with a displacement of 12,514 tons on the outbreak of war. Her peacetime complement was 690 officers and men, increased to over 800 in full wartime configuration.

On 13 April 1938 the *Effingham* was under dockyard control but on 15 June the ship was re-commissioned at Portsmouth with Captain Bernard Armitage Warburton Warburton-Lee in command, as Flagship of Vice-Admiral Max Kennedy Horton, Commander-in-Chief Reserve Fleet. After an initial shakedown cruise she returned to Portsmouth on the 23rd and remained there from the 30th for Navy Week, where she was open to the public.

In April 1939 Captain B. A. W. Warburton-Lee relinquished command, being appointed to command the flotilla leader *Hardy* from 28 July, and he was succeeded by Captain John Montague Howson, who, at the age of forty-seven, was an experienced officer who had served both in the Mercantile Marine and the Royal Navy at intervals for many years. During the First World War he had served with the Harwich Force at

---

5. Unfortunately, when refitting the new condenser tubes inserted proved to be from a faulty batch, a weakness very quickly revealed in a period of hard steaming in severe weather conditions during the first winter of the war, and she had to be re-tubed at Portsmouth Dockyard between January and March 1940.

the Battle of Dogger Bank in 1915, and at The Nore, and commanded a hospital ship in the Black Sea in 1919. He was appointed in command of *Effingham* and as Chief of Staff to Vice-Admiral Sir Max Horton, Commander-in-Chief Reserve Fleet on 17 April 1939.[6]

On 9 August 1939, the cruiser attended a Royal review of the Reserve Fleet of 133 ships in Weymouth Bay, she being manned by reservists and the fleet being inspected by HM King George VI from the Royal Yacht *Victoria and Albert*. His Majesty went aboard the *Effingham* and was presented to sixty commanding officers. On dismissal of the fleet *Effingham* was retained in commission and sailed north to work up her reserve crew with the Home Fleet, arriving at Scapa Flow itself on 25 August 1939. On arrival *Effingham* was assigned to the 12th Cruiser Squadron. The cruisers of this unit, *Cardiff* (Captain Philip King Enright), *Dunedin* (Captain Charles Edward Lambe CVO) and *Emerald* (Captain Augustus Willington Shelton Agar VC DSO) with *Effingham* flying the flag of Vice-Admiral Sir Max Horton, now designated Vice-Admiral Commanding Northern Patrol, were assigned to duty with the Northern Patrol, whose main tasks were to intercept German merchant ships attempting to get home prior to the outbreak of war, and to intercept any German raiders being pre-deployed to attack Allied shipping in the North Atlantic. They were joined in this task by the *Delhi* (Captain Louis Henry Keppel Hamilton DSO) and *Enterprise* (Captain Henry Jack Egerton) of the 11th Cruiser Squadron as soon as those two ships had completed emergency refits.

On the declaration of war on 3 September 1939 the ships of 12th Cruiser Squadron were already at work on their assigned tasks and, during a three-week period, intercepted 108 suspect merchant vessels, twenty-eight of which were sent into Kirkwall; however *Effingham* did not contribute much to this effort, being forced to return to Scapa after her first patrol stint on the 6th with damage. She had to be sent south to Devonport on 2 October, arriving the next day. For the next few days she was in dockyard hands

---

6. He subsequently saw service at the Dunkirk evacuation, for which he received an MiD and, on 10 June 1940, joined the staff of Admiral Sir Martin Dunbar-Nasmith, C-in-C Western Approaches, at HMS *Drake* at Plymouth. On 17 February 1941 he moved to become Deputy Chief-of-Staff to Admiral Sir Percy Noble, the new Commander-in-Chief Western Approaches, at HMS *Eaglet*, Liverpool. On 15 February he was appointed Chief-of-Staff to Admiral Commander Force H (Vice-Admiral Sir Neville Syfret) aboard the battleship *Malaya* (Captain John William Ashley Waller) and, from 27 August 1942, aboard the battleship *Nelson* (Captain Humphrey Benson Jacomb). He saw service in the Mediterranean, at Madagascar during Operation IRONCLAD, for which he received another MiD, and on Malta convoy Operation PEDESTAL in 1942 and the North African landings, followed by the landings in Sicily and at the Straits of Messina, Italy, in 1942 and 1943. On termination of Force H, he received his third MiD and, on 1 January 1944, was appointed Senior Naval Officer Persian Gulf in HMS *Euphrates* at Basra and in September moved to become Senior Naval Officer East Indies Fleet at HMS *Hathi*, Delhi. Post-war he was briefly naval *Aide de Camp* to His Majesty King George VI and retired on 2 January 1946, dying in 1948. See *Memoirs relating to Service in World War I and World War II of Captain John Montague Howson RN Rtd*, Ref: 96/56/1, *GB 0099 KCLMA Howson*, held at Liddell Hart Centre, King's College, Strand, London.

while essential repairs were attended to. She left Plymouth on the 9th and, six days later, relieved the heavy cruiser *Berwick* (Captain Irving Montgomery Palmer DSO) as main ocean escort for convoy KJ3 *en route* from Kingston, Jamaica. She remained with this convoy until the 25th but was still experiencing worrying engine problems and once more had to be detached, returning yet again to Devonport where she underwent boiler cleaning between 26 October and 7 November.

Effingham's size and internal capacity was to make her a natural choice for all manner of duties not normally associated with her type and one of the most important at this time was the transportation across the dangerous North Atlantic of £2 million of Britain's gold reserves, needed to pay for American war materials. The USA insisted on a 'cash and carry' system and, to pay for it, *Effingham* embarked this bullion on 7 November in Devonport dockyard under heavy security. She sailed and arrived safely at Halifax, Nova Scotia, ten days later, mission accomplished.

At Halifax Howson was appointed Senior Officer West Indies Patrol and, on the 24th, sailed to Bermuda dockyard in company with the Australian light cruiser *Perth* (Captain Harold Bruce Farncomb MVO). From Bermuda the two ships were employed on interception patrols between Kingston and Halifax from 3 to 6 December but it was not long before her troublesome condensers were again making themselves known and she was forced to go for more repair work at Bermuda from the 9th onward. After four days it was found that the problem was beyond the power of Bermuda to rectify. That 'bad batch' of condenser tubes fitted during her major re-construction were such that no amount of tinkering with the problem would suffice to make her reliable. Accordingly, the decision was taken to send *Effingham* home and have a complete new set fitted at Portsmouth dockyard. Accordingly she sailed to Halifax, where she picked up another trans-Atlantic convoy, HX14, on 29 December, staying in company until 9 January when she was detached and finally arrived at Portsmouth on the 10th, where she was taken in hand the following day. It proved a major job, her engines having to be totally stripped down and the tubes removed and replaced, and it was not until three months later, on 13 April 1940, that she was ready to re-join the war. It could be said that *Effingham*'s war-time career up to this point was scant, she having spent more time in dockyard hands than on actual operations. Post-repair trials were conducted in April and *Effingham* had already been allocated to take part in Churchill's plan to violate Norwegian neutrality by occupying the port of Narvik, Operation R4.

She duly sailed to Scapa Flow on 12 April to join this group; however, all such schemes were rudely interrupted by the surprise German invasion of Norway on the 8th which beat the British to the punch. Supported by overwhelming air power, to which the Allies could offer little or no response, the Germans were soon well established in the south of the country and began a steady progress northward to relieve their bridgehead at Narvik, where two British naval victories had left the tough Bavarian commander of the *Heer*'s 3rd *Gebirgs-Division* (3rd Mountain Division), *Generalmajor* Eduard Dietl, and his men stranded in the hills above the town but still, after a very brief period of demoralisation, increasingly resolute. The British army commander, Major-General Pierse Joseph Mackesy, and the British Flag Officer,

Admiral of the Fleet William Henry Dudley 'Ginger' Boyle, The Lord Cork and Orrery, GCB GCVO, were constantly at loggerheads on how to proceed to evict the enemy, the former favouring a carefully-prepared and measured step-by-step advance, the latter urging action before the rest of the German army arrived. In the end the 'Hawks' back home, led by the ever-impatient Churchill, had Mackesy replaced, but even then, in the end, little practical was achieved until too late.

On Tuesday 16 April Lord Cork & Orrery reported that, until the conditions of snow and ice improved, which was not expected until the end of the month, operations across country were not possible. In co-operation with the military commander he therefore intended to start redistributing the forces on 19 April to positions closer to Narvik, in readiness for an attack on the German forces at Bjerkvik, eight miles up the Herjangs Fjord from Narvik. On that same day at 1900 an Allied aircraft reported five enemy destroyers steaming northward at high speed off Stavanger. It was thought possible that they might be on their way to occupy Ålesund and so a striking force comprising the heavy cruiser *York* (Captain Reginald Henry Portal DSC), the *Effingham*, and the destroyer *Ashanti* (Commander William Gronow Davis) was diverted to that port 'with all despatch'.[7] This force covered the disembarkation of 700-strong landing parties from the sloops *Auckland* (Lieutenant-Commander Kenneth Adair Beattie DSO), *Bittern* (Lieutenant-Commander Robert Henry Mills), *Black Swan* (Captain Albert Lawrence Poland DSC) and *Flamingo* (Commander John Herbert Huntley) and was joined by the AA cruiser *Calcutta* (Captain Dennis Marescaux Lees) with a further fifty-strong landing party intended to forestall any enemy moves.[8] On the night of 19 April the *Effingham* was unsuccessfully attacked while on patrol off Harstad with the *Aurora* and destroyers *Faulknor* (Captain Antony Fane De Salis), *Escapade* (Commander Harry Robert Graham) and *Jupiter* (Lieutenant-Commander Derek Bathurst Wyburd), by the *U-38* (*Kapitänleutnant* Heinrich Liebe KC). Anchoring at Harstad next day Lord Cork and Orrery embarked aboard her and remained until she was relieved by the light cruiser *Enterprise* (Captain John Campbell Annesley DSO).

On 24 April *Effingham*, along with the battleship *Warspite* (Captain Victor Alexander Charles Crutchley VC), light cruisers *Aurora* and *Enterprise* and destroyer *Zulu* (Commander John Stuart Crawford) conducted a prolonged, but ineffective, bombardment of German army positions around Narvik. However, results were nebulous and Allied troops embarked aboard the repair ship *Vindictive* (Captain Arthur Robert Halfhide) were not landed to follow up.

On 1 May and 3 May *Effingham*, with Lord Cork embarked once more, and along with the battleship *Resolution* and light cruiser *Aurora*, shelled German positions around Akenes, and were heavily attacked from the air at Beisfjord, Narvik. She covered the landings of French troops on the 7th and on the 12th/13th, two battalions of the French Foreign Legion were transported to Bjerkvik at Herjangsfjord by the

---

7. See War Cabinet, 'Weekly Resume (No.33) of the Naval, Military and Air Situation from 12 noon April 11th to 12 noon April 18th, 1940.' W.P. (40) 131.

8. W.P. (40) 131, *op. cit.*

Effingham flying the flag of Lord Cork, and *Aurora*. The *Resolution* landed some tanks by means of two motor landing craft (MLCs) under covering fire.

Howson's officers aboard *Effingham* by this date included Commander Humphrey Gilbert Scott and Lieutenant-Commanders Richard Isacke Clutterbuck, a veteran of the Jutland battle and the post-war Baltic operations against the Bolsheviks[9], Geoffrey Percival Packard, the gunnery officer,[10] George Moir Donan Hutcheson (Rtd)[11] and the ship's navigator, Thomas Michael Blake. Blake had been a midshipman aboard the battle-cruiser *Hood* pre-war, and on promotion to sub-lieutenant had specialised in navigation. By this date he had received two promotions, the latest to lieutenant-commander (N), on 15 February 1940 aboard the sloop *Scarborough* (Commander Charles Thorburn Addis), before joining *Effingham* on 21 May 1940. In normal conversation he usually referred to himself simply as Michael Blake. Howson called him 'my young and very capable navigator'.

Between 11 and 13 May the new Commander of IV Corps, Lieutenant-General Sir Claude John Eyre Auchinleck, met with Lord Cork aboard *Effingham*[12] and it was decided to attempt to retrieve an already dire situation by sending the 2nd South Wales Borderers from Harstad to Bodø (Blikovær), some 100-odd miles to the southward, as soon as they could be disentangled from the debacle at Ankenes.[13] They were to take with them the HQ cadre of 24 Guards Brigade and associated units plus a small number of French *Chasseurs Alpins* from 5 *Demi-Brigade*. The Admiralty duly issued the appropriate instructions with the consideration that slow troopships would be too vulnerable to air attack and that the troops should, therefore, be conveyed in fast and more strongly-armed warships. The *Effingham* was large enough to have the required carrying capacity and she duly embarked these army personnel. She was given an escort with the emphasis on AA defence. Howson recorded that he had insisted on a maximum of forty tons of stores, but that the Army totally ignored this and kept piling additional equipment on the quay so that, when *Effingham* did sail, she had 130 tons embarked. This overloading prevented some of the anti-aircraft guns and also some of the main 6-inch guns from being operated.

In compliance with Admiralty signals timed at 2025 and 2325 on 16 May, the 20th Cruiser Squadron therefore sailed from Harstad at 0100 on Friday 17 May at

---

9. Richard Clutterbuck ended the Second World War as Commander for Flotilla Duties from April 1943 and died on 30 December 1964. He is buried at Boldre, Hants.

10. According to Howson, Packard was Fleet Gunnery Officer as well as *Effingham*'s gunner; extremely hard-working he had worn himself out and had had to be relieved from that duty, but had volunteered to stay on in a reduced capacity until his relief arrived.

11. George Hutcheson later served at HMS *Drake*, Plymouth and at HMS *President*, London.

12. Note from Admiral of the Fleet Lord Cork & Orrery to Lieutenant-General Auchinleck, views on proposal to capture Narvik (2 pps) and *Report* by Lieutenant-General Auchinleck to General Sir John Greer Dill CMG DSO, Vice-Chief Imperial General Staff, dated 13 May, (3pps). See *The Military Papers 1940–48, of Field-Marshal Sir Claude Auchinleck*, AUC3/69, John Rylands Library, University of Manchester.

13. Adams, Lieutenant-Colonel Jack, *The Doomed Expedition: The Campaign in Norway 1940*, p.66, 1989, London, Leo Cooper.

an initial speed of 20 knots, increased at 0503 to 23 knots, with an intended ETA off the Svartoksen Light[14] of 2000. The diversionary 160-mile route selected passed far offshore from the southernmost extensions of the Lofoten Islands, before turning east across the mouth of Vestfjord. It was thus hoped this extended route, a far greater distance to traverse than the inner Tjedsundet route, might avoid the squadron being detected by the Luftwaffe which had almost total dominance of the air. Howson recalled that this extended route meant 'our maintaining a speed of 22 knots if we were to reach Bodø at midnight'.

The 20th Cruiser Squadron was under the command of Rear-Admiral John Guy Protheroe Vivian, Admiral Commanding Anti-Aircraft Ships,[15] flying his flag in the *Coventry* (Captain David Gilmour) as the squadron flagship with the AA cruiser *Cairo* (Captain Patrick Vivian McLaughlin);[16] the destroyers *Matabele* (Commander George Kelvin Whitmey-Smith) and *Echo* (Commander Stanley Herbert King Spurgeon RAN) completed the force.[17] The *Effingham* had embarked Brigadier James Andrew Harcourt Gammel, on the General Staff of IV Corps, Allied Forces Norway, along with 1,020 troops of the South Wales Borderers, under Lieutenant-Colonel Philip Gottwaltz MC, plus the HQ unit of 24 Guards Brigade, and 167th Field Ambulance, along with some French *chasseurs*, ten Bren-gun carriers and 130 tons of associated equipment, principally stores and ammunition. Initially the journey was uneventful, save for *Coventry* reporting the sighting of a submarine periscope one mile off the starboard quarter at 0910. By noon they were in position 68° 41′N, 12° 40′E, on a mean course of 190°, with a partly cloudy sky, excellent visibility, a smooth sea and a force 4 wind from the south-west. An aircraft was sighted to the east by the *Effingham* and the Flagship was duly informed.

A signal, time of origin 1245, was received from Flag Officer Narvik, to detach one of his two destroyers to proceed to Silbasan and destroy an armed enemy transport reported there and, at 1418, the *Matabele* was accordingly detached. At 1422 the battleship *Resolution* (Captain Oliver Bevir) and destroyers *Wren* (Commander Harold Thomas Armstrong) and *Vansittart* (Lieutenant-Commander Walter Evershed)

---

14. A small lighthouse on a rocky Skerry, about 2.2 miles (3.5km) from the entrance to Bodø.

15. Vivian had commanded the light cruiser *Newcastle* in the immediate pre-war years and was appointed to his new position on 20 March 1940. He later served with the Western Approaches at Plymouth and, from March 1941 until the end of the war, was Admiral Commanding Reserves.

16. Following revelations about the scarcity of anti-aircraft capability during the Abyssinian crisis, and the approaching scrapping date of the old C-class cruisers, the Admiralty took the wise decision to convert them by landing their 6-inch guns and shipping what was considered, for the period, a good AA armament of eight 4-inch QF guns and eight 2-pounder pom-poms.

17. *Echo* was a very late addition, having only just arrived at Harstad after having been part of the escort for troop convoy NP1 from home, and then operating patrols from Harstad. On this occasion Spurgeon did not have time to be briefed but just followed immediate orders 'on the hoof' as they went along. See Spurgeon, Commander S. H. K., DSO RAN, *Private Papers*, Imperial War Museum, London, 90/23/1. Ref: 370. RWAS, dated May 1990. Spurgeon was not alone; Howson recalled that *Cairo* was also in the dark, signalling to him while they were *en route* 'Where are we going?', Howson, *op. cit.*, p.222.

passed the force off the starboard bow, on a reciprocal course.[18] The Admiral's signal was then cancelled and *Matabele* rejoined the squadron at 1515. By 1600 the force was steering 150° and a quarter of an hour later the welcome sight of two escorting Navy aircraft were seen overhead.

In the interim period the flagship had exchanged a series of signals with *Effingham* detailing arrangements for the landing of the troops on arrival there and the ship's subsequent patrols and intended movements in support once this had been accomplished. In the light of several reports of U-boats lurking off their port of destination, Captain Howson made the suggestion that, as there seemed a high likelihood of enemy submarine activity threatening the normal conventional approach to Bodø, an alternate ['back door'] route might be adopted, passing between Briksvaer Island to the south and the Terra Archipelago, a veritable maze of tiny islets, reefs and shoals, to the north. He informed Vivian that he had the Norwegian large-scale chart No. 65 to which to refer, something *Coventry* did not possess herself. Reference to the index of the Admiralty folio showed Vivian that this chart was on their approved list, even though his flagship had not yet been issued with it. *The Norway Pilot*[19] noted that the selected route, the Briksvaer Channel, was more strewn with navigational hazards than was the regular route, but that 'vessels with local knowledge can make this passage'. This was all known at the time by Howson, and acknowledged as so in his subsequent report made to the Flag Officer Commanding Allied Force in Norway, Admiral of the Fleet The Earl of Cork and Orrery), dated 20 May 1940, sent while *en route* home after the accident. Howson, however, expressed the opinion that this 'local knowledge' qualification was not specific to the Briksvaer Channel, but was applied generally in all Norwegian waters, save for the main shipping routes, and that 'hitherto, experience had shown that no extreme regard need be paid to it, provided normal pilotage precautions were observed'. And here was the rub! Howson himself stated that, while he had no previous experience of the route:

> I did have in my possession a large-scale Norwegian chart, number 65; on which the navigational features are clearly marked in a much clearer manner and on a large scale than Admiralty Chart No.2311. On that basis, I considered that the navigation of Briksvaer Channel was perfectly practicable and recommended its use to the Rear Admiral accordingly.[20]

---

18. The battleship had been hit while anchored at Tjedsund at 1130 on 16 May by a 550lb (1,100kg) bomb in an attack by Junkers Ju88A bombers of the II/KG 30 (*Hauptmann* Klaus Hinkerbein) operating from Vaernes airfield. The bomb penetrated through three decks before detonating in the Royal Marine messdeck. Two men were killed and twenty-seven injured but the battleship was not badly hurt and continued operations. The Germans lost two aircraft from 6 *Staffel* in this raid, those piloted by *Staffelkapitän Hauptmann* Günther Noll and *Leutnant* Heinrich Diemeyer, along with their entire crews.

19. p.204, Part III, lines 21 *et seq*.

20. The fact that the light cruiser *Penelope* (Captain Gerald Douglas Yates) had gone aground on 11 April off Fleinvær, Vestfjord, not that very far from Bodø, while hunting German troopships in

Mulling over the proposition, at 1401 Vivian queried Howson whether he had any reliable information regarding the enemy dispositions to which the latter responded at 1433 'Nothing reliable'. The C-in-C then asked Howson at 1449 whether there was a possibility that the Germans had mined that particular channel, which was a mere five cables in width, with the islets of Faksen and Flua respectively marking the western entrance and the eastern exit. Howson's reply, however, was that mining was considered most unlikely. Vivian considered that, in the absence of aircraft sightings thus far, his squadron remained undetected and the advantages of avoiding submarine attacks by such an unexpected approach to Bodø were considerable. He therefore decided to adopt Howson's recommendation. As Howson had the charts and Vivian did not, it was decided that *Effingham* would take over the role of 'Guide of the Fleet' and lead the way.

At 1555 Vivian signalled to all units:

When ordered to proceed in execution of previous orders at about 1945 today, Friday, *Effingham* is to take *Matabele* and *Echo* under her orders and proceed to Bodø. *Matabele* is to provide close AA support during disembarkation. *Effingham* is to leave Bodø not later than 0001/18. *Coventry* is to patrol north-west of Bodø, *Cairo* north side of Saltfjorden to the south of Bodø. A.A. ships are to take A/S precautions while patrolling. Unless otherwise ordered, all ships are to rendezvous with my Flag off Svartoksen Light by 0030/18.

A further signal informed Howson that *Coventry* and *Cairo* would remain in *Effingham*'s wake until the squadron was clear of the channel.

Howson wrote:

In *Effingham* we happened to possess a large-scale Norwegian chart showing the details of the 'back door' entrance which up to then the Admiralty charts did not give and leading marks and navigational considerations seemed quite practical. I set course with all leading marks clear and led the cruisers on the necessary course, keeping an eye on them over my shoulder and manoeuvring them by signal. Our course necessarily left the Faksen shoal rather close on my port hand but all bearings were clear. We were still going 22 knots and all seemed set fair.[21]

By 1912 the force was in position 67° 13'N, 13° 28'E and *Coventry* dropped back astern of *Effingham* so she could lead the line and at 1922 Vivian duly signalled 'Proceed in execution of previous orders'. In compliance *Effingham* changed course to 080° and placed *Matabele* ahead and *Echo* close on her starboard bow. The speed of the squadron was 23 knots with all ships in open order. As she led off, the more elderly C-class cruisers had shown difficulty in keeping up with the *Effingham*, who was proceeding at 300 revs (22 knots) and she therefore reduced to 290 revs to make things easier for them. By 1935 Svartski Island was in clear view and course was altered by signal 10°

___

these restricted waters apparently also aroused no misgivings in Captain Howson or his superior.
21. Howson, *op. cit.*, pp.223–4.

to port together and shortly after back 10° to starboard and steadied on 080°. The *Matabele* was at this time slightly to port of the line of advance and was ordered to get ahead, which she increased speed to do and altered course to 097°. *Echo* was out of station, having drifted to starboard, which proved just as well as things fell out.

On the bridge of the *Echo* grave reservations were being felt; Spurgeon discussed with his own navigation officer, Lieutenant (N) Francis Warrington-Strong,[22] the dangers of such an inflexible approach at high-speed. Spurgeon wrote:

> My Navigator Lieutenant Warrington-Strong (pilot) pointed out that two alternative openings lay some distance ahead either of which we might be called upon to take. I checked the very small-scale chart with him and commented on the lack of flexibility our position ahead of *Effingham* entailed. About this time he pointed out a rock marked 'Faksen' on the chart, somewhere well ahead, also a wide opening off to starboard down which I felt surely we must turn. In anticipation we reduced speed to lose bearing on the two ships to port and started turning to starboard expecting *Effingham* to hoist a new course signal. Instead she hoisted '*Echo* take up your appointed station.' This immediately created a situation amounting to an order for the three ships in company to continue on what I considered, according to our chart, a very hazardous route, especially at high speed in the vicinity of one charted submerged rock marked 'Faksen' and other visible outcrops dispersed over the area.

Spurgeon nonetheless decided on a compromise course that meant he would resume that position, but not immediately.

> By this time *Echo* had dropped back to a position close on *Effingham*'s beam so I ordered a high speed of 28 knots to catch up. I told our pilot 'Take a fix', and by eye set *Echo* on a course approximating to one that would, in due course, regain station of *Matabele*. Meanwhile pilot had fixed our position on the chart – a very quick and difficult job in the circumstances and together we checked our present course for danger. We agreed that, with any luck, deep water should continue under *Echo* for several miles so long as we remained within about 50–100 yards of the rocks to starboard. We estimated that we would pass the Faksen about 3–400 yards to port. Both *Effingham* and *Matabele* should have seen *Echo*'s high stern wave breaking dangerously over adjacent rocks as we raced closely by. I could not understand their signal to us and the necessity to run so close to danger at high speed and presumed they must have had some very strong reason unbeknown to me. I was watching *Matabele* as she was gradually coming on to correct bearing for reducing speed to 17 knots. Suddenly her masts and yards commenced waving, indicating one or both propellers had touched.[23]

---

22. Warrington-Strong was a very accomplished navigator; as a commander post-war, he became Queen's Harbourmaster at Hong Kong between 1957 and 1959.
23. Spurgeon, *op. cit.*, pp.9–10.

Although the chart showed very deep water, the destroyer *Matabele*, which was the leading ship, was seen to suddenly veer off course to starboard and reduce speed. It transpired that *Matabele* had touched hard on what later proved to be the Faksen Shoal and was badly damaged. She managed to extract herself and continue operations, but in a rather reduced capacity, although she could still make 20 knots (37.04 km/h) on one engine.[24]

The *Coventry* also reported she had touched but only lightly and suffered no damage, save for a slight rupture to one fuel tank.[25]

When *Effingham* had seen *Matabele* stumble and turn, she put her own wheel over to starboard to sheer off her, and almost immediately afterward, at 1948, *Effingham* herself hit the southern edge of the Faksen Shoal off Bodø and swung sharply to port. Spurgeon recorded:

> *Effingham* must also have seen this as she started to turn away. Almost immediately a great puff of smoke billowed from her funnels as she also hit the Faksen Rock on to which she had followed *Matabele* – a few months later I heard the reason for the incredible double calamity; it was their misreading the meaning of signs on the large-scale Norwegian chart they then carried and which led them to believe no rock existed.[26]

Effingham immediately sounded a long blast on the ship's siren to warn the others. One of the soldiers on board recalled many years later:

> There was a tremendous crash and the ship tilted to port at an alarming angle before coming back to even keel. For a moment, except for the hissing of steam, there was almost complete silence, then naval officers began calmly issuing instructions. This cue was quickly followed by the officers and NCOs of the

---

24. *Matabele* reported that she had damaged her 'A' bracket and propeller and her oil sprit storage room was making water slightly. She could continue to operate, but only on one engine which was clearly a liability. On return home she was sent to Messrs Silley Cox Ship Repairers at Falmouth for repairs on 27 May, during which time her X 4.7-inch mounting was replaced by a twin 4-inch HA mounting and she rejoined the fleet on 19 August 1940.

25. Macleod, Lieutenant-Commander Kenneth John, DSC RNVR, *Memoirs*, Imperial War Museum, London, Document 6361 RWAS, dated February 1997 – Macleod being a Lieutenant serving aboard *Effingham* at the date of her loss – and Admiral-of-the-Fleet Lord Cork & Orrery, *Report*, ADM 199/485. Haarr, *op. cit.*, pp 439, maintains that Vivian made no mention of this fact but this is certainly not the case: he specifically *did* do so, see *Report*, Rear Admiral Commanding 20th Cruiser Squadron on circumstances attending the loss of HMS *Effingham*, G. Vivian, Rear-Admiral, to Admiralty, dated 19 May 1940. See also ADM 199/378.

26. Spurgeon later put on record that it was at the subsequent Board of Enquiry itself that 'For the first time I was made aware of the causes that led up to *Effingham*'s loss. As I recollect *Matabele* was not mentioned.' Spurgeon is quite specific in his memoirs that he did not see the actual report, so that was not the source of his information. He categorically recorded 'No copy of the findings of the Board has ever been received by me'. Spurgeon, *op. cit.*, pp.11–12.

South Wales Borderers and company groups soon began to form up on the decks.[27]

Howson recorded:

> to my devastating consternation I realised with horror I had ripped the bottom out of the ship, and worse had lost all motive and steering power. I was a wreck. We had gone over an uncharted rock and were now in 55 fathoms of water ... useless and unmanageable and liable to sink at any moment.[28]

Howson's command was seriously damaged, having apparently hit first on her port bow, between bulkheads 10 to 19. There followed a succession of heavy thumps from astern of 62 bulkhead. Once aground, the *Effingham* began slowly settling on an even keel with all engines stopped. Not immediately realising the *Matabele*'s own difficulties, Vivian's initial reaction to this unexpected disaster was to order her to go to *Effingham*'s aid and attempt to tow her off while *Echo* acted as an anti-submarine screen. The *Cairo* was sent with all despatch to Bodø and, on arrival, to ensure the despatch of every available trawler and 'puffers'[29] in order to transfer the troops and their stores safely back in.

Meanwhile the rapid flooding of both boiler rooms and the engine rooms was taking place aboard Howson's command and seawater spread both forward and aft of these large spaces and all electrical power failed. She remained on an even keel and watertight doors were closed and bulkheads shored up but this only served to delay the influx of water into the ship; 'it was clear that the bottom was ripped open for much of the ship's length and water was entering in many places at a speed which could not be controlled.'

The shoal that had knocked the 'A' bracket off the shallow-draft *Matabele* and ruptured the fuel tank of the 3,500-ton *Coventry* was more than sufficiently lethal to rip the bottom out of the deeper-draft *Effingham*, already sitting far deeper in the water due to her additional loading of troops, vehicles and munitions, for a third of its length.

Captain Howson considered attempting to beach the ship in order to save the lives of the soldiers and crew but this was countermanded by Vivian for fear the Germans might capture her later. The *Effingham*'s steering power was lost and the cruiser drifted south-east for a considerable distance with the tidal flow, enhanced by the

---

27. Adams, *Doomed Expedition*, pp.69–70, *op. cit.*
28. Howson, *op. cit.*, pp 224.
29. 'Puffers' – Small coastal trading vessels known as *Skøyter* in Norway. It is claimed by Sub-Lieutenant Patrick Dazel-Job that he invented this name for them, as they reminded him of the 'Clyde Puffers' that did the same job at home on the west coast of Scotland and the Hebrides and made famous by the fiction of Neil Munro, and that, after he had reported them as such, the authorities in the UK thereafter assumed that this was the Norwegian name for them! See Dazel-Job, Patrick, *From Arctic Snow to Dust of Normandy*, 1992, Plockton, Ross-shire, Nead-An-Eoin Publishing.

effect of the light wind on her high side. Attempts at towing proved unsuccessful. She finally grounded at the northern end of Skjoldsh Island, in about five fathoms of water, some one-and-half cables south of Faksen Shoal. Her position was 67° 17′N, 13° 58′E, still some distance from Bodø. The detonators to the ship's own demolition charges were found to be in the submerged part of the ship and could not therefore be used to scuttle her and, likewise, the primers for her depth charges, themselves stowed in the torpedo flat, were also separately secured in a compartment that was already underwater. The same problem of inaccessibility prevented the Kingston valves being opened or the main circulator inlet. No anchors had been let go.

Vivian signalled to both Admiral-of-the-Fleet The Lord Cork and Orrery, Flag Officer Narvik, repeated to Admiralty, at 1951 that *Effingham* was aground, adding in a later communication that the cruiser would become a total loss and that *Matabele* was also damaged. He also instructed Howson at 2004 to destroy all secret documents, to which Howson replied that all the ship's confidential books (CBs), cyphers, signal books and logs, and message files, some five steel boxes worth, had been transferred to the *Echo* or, if loose, burnt and the H/F D/F[30] was wrecked. Gunsight telescopes and binoculars and the ship's rifles were transferred to the *Echo*.[31] Vivian also instructed Howson to abandon all attempts by *Echo* to tow her into shallow water, deeming that, as she was irredeemably damaged, it was better for her to go down to a deeper depth, the better to prevent any future German salvage.

Acutely conscious that, with the departure of the *Cairo* for aid, he commanded the only remaining undamaged vessel of the squadron, it behove Spurgeon to take care. Nonetheless, somehow the resourceful Aussie Commander Spurgeon managed to cram all the 1,020 or so soldiers and one watch (*circa* 250–300 men) of *Effingham*'s crew into his little ship, which was done by 2045; he ferried them over to the *Coventry* for transfer, before, around 2210, returning for the remainder. In the interim, ships' boats from *Effingham* herself, *Echo* and *Matabele*, plus the stricken ship's Carley floats and some makeshift rafts, had managed to evacuate a limited number of additional personnel from the ship. Meanwhile *Cairo* signalled at 2234 that she had managed to round up and despatch no fewer than five trawlers and thirteen puffers to come to their aid.

The *Echo* took the remainder of *Effingham*'s complement over to *Coventry*, but, as she was nearly full, was instructed to transfer the bulk of them to the *Cairo* who was returning. Howson himself was among those who went aboard the flagship where he, Vivian and the senior Army officers had a conference as to what to do next. Howson and his worried navigator, Lieutenant-Commander Blake, took the offending chart over with them, but, on studying it, Vivian had to agree that there was apparently a deep channel of more than 100 fathoms (182.88m+) in depth running between the

---

30. High-Frequency, Direction-Finder, commonly termed 'Huffduff' in the Royal Navy.
31. Spurgeon recorded in a hand-written addition to his private notes, how 'I also salvaged the Navigating Officer's [Blake] sextant which I was able to return to him later'. Spurgeon *op. cit.*, p.12.

islands of Briksvaer and the Terra group. He later reported to Their Lordships that 'I consider that Captain Howson was fully justified in making his suggestion that the squadron should use this channel'.

Howson also reported that his ship was touching forward but her stern was in deep water, though two trawlers might pull her into the channel before she sank. In truth there was very little chance that the 12,514-ton (12,714 tonnes) vessel (plus the extra vehicles and equipment embarked) could be shifted by two ancient trawlers. These little vessels, under the overall command of Lieutenant-Commander William Richmond 'Tiny' Fell, aided by Lieutenant-Commander Harry Ernest Huston Nicholls, were to become known as the 'Gubbins Flotilla' after the Army commander ashore there, Colonel Colin McVean Gubbins, which comprised five very small and elderly Admiralty *Strath*-class trawlers, of ancient First World War vintage, all of which had been hauled back into active service after a twenty-year interval.[32]

However, if *Effingham* was torpedoed where and as she lay it was feared that she would simply turn over on her beam ends. Vivian ordered an attempt to try and tow her off before the *Echo* put her down with torpedoes, but he was in no way to endanger the *Echo*. Vivian then asked Gammel and the colonel whether, as they were so close to their destination, they would like to be put ashore from the ships they were on. However, the military men were of the considered opinion that, because so much of their equipment was still aboard the *Effingham* and would be lost (as, with her quarterdeck under water, they were deemed unrecoverable), such a course was not desirable as the men would be poorly equipped. It was therefore decided that the safest course was to get the troops safely back to Harstad aboard the *Coventry* at 23 knots, hoping to arrive there before the routine Luftwaffe morning air attacks commenced. Once back there, the soldiers could regroup for another attempt. Auchinleck was soon forced to bemoan to Dill that this disaster meant that he would be unable to reinforce Bodø in the immediate future.[33]

Meanwhile the *Cairo* was instructed to provide the *Matabele* with AA protection while she limped back to Harstad at her best speed. Air cover was requested for *Echo* while she dealt with the *Effingham* and then rejoined. Vivian notified his superiors that the operation had been temporarily abandoned. *Coventry* returned without incident at 0545 on Saturday 18 May, and the other ships followed in safely.[34] Just four of the

---

32. See The Papers of Captain William Richmond Fell, 1915–1969, GBR/0014/FELL, (6 boxes), Churchill Archives Centre, Cambridge. They were the 1915-built *Strath Devon* (Skipper Robert Cooper RNR), *Strath Derry* (Skipper Harold Acum), dating from 1911, *Newhaven* (Skipper Albert Ernest Youngman, built in 1909), the *Eldorado* (Skipper Arthur Christy, dating from 1918), and the *Dulcibelle*, (Skipper Alexander Bruce) which was also built in 1918. Fell soon tired of these and organised the local 'Puffers' instead.

33. Auchinleck to Dill, dated 17 May 1940, AUC3/69, *op. cit.*

34. The re-supply of the Army units was commenced the night of the day after, with the leading echelon of the South Wales Borderers embarked aboard the destroyers *Firedrake* (Lieutenant-Commander Stephen Hugh Norris) and *Wrestler* (Lieutenant-Commander Arthur Andre Tait) with others following in batches after that until the last, which arrived in destroyers and Puffers on the 25th, but still mainly equipped with small arms as the available warships were small and

Bren-gun carriers were finally safely removed from aboard the *Effingham* before she was abandoned.[35] These Bren-gun carriers were driven by Midshipman John Charles Rushbrooke,[36] with no previous experience, up a makeshift ramp and onto the upper deck of the puffers aided by their flimsy derricks. These carriers, plus some mortars and a small percentage of the stores, were subsequently piled on the quay at Bodø where they were exposed to the attentions of the Luftwaffe and marauding army personnel from other units, like the Irish Guards, alike. Among the blessings of this incident was that all the Army personnel reacted with speed and the traditional British phlegm in the face of adversity; there was no panic. Nor, even better, was a single life, sailor or soldier, lost, despite postwar claims to the contrary. Howson later reported that:

> There was no likelihood of her being towed off, and so I decided to endeavour to assist her disintegration by firing a torpedo into the region of her mainmast to break her back. Although only in some five fathoms of water I felt this action was desirable and might assist in turning her on her side. Accordingly, one torpedo was fired[37] and she at once commenced to list to starboard and sink further. When last seen her quarter-deck was awash.

The need for an early departure had been emphasised earlier by the (not unexpected) appearance of the malignant form of a German Dornier Do17 bomber which was sighted in the distance, but this particular snooper was engaged and chased away by two Fleet Air Arm Blackburn Skua aircraft, although they could not catch her,[38] from No. 800 Squadron, operating from the carrier *Ark Royal* (Captain Cedric Swinton Holland). Fearing a greater response would follow now they had been sighted, Vivian ordered the *Effingham* destroyed forthwith.[39]

---

could not carry anything larger. Thus, the decision to return *Effingham's* troop passengers back to their original starting point actually gained nothing at all but merely caused yet further delay and their ultimate arrival in penny packets instead of *en masse*.

35. Three of these little lightly-protected tracked vehicles were later taken into action against advancing German forces but some of the mortars had 'vanished' from the quayside dump before the Borderers could re-acquire them.

36. Rushbrooke had an outstanding career including, at one time, commanding the oldest destroyer in the Royal Navy, the R-class veteran *Skate*, which managed to see service at Normandy, being awarded the DSC. He was made commander in 1954 and finally retired in 1970.

37. In fact *two* torpedoes were fired into her by *Echo*. See Spurgeon, *op. cit.*

38. The Admiralty had ordered the Skua as a dive-bomber, with some additional capacity as a fighter aircraft from the RAF, who controlled all aircraft production between the wars. But, in Norway, for want of anything other than a token Allied land-based fighter aircraft contribution, these Navy dive-bombers were forced to abandon their main designed role for most of the time, and act principally as fighter aircraft, even though they were slower than most of the German bombers they tried to intercept. See Smith, Peter Charles Horstead, *Skua!: the Royal Navy's Dive Bomber*, p.132, 2006, Barnsley, Pen & Sword Aviation.

39. As well as the bomb damage to *Resolution*, already noted, the Polish troopship *Chrobry* (Captain Sigmund Deyczakowski), packed with soldiers, had been destroyed by Stuka dive-bombers on 15 May, which increased the tension the Navy was feeling about the safety of their Army guests.

Accordingly Spurgeon, with Howson and a small team including volunteer Geoffrey Packard,[40] was sent back at 0345 to complete the job. Approaching the abandoned ship at around 0700 Spurgeon sent a team across that removed all locks and strikers from her 6-inch and 4-inch guns so they would be unusable, sand was rammed into other working parts and all her ready-use ammunition was thrown overboard. At 0800 on the 18th the *Echo* torpedoed her twice and she sank in 30 feet (9.144m) of water and left the scene an hour later.[41]

On 21 May 1940 the Admiralty issued an official communiqué that read:

The Secretary of the Admiralty regrets to announce that as the result of damage sustained through striking an uncharted rock off the Norwegian coast, HMS *Effingham* (Captain J. M. Howson RN), has become a total loss.

Captain Howson and the navigator, Lieutenant-Commander Blake, were sent home aboard the 11,030-BRT troopship *Sobieski* (Lieutenant-Commander Walter Charles Blake RNR, Liaison Officer as Temporary Acting Captain) which sailed in convoy with the 14,287-ton troopship *Batory*.[42] The damaged *Matabele* returned home escorting a convoy and her commanding officer was called as a witness, as was the captain of *Echo* when his ship returned from Norway and subsequent operations with the Home Fleet from Scapa.

Meanwhile the war had not stood still and, due to pressure of momentous events elsewhere, the Board of Enquiry was not held until 27 July 1940,[43] by which time much greater disasters had occurred and *Effingham*'s loss appeared relatively less important in the grand scheme of things. Howson had already redeemed himself commanding the naval beach parties on the evacuation beaches at Dunkirk, Bray Dunes and la Panne, having crossed over aboard the destroyer *Sabre* (Lieutenant-Commander Brian Dean) on 29 May, with a team of two commanders, two lieutenant-commanders and three lieutenants, which were split into two sections. These teams liaised with Senior Naval

---

40. Packard later spent time at the HMS *Excellent* Gunnery School writing manuals until fully recovered; he then went to HMS *Sultan* at Singapore in June 1941, again as Fleet Gunnery officer. He was captured there and imprisoned as a PoW at the notorious Zentsuji Camp. Howson stated in his memoirs that he died in captivity there, but this was *not* the case. Packard survived and retired with the rank of commander on 8 June 1946. He died at home in Suffolk in 1960.

41. Despite post-war claims that the wreck of the *Effingham* was shelled, the *Echo* carried out *no* such gunnery at the time, and nor did the cruiser *Aurora* (Captain Louis Henry Keppel Hamilton, DSO) when she passed close by the site on 25 May, having been ordered by Cork to make a brief survey with a view to salvage. Contemporary photographs and later aerial views reveal absolutely no evidence of shelling.

42. Howson recorded that, while writing up his report prior to sailing, he suddenly remembered to get the Norwegian chart as it would be required as evidence; he collected it from *Coventry* where the Commander-in-Chief told him, 'Tell Blake that I am very sorry about this. That I have always had a high opinion of him as a navigator and my opinion is no less high now.' Howson, *op. cit.*, p.225.

43. D.3A. Losses 17.5.

Officer Dunkirk, Captain William George Tennant MVO, and performed heroically, speeding up the loadings significantly.[44] Likewise the *Echo* was fully engaged as part of the Home Fleet Destroyer flotillas, including assisting in the rescue of survivors from the 17,046-ton Armed Merchant Cruiser *Scotstoun* (Captain Edgar Wallace Moulton) on 13 June and the hunt for German and Italian deportee survivors when the 14,694-ton liner *Arandora Star* (Captain Sidney Keith Smyth OBE RN Rtd) was sunk on 2 July, both U-boat victims, and escorted the *Ulster Prince* (Commander Frank Albert Bond DSC RNR Rtd) with occupation forces to Iceland and back.

Howson recorded 'Eventually in July, 2½ months after the disaster and when we had gathered that no Board of Enquiry would be held, I was ordered to go to Rosyth to attend an Enquiry'. This was held at HMS *Cochrane*, the shore base at Rosyth, under the auspices of Vice-Admiral Sir Charles Gordon Ramsey, C-in-C Rosyth. Howson was far from happy with the way the enquiry was carried out.

> Indeed I had to make several protests to get certain unjustified evidence expunged from the record. I felt strongly that the members were biased and behaved in an improper way in numerous respects; but essentially I felt convinced that they wholly failed to take note of the indisputable fact that, navigationally speaking, my navigator and I had taken all proper precautionary measures. On the conclusion of the proceedings I met my navigator outside, and found that he and I shared the same views. Later he happened to have an opportunity to discuss the matter with one of the members of the board when crossing the Forth after the enquiry and as a result he became even more strongly impressed with the false and 'unfair' attitude adopted by the Board. (They consisted of three retired captains, two being individuals of no distinction but undoubted prejudice.)[45]

Spurgeon noted that:

> As I recollect *Matabele* was not mentioned. *Effingham* was using a larger scale Norwegian chart than *Echo*'s Admiralty small-scale chart of the area ... In fact, the course drawn on the Norwegian chart she used and along which she planned

---

44. Howson's Report, RO 111, p.304.
45. Howson does not specifically name the officers in question, but on Dunbar-Nasmith's staff at Rosyth at this time were four Captains, William Ogilvy Scrymgeour-Wedderburn DSC, Chief-of-Staff; Christopher Hooper Phillips (Rtd); Kenneth Noel Humphreys CB (Rtd) from the Hydrographic Office's Navigation Department; and Harold Douglas Briggs, MG (Rtd) at HMS *Helcion* at Aultbea near Loch Ewe. As the original Board proceedings do not appear to have been preserved for some reason, it remains unclear which of these officers, if any, served on the Board. Blake was so indignant on how they had been treated that he later revealed he had taken the unusual step of unilaterally writing a Service Letter to the President of the Board, pointing out the facts. Howson, after taking advice, decided not to forward the letter, 'although I was extraordinarily grateful to Blake for his unorthodox proposal and his action'. Howson, *op. cit.*, p.229.

to pass, went directly through the centre of '+ Faksen'. This word 'Faksen' was not understood by *Effingham* to mean 'Rock'. The + had been accepted as a simple crossing of latitude and longitude degree line only, and nothing to do with the 'Brekubakke' which was its real name.

He added, 'It seems incredible that *Matabele* and *Effingham* should hit the same rock making the same errors.' He makes no comment on the fact that *Coventry* also struck; perhaps he did not know as he does not mention the damage to the two AA cruisers at all in his private notes. He also confuses Dunbar-Nasmith with Sir Victor Alexander Charles Crutchley VC KCB, who was Commodore Royal Naval Barracks, Devonport, at this time.[46]

In due course their deliberations were promulgated and the Admiralty notified all three principals, Vivian, Howson and Blake, that they had all incurred Their Lordships 'extreme displeasure' at their handling of affairs, in Howson's case specifying three pertinent points – a) he had not allowed enough clearance from a charted shoal ('I had, in fact, kept all my leading marks clear'); b) not queried the speed set by Vivian for the squadron in such restricted waters; and c) not correctly aligned his two escorting destroyers. Howson found these points:

all very queer! Nor was I ever court-martialled which, in the light of later events, it would perhaps have been wiser for me to have made application for. I *believe* that Admiral Vivian, who backed me to the hilt at the enquiry, also received Their Lordships' displeasure, as did Michael Blake, but I am thankful that Michael suffered no permanent 'injury' as a consequence. When Admiral Nasmith, the C-in-C Western Approaches, on whose staff I was serving when the Board's findings and Their Lordships' displeasure were forwarded, told me the results, he said that I need not worry unduly about it. I only wish that his views had subsequently proved to be right! [47]

Vivian never got another sea-going command. He first went to the staff of Western Approaches at HMS *Drake*, Plymouth, and was placed on the retired list on 29 October 1942, becoming Admiral Commanding Reserves until 1 October 1945. He was a KCB and CB and promoted to vice-admiral. The Norwegians awarded him the 1st Class Order of St Olaf for his part in getting their gold reserves safely out from under the noses of the Germans and to England. He died in 1963. Howson meanwhile survived the carnage at Dunkirk, in which he had shone, and had a distinguished wartime career as outlined above. Blake's career was in no way affected and, after a short spell at HMS *Dryad*, the Navy's Navigational School at Portsmouth, on 16 August 1940 he was appointed as navigation officer of the light cruiser *Despatch* (Captain Cyril

---

46. Spurgeon, *op. cit.*, p.12.
47. Howson, *op. cit.*, p.230.

Eustace Douglas-Pennant DSC), seeing service against the Italian fleet at the Battle of Spartivento in November, and continued to serve aboard her until April 1942.[48]

On 4 October 1943 aircraft from the US carrier *Ranger* (CV-4, Captain Gordon Rowe USN), engaged in sortie No. 7, an anti-shipping strike off Norway, Operation LEADER, photographed the wreck in position 67° 22'N, 14° 10'E. The occupying Germans did not bother with the wreck themselves and it lay undisturbed until after the war, when she was finally salvaged by Høvding Skipsopphugging (Chief Ship Scrapping Company) of Sandessjøen who also worked on the German warship wrecks *Tirpitz, Blücher, Konigsberg* and the merchant ships sunk at Narvik. The main components had been removed during the 1950s but a few plates and artefacts still remain at the wreck site today.

As with most of the incidents described in this book there has been a great deal of post-war theorising and speculation. Some of the stories are rank nonsense of course. Allegations that the Norwegian pilot was responsible for the accident because he had pro-German sympathies have appeared on the BBC,[49] one woman claiming that this (totally mythical) figure was immediately shot out-of-hand on *Effingham's* bridge. Leaving aside such typical internet *non sequitur*, some rather more sober judgements merit examination. The *Effingham's* navigation officer is alleged to have ruled a pencil line of the cruiser's track that obscured the offending 'rock' on the Chart No.65, a theory promulgated by Paul Kemp[50] and attributed to court martial evidence. On the other hand the 'traitor' theories have the same weakness – in that it was the destroyer *Matabele* that actually led the line, being approximately 800 yards (4 cables or 731.5m) *ahead* of the *Effingham,* and it was she who touched ground first; so unless there was also a second Nazi-sympathising Quisling pilot,[51] or alternatively, an inefficient navigator with a thick HB pencil present on that destroyer's bridge as well as aboard *Effingham,* then both speculations are equally questionable, if not bizarre.

---

48. With regard to his later career Blake subsequently became navigation officer of the famous battleship *Warspite* (under three respective captains, Captain Fitzroy Evelyn Patrick Hutton, Captain Herbert Annesley Packer and Acting-Captain The Hon. David Edwardes) on 19 May 1942, where he served until February 1945. He navigated her off Sicily, Salerno and back home during the D-Day landings at Normandy as well as the bombardment of the German batteries on Walcheren Island in Holland. He was then appointed to HMS *Saker* with the British Admiralty Delegation in Washington DC for the drive on Japan, for his contribution to which he received an MiD; and he was later *was* sent to the Navy's Signal School, HMS *Mercury*, by which time Their Lordships had forgiven him sufficiently to award him a gong. He married in June 1947 and had three children. Blake retired from the service at his own request on 1 September 1948 as a lieutenant-commander and finally passed away in 1984.

49. BBC *WW2 People's War, Sinking of HMS* Effingham, Angela Ng, A4460645, 15 July 2005.

50. Kemp, Paul, *The Admiralty Regrets: British Warship Losses in the 20th Century*, pp.115 & 270, 1999, Stroud, Sutton Publishing Ltd.

51. Vidkun Abraham Lauritz Jonssøn Quisling, Norwegian Defence Minister and leader of a far-right nationalist party, allied himself to the Nazi invaders in 1940 and his name has since become a by-word for treachery. He did have some supporters among various arms of the Norwegian authorities but this was pretty insignificant.

It is, however, on record that *Effingham*'s captain was vehemently opposed to embarking *any* Norwegian whatsoever, either as a pilot or even as a liaison officer, for fear that they would be unreliable and have pro-German sympathies. So *no* Norwegian was actually embarked in any ship of the force, a fact which has drawn much retrospective criticism from Norwegian historians of the case.

Lieutenant-Colonel Jack Adams, who was present as the signals sergeant of 2nd South Wales Borderers, also dismisses this rumour, as 'completely without foundation'.[52] The fact that three ships of the five-ship force touched almost simultaneously, although at some distance from each other, proves that the Admiralty statement about the incident was a complete falsehood, there being no way that a *single* pinnacle of rock could affect so many ships at the same time. One senses the political machinations of the First Lord of the Admiralty behind that bland misleading of the British public. A shallow shoal that was duly marked, but somehow overlooked, was, however, a different matter.

With regard to the pencil line, Geirr Henning Haarr is quite specific, following the same line as Spurgeon's notes, and alleging that Blake:

> put his trust in an English copy of the Norwegian Pilot Guide-Sailing Instructions[53] and a 1:50,000 scale chart. Unfamiliar with Norwegian charts, though, Blake pencilled in his course-line using a convenient cross as a marker, believing this to be part of the reference grid. It was not. Had he checked the list of symbols properly, he would have seen a small cross represented a shoal or shallow that might become awash at low tide and that he had now set his course straight onto it.[54]

A totally different conclusion is reached in a more recent analytical study. In former Royal Navy Lieutenant-Commander and Queen's Messenger Richard Noel John Wright's detailed study, he totally demolishes the isolated rock theory by examining the 1991 Royal Navy Hydrographer's Chart No. 3888, *The Approaches to Bodø*. This, he said, shows no such obstruction whatsoever, thus confirming what Vivian, Howson and Blake found when consulting their own large-scale chart on the bridge of the *Coventry* in the immediate aftermath of the accident. The rock, it seems, just did not exist and therefore Blake's ruled pencil line could not have obscured it; both mainstays of all the speculation and allegation over the previous seventy years were shown to be totally without foundation. But if it were a whole shoal?

Spurgeon of the *Echo* and his navigation officer had, as we have seen, expressed the opinion in his own recollections of the event that the speed had been too high to prudently penetrate such a narrow channel and that he felt the symbol that denoted the

---

52. Adams, Jack, *The Doomed Expedition*, op. cit., p.70.
53. *Den Norse Los*. 2013: Hønefoss. Karjverket – Norwegian Mapping & Cadastre Authority.
54. Haarr, Geirr Henning., *The Battle for Norway April–June 1940*, pp.292–6, 2010, Barnsley, Seaforth.

Faksen shoal had been, if not actually obliterated by the pencil mark on the chart, not properly understood. Wright postulated that this theory, too, failed to accord with the facts, requiring a course of 085° to make it valid, whereas the squadron's *actual* course was 080° to leave a safe distance of approximately two cables south of the shoal and this was determined by fixing the progression on the left hand side of the islet of Svartskj, as Howson had reported. How then did *Effingham* and two of her companions come to touch ground?

Wright proposed a different scenario. Some ten miles west of Faksen, but to the east of Svartskj, lies the southern base of the larger island of St Terranuken, the southernmost island of the Terra group, and at that distance its edge apparently interposed itself between *Effingham* and Svartskj. The difference this misidentification caused would have been sufficient to have caused an error of 0.5° which translated into two cables, proved deadly. Wright dismisses the respective 'fixes' made by both *Effingham* and *Coventry* at the time as being either distorted or inaccurate and he concluded therefore that the accident came about simply because Blake mistook a leading mark.[55] It remains the case, of course, that Wright's theory, of an accidental misalignment of a crucial navigational sight, detailed and thought-provoking as it is, remains just that, a *theory*, to be accepted or rejected. It seems likely that we may never know, with *total* certainty, what led to the loss of the *Effingham*.

---

55. Wright, Richard Noel John, *The Stranding, Grounding and Destruction of HMS Effingham, 1940*, article in *Warship 2011*, pp.165–74 (Editor John Jordon), 2011, London, Conway.

Chapter 14

On No Account Leave the Ship!

The *Sturdy*, 30 October 1940

The feeling of *déjà vu* brought about by the stranding of two cruisers of the same class, *Raleigh* and *Effingham*, many years apart, is even more poignant when one examines the loss of the destroyer *Sturdy* in 1940 and compares it with the tragedy of the *Narborough* and *Opal* some eighteen years earlier. The ships were very similar, all being 1,000-ton destroyers built to the same basic design and their fates were also startlingly alike, running aground in bad weather off the Scottish coast. Happily, *Sturdy*'s loss occasioned a far smaller loss of life than did the earlier tragedy.

The Admiralty-designed destroyers, which belonged to the 11th & 12th Emergency Wartime Programme of 1917–18, were known variously as the Modified *Rosalind*-Modified *Trenchant*- or Modified *Ulleswater*-class while design work was underway. Thankfully Their Lordships finally decided, in November 1917, to simplify things by designating them as the S-class, even though many of their predecessors carried names beginning with R, S, T and U and that, from a total of sixty-eight ships, twenty-six had names beginning with 'T'. The larger V-class destroyers were also under construction at this time in response to bigger German ships reported to be building, but these fifty-plus vessels, welcome though they were in the Grand Fleet, were more expensive, took longer to build and had speeds at least two knots slower than the 'standard' destroyers of the day which had gradually increased to over 1,000 tons (1,016.5 tonnes) since the first M-class ships of 1914. The need was felt for both types, the smaller, faster S-class, designed for 36 knots, being more suitable for operations in the southern North Sea and English Channel, based at Dover and Harwich, where their extra speed could enable them to intercept the 'hit-and-run' tactics adopted by the Germans in that area, while the larger V-class destroyers, with their heavier gun and torpedo armaments, operated with the Grand Fleet in the rougher conditions to the north.

Various proposals were adopted for this group, including the mounting of two single short-range 18-inch (45.72cm) torpedo tubes, carried on either side of the break in the fo'c'sle. These were capable of being fired directly ahead from the ship's bridge during close-range actions, although these weapons only delivered a 320-lb (145.149kg) warhead instead of 500-lb (226.796kg) . The bridge structures of these ships were constructed with solid steel, having curved frontages, rather than having canvas screens; sea-keeping qualities were to be improved by the adoption of a 'turtle-back' (slightly domed) fo'c'sle to clear water (a sea-keeping feature already widely adopted by deep-sea trawlers) and this was combined with a three-foot sheer, while the foremost 4-inch gun was to be mounted as far back along it as possible; also the ram stem was to be done away with. They were twin rather than three-funnelled, with the 'X' mounting placed between them and they carried a 2-pounder pom-pom on an HA II mounting abaft the two Mk IV 21-inch (53.340cm) torpedo tubes. They were ordered in two batches of thirty-three and thirty-six apiece and, of the second batch, Scotts were entrusted with the construction of three, *Strenuous, Stronghold* and *Sturdy*, with orders being placed in June 1917.

Laid down in March 1918, the dimensions of *Sturdy* were an overall length of 276 feet (84.125m), a beam of 26 feet 8 inches (8.128m) and a draft of 16 feet 3 inches (4.953m). As well as her three 4-inch (10.16cm) QF Mk IV guns on CP III mountings and the 2-pounder, she also carried a .303-inch (0.769m) Maxim and four 0.303-inch Lewis guns. Her propulsion plant was Brown Curtis single reduction turbines with 27,000shp. They carried 210 tons (2,133 kg) of oil fuel and had three Yarrow-type boilers. She carried a crew of around 100 officers and men. *Sturdy* was the first Royal Navy warship to be so named. Initially, she carried the pendant number F96 and later became H28.

Scotts Shipbuilding and Engineering Company Limited was based at Greenock on the Clyde and was usually known as Scotts. With the end of hostilities all warship building went into a hiatus and those ships still on the stocks that were not immediately cancelled were proceeded with at a leisurely pace. *Sturdy* was not launched until 16 June 1919, had a displacement of 1,017-tons (1033.32 tonnes) and achieved a speed of 34.21 knots (63.356 km/h) on her trials on 15 October before being commissioned at Princes Pier.

Between the wars their small complements and economic running costs made these little vessels popular with Their Lordships, who were faced with ever-declining budgets, and many went out to the Mediterranean and Black Sea in the immediate aftermath of the war. Others served in the Baltic, preserving the little states of Estonia, Latvia and Lithuania against the predations of the Bolsheviks and *Sturdy* was one of these. They remained there, and in the Eastern Mediterranean, until 1923, two of them, *Stonehenge* (Commander George Osborne Hewitt) and *Tryphon* (Lieutenant-Commander Walter Clark Clark-Hall) being wrecked in the Eastern Mediterranean, *Tobago* (Lieutenant-Commander Humphrey Edward Archer) being mined and *Speedy* (Commander Hubert Henry de Burgh DSO) sunk in a collision in the Sea of Marmora. Five more, *Stalwart, Success, Swordsman, Tasmania* and *Tattoo*, were given to Australia. Two more, *Torbay* and *Toreador*, went to Canada in 1928. Another flotilla was sent to China in 1972 during the troubles there. A further thirty-three S-class ships were held in the Maintenance Reserve, Rosyth, from 1928, but only fourteen were in commission. The *Sturdy* was also employed on 'rough-weather' trials out of Portsmouth in the late 1920s, only going to sea in the most awful conditions, ironic really, considering her ultimate fate. They were also used for specialised duties: *Senator* (Lieutenant-Commander Henry Victor Hudson) was fitted with a flying-off platform for aircraft astern while, later, both *Stronghold* (Lieutenant-Commander

Cuthbert Patrick Blake DSO with the Folland aircraft and Lieutenant-Commander Trevor St Vincent Frederick Tyler in 1927 with the LARYNX machine) and *Thanet* (Lieutenant John Docker Hayward Manly on September–October 1927 also with the LARYNX machine) being fitted with catapults on the fo'c'sles for radio–controlled UAV experiments in the 1920s.[1] Several of the S–class were equipped for minelaying and could be quickly adapted for this role when required, and these included *Sturdy*. Some had minesweeping adaptations, while *Shikari* (Commander Franklin Ratsey) was not finally completed until February 1924 as a W/T control vessel for the old battleships *Agamemnon* and *Centurion*, which were used as fleet target ships, in which role she served until September 1939.

Sturdy was also employed out of Portsmouth as 'plane-guard', or tender for the aircraft-carrier *Furious* for several years. She was laid up in reserve at Rosyth between 1927 and 1928 and, from 16 August 1930, was at Dartmouth Naval College as a tender under the command of Lieutenant-Commander John Graham Crossley. *Sturdy* was re-commissioned by Lieutenant-Commander William Gronow Davis on 11 March 1931 at that port, serving in Irish waters until being paid off again in June 1932 and put into reserve at the Nore. In the mid-1930s *Sturdy* was still listed as a Home Fleet unit.[2] But, aside from those kept in full commission, the class gradually deteriorated and were scrapped wholesale. The biggest cull took place in 1936 when, in exchange for the ancient liner *Majestic* (the former German *Bismarck*), due to be scrapped, the Admiralty sacrificed two dozen destroyers.[3] This vessel had a lot of money spent on her and she was turned into a static 'Boys' & Artificers' Training Ship' at Rosyth, being re-named *Caledonia*. After conversion she lasted just two years before being abandoned as too risky a target for the Luftwaffe, but this didn't save her as she caught fire, burned out and sank on 29 September 1939, at the very time those two dozen destroyers would have been welcomed with open arms in the fleet.[4] By the outbreak of the Second World War only eleven ships of the class remained.

---

1. The Royal Aircraft Establishment experimented with Folland light aircraft in 1924 and 1927/28, with the Armstrong Siddeley-engined LARYNX unmanned aerial vehicles, or drones, as anti-ship weapons in the Bristol Channel.

2. Among her officers at this time was a young sub-lieutenant, Richard Michael Smeeton, ultimately to end his naval career as Admiral Sir Richard and Deputy Supreme Allied Commander, Atlantic, in the 1960s.

3. Among the S-class ships that went at this time were *Scotsman, Seafire, Searcher, Serene, Shamrock, Spindrift, Sportive, Tactician, Thisbe, Torrid, Trojan, Trusty* and *Tyrant*.

4. The accepted 'life' for a destroyer at this period was fifteen years of peacetime work, halved under wartime conditions, and, as most of these little ships had been commissioned in 1918–22, their 'natural' lifespan was up anyway. The boiler life was a more restricting factor and so most of the class were laid up and then sold off. However, the mass scrapping came about just before they would have been really needed in the early years of the Second World War. Instead, fifty old American four-pipers, of the same vintage but infinitely inferior vessels, had to be substituted at the humiliating cost of leasing British bases to the Americans, a typical result of short-sighted British defence policies.

Lieutenant-Commander George Tyndale Cooper RN was appointed in command on 31 July 1939 and commissioned her for service from reserve. The refit took longer than anticipated. She was still working up when she was pressed into action. Her earliest wartime operation was therefore escorting the ill-fated battleship *Royal Oak* (Captain William Gordon Benn) during the last sortie from Scapa Flow. The German battle-cruiser *Gneisenau* (Flag of *Generaladmiral* Hermann Boehm; *Kapitän-zur-See* Erich Förste), light cruiser *Köln* (*Kapitän zur See* Theodor Burchari) and nine destroyers[5] had made a brief foray off the southern coast of Norway on 8 October and the Home Fleet was sailed in a vain attempt to intercept them. In company with the destroyer *Matabele,* the *Sturdy* sailed on 9 October escorting the old battleship, which was too slow to accompany the main fleet and was therefore delegated to act as a 'longstop' to the west of the Shetlands, patrolling the Fair Isle Channel. The weather proved vile and, in the very heavy seas, both destroyers lost touch with the *Royal Oak,* who returned to Scapa without them. There she was sunk at her moorings by the *U-47* commanded by the audacious *Korvettenkapitän* Günther Prien. This was not the last time that this gentleman crossed the path of the *Sturdy.*

On completion of her work-up, the *Sturdy* was due to join the China Squadron at Hong Kong and duly set off for that station but, while on passage through the Mediterranean in September, that assignment was cancelled and she was instead allocated to the local flotilla for employment as 'plane guard' for the Mediterranean training carriers like the *Argus* (Captain Henry Cecil Bovell) which was working out of Toulon at this time with both Skua and Swordfish aircraft embarked.[6] She also found employment on contraband control work, intercepting neutral ships and sending them into Gibraltar for examination of their cargoes. She continued on these duties for the first eight months of the war, but was found to be in urgent need of refitting and so was sent to Malta dockyard for this in April, a job which lasted until June. Here opportunity was also taken to fit her with the ASDIC anti-submarine detection device, but there were not enough sets to equip her with radar at that date.

Harry Springett was a young leading seaman whose duties included torpedoman/ electrician. He recalled that:

The *Sturdy* was generally in a bad state of repair and looking back one wonders how we ever kept her going. She leaked just about everywhere and during bad weather life on board was atrocious. *Sturdy* was, though, a very good sea boat.

---

5. The German destroyers were the *Bernd von Arnim* (*Korvettekapitän* Kurt Rechel) , *Dieter von Roeder* (*Kapitänleutnant* Erich Holtorf), *Erich Steinbrinck* (*Korvettenkapitän* Rolf Johannesson), *Frederick Eckoldt* (*Korvettenkapitän* Alfred Schemmel), *Frederick Ihn* (*Korvettenkapitän* Rudolf von Pufendorf), *Karl Galster* (*Korvettenkapitän* Theodor Freiherr von Mauchenheim*)*, *Max Schultz* (*Korvettenkapitän* Claus Tramfedach*)*, *Paul Jacobi* (*Korvettenkapitän* Hans-Georg Zimmer) and *Wilhelm Heidkamp* (*Korvettenkapitän* Hans Erdmenger).

6. This duty had been performed by a number of different R- and S-class destroyers between the wars, their speed and ease of handling making them very suitable for rescuing ditched aircraft crews from the drink.

She was very fast, probably one of the fastest boats the Navy had. She had sleek greyhound lines and could do 34 knots. She had oil-fired boilers but it was shocking in the boiler room with no room, no air conditioning and only fan forced air from the upper deck. She had a steam-driven capstan.

Whilst in Malta in dry dock Italy declared war on England and the Fleet left Malta and left *Sturdy* high and dry. The refit was pushed along and we eventually left and proceeded to Gibraltar and thence back to England to take part in the retreat from France.[7]

With the debacle on the continent, the fall of Norway, France and the Low Countries, and the heavy loss and damage of destroyers off Norway and Dunkirk, every destroyer became doubly valuable. After escorting convoy HG52 from Gibraltar to Cape Finisterre, she joined the 22nd Destroyer Flotilla at Portsmouth and joined convoy HG034F on 13 June for three days. Along with the destroyer *Mackay* (Commander Graham Henry Stokes RN), she was part of the naval force sent to carry out the evacuation of the British troops from St Valery (Operation AERIAL). However this was cancelled and, on 19 June, *Sturdy* was instead ordered to escort the French submarines *Junon* (*Lieutenant de Vaisseau* Jaume) and *Minerve* (*Lieutenant de Vaisseau* Bazin) who were under tow from Brest to Plymouth by the requisitioned War Department tugs *Queen's Cross* and *Watercock*. Off Pieres Noires, the *Watercock* (Master William Gerrard Fothergill) ran out of coal and *Sturdy* was ordered by Commander Bryan Gouthwaite Scurfield RN, who had joined them aboard the destroyer *Broke*, to take over the tow for the remainder of the passage to Plymouth. This done, *Sturdy* entered Portsmouth on 23 June and had her amidships Y 4-inch gun replaced by an AA gun, while some crew members participated in the storming and taking-over of pro-Vichy French warships in the port to prevent them being sailed to German-held ports.

For the rest of the summer *Sturdy* continued to patrol, having a brief brush with a trio of German E-boats on 18 July, and escort coastal convoys working from Newhaven, Portsmouth, Dartmouth and Plymouth. She also took part in anti-invasion patrols on the night of 2/3 October, working with the destroyers *Vanoc* (Lieutenant-Commander James Godfrey Wood Deneys) and *Sardonyx* (Lieutenant-Commander Robert Basil Stewart Tennant). Patrols off Dover remained continuous, interspersed with coastal convoy work, she escorting CE12 before receiving a boiler-clean at Portsmouth. Following these anti-invasion patrols in the Channel, *Sturdy* was allocated to Western Approaches Command at Londonderry, despite the unsuitability of these small vessels for the Atlantic winter weather conditions and her short range.

Sturdy was part of the escort for convoy OB229 between 15 and 18 October along with the destroyer *Whitehall* (Lieutenant-Commander Archibald Boyd Russell) and the ex-American *Chelsea*, (Lieutenant-Commander Richard Dixon Herbert Stephen Pankhurst) plus the corvettes *Arabis* (Lieutenant-Commander Arthur Blewitt DSC

---

7. Springett, Harry, *Some Personal Reminiscences*, dated August 1998 and prepared and edited by his daughter, Dawn Springett.

RNR) and *Heliotrope* (Lieutenant-Commander John Jackson RNR) before being hastily despatched to assist with the defence of convoy HX73 from Halifax to the UK, on the 19th. She worked under command of the destroyer *Whitehall* and with the corvettes *Arabis, Coreopsis* (Lieutenant-Commander Alan Holt Davies RNR), *Heliotrope* and *Hibiscus* (Lieutenant Charles George Cuthberton RNR), the minesweeper *Jason* (Lieutenant-Commander Reginald Ernest Terry) and trawlers *Angle* (Lieutenant Alexander Cumming Lister RNR), *Blackfly* (Lieutenant Mervyn Isdale Miller RNR) and *Lady Elsa* (Temporary-Lieutenant Sidney George Phillips RNVR), to which the Dutch submarine *O-21* (*Luitenant ter zee 1ste klasse* Johannes Frans van Dulm RNN) was attached as a deterrent in case the convoy was attacked by surface raiders.[8] Attacked by a group of U-boats, no fewer than twelve merchant ships totalling 75,069 tons were sunk, almost one ship in four, a disaster which resulted in a total rethinking of convoy defence. *U-47* alone sank four ships and *U-100* (*Korvettenkapitän* Joachim Schepke) three, *U-46* (*Korvettenkapitän* Englebert Endrass) sank two as did *U-38* (*Korvettenkapitän* Heinrich Liebe) while *Korvettenkapitän* Heinrich Bleichrodt (*U-48*) also sank one between the 19th and 20th, two more being badly damaged. The *Sturdy* rescued the few survivors from one of Prien's victims, the 5,026-ton *Whitford Point* (Captain John Edward Young), some ninety miles south-west of Rockall.

On 25 October *Sturdy* joined the escort of fast convoy OL009 along with the destroyers *Viscount* (Lieutenant Michael Southcote Townsend) and *Shikari* (Lieutenant-Commander Hugh Nicholas Aubyn Richardson) with which she had sailed from Liverpool at 0530. She remained in company for three days before being despatched to join the escort of slow convoy SC008 from Sydney, Cape Breton, Nova Scotia, to Liverpool.[9]

---

8. This was an unfortunate experiment, the submarine merely confusing the surface escorts who depth-charged her twice, fortunately without success!

9. The ships of SC008 comprised the following vessels: *Anvers* (4,398 tons); *Baron Dechmont* (3,675 tons); *Baron Tweedmouth* (3,357 tons); *Beaumanoir* (2,477 tons); *Bifrost* (1,781 tons); *Cara* (1,760 tons); *Coulmore* (3.670 tons); *Dallington Court* (6,889 tons); *Empire Cheetah* (5,506 tons); *Empire Springbuck* (5.591 tons); *Facto* (1,522 tons); *Favorit* (2,826 tons); *Frank B. Baird* (1,748 tons); *Gironde* (1,770 tons); *Ila* (1,583 tons); *Jura* (1,759 tons); *Leonidas Z. Cambanis* (4,274 tons); *Lyra* (1,474 tons); *Marga* (1,583 tons); *Mathilda* (3,650 tons); *Merchant* (4,615 tons); *Michael L. Embiricos* (5,202 tons); *Mirupanu* (2,539 tons); *Newton Ash* (4,625 tons); *Parthenon* (3,189 tons); *Penolver* (3,721 tons); *PLM 27* (5,633 tons) a 'liberated' French vessel – the initials PLM stand for Paris-Lyon-Marseille; *Penolver* (3,721 tons); *Philip T. Dodge* (5,047 tons); *Ringhorn* (1,298 tons); *Rushpool* (5,125 tons); *Saturnus* (2,741 tons); *Sirce II* (4,966 tons); *Suecia* (4,966 tons); *Tautra* (1,749 tons); *Thistleglen* (4,748 tons); *Trompenberg* (1,995 tons); *Vassilios A. Polemis* (3,429 tons); *Vespasian* (1,570 tons); *Widestone* (3,192 tons); *Winona* (6,197 tons); *Winterswijk* (3,205 tons); *Zephyros* (4,796 tons). The escorting warships were the destroyers *Harvester* (Lieutenant-Commander Mark Thornton) and *Highlander* (Commander William Alexander Dallmeyer), which were due to be relieved by *Scimitar* (Lieutenant Robert Denys Franks) and *Sturdy* on this side of the Atlantic, the sloops *Sandwich* (Commander Morgan John Yeatman) and *Weston* (Commander Alastair Gordon Davidson Rtd), corvettes *Campanula* (Lieutenant-Commander Richard Vere Essex Case DSC), *Clarkia* (Lieutenant-Commander Frederick John Gwynn Jones RNR), *Gladiolus* (Lieutenant-Commander Harry Marcus Crews Sanders RNR), the Canadian

The two destroyers, maintaining a speed of fifteen knots in line-ahead formation, left at sunset, reducing to twelve knots at 1215 the next day to conserve fuel when the convoy was not located in the worsening weather conditions. According to the previous night's situation report *(sitrep)* the convoy was on time, so *Shikari* therefore ordered both destroyers to alter course to the south and hold that course for five miles, and then to sweep 90 degrees which, it was expected, would bring them up astern of the elusive convoy. The weather continued to go downhill and by dusk a Force 7 gale was blowing and the *Sturdy* closed to within three cable lengths of *Shikari*'s port beam in an effort to maintain visible contact. Alas, this proved impossible and all sight was lost as night fell.

Telegraphist Stanley Walter Ibbott gave this account of conditions aboard:

The weather steadily deteriorated. Ships wallowed in the heavy seas. The gale force wind was bitterly cold. Those of us who possessed them wore balaclava helmets and warm gloves. Due to the high-speed manoeuvring our decks were constantly under water, a lot of which washed below decks and made the messdeck most uncomfortable.

I was a radio Telegraphist. Our radio office was two metres above deck level and immediately below the flag deck and bridge. The office was small and compact. The receiving apparatus was fixed to the forward bulkhead. There was a five-foot bench at which two men could sit. On the port side of the office was a rotary spark transmitter and on the starboard side an Arc transmitter. To the modern radio man this will sound prehistoric but it was all we had in those days. We possessed two wooden swivel armchairs which could be bolted to the deck in rough weather. Our contact with the Bridge was by voice-pipe. If some clot on the Bridge left the lid off in bad weather, we would get a cold salt shower whenever the ship ploughed into a large wave.

Lifelines were stretched taut above the decks fore and aft with slip rings which each had six feet of rope to which ratings could cling while traversing the deck, to avoid being washed overboard. All men wore deflated rubber lifebelts which had long tubes so that a man could inflate his belt if he had the misfortune to be thrown into the sea. There was also a red single-cell torch light which could be switched on at night.

When they altered course, things worsened.

The gale was now Force 9. Spume was blown from the surface by the wind and made it impossible to see the surface of the sea. Our decks were only two

---

armed yacht *Elk* (Acting/Lieutenant-Commander Norman Vincent Clark RCVR) and armed trawlers *Fandango* (Temporary-Lieutenant Frank Clifford Hopkins RNR), *Man O'War* (Skipper Edward Robert Harris RNR), *Stella Capella* (Temporary-Sub-Lieutenant Arthur Lionel Waldegrave Warren RNR) and *Vizalma* (Temporary-Lieutenant Ronald Ian Taylor McEwan RNR).

metres above sea level! We battled on throughout that day, the 29th, struggling to maintain our course against the southerly gale. No hot meals were possible because our galley was continually flooded. We managed to get some tinned corn beef sandwiches and we drank water, which had been contaminated by sea water. Fortunately I did not suffer with 'Mal de Mer'. Many poor fellows did. A few were at sea for the first time! We radio operators stayed in the office where we were out of the wind and had reasonably dry decks. All hands wore their warmest clothing (which had been soaked time and time again). Below decks they huddled together for warmth with water swilling around their sea-boots.[10]

Lieutenant-Commander Cooper considered it too risky to try and close *Shikari* again, even if he could locate her, the danger of collision being too great. The decision was made to reduce speed to 8 knots and maintain his existing course until dawn. The position of the ship's oil fuel was approaching critical and the weather continued to worsen. Standing orders were that no ship's bunkerage should be allowed to fall below eighty tons (81.283 tonnes) and, with only 100 tons (101.604 tonnes) left and in such a lightened condition, her already lively motion was getting ever more skittish. There was still no sign of the convoy or his companion. Cooper took the decision to make for Londonderry to refuel. He accordingly signalled this intent to both the Commander (D) at that base and *Shikari*.[11]

The conditions were by now atrocious, with winds gusting in excess of 50 knots (92.60 km/h) and thirty-foot (9.144m) waves which threatened to swamp or poop the little vessel. Cooper had been unable to obtain any reliable 'fix' for twenty-four hours and, with the expected drift, no estimate he could make would have much relevance. He discussed the situation with his leading telegraphist and considered requesting a D/F 'fix' from the Admiralty as a last resort. He decided to postpone this option until first light if they had not achieved landfall by then. It might have been well had he grasped the nettle there and then however. Instead, Cooper set his course for Inishtrahull Island, off the most northerly point of Ireland, which at that date had a lighthouse, at a speed of nine knots.

'Darkness fell around 4 p.m.,' recalled Telegraphist Ibbott,

and those who were not on duty, tried to sleep as best they could. In the office we had one operator on watch and the other two lay on the deck. We found sleep impossible on that heaving, pitching, rolling deck. Men who were in the aft or fore part of the ship were ordered to remain where they were. This meant that those offices and men on watch could not be relieved. It was alright for us in the

10. Ibbott, Stanley Walter, *Personal Account*, dated January 2012, transcribed by Dawn Springett.
11. *Sturdy* and *Shikari* were the mainstays of the 42nd Escort Group whose other ships were the sloops *Folkestone* (Lieutenant-Commander Charles Fraser Harrington Churchill), *Wellington* (Commander Ian Hamilton Bockett-Pugh) and *Weston* (Commander (Rtd) John Gilbert Sutton).

wireless office because we were all together. The one on watch merely booted his relief to wakefulness and they swapped places.

During daylight hours our navigator had been unable to obtain a fix on the sun because of cloud cover. We were under 'radio silence'. This meant that we were unable to transmit a request to a shore station for a radio bearing. We were steering blindly ahead not knowing whether we were on course or not. The Captain and Navigator could only guess our position. They considered that we would reach Londonderry at around 9 a.m. on the 30th. I had the morning watch (4 a.m. to 8.a.m.). [12]

Sturdy was lost on 30 October 1940, running aground on Sgeir Nan Latharnaich off A'Dhorlainn Bheag, Sandaig, Tiree Island, the most westerly of the Inner Hebridean islands, in position 56° 28'N, 6°, 59'W. This was far to the north of her intended landfall and little warning was received of her fate due to the continuing severity of the gale-force conditions that had driven her so many miles off course. At 0430 on the 30th a white line of foam was sighted off *Sturdy*'s port bow and this was initially taken as merely being the wash of one of the enormous waves she had been ploughing through. But it was not, and within a few seconds *Sturdy* was ashore.

Cooper reported that a there was 'a slight bump' at first, followed almost immediately by a heavy crash beneath the ship's bridge. Many thought that the *Sturdy* had been hit by a torpedo so abrupt was the blow. The engines were rung to stop, watertight doors were closed and the Carley rafts were broken out in anticipation of abandoning ship. Cooper went out on to the bridge wing to see the worst and duly found it. His command was jammed hard aground, with a 10-degree starboard list, obviously in mortal extremis with the propellers damaged and they failed to respond to go slow astern. It was felt that, even if she had come away, she would have slipped back into deep water and foundered, just as the unfortunate *Narborough* had done. The huge seas were pushing her over and grinding her hard into the shore while the waves continued to pound over her.

Harry Springett recalled:

What we were doing in that neck of the woods I do not know and I do not think the captain did either. His name was Lieutenant Commander Cooper – not a very impressive man and [he] was not liked by the ship's company. He was a career sailor and was known as 'the man with the glaring eyes' and he was commonly called 'Gladys Cooper'. [13]

---

12. Ibbott, *Personal Account, op. cit.*
13. After Dame Gladys Constance Cooper DBE, a very famous actress of both stage and screen at the time, usually playing highly-dramatic roles; her films included *Rebecca*, *Now Voyager* and *My Fair Lady*.

He was not only a terrible captain, he used to get seasick![14] The night we ran on to rocks was a vile night – heavy seas, raining, blowing etc. *Sturdy* was well damaged by the weather and her mast may have been down or we may have had to keep radio silence and we could not get a sighting because of poor visibility. The first we knew was a bang/clang and the ship suddenly tipping over. It was the early hours of the morning and I was lying down somewhere below deck as I had just come off watch. There was quite a bit of panic when we first struck because everyone thought it was a torpedo. There was a mad rush to get up on deck but we could see very little. We did not even know if we were near land as there was a very high tide at the time. The bridge shouted to the LTO[15] to switch the searchlight on. The engine was still going and the searchlight operated for about five minutes. *Sturdy* began to break up rather quickly and was pounded by heavy seas.[16]

Ibbott had similar recollections:

At about 4.25 there was a terrific crash. The ship shuddered and stopped, lifted and crashed again and again. Seas coming from our starboard quarter began to break solidly over us. I heard the Captain call down the voice-pipe, 'Break silence! Make a distress call and ask for a radio bearing.' I yelled to the other operators to get weaving. I adjusted the spark transmitter to [emergency] frequency and transmitted our distress signal. I did this several times and asked for a radio bearing. Then came a heavy crash outside the wireless office door. The mast had snapped and fallen between the foremost funnel and the wireless office. We had no aerial!

The two men off watch grabbed a length of aerial wire and a couple of insulators and went out to rig an emergency aerial. They did this by fixing the wire to a davit top and attaching the other end to where the normal aerial entered the office. I shifted the wavelength again and again transmitted our signal on each occasion several times. I later learned that I had been heard by a shore station, a ship (HMS *Rhododendron*) and by an aircraft. Our signal had been passed on by the aircraft. The shore station had fixed our position as having hit the Isle of Tiree, a small island 110 miles north of Londonderry. The gale had blown us that far off course![17]

Cooper's prime concern now was to get his crew safely ashore and, after firing off distress rockets, the 24-inch searchlight was shone along the coast to see whether or not this was possible. In order to get a line ashore a raft with two men aboard was launched

---

14. But there, of course, so did Lord Nelson and many other celebrated naval heroes.
15. Leading Torpedo Operator.
16. Springett, *Reminiscences, op. cit.*
17. Ibbott, *Personal Account, op. cit.*

but almost immediately upturned in the wild water and the two brave volunteers were immersed. Luckily, they survived this experience and both men managed to struggle ashore. They set off inland seeking help. One of the Carley floats was also launched in an effort to get more men off the ship, but the backwash from the seas sucked it back toward the ship and it proved totally uncontrollable.

Ibbott recalled that:

> The Captain ordered a Carley raft to be launched from aft with volunteers who were to take a rope with which, once they were ashore, they could pull a heavy hawser to anchor the ship, to the shore. The raft was launched upon the crest of a large wave in the hope that it would be carried high over the reef. It was not! The raft was flung end upon end ... over and over. The men were flung into that raging sea and, from memory, I heard that there was only one survivor. The bodies were recovered in daylight when the tide had ebbed and the seas had gone down. The daylight also showed that our ship lay across three exposed reefs. The keel had been smashed from the boat stowage to a spot somewhere below the bridge.[18]

The ship was now clearly on her last legs and, in desperation, yet a third attempt was made, this time utilising the ship's whaler with a crew of thirteen embarked. At this time all lighting aboard *Sturdy* failed because the boilers had become flooded with seawater. The whaler was lowered with enormous difficulty but suffered exactly the same fate as the previous two attempts, being swept ahead of the ship before capsizing. The ill-fated occupants joined those of the float in the swirling maelstrom and in the confusion and darkness of the early morning not all made it to the beach alive.

Harry Springett was in the thick of it.

> Because *Sturdy* was tipped right over a boat could only be launched from one side and as I was coxswain of the only sea boat, a whaler, they could launch, I took my place. We had hardly hit the sea before the whaler was swamped by the huge waves and we were all in the water, fully clothed.... We started swimming with the sea/surf and eventually got a foothold on the rocks/sand and realised we had reached shore – I wasn't a bad swimmer in those days. I think it may have been a half an hour since the ship had struck....
>
> I remember the names of two men who were drowned – one, Percy Cornford, I think from Brighton on the South Coast and 'Ginger' Greenshields, I think from Leeds. I remember Greenshields imploring Cornford to get off his back. 'Let go! Let go! You're choking me!' Apparently Cornford couldn't swim and just got the death grip on Greenshields. I remember afterwards thinking it could have been me that Cornford grabbed for we were all very close in the water.

---

18. Ibbott, *Personal Account, op. cit.*

Another instance I remember is with a man called Samwells.[19] When I crawled up the beach absolutely exhausted I remember Samwells had not quite made it out of the water and just did not have the strength to go any more. When some strength returned a couple of us tried to drag him clear but we were so weak we hardly moved him and there he lay. I do not know who or when but one of the islanders came down to the shore, picked up his body and placed it in a wheelbarrow and wheeled him away. He eventually survived, only to die a couple of years after with cancer at an early age. He was a postman from somewhere near Croydon and a very fine man. I was not able to walk very well because I had cut my feet on the rocks but the islanders seem suddenly to appear. I was taken to a cottage where the people were very kind, my clothes were dried and I had a hot bath. I fell asleep exhausted in a beautiful bed.... .[20]

In total there were five of her crew who died tragically while attempting to get ashore, these being Able Seamen Frederick 'Ginger' Greenshields and Percy Reginald Cornford RNVR, from the whaler, Stoker 1st Class Thomas William Cowler and Leading Stoker Albert Thomas Trahearn from the Carley float and Ordinary Seaman John Herbert Rivett.

The late Hugh McLean from Baranpol recalled:

It was a Thursday. I remember it well. Willie got up – he heard something moving outside, something being blown by the wind.... This would be about 6 or 7 o'clock in the morning. It was quite a rough morning and it was raining. I would call it force 9–10, a severe gale. Just before we got down there we could make out it was a naval vessel – the paint, the colour, you see. There were a lot of people there; you'd hear 'Help'. I remember the first thing we met there, a body, a beautiful, young fellow. I picked him up and took him beyond the reach of the ocean and put him on the grass.

At 0510 *Sturdy*'s tormented hull gave up the ghost and broke in half. Fortunately, the surviving crew had all been concentrated in the forepart of the ship, where the heavy surf continued to break over them. The empty stern section of the destroyer was pummelled round to port by the continuing breakers and ended up at right angles to the ship's stem. The need for a line to be got ashore to save the rest of the crew was paramount and another volunteer, Able Seaman E. J. Smith, ignoring the fate of his predecessors, made the attempt. Despite being lifted an estimated ten feet into the air by the breakers Smith somehow survived and, seeing his struggle, a second man, Leading Stoker Mitchell, also went over the side to try and help him. Incredibly both these heroes managed to get across the rocks with only minor contusions and cuts and a line was finally got aboard the forward section of the *Sturdy* and made fast. It was

19. This would actually be Petty Officer Walter Joseph Samells, who later served aboard the destroyer *Echo*.
20. Springett, *Reminiscences, op. cit.*

still a daunting prospect to actually contemplate using this escape route but, before the first man attempted it, there was a dramatic intervention from ashore.

Those of the second party who had managed to scramble ashore made their way to the home of Mairi Mohoreasdal. She alerted Captain Donald Campbell Sinclair (Domhnall an Ban), a Merchant Navy officer, who happened to be home on leave in the area, at Greenhill, at the time of the loss. He used his torch to send a Morse code signal to the ship advising 'On no account attempt to leave the ship – tide is going-down'. Accepting this local advice, the crew stayed on board until daylight when the tide proved to be far enough out to prevent further casualties. The Admiralty commended Sinclair for his prompt action which undoubtedly prevented heavier loss of life. Sadly, Sinclair himself was lost at sea when his ship, the *Empire Eland* (5,613 tons), was sunk by two torpedoes from the *U-94* (*Oberleutnant* Otto Ites) while straggling from convoy ON14 on 15 September 1941.[21]

The bulk of the remaining crew duly abandoned ship at daybreak using Smith's rigged line as their escape route, but in much safer (and rather drier) circumstances. Lieutenant-Commander Cooper himself remained aboard what was left of his command, with some of his officers and signalmen, to ensure the safe collection of confidential codebooks, charts, logbooks and pay books.

Commissioned Engineer Edward James Alfred Gibson suffered a broken knee when a huge wave threw him against the machinery and was sent to Oban Cottage Hospital. His son, later Lieutenant-Commander Michael Gibson, was sent with his mother to recover his father's possessions and recalled that the bow of the *Sturdy* was on the grass on the shore while the stern was forty yards offshore. Gibson and most of the uninjured members of the crew, who had been magnificently cared for by the villagers, were all later picked up by the corvette *Rhododendron*, (Lieutenant-Commander William Nelson Mitchell Falchney RNR) which had arrived on the scene with the rescue tug *Marauder* (Temporary-Lieutenant Walter James Hammond). The *Rhododendron* later transferred four officers and seventy-seven of the surviving crew members to Oban, leaving behind a small detachment when they left. This latter party was left to guard the wreck and supervise the removal of her explosives and comprised Lieutenant-Commander Cooper, First Lieutenant, Lieutenant Daniel Will Ungoed, John Wesley Bratley, the Gunner (T) along with nineteen experienced crew members to work on salvaging what vital equipment could be saved from the wreck[22] with nineteen senior ratings who stayed behind to de-store their ship to the best of their

21. The first torpedo brought her to a halt but, before all the crew could get clear, she was put down by a second and Sinclair, thirty-two crewmen and five DEMS (Defensively Armed Merchant Ships) gunners were all killed.

22. The other officers were Lieutenant Brian Cochrane Longbottom, Lieutenant Michael Vyse, Sub-Lieutenant Michael John Lyndon Blake, Temporary-Sub-Lieutenant Ronald George, Commissioned Engineer Edward James Alfred Gibson, Midshipman John Birch Leeming. Leeming later transferred to the Fleet Air Arm and became an instructor. On 15 May 1943 he and an Australian pilot, Sub-Lieutenant Alan Cairnhill McCracken, were conducting low-level training flights in Hawker Sea Hurricane fighters from HMS *Heron* at RNAS Yeovilton, when the Australian crashed into Downside School, Stratton-on-Fosse, in Somerset, killing nine

ability. The stern section was some forty yards offshore and could only be accessed by breeches buoy.

On 31 October the five men who had died were laid to rest at Soroby burial ground, Balemartine, with the salvage party and many local residents in attendance.

As related, the rescue corvette had arrived, picked up the crew and left behind a salvage party. Aboard the *Rhododendron* Telegraphist Ibbott found a secure billet.

> The ship's doctor had orders piped around the ship for all survivors to muster under the fo'c'sle for an issue of rum. You see, oil fuel, if swallowed is poisonous. Rum nullifies the toxin. I dressed and went up. I didn't tell the doc that I had not been near oil fuel. I got my tot … and ran into our Midshipman; his name was Leeming, son of the manufacturer of Tootal ties. He shouted out to me 'Hey, Stripey', I have been looking for you everywhere. I need your help badly. The Captain has given me half a bottle of Port and half a bottle of whisky to drink and to stay in the wardroom out of his way until we reach harbour. You know I can't drink that lot. Help me for God's sake!' So, for heaven's sake and for his sake, I went to the wardroom and helped him. He was happy and relieved … I was happy and loaded!

A little light relief after such a harrowing ordeal.[23]

The Board of Enquiry was duly convened and sat on 9 November 1940 aboard the light cruiser *Cardiff* (Captain Philip King Enright) under the auspices of Vice-Admiral Bertram Chalmers Watson CB DSO (Rtd), the Flag Officer in Command (FOIC) Greenock.[24] The members of the Enquiry were Captain Enright himself, Commander Errol Concanon Lloyd Turner,[25] and Lieutenant (N) Francis Brian Price Brayne-Nicholls, (*Cardiff*).[26]

Cooper had a large number of recommendations and endorsements from former commanding officers, all of whom thought highly of him as a destroyer man and worthy of command. These included Commander Edward Bruce Chicheley Thornton of the destroyer *Wryneck* (November 1930 to December 1931), Commander Percy

---

pupils. At the subsequent court martial Leeming was severely reprimanded and dismissed his ship.

23. Ibbott, *Personal Account, op. cit.*
24. This was HMS *Orlando*. Watson had had a distinguished career. At Greenock his fiefdom included the top-secret Naval Signals Citadel, *Bagatelle*, where much of the success of the Battle of the Atlantic was later achieved. On being relieved in January 1942, Watson became a convoy commodore and survived his command ship *Jeypore* (Master Thomas Stevens) being torpedoed and sunk SSE of Cape Farewell by the *U-89* (*Korvettenkapitän* Dietrich Lohmann) on 3 November 1942.
25. Commanding officer of the destroyer *Active* which had just returned from 13th Destroyer Flotilla at Gibraltar and was undergoing a long refit at Liverpool prior to joining Western Approaches Command.
26. ADM 1/11542, Loss of HMS *Sturdy*, 30 October 1940. Board of Enquiry November 1940. National Archives, Kew, London.

Frank Pilkington Wood of the destroyer *Crescent* (April 1932 to July 1934),[27] Captain Lancelot Ernest Holland of the battleship *Revenge* (July 1934 to January 1936), Captain Arthur John Power, Commanding Officer of HMS *Excellent* (February 1936 to May 1936) and Commander Roderick Cosmo Gordon of the destroyer *Hereward* (June 1936 to June 1939). None of their ringing endorsements, nor the sympathy of the Board, did much good. It was pleaded that 'the Sub-Lieutenant was sick, her officers young and inexperienced', but that cut little ice either, nor did it save Cooper from Their Lordships' wrath.

The Board itself, although sympathetic in that they fully recognised that the appalling weather was a mitigating feature of the tragedy, and indeed had been a major contributory factor, nonetheless found that Cooper had failed to make sufficient allowance for drift; nor had sufficient allowance been made for the ship's speed over the ground due to a misunderstanding over the engine revolutions; and the unreliability of the ship's compasses due to the extraordinary heavy roll of the ship, in which factor the degaussing of the ship against magnetic mines may have been a factor.[28]

The verdict was negligence and Cooper duly received Their Lordships' 'severe displeasure' for his 'serious neglect' and was placed on half-pay for six weeks.

In further mitigation, Admiral Sir Martin Eric Dunbar-Nasmith VC KCB KCMG, Commander-in-Chief, Western Approaches Command, Plymouth, himself having a navigating background, forwarded the remarks of Rear-Admiral Alexander Robert Hammick (Rtd), the Second-in-Command to Flag Officer-in-Charge Greenock, who opined to the Secretary of the Admiralty, that:

An error of judgement, involving the loss of his ship, must always be the responsibility of the Commanding Officer, and Lieutenant Commander Cooper, both in his report and in the frankness of his evidence before the Board, has not hesitated to give a full and clear picture of the circumstances leading up to this unfortunate occurrence, and the factors which governed his decision at the time.

His action during the harassing period after his ship had grounded until his crew were safely ashore showed him, however, to be capable of calm and sound judgement in an emergency, while the exemplary bearing of his ship's company throughout testifies to the powers of leadership.

Although the loss of a destroyer now is a matter of great concern, I feel that the lessons learned from this experience will be of lasting benefit to Lieutenant Commander Cooper, and I would therefore commend for Their Lordships' favourable consideration lenient treatment on the findings of the Court, particularly in view of the last sentence of paragraph 2 of Flag Officer-in-Charge,

---

27. *Crescent* served pre-war in the 2nd Destroyer Flotilla at Home and in the West Indies, but was then sold to Canada who renamed her *Fraser*.

28. In connection with the latter theory, Harry Springett wrote many years later, that 'I do not remember seeing an officer again from that day to this and I was never asked anything about the ship, but I heard stories about the inquiry. One of the crew who had been in charge of me told the Captain had asked him to say the compass was faulty....' Springett, *Reminiscences, op. cit.*

Greenock's remarks. An officer of this calibre can ill be spared in small ships at the present time.[29]

Their Lordships felt no such thing. One *very* senior officer was less inclined to be so charitable; the First Sea Lord, Admiral-of-the-Fleet Sir Alfred Dudley Pickman Rogers Pound GCB OM GCVO, despite all his many cares and responsibilities worldwide, immersed himself in the case. He seemed to have become fixated on the *Sturdy* and severely castigated Cooper for the loss 'of this fine destroyer' at a time when every such ship was worth its weight in gold when Britain was fighting for her very existence.[30] He enquired whether every precaution had been taken, these destroyers were equipped with the Chernikeeff Log pre-war; 'was it not employed?' he demanded to know.[31]

It transpired that what *Sturdy* was equipped with for this purpose was a device known as a hand-sounding machine, or, to be more precise, Lord Kelvin's Sounding Machine.[32] Also named after its inventor, this was a typical piece of complex Victorian innovation designed to replace the age-old hand-swung lead for taking depth measurements at sea while underway. Motor-driven, this device mechanically lowered a 24lb lead weight on a drum-wound wire. There was a brace of winding handles, each with a Kelvite Sinker lead and a pair of feelers. Their Lordships considered that Cooper should have been court-martialled, indeed still wanted to do so. The Admiralty expressed their 'strong disapproval of the manner in which the Inquiry was

29. Loss of HMS *Sturdy*, Report of Board of Enquiry, Enclosure 7021/M.595, dated 6 December 1940, National Archives, Kew, London.
30. Boards of Enquiry and Disciplinary Courts (29). Loss of HMS *Sturdy*: Board of Enquiry and expression of Their Lordships' strong disapproval of manner in which the case was handled, 1940/41, ADM1/11542/NL 1718/1941, National Archives, Kew, London.
31. The Chernikeeff Log was a valve-rotating propeller device contained in a retractable tub lowered a few metres below the ship's hull. It was named after its inventor, Captain Vasily Chernikeeff of the Imperial Russian Navy, who had introduced it in 1917. There was also the Walker Patent Log that performed the same basic task, this being an instrument used to measure nautical speed and distance traversed within a set period. It was based on a small rotator contained within a torpedo-shaped tub about twelve inches in length with stabilising fins, which had a long, braided line attached. This line was connected to a geared counter bolted to the afterdeck. When this device was paid out astern of the parent ship to a depth of about a metre or so, it rotated, which gave a reading of the ship's speed through the water. The two devices were often confused, the latter frequently being referred to as the Chernikeeff. Most Royal Navy destroyers had been fitted with this device during the First World War. Whether *Sturdy*, completed late, was ever so equipped, and, if so, still retained hers at this period, is not known. Both devices were still in common use at sea as late as the 1970s.
32. In 1876 Sir William Thomson (later Lord Kelvin) took out a patent (no. 3452) for a sounding device that improved on the earlier machine invented by Edward Massey three-quarters of a century before. Lord Kelvin subsequently further adapted this in conjunction with the Royal Navy and, between 1903 and 1906, he worked with the Royal Navy to develop the Kelvite Mark IV Sounding Machine specifically for use on fast-moving ships like destroyers. It was still in production by Kelvin, Bottomley & Baird Ltd, Glasgow, as late as the 1960s.

dealt with'. Their Lordships' opinion was that 'a court-martial should have been held' although they realised that it was clearly impractical to re-assemble the now-scattered ship's company and because of the non-availability of the *Shikari*'s officers and others, all making this course impossible under the current circumstances. Indeed Nasmith himself was censured for his defending comments and slated for the words he had used, being forced to defend himself. He had said that Malin Head D/F station was only to be used in extreme emergencies according to standing instructions and Cooper had not deemed it to be so at the time; the Kelvin apparatus could not have been successfully deployed in the existing weather circumstances, and so on.

Captain Ronald George Bowes-Lyon, the Director of Navigation, Navigation Branch, Hydrographic Department at the Admiralty since 15 October 1940, wrote on 12 December that:

> The Commanding Officer's error lies in the fact that at *no* time during the sea passage was he prepared for sounding. If the preparations had been made and subsequent events had rendered actual soundings impossible, it could then fairly be pleaded that all reasonable precautions in this respect had been taken.

However, Bowes-Lyon continued, 'At no time during the sea passage in question was the Kelvin Sounding Machine prepared for use'. He went on, 'soundings should have been attempted and the best time for this was during the night of 29/30 October when Dead Reckoning had shown the ship to be proceeding toward the land across the 100 fathom line, and subsequently the 50 fathom line'.

Moreover, 'D/F bearings from Malin Head being available, steps should have been taken to obtain them during the night of 29/30th, particularly since the sounding machine could not be used. By this time the ship's position was, inevitably, a matter of conjecture....'

Rather than going easy on Cooper, The Admiralty increased their measure of displeasure by changing the charge of 'serious neglect' to one of 'grave neglect'.

Dudley Pound wrote on 30 December that the question of the sickness of the sub-lieutenant and the inexperience of the officers, would, due to the rapid expansion of the fleet in the face of all-out war, 'soon apply to all our destroyers, and, if allowed to pass, the same arguments may be used to excuse other ships which might be lost or damaged' in the future. Pound also stated that:

> With regard to the future employment of Lieutenant-Commander Cooper I feel most strongly that his next appointment should be to a large ship or a ship of a class smaller than a destroyer, as it is important to make everyone realise that incidents such as these will not be treated lightly.

As a direct result of Pound's hostile intervention, Lieutenant-Commander Cooper was not given another command during the war, but was later assigned as a commander aboard the heavy cruiser *Exeter* (Captain Oliver Loudon Gordon), which had earlier suffered severe damage at the Battle of the River Plate in 1939 and was being extensively rebuilt. He went out East with her and was a survivor when she was sunk by Japanese cruisers north of Java in 1942.[33] After a torrid period as a PoW of the Japanese, during which time he acquitted himself very well, he and 400 other internees sailed home via Freemantle aboard the submarine depot ship *Maidstone* (Captain Lancelot Milman Shadwell).

Cooper returned to a different world. The war was won but the nation was bankrupt, there was a change of government and Admiral Pound had died. The new Admiralty Board considered his actions while a PoW and were generous to him in the end. Cooper received an MiD on 8 June 1944, was promoted to commander on 21 December 1945, and was made captain of the destroyer *Onslaught*. He received an OBE on 16 July 1946 and was appointed to command the new *Weapon*-class destroyer *Scorpion* on her completion.[34] Commander Cooper was then appointed as Chief Staff Officer Coastal Forces and subsequently Executive Officer of the *Daedalus* Fleet Air Arm station at Lee-on-Solent. He was promoted to captain and commanded the shore-base *Safeguard* at Rosyth. He retired, at his own request, on 3 July 1957 and died on 25 September 1999.

Much *Sturdy* memorabilia is held at An Iodhlan, Scarnish, Tiree. This memorial, organised by Commander Michael James Gibson RN RD (Rtd) and built by the late Bernie Smith, has been erected above the beach in Sandaig and was dedicated on Saturday 30 October 2010, attended by Commodore Charles Stevenson CBE, Naval Regional Commander Scotland and Northern Ireland.

As for *Sturdy* herself, on 17 March 1970 a tender was received to purchase the remains from DGDC and the wreck was subsequently sold. By 29 April it was reported that the vessel had been broken up ('smashed to smithereens' according to a report by Mark J. Brooks BA, dated 26 April 1970) and much metal recovered. Some items from the wreckage could still be traced in the rock pools in the vicinity.

---

33. See his book, *Ordeal in the Sun*, 1963, London, Robert Hale Limited, re-published as *Never Forget, nor Forgive: A Japanese Prisoner-of-War remembers*, 1995, Ringwood, Navigator Books.
34. One of the earlier destroyers of this name, of which there have been three, had been commanded by Andrew Browne Cunningham, and this new destroyer was named in honour of her, as he was by now Lord Cunningham of Hyndhope, First Sea Lord. An existing destroyer of the name, which had served at Normandy, was given to Holland, so the name became free again. The term 'Scorpion' is of legitimate inclusion as a weapon because this name was applied to an ancient ballista-type siege instrument. Three flotillas were planned, but the Labour government axed all except four of these ships along with all of the *Gauntlet*-class, many *Battle*-class and half the *Daring*-class. This involved hasty re-naming of *Tomahawk* as *Scorpion*.

Chapter 15

Who has the Helm?

The *Nottingham*, 7 July 2002

Lord Howe Island is a rocky narrow outcrop just six nautical miles long (11.12 km) and two nautical miles (3.706 km) across at its widest point, situated in the Tasman Sea, some 420 nautical miles (778 km) north-east of Sydney, New South Wales, and is the most southerly of the outlying islands off eastern Australia. To the east of this island are some notorious shoals and rocks linked underwater to the tiny Mutton Bird Island a mile farther north. The Admiralty Pilot states clearly that this area is 'very foul ground'.[1]

On 6 August 1837 the 251-ton (255 tonnes), 264-feet (80.46m), three-masted, wooden whaling ship *Wolf* (Captain John Evans), owned by William Walker & Co., Sydney, was in these waters with three of her crew sick and others ailing.[2] She had been out on an eighteen-month voyage and all was not well aboard. The *Wolf* sighted Lord Howe Island at a distance of twelve miles (19.512 km) at 0380 next morning and, during the morning, Evans went ashore to procure water and fresh provisions for his men as more of them were ailing. The weather was rough and squally and a fresh breeze was blowing. At daybreak the *Wolf* stood under the eastern side of the island and, at 0830, sent three boats ashore with casks for water while the ship herself stood some two-and-a-half miles (4.0234 km) offshore. As they passed the reef Evans noted in his log that 'observed strong currents setting towards it'. At 1100 the *Wolf* was tacked in toward the shore and, an hour later, she hove to to await the return of her boats. The wind had strengthened and it was hazy. On 8 August the winds freshened further but the boats had not returned. At 0030 the *Wolf* filled her sails and stood inshore, passing the shoal one point before her starboard beam three-quarters of a mile (1.207 km) off, passing it rapidly due to 'the strong current' to the southward.

A single boat came off to her from ashore, the crew stating that the water casks could not be towed due to the strength of the current. The shoal was logged on her lee

---

1. See *British Admiralty Australian Nautical Chart – Approaches to Lord Howe Island* (AU610).
2. The *Wolf* was originally a Royal Navy vessel, a gun-brig built in 1814 at Woolwich Naval Dockyard on the Thames, one of the 14-gun *Crocus* class. These ships were sometimes referred (inaccurately) to as the 'Croker' class, probably because John Wilson Croker, an Irish-born politician, was appointed as Secretary to the Admiralty at the time they were constructed. See ADM 359/31B/170 (ADM BP/31B) dated 30 November 1811, National Maritime Museum, Greenwich, London. The *Wolf* was completed too late for the Napoleonic Wars for which she had been designed and, after ten years' service, had been sold out of the service into commercial use in 1825.

beam about a quarter of a mile off and, at around 0045, the current appeared to shift suddenly, 'setting ship rapidly on weather bow down to shoal'. The speed took them by surprise and there proved no room to wear the ship under double-reefed topsails, jib, foretopsail, and main trysail. Evans had the reefs shaken out of the fore topsail and made all sail possible to try and claw back but in the end had no option but to run in between two visible sections of the reef, with the wind hard to the southward. The captain put the helm up and ran the ship, but lost his last gamble and she struck and 'hung about ten minutes on her starboard bilge' before starting ahead again and striking for a second time aft, more severely than before. The ship's rudder was carried away together with some pintels.[3] What the unfortunate vessel had hit later turned out to be a 350 yards (320.04m) long by 200 yards (182.88m) wide, submerged rock, of about thirty-two feet nine-and-a-half inches (10-m) diameter, situated about eight cables (1.48 km) from the island whose peak attains a height of forty-seven inches (1.2m) above Mean High Water Springs (MHWS).

The *Wolf* finally cleared the reef and was headed offshore, apparently making no water, and a spare rudder was shipped with a view to making it to Sydney some 486 miles (781 km) to the WSW. Alas this intent proved illusory for it was quickly found she had indeed been severely holed, and soon had four feet (1.219m) of water in her hold despite all pumps being set to work. Soon this inrush was within four feet of the second deck and so Evans decided to beach her. The mizzen mast was hacked down with every sheet aft cleared away and as much sail as possible set forward. They launched a spar to the lee quarter, but water continued to pour inboard and the inevitable quickly had to be faced. The captain and crew mustered clothes in the ship's boats and abandoned the wreck, for such she had now become, and, within half-an-hour of striking, the *Wolf* had capsized and sunk, taking with her all the crew's possessions and eighteen months' work, 1,650 barrels of sperm oil. Evans and his crew landed on Lord Howe Island where the inhabitants received them with great kindness for five weeks until the *Psyche* (Captain Stephen Norris) arrived and took them to Sydney. The wreck of the *Wolf* (valued, without cargo, at £16,000 but only insured for £8,000) has never been located.[4] Since that date the pinnacle where she first impacted, located to the east of Mount Lidgbird, has carried the name Wolf Rock.[5]

Fast-forward 165 years and another ship was operating in the area and also suffered a sick crew member. Not a former Royal Navy ship, but a fully active fleet unit; not a frail wooden sailing vessel she, but an ultra-modern, state-of-the-art warship of the Royal Navy equipped with every conceivable electronic navigation aid and a

3. Pintels – alternative spelling of pintle, a bolt which fits into a gudgeon attaching the moveable section of a ship's rudder section, so enabling it to be easily lifted in and out.

4. See 'Records of Wrecks. No. 106' in *The Nautical Magazine: A Journal of Papers on Subjects Connected with Maritime Affairs*, Vol 7, p.282, 1838, London, Simpkin, Marshal & Co. Also *The Sydney Gazette and New South Wales Advertiser*, Saturday 16 September 1937, p.2.

5. *Not*, it should be noted, Wolfe Rock, because the rock was originally named for the ship and *not* after Major-General James Wolfe, the conqueror of Quebec; however, nowadays, Wolfe is the version more in common use locally.

formidable array of additional high-technology. She was the 3,500-ton (3,556-tonne) Type-42[6] destroyer *Nottingham* (Captain Richard Farrington)[7] with a crew of twenty-seven officers, seventy-one senior rates and 173 junior rates for a total of 271. She had been built by Vosper Thorneycroft's Woolston shipyard at Southampton, being laid down on 6 February 1978, launched on 18 February 1980 and commissioned on 14 April 1983. She had an overall length of 410 feet (125m), a beam of 47 feet (14.3m) and a draught of 19 feet (5.8m). She was powered by two Rolls-Royce Olympus TM3B gas turbines, with two Rolls-Royce Tyne RM1C gas turbine cruising engines capable of speeds of up to 18 knots (33 km/h). Her top speed was 30 knots (56 km/h). She carried a single Vickers 4.5-inch (114mm) Mk 8 automatic gun and two Vulcan Phalanx close-in weapons systems for her own air defence, along with a single twin Hawker Siddeley Dynamics Sea Dart missile launcher. She also carried a Westland Lynx HMA8 helicopter in an inbuilt hangar. Her pendant number was D91 and she was the sixth Royal Navy ship to carry that name. She had cost £300 million to build. Her first commanding officer was Commander Nigel Essenhigh, who later became a distinguished First Sea Lord. Her internal equipment included an Echo Sounder 778 and associated Bridge Unit (BU). She was also equipped with a Wordsafe Voice Recorder on her bridge.[8]

The *Nottingham* had undertaken a major refit from which she had emerged in September 2000. For the next six-month period the destroyer conducted trials at sea and underwent a range of Safety Readiness Checks (SRC) and, between April and May 2001, undertook Basic Operational Sea Training (BOST), followed by a Joint Maritime Course (JMC) in June. She then began operational duties by joining Exercise ARGONAUT 01/SAIF SARREA in August 2001. The *Nottingham* returned to Portsmouth for Christmas. In 2002 she carried out a High Seas' Firing (HSF) programme and on 18 March sailed to conduct a full-month deployment to the Far East. On her schedule was participation in the planned Five Powers' Defence Arrangement Exercise and courtesy visits to both Tokyo and Shanghai after which similar visits were planned for Australian and New Zealand ports.

The ship's officers had undergone some change during this period. Forty-one-year-old Commander Farrington had joined the ship in September 2000, Lieutenant-

---

6. Of light cruiser tonnage all fourteen of them carried cruiser, rather than destroyer, names, being *Birmingham, Cardiff, Coventry, Edinburgh, Exeter, Glasgow, Gloucester, Liverpool, Manchester, Newcastle, Nottingham, Sheffield, Southampton* and *York*. Two, *Coventry* and *Sheffield*, were sunk in the Falklands in 1982.

7. Commander Farrington had formerly been with the Directorate of Naval Operations at the Ministry of Defence, Whitehall, London, since 1997 and at HMS *Dryad*, the Naval Warfare School at Southwick House and had been appointed to stand by the *Nottingham* in 2000.

8. The echo sounder had been reported as suffering from an intermittent fault during Standard Operator Checks (SOC) on 24 June on readings below a depth of 65 feet 7.5 inches (20m), but, when checked that day, no faults were discovered. Likewise, the ship's Radar 1007 aerial had exhibited water ingress problems to its rotating joint, and these were due to be rectified on arrival at Wellington.

Commander John Lea, the Executive Officer, had joined in February 2002,[9] Navigation Officer Lieutenant Andrew Richard Ingham arrived in May 2002, the Officer of the Watch, Lieutenant James Robert Denney, was appointed in December 2001[10] and the Marine Engineer Officer, Lieutenant-Commander (FTC) Ian Stuart Groom BEng CEng MIMarE, had been appointed in March 2000. The flight commander of the Lynx aboard was Lieutenant (CC) Philip David Nash, who had performed the same function aboard the *Glasgow* and then on the staff of No. 815 Naval Air Squadron's 2 Flight.[11] On 4 July the *Nottingham* left Cairns, Queensland, to sail for Wellington, New Zealand, where she was due to dock on 9 July.[12] The planned route was southward along the Great Barrier Reef to Lord Howe Island where it was planned to anchor off Ned's Beach, off the island's north-eastern coast, with an alternative choice at Middle Beach, at 1600 on 7 July for visits by the ship's company for recreation and goodwill. The ominous threat of Wolf Rock lurked some three nautical miles (1559.6m) south of the intended anchorage, however. The *Nottingham* was due to pass this almost-invisible hazard at a range of one-and-a-half nautical miles (779.8m) that day, but the rock had failed to be noted as a danger, although Farrington later told the press that 'they were all aware of it'. The navigating officer had not 'hatched off' this potential threat, nor were there any clearing bearings drawn on the chart while the strength of the tidal stream (which had so concerned Captain Evans over a century-and-a-half earlier but which had still proved his bane) was also not noted. Nor had the rock's position been input into any of the electronic navigation aids, the command system or the command support system. Despite these omissions, the *Nottingham* duly made her planned landfall at 1400, and anchored safely at 1534 without any problems being encountered.

The scheduled programme was, however, abruptly interrupted when Commander Farrington was notified that morning that an injured crew member, suffering from a slipped disc, was to be sent ashore urgently for onward transfer to the UK for specialist treatment. Special sea dutymen were not closed up but Damage Control State was changed to 3, condition *Yankee* and the Blind Pilotage Safety Officer (BPSO) had been closed up twenty minutes ahead of arrival.

Departure time for Wellington was arranged for 1900 (the clocks having been advanced one hour) and, while anchored, the weather remained good, with good

---

9. He had been awarded a Bridge Watchkeeping Certificate while in the *Exeter* in 1994–95 and had been NBCDO of the *Fearless* between 2000 and 2001.
10. He had been awarded a Bridge Watchkeeping Certificate in OPV.
11. Appointments, see *The Navy List 2000* (Corrected to 12 April 2000), 2000, The Stationery Office, London.
12. The details of the accident that follow are principally derived from the now unclassified Official *Board of Inquiry Report into the Grounding of HMS* Nottingham *at Wolf Rock, Lord Howe Island, Australia on 7 July 2002*, Report FLEET/259/2/1, dated 21 July 2003, now in the Public Domain, based on the findings of the Board of Inquiry which was convened aboard HMNZS *Endeavour* (Commander John Campbell, RNZN) between 13 and 16 July, with the full co-operation of the Commanding officer and the ship's Company of HMS *Nottingham*.

visibility, and a 12–16-knot wind. There was a long swell running from the south which made operation of the Westland Lynx helicopter difficult while the ship remained stationary. After the Lynx had had to have been 'waved off' on three consecutive attempts, earnest discussion was made about whether to up-anchor and set *Nottingham* in motion to counter the roll and preparations were made to do this, the main engines being started. In the end this proved unnecessary for at 1714 the Lynx finally managed to land aboard with the executive officer, who had been ashore, back on board. Commander Farrington then decided to leave with the casualty and instructed his navigator that he would return around 2100 and he should, in the captain's absence, 'run a racetrack in her, and stay out to the east'. On his way to the Lynx the skipper and XO met, and the latter was told to get the ship underway and proceed down the navigation track ('navtrack') where the returning Lynx could be recovered *en route*. Unfortunately, this ran at variance to what the Navigator had been ordered to do earlier. No entry was apparently made in the Sea Order Book. The Lynx, with Farrington aboard, departed again at 2005 while the XO went to the bridge to assume command. He and the Navigation Officer made the decision to weigh anchor, which was done at 2057 local time, and to head out eastward and await the return of the helicopter.

Events now moved with the inevitability of a Greek tragedy. The second officer of the watch, a young sub-lieutenant who had only joined the ship in January 2002, drew a track 090° from Ned's Anchorage toward a point where *Nottingham* would interdict her pre-planned track to Wellington. The officer of the watch approved the plan, but without any reference to the chart. The officer of the watch manoeuvred the *Nottingham* out from her anchorage under the supervision of the navigator and executive officer and the second officer of the watch took a final radar fix at 2057, but this was not reported to the officer of the watch. Unbeknown to any member of the navigating team the ship was now placed just 300 yards (274.32m) from the limiting danger line. The destroyer then proceeded out from the anchorage and moved down the racetrack at a speed of twelve knots (22.224 km/h).

The use of chart references was minimal over the next hour, neither the XO nor navigator doing so, nor did they take any fix or request one. The OOW did consult the chart, at 2144, but did not fix the ship or supervise the Second Officer of the Watch. Nor were any soundings taken and the 778 echo-sounder remained switched off. Once clear of Ned's Anchorage the navigator left the bridge. The communication between the Lynx and the ship was maintained, with the bridge control planning the conduct of flying operations for recovery while being monitored from the operations room by the Principal Warfare Officer. The *Nottingham* reverted to State 3, condition *X-Ray*.

At 2125 the destroyer changed course 140° onto the track for Wellington, but no hazard checks, on the chart, visual or by radar, were conducted covering this new alignment. When the navigation officer returned to the bridge at 2137 he was irked to discover that he had not been notified of the change of plan 'from running an east/west racetrack to proceeding down the navtrack'. With a 'considerable swell' and the existing direction of the wind, the late arrival of the Lynx at the rendezvous point caused a further alteration of course of 230°, which, the officers agreed, would provide a suitable flying course and ensure Lord Howe Island was left safely on *Nottingham*'s starboard bow. After being checked, this plan was adopted at 2144 but, at 2149, this was again modified to 235°. The *Nottingham* was now off the navtrack, and just two nautical miles from 'significant danger with no safety considerations or plan in place'.

Recovery of the Lynx with Commander Farrington was safely accomplished at 2153, and the helicopter shut down at 2155. With the skipper safely back aboard all seemed well, but it was far from it. In order to safely stow the Lynx in her hangar, and also regain the navtrack, the navigation officer agreed with the executive officer yet another alteration of course, to the north-west to get into the lee of Lord Howe Island. On agreement the XO left the bridge at 2155, while the Principal Warfare Officer, with the flying operations terminated, simultaneously left the operations room and the captain was making his way to the bridge. Wolf Rock was now just over one mile distant. On the island, harbourmaster Clive Wilson recalled that conditions were bad: 'It was rough winds, wild seas, breaking waves that night.'

The navigator ordered the officer of the watch to alter course to 350° to comply with what he had just agreed but, before this had been completed, modified it to 320°. The *Nottingham* then steadied on this course and the two officers decided to shut down the starboard engine and were involved in a detailed four-minute discussion on the best procedure of how this could be done. In their involvement with this debate, neither one appeared to have noticed that the second officer of the watch had fixed the ship, at 2200, in a position four cables south-east of Wolf Rock and steering directly for it still at 12 knots (22.224 km/h). This 'fix' was plotted onto the 1:150000 scale chart, with the officer 'inadvertently drawing part of the fix over Wolf Rock, completely obscuring it from view'.[13]

While the OOWatch was fully engrossed with watching the pitch-and-roll gauges lest he lose the helicopter overboard in the swell before she could be safely secured, yet a further distraction came when the flight deck requested his permission to move the Lynx to the 'Fly 2' position. At the same time the machinery control room also requested his permission to shut down the port steering motor. When he finally sorted these problems out at 2202, he looked out of the bridge windows and immediately was aware of 'a pale white glow on the water' just 100 yards (91.44m) off *Nottingham*'s starboard bow. He initially assumed it was the reflection of moonlight on the sea and looked upward to the sky to verify this. With a mere twenty seconds remaining until impact, the navigator finally observed white foam and rushed to the chart to check the ship's position. He shouted to the officer of the watch 'Come Right, mate' but, at 2202, *Nottingham* hit the western edge of Wolf Rock.

The shock throughout the ship was severe and also severe was the damage to the *Nottingham*'s thin starboard plating. 'Emergency, Emergency, close all red openings' was piped by the navigating officer and he ordered the officer of the watch to come

---

13. It will not be lost on the reader that this is exactly the same error that the navigating officer of the *Effingham* had been accused of making sixty-two years earlier.

astern, just as both the commanding officer and the executive officer arrived on the bridge. Below, the marine engineering officer of the watch started up all the high-pressure salt-water (HPSW) pumps and the standby diesel generator. A heavy inrush of water was reported entering the compartments in the region of the starboard stabiliser in the forward engine room (FER), and several flood alarms were sounding.

Commander Farrington immediately realised his ship was firmly aground, although not yet knowing the full extent of her harm. The engines were ordered stopped, the officer of the watch complying and then starting the starboard one. The marine engineering officer piped 'Hands to Emergency Stations'. Commander Farrington ordered all hands to be issued with lifejackets. By this time *Nottingham* was listing between 10 to 15 degrees to starboard with water continuing to inflow forward. The yeoman made contact with Lord Howe Island and informed them *Nottingham* was aground on Wolf Rock. The captain then ordered the engines to full thrust astern.

By 2209 the destroyer had come clear of Wolf Rock and an initial damage situation report was sent to command by the weapon engineer officer. Slow flooding was taking place in the DER, and free flooding in the Sea Dart Spray Compartment and the 4.5-inch magazine. The marine engineering officer ordered power isolation in order to stem the flooding in Conversion Machinery Room (CMR) 4G, doing so without requesting permission or informing command of his action. Both gyros, steering-gear control, and shaft and telegraph indications went out. Steering control was switched to mechanical and the *Nottingham* was halted south of Wolf Rock to assess the damage more completely. Commander Farrington then requested a suitable place to beach the vessel and Sydney Maritime Co-ordination Centre was notified via the Global Maritime Distress and Safety System (GMDSS).

The immediate crisis contained, ideas of beaching the ship were abandoned as the marine engineer officer advised that the ship was not in danger of sinking or plunging. C, D, E, F and G sections of 4 and 5 decks were free flooded, and there was seven feet (2.1336m) of water in the Sea Dart Quarters, Sea Dart Hydraulic and Power Rooms and 3D messdeck, with five feet (1.524m) in the FER and rising. Instead, Commander Farrington conned the ship back to Middle Beach and anchored at 2340. By 2355 the main computer supply was gone, but the main broadcast and internal communication had been restored. Although at one point it had been feared that the *Nottingham* was within a mere six minutes of foundering, by 2359 the flooding had been stabilised, levelling off in the FER at eighteen feet (5.486m) while the after engine room had been pumped out to six feet (1.8288m), and her list had eased to just 2.5 degrees.

Fleet Headquarters was initially notified by INMARSAT, and, at 0342, Commander Farrington and the marine engineering officer went ashore to get better communications linking in order to obtain expert advice from Warship Support Agency (WSA) about stability options and obtaining specialist diving support teams. Allied naval help was quickly forthcoming. The Royal New Zealand Navy organised Task Group 648.1 with the fleet replenishment vessel HMNZS *Endeavour* and the frigate HMNZS *Te Mana* (Commander Anthony Jonathan Parr RNZN) to work under OPCON at the Military Co-ordination Centre (MCC). The former arrived at 0902 on the 9th from Australia and the latter reached the area on 10 June. The Royal Australian Navy supplied an eleven-man section of their clearance diving team who were conveyed to the area by the Royal Australian Air Force from No. 37 Squadron based at RAAF Richmond. They also transported the team's diving equipment, pumps, sheet metal for hole patching and welding gear the 450 nautical miles in one-and-a-half hours. Squadron Leader Dean Tetley confirmed *Nottingham*'s nose 'clearly below the water and you could see the bilge pumps in action'.[14] A single search and rescue (SAR) Lockheed Hercules C-130J had already overflown the scene in the early hours of Monday 8 July and delivered specialist salvage equipment.

In summary, it took ten minutes for the marine engineering officer, after his arrival at the main damage control centre, to receive damage information around the ship and produce an initial estimate of the extent of the damage. David J. McCarthy[15] noted that communications were lost with the outlying parts of the ship very rapidly. Flooding reports were obtained relatively quickly, but damage reports were limited as compartments were flooded and subsequently sealed. The forward engine room bulkhead was considered a structural priority, principally since its loss would have resulted in a significant loss in the ship's remaining stability. The priority in the initial response was to deal with the extensive flooding. Communications with shore-based authorities were complex and had to be made from ashore. Considerable effort and manpower was expended erecting shoring-up bulkheads and hatches. The flood was fully under control and the ship assessed as safe after four-and-a-half hours.

The ship's company had come together in a remarkable way and it was principally through their efforts that she was saved. This fact was recognised on 29 April 2003 with the award of the Queen's Commendation for Bravery to Petty Officer Marine Engineering Artificer Darren Philip Bennion, Operation Mechanic (Above Water Warfare) 1s James Clement Bowen and Alexander Stelios Michou for their bravery.

Ben Mitchell of Australia Search and Rescue was able to give reassurance after a preliminary examination. 'Some consideration was given to beaching the vessel to prevent sinking. The ship had been holed but the crew managed to stem the inflow of water and they got the situation under control.'[16] Once *in situ* the divers conducted an underwater survey and confirmed large structural damage from the stem through to K section, including the total loss of the starboard stabiliser fin. Only H section remained undamaged. Also quickly on site by the 8th was the Major Warship Integrated Platform Team (MWIPT) representative who conducted an interior survey. He noted the severe distortion of the ship's stem post and the partial loss of the vertical keel in A and B sectors.

The final verdict on *Nottingham*'s damage was that significant raking damage extended to over half the ship's length. Therefore, in order to assess whether the

---

14. *Air Force News*, 18 July 2002.
15. McCarthy, David J., *Response to a Damage Event*, Master of Science Thesis, 2006, London, University College of London.
16. Lynch, Jake, BBC Report, 'Battle to save stricken warship', Sunday 7 July 2002.

Nottingham could safely be towed the 425 miles to Sydney without danger 'an extensive structural analysis was required'. These calculations were carried out by QinetiQ, a privatised government defence work agency based at Thurleigh airfield near Bedford. 'They used in-house analysis tools capable of handling damage structure. Manual definition was required to digitise ship structural plans before the tools could be used.'[17]

Wolf Rock itself was not overlooked in all this concern. With inevitable predictability *The Guardian* was concentrated on impact on the environmental aspect of the accident, and stated that 'the ship had leaked a half-mile-long oil slick', but it had to admit that this pollution 'was being broken up by the propellers of small boats' and was also 'being blown away out to sea and away from the island'.[18] The Lord Howe Marine Parks Authority dived the rock and reported quite unequivocally that there had been *no* environmental impact on marine life from this incident.

Meanwhile the Ministry of Defence's Salvage Department (SALMO) had despatched a team of their own, who had learned their skills at HMS *Phoenix*, the Damage Repair Instructional Unit (DRIU), to stabilise the ship and ready her to make the journey across to Newcastle, New South Wales, a port at the mouth of the Hunter river, north of Sydney, where there were proper dockyard facilities to further attend to her. They were assisted in this not only by the ship's crew but by operations manager Graeme Mackenzie and local marine officials. Steel plates had been welded to her broken side where a 100-foot (30.480m) gash stretched from bow almost to her bridge. Wood and steel shoring was put in place and, finally, she was considered safe and ready. On 6 August she was towed across, stern-first, by Djakata-based Ocean Butana Lines 1,297-ton, 6,000hp anchor-handling tug *Pacific Chieftain*, with the Hong Kong Salvage & Towing Company's 4,000bhp tug *Yam O* providing the steering. A third tug, the 470-ton (477 tonnes), Sydney-based *Austral Salvor*, owned by Svitzer Australasia, stood by as reserve tug in case required but was not, in the event, needed.

On arrival at Newcastle, a supervisory team of Commander Anthony Holberry RN and Mr James Ward from SALMO ensured the safe unloading and disposal of her Sea Dart missiles, and additional repairs were done while her fate was pondered upon. Ultimately the cost of bringing another Type 42 destroyer up to the standard of *Nottingham*'s last refit was deemed considerably more than salvaging her and so she was given a stay of execution.

The Breda, Netherlands-based Dutch salvage company of Dockwise was given a £7 million contract to bring her back to the UK and they despatched the largest vessel in their fleet, the 22,428-ton (22,788 tonnes) heavy-lift ship *Swan*, which was based at Singapore at the time, to Sydney. The *Swan* had 29,526-tons (30,000 tonnes) of seawater pumped into her ballast tanks, which lowered her into Sydney Harbour and

---

17. See Bole, Marcus, 'Introducing Damage Structural Assessment to Onboard Decision Support Tools. 2.1 The Grounding of HMS *Nottingham*.' Abstract, pp.387–8, 2007, Farnborough, Graphics Research Corporation (GRS).

18. Norton-Taylor, Richard, 'Contrite captain is all at sea', article in *The Guardian*, 9 July 2002.

the tugs carefully manoeuvred *Nottingham* into a specially-constructed steel cradle which had been welded to her deck. Ballast was then pumped from the *Swan*'s tanks raising both ships together, and releasing trapped water from the destroyer's buckled bow section. On 28 October *Swan* and *Nottingham* commenced the long journey home 'piggy-back' style. They finally arrived at Portsmouth on 9 December and *Nottingham* was delicately unloaded and docked, whereupon Fleet Support got to work reinstating her.

While all this excellent work was being undertaken, the media and internet had been whipping themselves up into their usual frenzy with speculation, claim and counter-claim, all long before any evidence had been analysed. The harbourmaster at Lord Howe Island, Clive Wilson, was quoted as claiming that the 'the latest Royal Australian Navy chart of the island had the notation "inadequately surveyed"'. Wilson stated that 'some areas along the shore are not definitely charted'. The chart AUS 610, he claimed, and the Admiralty version of it carried a note that said Wolf Rock was 'reported to lie 1.5 cables (0.274km) NW in 1990'. This means, it was claimed, that Wolf Rock could actually be 900 feet (0.39km) northwest of the position shown on the chart. It was also stated in the press that the last survey was conducted as long ago as 1837 by HMS *Benham*. 'Wolf Rock may not have been precisely marked.'[19]

Another old favourite was rolled out by the press, eager to make the biggest possible mountain out of any mole-hill by claiming that *Nottingham* was 'in the South Pacific to escort a shipment of nuclear waste through the area'.[20] But of course this was complete rubbish also; *no* other ship was present and *no* such cargo was being transported from Australia to New Zealand. Even more bizarre was the media's accusation that the damage to HMS *Nottingham* had affected Britain's contribution to the war in Iraq. Quite how a ship travelling from Australia to New Zealand was supposed to have been contributing to that particular operation in the Middle East is something only a television journalist could have envisaged; nonetheless the Ministry of Defence was forced to issue a straight-faced denial of any such impact.

At the other media extreme, defence correspondent Sean Rayment, writing in the *Daily Telegraph*, stated categorically that 'A Senior Naval Official [unnamed] based in Portsmouth, the home port of the *Nottingham*, said "Commander Farrington will not be punished for the accident"'. This was obviously incorrect: *all* such accidents are

19. Ware, Hugh, 'Royal Navy destroyer hits rock, nearly sinks off New Zealand', article in *Professional Mariner*, 1 May 2007 edition. A remarkable document, Lord Howe Island being off Australia rather than New Zealand, there being no such Royal Navy warship as HMS *Benham*, survey or any other type of ship. The first survey was conducted by HMS *Supply* (Lieutenant Henry Lidgbird Ball) a 168-ton, 8-gun brig acting as tender to the 6th-rate HMS *Sirius* (Captain John Hunter), flagship of the First Fleet. This work was done between 1788 and 1791. The *Supply* was later sold out of service and became the *Thomas & Mary* and worked on the Thames. The first hydrographic survey was done by Captain Henry Denham aboard HMS *Herald* with biologists William Milne, John Macgillivray and Denis Macdonald.

20. Cornford, Phil, 'The night Wolf Rock ripped into Britain's finest', article in *Sydney Morning Herald*, Tuesday 9 July, 2002.

investigated in the Royal Navy. The *Telegraph* story continued, with a greater degree of accuracy, that:

> The accident was not his fault. That is a fact which has now been accepted. He quickly took command of the vessel and made a brilliant assessment of the situation. It was his leadership and clear thinking that prevented the ship from sinking and endangering the lives of his crew.

'The *Telegraph*,' Rayment continued:

> understands that Commander Farrington publicly suggested that the accident was his fault in part to protect the reputation of the Lieutenant in charge of the ship. The naval official said – Commander Farrington was attempting to deflect criticism from the young Lieutenant in charge of the vessel. He had agreed with the Ministry of Defence in London that the press line must be that the accident was his fault and that they should reiterate the public statement he had made after the accident.

'Commander Farrington's actions have attracted considerable praise from within the service: senior officers have privately let it be known that they believe he had upheld the best traditions of the Royal Navy,' wrote Rayment.[21]

Commander Farrington's predictions proved a rather more correct prophecy of what was to occur. He confessed to the media, including Rayment, in the immediate aftermath of the accident:

> Just as the sun comes up in the morning, if you run your ship aground you get court martialled. It hazarded the lives of 250 men and women. We have done significant damage to a major British warship. This is quite the worst thing that's ever happened, quite the worst character-building stuff. I'd say it's the worst feeling in the world.

He could not have been clearer and, in the final analysis, Farrington was to be proved rather more accurate in his prediction than was the *Telegraph* and the inevitable court martial most certainly did follow.

Nobody had died; outstanding work by the ship's crew had saved the ship from what appeared to be an irretrievable disaster; the captain had accepted full responsibility and the other officers charged had all pleaded guilty. Whatever were the world's press, used to dealing with the self-promotion and self-importance of politicians and show-business personalities, to do in order to work some meaty drama out from such honesty and endeavour?

---

21. 'Commander 'who ran aground' revealed to be ship's Saviour', article in *Daily Telegraph*, London, 11 August 2002.

The British media had a field day, it being sadly noted in *The Naval Review* that more sympathy was shown in Australia than at home; one typical report stating that:

> The ignominy of the grounding was compounded last week as pictures were beamed around the world of the crippled vessel being towed towards port by two Australian tugs. The priority is to safely dispose of the Sea Dart missiles, the ship's main armaments, which were damaged by water. Royal Navy technicians will spend the next two weeks removing the weapons, which could become unstable and explode if they dry out.

Commander Richard Farrington and three of his senior officers from the ship appeared before a courts martial hearing at Portsmouth Naval Base on 11 September. Prosecutor[22] Commander Stuart Crozier stated at the hearing that not one of the three officers on the *Nottingham*'s bridge that night knew where the ship was in relation to the chart. Although not on the bridge at the time, as he had returned aboard just nine minutes before the impact, Commander Farrington pleaded guilty at the court martial to delegating conduct of the ship without ensuring a sufficient navigational plan was in place.

The formal charges were that: Commander Farrington did on 7 July 2002 neglect to perform the duty imposed on him by the Queen's Regulations for the safe direction and management of HMS *Nottingham* by failing to properly delegate conduct of the ship to his Executive Officer; Lieutenant Commander Lea and Lieutenant Ingham did on 7 July 2002 by negligence allow HMS *Nottingham* to be stranded; Lieutenant Denney did on 7 July 2002 by negligence cause HMS *Nottingham* to be stranded.

The court's verdicts were comprehensive on all four men. Lieutenant Denney (OOW) was dismissed ship; Lieutenant Ingham (Nav) received a severe reprimand; Lieutenant Commander Lea (XO) was dismissed ship and Commander Farrington (CO) received a reprimand. Sentencing Farrington, Commodore Philip Wilcocks criticised him for failing to give a proper handover to his XO by checking sea charts with him for potential hazards and providing clear instructions. Lieutenant James Denney, the officer of the watch, pleaded guilty to negligently causing HMS *Nottingham* to be stranded. Lieutenant Andrew Ingham, the navigation officer and Lieutenant Commander John Lea, the executive officer, both pleaded guilty to negligently allowing the ship to be stranded. Denney and Lea were dismissed from the ship by the court martial, and Ingham was given a severe reprimand.

Speaking to all four defendants, Wilcocks said the accident 'undermined the high reputation of the Royal Navy and caused significant embarrassment, wasted resources, and took an operational warship out of active duty for a long period'. He added,

---

22. At the rank of commander, the Naval Prosecuting Authority (NPA) was a statutory appointment by Royal Warrant, answerable to the Attorney-General, with worldwide jurisdiction for prosecution of naval courts martial and response to summary appeals. It has since been superseded by the Services Prosecuting Authority (SPA).

'The most important message from this court martial is that the highest navigational standards must be maintained at all times to ensure safety at sea. They are ignored at our peril.'

The *Guardian* stated:

The commander of a naval destroyer that struck rocks off Australia in July last year was yesterday reprimanded by a court martial for his part in the collision. Richard Farrington – who was not on board at the time – was told that his culpability was 'at the very lowest end of the scale' but he had not handed over control correctly. HMS *Nottingham* ran aground when a junior officer, plotting a route on the ship's map, inadvertently placed a navigational instrument on top of a location, hiding the rocks.

The first the crew knew of them was moments before the crash when Lieutenant James Denney, the officer at watch, spotted something ahead of the ship and said: 'What the hell is that? It looks like moonlight on the water.' Seconds later the ship ran aground, causing £26m of damage.[23]

The MoD issued an official statement confirming these findings which read:

At today's Courts Martial following the grounding of HMS *Nottingham*, four of the Ship's Officers were charged, pleaded guilty and have been sentenced accordingly. The Royal Navy places a strong emphasis on the importance of safe navigation and this is reflected in the extremely high quality of Navigation Training conducted today. Royal Navy ships operate safely across the globe on a daily basis, in sometimes hostile, always demanding, navigational and operational situations. Royal Naval Training takes these constant hazards into account in order to prevent instances of this nature. The excellence of the design and build of the ship combined with the high quality calibre of the ship's company assured the safety of the ship and crew. The prompt and courageous actions of the ship's company in dealing with this incident reflect the high standard of training conducted both regularly at sea and ashore.[24]

The most acerbic comments on the case came, not from the press, but from British Merchant Navy officers and amateur yachtsmen.

Speaking after the court martial, Commander Farrington spoke on behalf of all four defendants, saying they were pleased to be able to put the incident behind them and to continue with their careers. Farrington was quoted as saying:

This incident reminds us all that the sea is an unforgiving master and all those who follow this rewarding profession must treat it with respect, regardless of the

---

23. *The Guardian*, Friday 12 September 2003.
24. AP/PA, 12 September 2003.

technology that might be available. As I think I said at the time, the grounding marks the coincidence of unfortunate circumstances and basic human error. This court martial has reinforced that view. We made mistakes, omissions. We all could have done more. We accept responsibility and the inevitable consequences but there is little more to be said on why it happened. But I would like to say that I hold my fellow officers in the highest regard. They were thoroughly professional before this all happened and they remain thoroughly professional. I would relish the opportunity to serve at sea again with any of them.

Commander Farrington also expressed his gratitude to the navies and air forces of New Zealand and Australia which assisted with the rescue of HMS *Nottingham*, as well as the people of Lord Howe Island and the people of Newcastle, NSW, where the ship's company was put up before returning to the UK

Praising his ship's company, Commander Farrington said:

I would like to recognise and applaud a magnificent ship's company who responded better than any captain could have wished. Anyone who doubts the training and professionalism of the Royal Navy need look no further than their efforts to save the ship in the hours, days and weeks following the grounding and the achievements in bringing her safely to harbour with no injuries or loss of life.

On the practical side the *Nottingham* accident stimulated vigorous action to be taken across the Royal Navy in an effort to improve standards of navigational safety. There was an internal review which resulted in the advanced procurement of electronic charting systems for all naval vessels. The internal review examined in detail the full range of both individual and bridge-team training across the Fleet, and came to the conclusion that there were areas for improvement. A thirty-point action plan resulted from this study which was duly implemented, the key elements of which included improvements to both individual and team training as well as the introduction of routine inspections to deployed units. In parallel with this, action was taken to improve navigational safety in the short term by introduction into service of forty-two laptop-based electronic charting systems. These 'Navigational Command Aids' were a stop-gap measure to enhance navigational safety pending the full introduction into service of the Warship Electronic Chart Display Information Systems (WECDIS).

As for the *Nottingham* herself, she also was to receive a verdict on her future, and that was that she was to be made good and put back into service.[25] She had arrived back in Portsmouth just before Christmas. Repairs to the hull involved the removal and replacement of 98.42 tons (100 tonnes) of steelwork as well as the removal of the ship's turbines. When the bow by the Sea Dart magazine was opened up the repair team found

---

25. Written Ministerial Statements Defence. HMS *Nottingham* to be repaired at HM Naval Base Portsmouth, House of Commons, *Hansard*, 3 December 2003.

almost half-a-ton of Wolf Rock embedded inside. Not only the hull itself required attention for the inspection discovered a great deal of additional work; for example, it was found necessary to repair wiring and other internal structures affected by the salt water. During the period of her rebuilding, the older Type 42, *Glasgow*, herself due for the scrapyard, was renovated sufficiently to take her place on a temporary basis.

The final total rebuilding was at a cost of £39 million and this expenditure was intended to extend her active life until 2012. The work was finally completed on 7 July 2003, the anniversary of her grounding. She was re-commissioned in April 2004 and began active duty once more in July that year. After three-and-half years' further active service, *Nottingham* was placed in reserve at Portsmouth[26] in April 2008. Her final commanding officer, Commander Andrew Price RN, said on paying her off that *Nottingham* had served the nation well over her twenty-five-year service lifetime, but others queried whether the rebuilding cost had been justified at a time of an enormous retrenchment in the Navy's strength from a series of hostile Government decisions. *Nottingham* certainly never put to sea again after that date and was decommissioned on 11 February 2010. She was sold for scrap on 28 March 2011 by Leyal Ship Recycling[27] and was towed from Portsmouth for Turkey on 19 October 2011.

The four defendants were by no means the first, nor will they be the last, to undergo court martial for accidents that occurred on their watch. Many a famous admiral has undergone a similar ordeal, yet gone on to achieve notable and valuable subsequent careers in the service.[28] It was so with all four of *Nottingham*'s officers, who all achieved great things subsequent to this ordeal.

Commander Farrington's career continued and in November 2002 he became Second Sea Lord Chief Programmer at Portsmouth, a position he held until September 2004 when he was appointed as UK Maritime Advisor to US Central Command, based at Tampa/St Petersburg, Florida, until June 2005. After eight months here Farrington returned to Portsmouth as Commander UK Amphibious Forces – Staff Officer Operations Support, working with the Royal Navy and Royal Marines. Two years later, in May 2007, Farrington became Chief of Staff, Maritime Battle Staff, a position he held for thirty-two months. His next naval appointment was as Captain Surface Ships, Portsmouth Flotilla between December 2009 and December 2011. In March Farrington became Commander Devonport Flotilla and then Portsmouth Flotilla. As a captain and a CBE, Richard Farrington became Chairman of the Royal Naval Sailing Association and, after qualifying as a yacht surveyor through the International Institute of Marine Surveyors, he established his own private company, Compass Yacht Services at Portsmouth, which expanded into marine consultancy.

The navigator, Andy Ingham, has had an equally distinguished career. His previous command had been the 740-ton (751 tonnes) *Hunt*-class mine-countermeasures vessel *Chiddingfold* in 2000, and after *Nottingham* he became navigation officer of

---

26. The euphemism used by the MoD at the time was 'extended readiness'.
27. LEYAL Gemi Sökum, Aliaga, Aegean.
28. See many instances in – Smith, Peter Charles Horstead, *Sailors in the Dock, op. cit.*

the 5,300-ton (5,385 tonnes) frigate *Cornwall*. After a spell ashore he went out to the Middle East with the *Chatham*. He qualified as an air warfare officer, joining the 21,200-ton (21,540 tonnes) landing platform helicopter (LPH) assault ship *Ocean* (Captain Adrian Johns) in the Caribbean and then the 5,117 (5,200 tonnes) destroyer *Edinburgh*. The Afghanistan operation saw him at the Joint Headquarters team at Northwood, London and at Lashkar Gah as liaison officer. With 4 Mine-Countermeasures Squadron operations in the Gulf, Ingham commanded the mine warfare vessel *Cattistock*, along with sister ships *Atherstone* (Lieutenant-Commander Andy Smith) and *Middleton* (Lieutenant-Commander Steve Higham), and he was promoted to commander in 2012. Ingham was appointed in command of the 7,900-ton (8,026 tonnes) air-defence destroyer *Diamond* in February 2013. He is a Fellow of the Honourable Company of Master Mariners and a Member of the Royal Institute of Navigation.

Lieutenant-Commander John Lea also rose to become a commander and from May 2012 has been the Executive Commander of Royal Naval Air Station Culdrose. He co-wrote a book on Horatio Nelson[29] and is a director of two sports-related organisations in Cornwall.

Lieutenant Denney was the fourth of the quartet who went on to excel. He served as second-in-command aboard the 1,673-ton (1,700 tonnes) *River*-class offshore patrol vessel *Severn* and then the 1,448-ton (1,472 tonnes) *Castle*-class offshore patrol vessel *Leeds Castle*, including a period as Falkland Islands Guard Ship between 2004 and September 2006. In September 2007 he became Director of Operations aboard the 4,800-ton (4,900 tonnes) *Duke*-class Type 23 frigate *Westminster* during her NATO deployment in the Middle East. He then moved on to organise the Phase One Sea trials of the air-defence destroyer *Diamond* between April and December 2009. From then until September 2011 he was Senior Instructor, Principal Warfare Officer Course at the Maritime Warfare School before, having been promoted to commander, becoming Senior Operations Manager, UK Maritime Component in the Arabian Gulf for eight months, followed by a stint as Officer Commanding Initial Warfare Officer (IWO) Training at the Maritime Warfare School. More recently he has been Output Delivery Manager at the Defence Academy of the UK at Shrivenham.

Another of the new destroyers, *Defender*, has, as her commanding officer, Commander Philip Nash, who had served as the XO and second-in-command of *Daring*, having completed the Advanced Command Staff Course at the Joint Staff College, Shrivenham and gaining a Master's degree in Defence Studies.

Their subsequent achievements seem to prove that good can come from even the direst circumstances, which is an encouraging way to end our brief survey of the Royal Navy *in extremis*.

---

29. Lea, Lieutenant-Commander John, and McCarthy, Lily, *Remembering Nelson*, 1995, Portsmouth, Royal Navy Museum.

Further Selected Reading on Royal Navy Shipwrecks

Brown, David Keith, *Warship Losses of World War Two* (Arms & Armour Press, London, 1995)

Dalyell, Sir John Graham, *Shipwrecks and Disasters at Sea. (3 Vols)* (Longman, Hurst, Reese, Orme & Brown, London, 1812)

Gilly, William O. Stephen, *Narratives of Shipwrecks of the Royal Navy* (John W. Parker, London, 1864)

Gosset, William Patrick, *The Lost Ships of the Royal Navy 1793–1900* (Mansell Publishing, London, 1986)

Grocott, Terence, *Shipwrecks of the Revolutionary & Napoleonic Eras*, (Caxton Editions, London, 2002)

Hepper, David J., *British Warship Losses in the Age of Sail 1650–1859* (Jean Boudriot Publications, Heathfield, 1994)

Hocking, Charles, *Dictionary of Disasters at Sea* (2 Vols) (Lloyds of London, 1989)

Hodge, William Barwick, Vice-President of the Statistical Society, *On Shipwrecks in the Royal Navy* (Parker, London, 1857)

Hooke, Norman, *Maritime Casualties* (LLP Professional Publishing, London, 1997)

Larne, Richard & Bridget, *Shipwreck Index of the British Isles* (6 Vols) (Lloyds Register of Shipping, London, 1995–1998)

Redding, Cyrus, with de Perthes, Jean Louis Hubert Simon, *A History of Shipwrecks, and Disasters at Sea; from the most authentic sources* (Whittaker, Treacher & Co., London, 1833)

Royal Navy Museum, MSS 294: *Shipwrecks of the Royal Navy. Part 1 – 1660–1793, Part 2 1793 to 1850* (Portsmouth, No. 121, 1850)

Seaton, David, *Narrative of the Wreck of the Birkenhead: drawn up from Official Documents and other authentic evidence; with some additional details and an Appendix* (Hazell, Watson & Viney, London, 1890) (Original privately published Edinburgh, 1861)

Index

Abdiel, HM minelayer 189
Abercrombie Robinson, troopship 113
Abercromby, General Sir Ralph 52–53, 75
Aboukir, HM armoured cruiser 180
Achilles, HM ironclad 148
Active Class frigates 72
Active, HM destroyer 230
Active, HM frigate 72
Acum, Skipper Harold 209
Adair, Admiral Sir Charles 133
Adair, Captain Charles William 133
Adair, Captain Thomas Benjamin Stratton 133–135, 142–143, 145–149
Adair, General Sir Charles William 133
Adair, General Sir William 133
Adair-Hall, Lieutenant-Commander Harold Dallas 161
Adams, Captain Henry George Horner, CBE 178
Adams, Commander John 108
Adams, Engineer John H 130
Adams, Lieutenant-Colonel Jack 201, 207, 215
Adams, Midshipman William Leslie Graham 180, 188–189
Adams, Ordinary Seaman Herbert 131
Adamson, Assistant Engineer William 130
Adder, HM gun-brig 177
Addis, Commander Charles Thorburn 201
Addison, Albert Christopher (author) 88
Adventure, HM 4th-rate 8
Adventure, HM cruiser-minelayer 189
Advice, HM 4th-rate 35
Aeolus, French privateer 75
Aerial, Operation 221
Agar, Captain Augustus Willington Shelton, VC, DSO 198
Aikenhead, Seaman William 70
Albemarle, HM battleship 132
Aldridge, Able Seaman Francis 105
Aldridge, Seaman James 70
Alexander, French 3rd-rate 74
Allday, Island Agent Frederick William 138
Allen, Commander Hamilton Coclough 164
Allen, Leading Stoker Frederick 130
Allen, Private Peter 43rd Regiment 109
Allen, Private William Royal Marines 107
Alliance, HM Admiralty tug 166
Almindeligheden, Dutch privateer 75
Alterton, Able Seaman John 105
Amazon, HM 6th-rate 100
Ambrose, Captain Maintop Thomas 130
Ambrose, Private Edward 43rd Regiment 109

Ambuscade, Batavian 5th-rate 53
America, HM 3rd-rate 53
Amethyst, HM 5th-rate 55
Amphitrite, Batavian 5th-rate 53
Amphlett, Paymaster Edward Albert 121–122, 124, 126, 129
Andersen, Master 76
Anderson, Able Seaman George 130–131
Anderson, Captain John 35
Anderson, Private George 74th Regiment 107
Anderson, Private John 43rd Regiment 107
Andrews, Private James Royal Marines 131
Andrews, Sergeant David 60th Regiment 109
Andrews, Stoker 1st Class Alfred Percy 156
Angerstein, Underwriter John Julian 65
Angle, HM anti-submarine trawler 222
Ankelt, Ordinary Seaman Alfred 130
Ann Rebecca, Dutch brig 100
Anna Dorothea, Danish privateer 76
Anna Wilhelmine, Danish privateer 75
Anne and Catherine, Danish merchantmen 76
Anne and Margaret, Danish merchantmen 76
Anne, Queen 48
Annesley, Captain John Campbell, DSO 180, 188, 200
Anson, Admiral of the Fleet George, Lord Anson 21
Anson, HM battleship 189
Antelope, HM 4th-rate 42
Anthers, Private Andrew 2nd Regiment 109
Antrim, HM protected cruiser 152
Anvers, Belgian freighter 222
Apollo, HM 5th-rate 74
Apollo, the Sun God 115
Appleyard, Ordinary Seaman Hilton 175
Aquarius, RFA water-carrier 137
Arab Class, HM compostie gunboats 183
Arab, HM 6th-rate 73
Arabis, HM corvette 221–222
Arbuthnot, Commander Geoffrey Schomberg, CB, DSC 188
Archbold, Gunner John 86, 101
Archer, Lieutenant-Commander Humphrey Edward 218
Archer, Ordinary Seaman Harold Percy 176
Archer, Private Thomas 12th Regiment 106
Ardent, HM 3rd-rate 53
Argus, HM aircraft-carrier 146, 189, 220
Arizona, US battleship 179
Ark Royal, HM aircraft-carrier 189, 210
Armstrong, Commander Harold Thomas 202
Armstrong, Private James 12th Regiment 106

Arris, Captain Robert 25
Arrogant, HM frigate 101
Arrow, HM sloop 58, 61, 63–64, 66
Arundel, HM 5th-rate 25, 42, 44, 46–47
Ashanti, HM destroyer 200
Ashbolt, Stoker John 101–103, 108
Ashen, Stoker 1st Class Charles Herbert 176
Ashwood, Boy 1st Class James 131
Asia, HM 2nd-rate 125
Askew, Stoker 2nd Class John 176
Asser, Captain Cyril 148
Association, HM 2nd-rate vi, 33–34, 37, 39–42,
    44–46, 48–49
Astley-Rushton, Vice-Admiral Edward Astley 196
Astraea, HM frigate 71–82
Atherstone, HM minehunter 250
Atkins, Seaman Thomas 29, 33
Atkinson, Able Seaman Frederick 175
Atlantic, Battle of 230
Attye, Lieutenant Francis Lionel Octavious 106
Attye, Miss Augusta-Jeans 106
Attye, Miss Hannah-Lucy 106
Attye, Miss Harriett-Carolina 106
Attye, Miss Margaretta-Ellen 106
Auchinleck, Lieutenant-General Sir Claude
    Eyre 201
Auckland, HM sloop 200
Audacious, HM battleship 163
Aufrere, Lieutenant Charles Gastine 57, 60, 67
Augustin, Doctor George 21
Aurora, HM light cruiser 200–201, 211
Aurora, HMC light cruiser 178
Austral Salvor, tug 243
Avis, Boy 2nd Class John H 131
Aylen, Clerk Henry Nelson 130
Ayscough, Commander John 58

Bacon, Director James 23
Bagatelle, HM signals centre Greenock 230
Bailey, Commander William 180
Baker, Captain John 37
Baker, Commissioned Engineer John George
    Lightfoot 136
Baker, Ship's Cooper Henry 130
Baldwin, Lieutenant-Commander Charles William
    Augustus 183
Ball, Lieutenant Henry Lidgbird 244
Ball, Ordinary Seaman William 130
Ballam, Leading Stoker Jesse 175
Ballard, Captain George Alexander 138
Banden, Private John, 2nd Regiment 109
Bannister, Able Seaman Samuel 129
Barbara, Italian blockade runner 188
Barber, Able Seaman George Ellis 176
Barber, Chief Engineer Benjamin 89, 101, 108
Barfleur, Battle of 9
Bark, Private Abraham 6th Regiment 106
Barker, Captain Charles 100
Barkly, Midshipman Henry 124, 129
Barkly, Sir Henry, Governor of Victoria 124
Barlow, Chief Mate Edward 5
Barnaby, Naval Architect Kenneth Cloves 103

Barnes, Boy 1st Class William 131
Barnett, Lieutenant Benjamin 32
Baron Dechmont, British freighter 222
Baron Tweedmouth, British freighter 222
Barossa, HM wooden screw corvette 115
Barrett, Petty Officer Stoker William Henry 176
Barrett, Private Charles 12th Regiment 106
Bartlett, Ordinary Seaman Albert Percy 175
Barttelot, Captain Brian Henry Fairbairn 169
Bashford, Stoker 1st Class Herbert 184
Batavier, Batavian 4th-rate 53
Batory, Polish troopship 211
Bawes, Captain George 24
Baxter, Private Archibald 74th Regiment 107
Baylam, Private Henry Royal Marines 131
Bayliss, Painter William E 129
Bayly, Captain Symon 38
Bayton, Able Seaman Harry Lewis 175
Bazin, *Lieutenant de Vasseau* 221
Beach, Able Seaman George 175
Beach, Sir Richard 3
Beacham, Master C A 193
Beachy Head, Battle of 3, 6
Beames, Petty Officer Stoker George Henry 176
Beard, Lieutenant Charles Tachereau, RCN 178
Beattie, Lieutenant-Commander Kenneth Adair,
    DSO 200
Beatty, Admiral David Richard 174
Beaty-Powmnall, Captain Charles Pipton 171
Beaulieu, HM 5th-rate 56
Beaumanoir, British freighter 222
Beaumont, Rear-Admiral Basil 28
Beckensall, Able Seaman Albert William 176
Beckers, Salvage Engineer Frans 68
Beckett, Private Michael 6th Regiment 106
Beckford, Governor Peter 11
Bedford, HM 3rd-rate 4
Bedford, HM armoured cruiser 151–158
Bedford, Michael 65
Bedout, *Captaine de Vaisseau* Charles 74
Beens, *Citizen Lieutenant de Vaisseau* Francis
    Louis 73
Beer, Carpenter James 129
Beeston, Governor Sir William 12
Belam, Captain John 97
Belcher, Captain Edward 154
Belgrove, Commander Thomas 111
Bellairs, Captain Roger Mowbray 195
Bellars, Captain Edward Gerald Hyslop 189
Belleisle, HM 2nd-rate 74
Bellerophon, HM battleship 173
Bellingham, Private Thomas 12th Regiment 106
Belliqueux, HM 3rd-rate 53
Ben, Correspondent John 45
Benbow, HM battleship 145, 189
Benbow, Vice-Admiral John 13
Ben-my-Chree, HM seaplane-carrier 180
Benn, Captain William Gordon 220
Bennett, Captain Robert 111
Bennett, Engine Room Artificer Wesley
    Bramwell 176
Bennett, Isabella, Countess of Arlington 38

Bennett, Ordinary Seaman John 131
Bennie, Private John 74th Regiment 107
Bennion, Petty Officer Marine Engineering Artificer Darren Philip 242
Benson, Commander Howard Hartwell James 192
Benson, Commander Thomas 72
Bentell, Ordinary Seaman Henry 130
Bentlett, Boy 1st Class Henry 130
Berea, Battle of 97, 113
Berge Istra, Norwegian bulk ore carrier 70
Berge Vanga, Norwegian bulk ore carrier 70
Berlin, German minelayer 163
Bermingham, Private Henry Thomas 73rd Regiment 107
Bernard, M. Alleande vii
Bernard, Private James 73rd Regiment 107
Bernd von Arnim - German destroyer 220
Bertelli, Diver Brad 17
Berwick, HM armoured cruiser 151
Berwick, HM heavy cruiser 199
Beschermer, Batavian 4th-rate 53
Betts, Master Shipwright Isaac 3
Bevan, Historian David 112
Bevan, Journalist Pauline 112
Bevir, Captain Oliver 202
Bewhill, Ordinary Seaman Henry 108
Bibb, Captain Edward 8
Bickle, Ordinary Seaman William H 131
Bifrost, Swedish cargo ship 222
Bigg, Commodore Theodore Evelyn Johnstone 164
Biggam, Private James 73rd Regiment 107
Bignell, Leading Stoker Jesse 130
Binfield, Private Charles Royal Marines 131
Birmingham, HM destroyer 237
Birmingham, HM light cruiser 189
Birt, Private Joseph 91st Regiment 108
Bismarck, German battleship 70
Bismarck, German liner 219
Bittern, HM sloop 200
Black Swan, HM sloop 200
Black, Chief Engine Room Artificer Robert DSM 175
Blackfly, HM anti-submarine trawler 222
Blackie, Private Robert 74th Regiment 107
Blackwill, Ordinary Seaman William 131
Blake, Able Seaman Richard 105
Blake, Captain Eardley Wilmot 179
Blake, Captain Thomas 25
Blake, HM protected cruiser 179
Blake, Lieutenant-Commander (N) Thomas Michael 201, 208–209, 211–216
Blake, Lieutenant-Commander Cuthbert Patrick, DSO 219
Blake, Lieutenant-Commander Edward William Herford 180, 187
Blake, Lieutenant-Commander Walter Charles, RNR 211
Blake, Sub-Lieutenant Michael John Lyndon 229
Blanche, HM 5th-rate 58
Blanche, HM scout cruiser 165
Bleichrodt, *Korvettekapitan* Heinrich 222
Blenheim, HM 3rd-rate 101

Blewitt, Lieutenant-Commander Arthur, DSC, RNR 221
Blewitt, Ship's Master Thomas Henry 144
Bligh, Captain John 76
Blom, Fisherman Willem 60
Blonde, HM 5th-rate 58
Blucher, German heavy cruiser 214
Blues, Petty Officer John Alexander 176
Blythmann, Diver Finn 81
Blythmann, Diver Tage 81
Boadicea, HM scout cruiser 162–165, 167, 171, 173
Bockett-Pugh, Commander Ian Hamilton 224
Boehm, *Generaladmiral* Hermann 220
Boland, Ordinary Seaman Joseph 130
Bole, Marine Scientist Marcus 243
Bolton, Captain William 59
Bonaparte, Colonel Napoleon 51
Bond, Commander Frank Albert, RNR, DSC (Rtd) 212
Bond-Shelton, Cornet Ralph MacGeough 12th Lancers 86, 88, 92, 94, 96, 105, 113
Bonner, Master George Douglas 193
Boomah Pass, ambush at 85
Boorder, Captain James 60
Booth, Historian Tony 148
Booth, Lieutenant Audley Henry 73rd Regiment 86, 91–92, 94, 107
Booth, Lieutenant-Commander Richard Henry 192
Boothby, Captain William Osbert 152
Bornholm, Dutch privateer 75
Boscawen, HM parent ship (ex-*MB 3632*) 185
Bostock, Captain Nathan 27
Boswell, Private William 12th Regiment 106
Bosworthick, Blacksmith John 130
Bott, Commander (N) Leslie Charles 180–181, 185–186
Boult, Seaman Goodall Tame 70
Bourne, Historian Kenneth 116
Bovell, Captain Henry Cecil 220
Bowen, Able Seaman John 101–102, 108
Bowen, Assistant Surgeon Robert 86, 96, 98, 111
Bowen, Journalist David 69
Bowen, Petty Officer Operation Mechanic (Above Water) 1 James Clement 242
Bowes-Lyon, Captain Ronald George 233
Bowley, Lieutenant Edmund Mansel 162–163, 175
Boyce, Private William 74th Regiment 110
Boyden, Private James 2nd Regiment 98, 109
Boyer, Historian Abel 40
Boylan, Ensign George Augustus 2nd Regiment 86, 94, 105
Boynton, Able Seaman George Edward 176
Brackley, Private George 43rd Regiment 109
Braddell, Lieutenant John Tandy 64
Bradford, Captain Edward Eden 138, 142
Bradford, Dr. Charles 42
Bradley, Private George 12th Regiment 106
Brady, Gunner Thomas Royal Marines Artillery 131
Bramble Class, HM composite screw gunboats 185
Bramsdon, Sir Thomas 194
Bramwell, Able Seaman Edward 175
Brand-Eschauzier, Jean Pierre 67

Bratley, Lieutenant John Wesley 229
Brayne-Nicholls, Lieutenant (N) Francis Brian Price 230
Bremnet, Naval Engineer James 84
Brennan, Private Daniel 43rd Regiment 107
Brennan, Private William Edward 73rd Regiment 107
Bridge, Captain Arthur Robin Moore 187
Bridgeman, Interviewer William 162
Bridges, Captain Timothy 10, 11
Bridges, Private George, 12th Regiment 109
Bridle, Boy 1st Class William J 131
Brien, Stoker Daniel 105
Briggs, Captain Charles John 142
Briggs, Captain Harold Douglas, MG, Rtd. 212
Briggs, Carpenter Edward 129
Bristol Class, HM light cruisers 157
Bristol, HM 4th-rate 11
Britannia, HM 1st-rate 2, 179
Broadhurst, Captain Benjamin 72
Broadway, Boy 1st Class John T 131
Broadwood, Gunner John Royal Marine Artilley 131
Brockway, Historian James 59
Brockway, Leading Telegraphist Francis William DSM 176
Brodie, Acting Master William 87, 92, 94–95, 104
Brodie, Allan viii
Bromley, Captain Arthur, CMG 179, 182, 185–186
Bromley, Private Joseph 6th Regiment 106
Bronto, German blockade runner 188
Brook, Admiral Edward Errington 168
Brooke, Lieutenant-Commander Basil Richard 166
Brooke, Wireman Frederick William 176
Brookfield, Charles Mann 19–20
Brookland, Private James 60th Regiment 107
Brooks, Dr. Charles Edward Pelham 23
Brooks, Environmental Scientist Mark J 234
Broughton, Midshipman Thomas H 124, 130
Brown, Able Seaman James J 129
Brown, Captain Thomas 177
Brown, Ordinary Seaman John Metcalf 176
Brown, Private James William 60th Regiment 107
Brown, Private William 6th Regiment 106
Brown, Quartermaster Henry 103, 129
Brown, Stoker Alfred 130
Bruce, Private Walter 74th Regiment 107
Bruce, Rear-Admiral Henry Harvey 169
Bruce, Skipper Alexander 209
Brunel, Isambard Kingdom 84
Bryan, Private Edward 73rd Regiment 107
Bryan, Private James, 91st Regiment 108
Bryan, Private Joseph 6th Royal Regiment 106
Bryan, Private Patrick 6th Regiment 106
Bryan, Private William 6th Regiment 106
Buckingham, Private Charles James, 91st Regiment 108
Buckley, Private Daniel 73rd Regiment 107
Buckley, Private William 73rd Regiment 107
Budd, Private William 2nd Regiment 109
Budge, Private John Royal Marines 131
Budge, Willy 175
Bull, Stoker 1st Class James George 176

Bulldog, HM sloop 74
Bullen, Private William 43rd Regiment 107
Bullimore, Peter viii
Bulwark, HM battleship 157
Bunce, Boy 1st Class George 131
Bunker, Private Daniel Love 43rd Regiment 109
Bunn, Able Seaman Alfred 176
Burchari, *Kapitan-zur-See* Theodor 220
Burge, Gunner William Royal Marine Artillery 131
Burgin, Stoker 2nd Class Fred 175
Burke, Private Joseph Edward 2nd Regiment 105
Burke, Private William 73rd Regiment 109
Burlon, Private William 60th Regiment 109
Burnett, Commodore William Farquharson 115, 118–120, 122–127, 130
Burns, Charlotte Mary Emily 151
Burns, Shipping Magnet James Cleland 151
Burton, Boy 1st Class Thomas H 130
Burton, Captain Robert Heron 115, 122–124, 130
Burton, Ordinary Seaman James 105
Burton, Private William 73rd Regiment 107
Bushe, Private William, 73rd Regiment 107
Buss, Lieutenant-Commander Stuart Austin 188
Butcher, Able Seaman John 101, 105
Butler, Captain Thomas 10, 13–16, 18, 37
Butler, Ordinary Seaman William M 105
Butler, Private John 43rd Regiment 107
Butler, Quartermaster Frederick 121, 129
Butler, Sergeant William 91st Regiment 108
Butler, Trooper William 12th Lancers 105
Button, Ordinary Seaman Sidney 176
Byng, Vice-Admiral Sir George 37, 44
Byrne, Historian Timothy Brian 128
Byrne, Private James 12th Regiment 106
Byrne, Private John 43rd Regiment 107
Byrne, Private John, 73rd Regiment 107

Caboto, Italian blockade runner 188
Caesar, HM battleship 180
Caffery, Private Michael 73rd Regiment 107
Cairo, HM AA cruiser 202, 204, 207–209
Calam, Stoker 1st Class James Henry 156
Calcutta, HM light (later AA) cruiser 178–179, 184–185, 191, 200
Calcutta, HM screw steamship 117
Caldicott Castle, British merchantman 73
Caledonia, HM boys training ship 219
Calhoun, Commander William Lowndes, USN 192
Callaghan, Boy 2nd Class Thomas 131
Callaghan, Private James 60th Regiment 107
Calton, Telegraphist Frederick John 175
Calvert, Skipper James, RNR 170
Cambrian, HM light cruiser 178, 185, 188
Cambridge, HM 3rd-rate 6
Cameron, Captain John Even, MVO 185
Cameron, David British Prime Minister 21
Campanula, HM corvette 222
Campbell, Commander John, RNZN 238
Campeche, Battles of 84
Camperdown, Battle of 52, 56
Cannon, Historian Richard 12
Canopus, HM battleship 142

Canterbury, HM 3rd-rate 24–25
Canterbury, HM store ship 24–25
Capetown, HM light cruiser 184–185, 191
Cara, British freighter 222
Cardiff, HM destroyer 237
Cardiff, HM light cruiser 179, 198, 230
Carey, Private David 91st Regiment 110
Carleton, Captain James 25
Carlill, Midshipman Stephen Hope 180–181, 185–186, 189–190
Carpenter, Coxswain Robert 129
Carphin, First Mate George 111
Carr Laughton, Leonard George 34
Carrigan, Private Patrick, 6th Regiment 106
Carrington, Private Moses 12th Regiment 106
Carter, Captain William 27
Carter, Ordinary Seaman Charles 105
Carter, Sergeant Thomas Royal Marines 131
Carter, Signalman Cecil John 176
Carthew, Captain James 75
Carver, Able Seaman Eric Woodward 175
Cary, Henry, Viscount Falkland 17
Carysfort, HM 6th-rate 17
Case, Lieutenant-Commander Richard Vere Essex, DSC 222
Casement, Captain John 138, 142
Cash, Private Thomas 73rd Regiment 109
Caspal, Lieutenant William 63
Castle Class, Admiralty trawlers 170
Castle Class, HM offshore patrol vessels 250
Castor, HM 5th-rate 97–98, 110
Castor, HM 5th-rate 17
Castor, HM light cruiser 160–161, 166–167, 172
Caswell, David Ballantyne 193
Catford, Stoker 1st Class Henry 175
Cathcart, Major-General George 113
Cattaneech, Private John 74th Highlanders 107
Cattistock, HM mine countermeasures vessel 250
Caulfield, Evelyn vii
Caulfield, Private Dennis 6th Regiment 106
Cavanagh, Private Thomas 91st Regiment 108
Cave, Private Thomas 43rd Regiment 107
Cavendish Class, HM heavy cruisers 177–178
Cavendish, Captain Philip 42
Cavendish, HM heavy cruiser 177
Cazalet, Captain Peter Grenville Lyon 189
CE12, convoy 221
Cellars, Private Michael 12th Regiment 106
Cemortan, Dancer Ms Dominica 83
Centurion, HM 5th-rate 28
Centurion, HM battleship 219
Cerberus, Batavian 3rd-rate 53
Cerberus, HM 5th-rate 63, 72–73
Ceres, HM 5th-rate 72
Chads, Captain Henry Ducie 101
Chadwick, Private Thomas 2nd Regiment 109
Chaffer, Ordinary Seaman James Charles 175
Chamberlain, Captain Peter 27
Chamberlain, Captain William Charles 125
Chambers, Author Robert 25
Champion, Engine Room Artificer Owen 175
Chapman, Mrs Anne 110

Chapman, Private William Henry 60th Regiment 107, 110
Charles W Baird, barge 19
Charles, II, King 2, 33
Charles, HM galley 42
Charnock, Historian John 47
Chatfield, Captain Alfred Ernle Montacute 174
Chauncey, US destroyer 192
Cheeseman, Able Seaman Henry 108
Chelsea, HM destroyer 221
Chernikeef, Captain Vasily 232
Chesapeake, HM frigate 108
Cheshyre, Commander John 74
Chest, Rev Thomas 24
Chester, HM 4th-rate 9
Chiddingfold, HM minehunter 249
Childers, Author Erskine Hamilton 59
Child's Play, HM 5th-rate 10
Chilley, Captain John 35
China, British hospital ship 170, 172–173
Chisholm, Editor Hugh 71
Christal, Seaman George 70
Christian, Rear-Admiral Sir Hugh Cloberry 74
Christie, Stoker 1st Class Herbert 175
Christy, Skipper Arthur 209
Chrobry, Polish troopship 210
Churchill, Lieutenant-Commander Charles Fraser Harrington 224
Churchill, Sir Winston Leonard Spencer 70, 187, 199–200
Chuse, Stoker William 108
Cileman, Private Richard 2nd Regiment 105
Cinnamond, Private William Royal Marines 107
Clark, Acting-Lieutenant-Commander Norman Vincent, RCVR 223
Clark, Lieutenant-Colonel John, Commandant Royal Military Asylum Chelsea 113
Clark, Private William Chuse, 91st Regiment 108
Clarke, Historian James Stanier 31
Clarke, Private William 6th Regiment 109
Clark-Hall, Lieutenant-Commander Walter Clark 218
Clarkia, HM corvette 222
Clarkson, Assistant Surgeon James 130
Clay, Private William 2nd Regiment 105
Clear, Signalman Herbert William 176
Cleary, John 131
Clement, Lieutenant Edward 6
Clements, Private John 73rd Regiment 107
Clemson Class, US destroyers 192
Cleopatra, HM screw corvette 179
Clews, Stoker William 130
Clifford, Private Alfred 6th Regiment 106
Clince, Private Mathias 12th Regiment 106
Cloete, Colonel Abraham Josias 86
Clover, Midshipman Nelson 136
Clowes, Sir William Laird 73
Clutterbuck, Luieutenant-Commander Richard Isacke 201
Cobb, Captain Charles 75
Cobb, Chief Petty Officer Walter Edward 176
Cobra, HM destroyer 177

Cochrane, HM naval establishment Rosyth 212
Cochrane, Ordinary Seaman John George 130
Cochrane, Rear-Admiral Alexander 81
Cockcroft, Journalist Lucy 7
Cocker, Private George 45th Regiment 107
Codie, Private John 91st Regiment 110
Codrington, Captain Christopher 9
Codrington, HM destroyer 188
Coe, Private James 2nd Regiment 105
Coffin. Ordinary Seaman Thomas 88, 91, 101, 108
Coggershall, James Lowell 10
Cohn, Diver John 21
Coke, Captain Charles Henry 139, 142
Colbey, Trooper Charles 12th Lancers 86, 105
Cole, Ordinary Seaman Samuel 131
Coleman, Private Richard 2nd Regiment 105
Colledge, Historian James Joseph 84
Collins, Private Mathew 73rd Regiment 107
Collins, Private Thomas, Royal Marines 131
Collins, Seaman Timothy 70
Colossus, HM 3rd-rate 73
Colossus, HM battleship 158, 171, 173
Colpoys, Rear-Admiral John 73
Colrenshaw, Private John, 6th Regiment 106
Colson, Mathmatician Nathaniel 50
Columbus, Christopher 77, 80
Colundt, Master 75
Commins, Private Bernard 12th Regiment 106
Commonwealth, HM battleship 152
Compton, Captain Walter Burge 178, 184
Comus, HM sloop 76
Con, Private Thomas 6th Regiment 109
Coney, Captain William 37
Congham, Private John 91st Regiment 110
Conlan, Private Daniel 60th Regiment 107
Connor, Able Seaman James 175
Conqueror, HM battleship 145, 148
Conquest Class gun-brigs 64
Constance, American brig 72
Constance, HM light cruiser 178
Conte Rosso, Italian liner 146
Cook, Leading Seaman William 175
Cook, Stoker 1st Class William 156
Cooke, Agent Christopher 74
Cooke, Captain John 55
Cooke, Historian James Herbert 46
Cookney, Wardroom Stewart William H 131
Cooney, Private Patrick 73rd Regiment 107
Cooper, Able Seaman William 130
Cooper, Dame Gladys Constance, DBE 225
Cooper, Lieutenant-Commander George
    Tyndale 220, 224–226, 229–234
Cooper, Private John Royal Marines 109
Cooper, Skipper Robert, RNR 209
Coppinger, Captain Cuthbert 196
Corbett, Commander Godfrey Edwin 187
Corbett, Commander Noel Marcus Francis 188
Coreopsis, HM corvette 222
Cork & Orrey, Admiral of the Fleet William Henry
    Dudley Boyle, Lord, GCB, GCVO 200, 201, 203,
    206, 208
Cornell, Private Charles 2nd Regiment 105

Cornewall, Captain Charles 37
Cornford, Able Seaman Percy Reginald,
    RNVR 227–228
Cornford, Journalist Phil 244
Cornwall, HM armoured cruiser 151
Cornwall, HM frigate 250
Cornwallis, HM 3rd-rate 109
Cornwallis, HM battleship 132, 139, 142
Coronation, HM 2nd-rate 1–7, 49, 159
Corps, Quartermaster Henry 129
Cosgrave, Private John 43rd Regiment 107
Costa Concordia, Italian cruise liner 83
Costello, Private John 12th Regiment 106
Coston, Inventor Martha Jane 181
Coston, US Navy Scientist Benjamin Franklin
    181
Cottam, Captain George Frederick 117
Coulmore, British freighter 222
Coulomb, French ship designer Joseph-Marie-
    Blaise 51
County Class HM heavy cruisers 151, 196
Courier, HM armed cutter 56–57
Courier, HM armed cutter 75
Cousin, Private David 74th Regiment 107
Coventry, HM 4th-rate 25
Coventry, HM destroyer 237
Coventry, HM light cruiser 196, 202–204, 206–209,
    211, 213, 215–216
Cowan, Private John 74th Regiment 107
Cowen, Able Seaman William 130
Cowing, Able Seaman Francis Gill 175
Cowler, Stoker 1st Class Thomas William 228
Cozens, Corporal Benjamin 43rd Regiment 107
Crabb, Gunner Henry Royal Marine Artillery 131
Crabbe, Temporary-Engineer-Lieutenant(A) Charles
    John, RNR 166
Cracroft, Captain Peter 119
Cragg, Private John 12th Regiment 106
Craig, Sir James 194
Cramp, Gunner Lewis Royal Marine Artillery 131
Cranfield, Governor Edward 11
Craufurd, Sir James 54
Craven, Lieutenant Francis Worthington 168
Crawford, Commander John Stuart 200
Creech, Stoker 1st Class George 176
Crescent, HM depot ship 158
Crescent, HM destroyer 231
Cressy, HM armoured cruiser 180
Crocker, John Wilson 285
Crocker, Private John Wilson 6th Regiment 106
Crocus Class, HM gun-brigs 235
Croker, Able Seaman Edward 108
Cronin, Boy 2nd Class John 131
Cross, Rear-Admiral Charles Henry 142
Crossley, Lieutenant-Commander John Graham 219
Crouson, Royal Marine drummer Joseph 130
Crow, Captain Josias 28–29
Crow, Ordinary Seaman Alfred 131
Crozier, Commander Stuart 246
Cruizer, HM brig-sloop 75
Cruizer, HM 6th-rate 37, 39
Crust, Able Seaman Henry James 156

Crutchley, Commodore Sir Victor Alexander Charles, VC, KCB 200, 213
Crutchlow, Stoker 1st Class David 176
Cubiss, Engine Room Artificer Ernest Stanley 175
Cuckoo, Sopwith torpedo-bomber 146
Culebra, British freighter 193
Culhane, Surgeon Dr.William 86, 94, 96, 101, 103, 108
Cull, Private Henry 2nd Regiment 105
Cull, Petty Officer Henry George 175
Cumberland, HM 3rd-rate 25–26
Cumberland, HM armoured cruiser 151
Cumming, Captain Arthur 116, 125
Cummins, Private Bernard 12th Regiment 106
Cunningham, Captain Andrew Browne 191–192, 234
Cunnyngham, Private Patrick 91st Regiment 110
Curacoa, HM screw frigate 125–126
Curlew, HM light cruiser 196
Currigan, Private Patrick 6th Royal Regiment 106
Curtis, Corporal Francis 60th Regiment 107
Cuthberton, Lieutenant Charles George 222
Cyclops, HM depot ship 166, 170

Dacres, Captain Richard 74
Dacres, General Sir Richard 116
Daedalus, HM frigate 72
Daedalus, HM RNAS Lee-on-Solent 234
D'Aeth, Lieutenant-Commander John Reginald Hughes 189
Dailey, Private Daniel 91st Regiment 108
Daley, Able Seaman Patrick 129
Daley, Able Seaman Thomas 108
Dallington Court, British freighter 222
Dallmeyer, Commander William Alexander 222
Dampier, Captain Cecil Frederick 163
Dampier, Lieutenant-Commander Thomas Henry Fielder 175
Daniels, Private Thomas Royal Marines 109
Daring Class, HM destroyers 234
Daring, HM air-defence destroyer 250
Dark, Master Mariner William P M 143
Darkin, Drum-Major John Robert 110
Darkin, Master 110
Darkin, Miss Marian 88, 110
Darkin, Mrs Anne 110
Darkinman, Stoker James Robert 105
Darsey, Private George 73rd Regiment 107
Dartmouth, HM 4th-rate 25
Dartmouth, HM light cruiser 185
Dashing Wave, ketch 144
Dathan, Lieutenant James Hartley 135, 142–147
Davey, captain fore-top John 122–123, 130
Davidson, Commander Alastair Gordon, Rtd. 222
Davies, Lieutenant Oswald Harcourt 142
Davies, Lieutenant-Commander Alan Holt, RNR 222
Davis, Boy 2nd Class John H 131
Davis, Boy 2nd Class William 131
Davis, Commander Louis Poisson, USN 192
Davis, Historian Gill (Jill) M 149
Davis, Historian Roger C 149

Davis, Lieutenant-Commander (later Commander) William Gronow 200
Davis, Private Daniel Royal Marines 131
Davis, Second Master Jeremiah O'Dwyer 87, 94, 101, 104
Davis, Stoker Charles 130–131
Dawson, Captain Oswald Henry 191
Dawson, Private Charles 73rd Regiment 107
Dawson, Seaman Jacob 70
Day, Editor Kelvin 118
Day, Private William 2nd Regiment 105
Dazel-Job, Sub-Lieutenant Patrick 207
De Burgh, Commander Hubert Henry, DSO 218
de Contentin, Admiral Anne-Hilarion, *Comte* de Tourville 3
de Courcy, Commander Michael 80
de Florinville, *Citizen Lieutenant de Vaisseau* Jacob 73
de Freyer, Curator Hans Jan 59
de Joyeuse, Vice-Admiral Villaret 73
de la Conte, *Capitaine de Vaisseau* Henri 74
de Lagara, Admiral Juan 51
de Medina, Capitan Don Nicolas 63
de Meric, Captain Martin John Coucher 189
de Meric, French 6th-rate 37
de Montmorecy-Luxemboorg, Anne Henri Rene Sigismonde 58
De Ruyter, Batavian 3rd-rate 53
De Salis, Captain Anthony Fane 200
de Weerdt, Curator Gerald 62
De Wet, Sub-Lieutenant Eric Oloff 166
Deacon, Officer's Steward Albert Thomas 176
Dean, Lieutenant-Commander Brian 211
Deane, Sir Anthony 3
Debank, Private William 43rd Regiment 107
Deegan, Private Hugh 73rd Regiment 107
Deeley, Ordinary Seaman Thomas 101
Deely, Assistant Engineer 1st Class Edward 94, 105
Deering, Captain Unton 25
Defence, HM ironclad 125
Defender, HM air-defence destroyer 250
Defoe, Daniel (Fox) 23, 49
Delaney, Private James 91st Regiment 108
Delavall, Vice-Admiral Sir Ralph 3
Delft, HM troopship 75
Delhi, HM light cruiser 198
Delphy, US destroyer 192
Demmack, Private William 12th Regiment 106
Deneys, Lieutenant-Commander James Godfrey Wood 221
Denham, Captain Henry 244
Denham, Captain James 178
Denney, Lieutenant James Robert 238, 246–247, 250
Dennison, Captain John 133
Denyer, Officer's Cook John Ernest 175
Derham, Rev. William 24
Despatch, HM light cruiser 213
Devonshire Class, HM armoured cruisers 177
Dewar, Captain Kenneth Gilbert Balmain, CBE 185
Dews, Private Thomas 43rd Regiment 107
Deyczakowski, Captain Sigmund A 210

D'Eyncourt, Sir Eustace Tennyson 177
Diamond, HM air-defence destroyer 250
Diana, Princess of Wales 70
Dibble, Stoker Isaac 105
Dickens, Author Charles 95
Dickens, Vice-Admiral Gerald Charles 196
Dickson, Private Hugh 6th Regiment 106
Dictator, HM 3rd-rate 75
Dido, HM protected cruiser 138
Diemeyer, *Leutnant* Heinrich 203
Dieter von Roeder, German destroyer 220
Dietl, *Generalmajor* Eduard 199
Digby, Captain Noel Stephen Fox 179
Dilkes, Captain Thomas 10
Dill, General Sir John Greer 201, 209
Diomede, HM 4th-rate 72
Diomede, HM light cruiser 189
Dismukes, Captain Douglas Eugene 179
Disraeli, Benjamin, Chancellor of the
    Exchequer 113
Dixie, Lieutenant Albert Edward 153–154, 157–158
Djemnah, French troopship 183
Doble, Private Robert Royal Marines 107
Dobree, Captain Daniel 58
Dobson, Private William 73rd Regiment 109
Dockery, Private Martin 45th Regiment 107
Dodd, Trooper John 12th Lancers 109
Doherty, Richard viii
Dolphin, HM 5th-rate 25
Dolphin, Prussian hoy 75
Donald Stewart, British freighter 193
Donald, Private William 74th Regiment 107
Donaldson, Private David 74th Regiment 107
Donegal, HM armoured cruiser 151
Donna Paula, Spanish slave ship 78
Donnell, Private William 43rd Regiment 107
Donoghue, Boy 1st Class Denis 131
Doolan, Private Robert 12th Regiment 109
Dopson, Stoker John 105
Doren, Private Thomas Royal Marines 131
Dorey, Stoker Andrew 130
Doris, HM protected cruiser 139–140, 142
Dorling, Captain Taprell ('*Taffrail*') 161
Dornier Do.17 210
Dorsetshire, HM 3rd-rate 34
Dortnell, Boy 1st Class Charles 105
Double, Private Henry 2nd Regiment 109
Douglas-Pennant, Captain Cyril Eustace, DSC 214
Dowdall, Seaman John 70
Down, Fisherman Alan 7
Doyle, Private Patrick 73rd Regiment 107
Drake Class, HM armoured cruisers 151
Drake, Colour-Sergeant John Royal Marines 101,
    109
Drake, HM armoured cruiser 152
Drake, HM naval establishment Plymouth 198, 201,
    213
Draper, Captain John 9, 25
Dreadnought, HM battleship 132, 145, 150
Drew, Captain James 73
Drew, Ship's Cook George 130
Drew, Stoker Thomas 108

Driackford, Ordinary Seaman Thomas 108
Driver, HM paddle sloop 175
Drummond, Captain John Edmund 180
Drummond, Vice-Admiral John Ian Edward 191
Drury, Commander Byron 118–120
Drury, Private James 91st Regiment 108
Drury-Lowe, Captain Sidney Robert 179
Dryad, HM Navigational Training School
    Portsmouth 185, 213, 237
Du Cassee, French Governor Jean-Baptiste 9
Du de Chatillon, Anne Henri Rene Sigismonde de
    Montmorency Luxembourg 58
Duc de Chartes, French privateer 72
Duchess, HM 2nd-rate 6
Dudley, Private John William 73rd Regiment 107
Duffet, Boy 1st Class George 131
Duffy, Boys 1st Class John 105
Duggan, Gunner Edward 175
Duke Class, HM frigates 21, 250
Duke, Captain Robert Gordon 189
Duke, HM 2nd rate (ex-*Vanguard*) 35
Duke, HM 2nd-rate 30
Dulcibelle, HM anti-submarine trawler 209
Dummer, Draughtsman Edmund 2
Dunbar, Able Seaman John William 176
Dunbar, Captain James 76
Dunbar-Nasmith, Rear-Admiral Martin Eric 196,
    198, 212–213, 231
Duncan Class, HM battleships 132, 160
Duncan, Admiral Adam 52, 55–56, 66
Duncan, Captain Henry 52
Duncan, Historian Archibald 73
Duncan, HM battleship 132, 138, 142, 160
Dunedin, HM light cruiser 189–190, 198
Dunkirk, evacuation from 198, 211–213, 221
Dunkirk, HM 4th-rate 10–11, 13–19
Dunn, Able Seaman Thomas 101–103, 108
Durkin, Private John Royal Marines 131
Durkin, Private Joseph 12th Regiment 106
Duyf, Dentist Anne Jan 69
Dyke, Able Seaman John 108

Eagle, HM 3rd-rate 37, 39, 44–45
Eagle, HM advice boat 27
Eagle, HM aircraft-carrier 187, 189
Eaglet, HM naval establishment Liverpool 198
Early, Boy 2nd Class Albert 131
Eastwood, Stoker 1st Class Arthur Richard
    Austin 156
Eccles, Rev John Charles, Canon of Woodville 128–
    129
Echo, HM destroyer 202, 204–205, 207–213, 216,
    228
Eclipse Class, HM protected cruisers 139
Edinburgh, HM destroyer 237, 250
Edward the Confessor, King 28
Edward VII, King 113
Edwarde, Corporal Joseph, 12th Lancers 92, 105,
    113
Edwardes, Captain The Hon. David 214
Edwards, Captain Edwin Harold 162, 164–165
Edwards, Captain Ralph Alan Bevan 189

Edwards, Lieutenat-Commander John E, RNR 137
Edwards, Petty Officer Stoker Albert 175
Effard, Stoker Petty Officer Edward 184
Effingham, HM heavy (later light) cruiser 177, 194 et seq.
Effingham, Lord High Admiral Howard 195
Egerton, Captain Henry Jack 198
Eglinton, Barque 111
Egmont, HM special service vessel 148
Ekins, Thomas, Stewart 45
El Teb, Battle of 138
Eldorado, HM anti-submarine trawler 209
Elizabeth II, Queen 69
Elizabeth, HM 3rd-rate 4
Elizabeth, The Queen Mother 70
Elk, HMC armed yacht 223
Elliot, Seaman John 70
Elliott, Able Seaman James Lowrey 175
Elliott, Private Eli 60th Regiment 107
Ellis, Carpenter James 148
Ellis, Keeper John Lakey 137
Ellis, Ordinary Seaman James 131
Emerald, HM light cruiser 198
Emerald, HM steam frigate 116, 125
Emms, Captain Fleetwood (Eames) 32
Emperor of India, HM battleship 169
Empire Cheetah, British freighter 222
Empire Eland, British freighter 229
Empire Kudu, British freighter 193
Empire Mallard, British freighter 193
Empire Moon, British freighter 193
Empire Springbuck, British freighter 222
Empress of France, liner 184–185
Endeavour, HMNZ fleet oiler 238, 241
Endrass, *Korvettenkapitan* Englebert 222
England, Private John 12th Regiment 106
Englison, Trooper John 12th Lancers 86, 105
Enright, Captain Philip King 198, 230
Enterprise, HM light cruiser 198, 200
Erdmenger, *Korvettenkapitan* Hans 220
Erich Steinbrinck, German destroyer 220
Erne, HM destroyer 161
Ernest, Master-at-Arms John E 130
Erskine, Captain Seymour Elphinstone 152
Escapade, HM destroyer 200
Eschauzier, Wreck Receiver Pierre 67
Eskins, Constructor Thomas 38
Essenhigh, Commander Nigel 237
Essex, HM armoured cruiser 151
Esson, George 175
Eugene of Savoy, Prince 37, 49
Euphrates, HM naval establishment Basrah 198
Euryalus, HM armoured cruiser 138
Evans, Captain Frederick John 235–236, 238
Evans, Captain Frederick John Owen 100, 119
Evans, Private James 91st Regiment 108
Evans, Signalman Hugh 120
Evelegh, Commander Markham Henry 187
Evershed, Lieutenant-Commander Walter 202
Evertsen, Admiral Cornelis 4
Ewart, Captain Arthur Wartensleben 139
Excellent, HM 2nd-rate 101

Excellent, HMS Royal Navy Gunnery Establishment, Whale Island 133, 142, 176, 211, 231
Exeter, HM 4th-rate 34
Exeter, HM destroyer 237–238
Exeter, HM heavy cruiser 196, 233
Exmouth, HM battleship 132, 138, 142
Experiment, HM 5th-rate 13–15, 17–19, 56

Fabian, Shipwright Robert 72
Fabius, French privateer 75
Facto, Norwegian freighter 222
Fairborne, Vice-Admiral Sir Stafford 33
Fairburn, Historian Taylor 117
Fairclough, Lieutenant Samuel 86
Fairfax, Captain Robert 26–27, 30
Fairfax, Perry 90
Falchney, Lieutenant-Commander William Nelson Mitchell, RNR 229
Fama, Danish privateer 76
Fandango, HM anti-submarine trawler 223
Fantome, HMA sloop 180
Farbridge, Stoker 2nd Class Robert Bullerwell 176
Farncomb, Captain Harold Bruce, MVO, RAN 188, 199
Farquhar, Telegraphist Alexander Gordon 175
Farragut, US destroyer 192
Farrington, Commander Richard 237
Faulknor, Captain William 37
Faulknor, HM destroyer 200
Favorit, Norwegian freighter 222
Favourite, HM sloop 81
Fawn, HM sloop 80
Fearless, HM amphibious warfare ship 238
Feeley, Private Hugh 73rd Regiment 107
Fell, Lieutenant-Commander William Richmond 'Tiny' 209
Fellows, Ben viii
Ferguson, Leading Stoker Colin 156
Ferguson, Private Charles 74th Regiment 110
Ferris, Captain John 179
Fevyer, Historian William H 183
ffoulkes, Colonel Jonathan 12
Field, Lieutenant Arthur 40, 49
Field, Private John Thomas 12th Regiment 106
Field, Stoker 1st Class Silas 184
Fielding, Midshipman Bernal Whitley 122, 124, 126, 129
Fiford, Stoker William 105
Finch, Daniel, Earl of Nottingham 4
Finn, Able Seaman Robert 108
Finn, Ordinary Seaman Edward 131
Finn, Private Richard Thomas 6th Regiment 106
Finnis, Captain of the Maintop John 129
Fireball, Operation 187
Firebrand, HM fire-ship 10–11, 13–19, 27, 37, 39, 41–42, 44–45, 48
Firedrake, HM destroyer 209
Firman, Private Robert 12th Regiment 109
Fish, TV Weatherman Michael 22
Fisher, Able Seaman William 129
Fisher, Admiral John Arbuthnot 133
Fisher, Captain Douglas Blake, OBE 188

Fisher, Stoker 1st Class George 184
Fitzgerald, Private Thomas 12th Regiment 106
Fitzherbert, Captain Edward Stafford 138, 152–153, 155, 157–158
Fitzpatrick, Private James 73rd Regiment 109
Fitzpatrick, Private Matthew 73rd Regiment 107
Fitzroy, Henry, Duke of Grafton 38
Flamingo, HM sloop 200
Flanagan, Private Michael 73rd Regiment 107
Flanaghan, Private Michael Royal Marines 131
Flanaghan, Private Patrick 12th Regiment 106
Flanley, Private Thomas 12th Regiment 106
Fletcher, Captain John 10, 11
Fletcher, Miss V 59
Fletcher, Private William 6th Regiment 106
Fletcher, Salvage Engineer Johan J 58–59, 68
Flinn, Private Patrick 91st Regiment 110
Flower Class, HM minesweeping sloops 166
Flynn, Private William 73rd Regiment 107
Fogarty, Stoker 1st Class John Thomas 156
Foley, Ordinary Seaman Thomas 176
Folkestone, HM sloop 224
Forbes, Able Seaman Thomas 108
Forbes, Private William 2nd Regiment 105
Ford, Private Hugh 91st Regiment 108
Ford, Stoker 1st Class Andrew 176
Foreman, Able Seaman Reginald 176
Formidable, French 2nd-rate 74
Formidable, HM 2nd-rate 53
Forrest, Midshipman John William 180, 188
Forste, *Kapitan-zur-See* Erich 220
Fortescue, Editor John William 9
Foss, Private Henry 60th Regiment 109
Foster, Private William 91st Regiment 108, 110
Fosters, the Miss 110
Fothergill, Master William Gerrard 221
Foudroyant, HM 3rd-rate 66
Fovargue, Stoker 1st Class George 156
Fowler, Officer's Steward William Frederick George 176
Fownes, Lieutenant Henry George 74
Fox, Ernest vii
Fox, Able Seaman Charles 129
Fox, Derek vii
Fox, HM frigate 72
Foxhound, HM destroyer 188
Foyle, Private Stephen Royal Marines 131
Francis, Able Seaman George William 176
Frank B Baird, Canadian freighter 222
Frank, Private William 73rd Regiment 107
Franks, Lieutenant Robert Denys 222
Fraser, Captain Bruce Austin 195–196
Fraser, Captain Percy 60
Fraser, HMC destroyer 231
Frederick Eckoldt, German destroyer 220
Frederick Ihn, German destroyer 220
Frederick, Captain Thomas 72
Frederick, Dutch Greenlandsman 74
Freeman, Private Owen 12th Regiment 106
Freemantle, Captain Charles Albert 190
French, Private Michael 73rd Regiment 107
Frobisher, HM heavy cruiser 177, 187, 189, 196

Frost, Private Thomas 60th Regiment 107
Frou Eaagle, Dutch privateer 75
Fuller, US destroyer 192
Furious, HM battle-cruiser (later aircraft-carrier) 177–178, 180, 188–189, 219
Fury, HM bomb ketch 75
Furzer, Lieutenant John 49
Furzer, Master Shipwright Daniel 2
Fynn, Private William 12th Regiment 106

Gaddis, Commander William Peace, USN 192
Gaffee, Petty Officer Arthur George 176
Gaffey, Private Patrick 91st Regiment 108
Gaffney, Yeoman of Signals John Lund 175
Galatea, HM 5th-rate 80
Galatea, HM light cruiser 189
Galathea, Batavian Brig 53
Gale, Boy 1st Class William 108
Gamble, Captain Douglas Austin 142
Gammel, Brigadier-General James Andrew Harcourt 202, 209
Ganges, HM 3rd-rate 56
Gannaway, Ordinary Seaman William 131
Gardner, Lieutenant James Anthony 58, 65
Gardner, Private Henry Royal Marines 131
Gardner, Stoker Edward 108
Garner, Able Seaman William John 175
Garnett, Midshipman Richard Pennington 180, 187
Gate Pah Tauranga, Battle of 126
Gauntlet Class, HM destroyers 234
Gavin, Private Maleck 73rd Regiment 107
Gavin, Private Michael 73rd Regiment 107
Geary, Able Seaman Thomas 129
Gelder, Dutch schooner 67
Gelderland, Batavian 2nd-rate 53
George V, King 70
George VI, King 70
George, Stoker Thomas 105
George, Temp. Sub-Lieutenant Ronald 229
Gerrard, Captain's Cook Benjamin 105
Gibney, Lieutenant John Edward Francis 168
Gibson, Clare viii
Gibson, Commander (E) Edward James Alfred 229
Gibson, Lieutenant Daniel 63
Gibson, Lieutenant-Commander Michael James 229, 234
Gibson, Private James 74th Regiment 107
Gilbert, Able Seaman Henry 105
Gildea, Private James 2nd Regiment 109
Giles, Private Lawrence 73rd Regiment 107
Gill, Chief Petty Officer Edwin George 175
Gill, Leading Seaman Charles John 175
Gillham, Assistant Paymaster William Henry Patey Morgan 130
Gillham, Private George 43rd Regiment 107
Gilmour, Captain David 202
Gilmour, Lieutenant David 61
Gingall, Able Seaman George 176
Ginn, Private Francis Thomas 43rd Regiment 107
Gipps, Edmund Fredereick Estcourt 142
Giradot, Lieutenant John Francis 43rd Regiment 93, 109

Gironde, British freighter 222
Gladiator, HM protected cruiser 133, 148, 156
Gladiolus, HM corvette 222
Glasgow, HM destroyer 237–238, 249
Glatton, HM 4th-rate 53, 75
Gleeson, Private Patrick 6th Regiment 109
Gleeson, Private Terence 2nd Regiment 109
Glennie, Captain Sir Irvine Gordon 187
Gloria, Liberian motor vessel 70
Glorious, HM battle-cruiser (later aircraft-carrier) 183, 189
Glory, HM 2nd-rate 73
Glory, HM battleship 158
Gloucester, HM destroyer 237
Glover, Captain Thomas William 100
Gneisenau, German battle-cruiser 220
Godolphin, Sidney, Earl of Godolphin 44–45
Golden Peace of Dantzick, Prussian merchant vessel 35
Goldfinch, HM destroyer 161
Goldin, Private James 6th Regiment 106
Goldshmidt, Captain's Steward C 131
Goldsmid, Agent Abraham 54–55, 58, 64–65
Goldsmid, Agent Benjamin 65
Goodall, Sir Stanley Vernon, Director Naval Construction Admiralty 196
Goodall, Stoker 1st Class George William 156
Goodwin, Boy 1st Class James 131
Goodwyne, Earle of Kent (Godwin) 28
Goolden, Lieutenant-Commander Massey, DSC 180, 184, 188
Gordon, Acting-Commander William Everard Alphonso 111
Gordon, Captain Joseph 113
Gordon, Captain Oliver Loudon 233
Gordon, Commander Roderick Cosmo 231
Gordon, Corporal George Royal Marines 131
Gordon, Major Antony George Drumearn, Royal Scots Fusiliers, Rtd. vii, 92
Goree, HM sloop 81
Gorman, Private David R 74th Regiment 107
Gossage, Assistant Engineer George Frederick 130
Gostelo, Cartographer Walter 44
Gothland, Belgian liner 148
Gottwaltz, Lieutenant-Colonel Philip, MC 202
Gould, Private Thomas Royal Marines 131
Gould, William R, BEM, Gunroom Messman 180
Gowan, Private Charles 74th Regiment 108
Gowlland, Midshipman Geoffrey Langton 180, 189
Grady, Private John 6th Regiment 106
Graeme, Captain Alex 73
Graham, Commander Harry Robert 200
Graham, Ordinary Seaman Henry James 130
Graham, Ordinary Seaman James Henry 130
Graham, Private James Henry, 74th Regiment 107
Grana, HM convalescent ship 63
Grant, Leading Seaman Albert James 176
Grant, Ordinary Seaman Alexander Frazer 175
Grant, Private John 73rd Regiment 107
Grant, Private Joseph 91st Regiment 108
Graves, Lieutenant Thomas 49
Gray, Private George Royal Marines 131

Gray, Teresa viii
Graydon, Vice-Admiral Sir John 28
Great Britain, British paddle-vessel 84
Green, Able Seaman Albert Edward 175
Green, Private Patrick R 73rd Regiment 109
Green, Private William 2nd Regiment 105
Green, Stoker 1st Class George Alfred 176
Green, Stoker 1st Class Robert 176
Greenleaf, Private John 2nd Regiment 105
Greenshields, Able Seaman Frederick 227–228
Greenway, Captain James 32
Greenwood, Private John Royal Marines 131
Greetham, Sir George Lambum 101
Grenada, British prize. 75
Grey, Sir George, Governor of New Zealand 125
Grice, Master F Sydney H 193
Griffin, HM 5th-rate 38–39, 41
Griffith, Captain Edward 73
Griffiths, Able Seaman Richard Thomas 175
Griffiths, Captain Eric 185
Griffiths, Captain Richard 37, 41, 49
Grimshaw, Private Ambrose 12th Regiment 106
Grindall, Captain Richard 73
Grindle, Lieutenant John Annesley 180, 188
Groom, Lieutenant-Commander (FTC) Ian Stuart, Beng, Ceng, MIMarE 238
Guadeloupe, Mexican Navy steam frigate 84
Gubbins, Colonel Colin McVean 209
Guillemet, *Captaine de Vaisseau* Francois Charles 74
Gunman, Captain James 38, 41
Gunning, Sub-Lieutenant James Melhuish 175
Gurney, Captain Edward 11

Haarr, Historian Geirr Henning 206, 215
Hackenley, Private Francis 91st Regiment 108
Haddock, Captain Herbert James, RNR 163
Hager, Captain John 42
Haggan, Private Patrick 91st Regiment 108
Haggan, Private Stephen 91st Regiment 108
Haggart, Private John 91st Regiment 110
Haggis, Coxswain Arthur 129
Haher, Private John 73rd Regiment 107
Haile Selassie, Emperor of Ethiopia 196
Hajime, Captain Mizumachi 157
Hales, Private Samuel 2nd Regiment 109
Halfhide, Captain Arthur Robert 200
Halford-Forbes, Emma viii
Halfpenny, Private William 73rd Regiment 109
Hall, Able Seaman Joseph 105
Hall, Ordinary Seaman James 130
Hall, Ordinary Seaman John 130
Hall, Private William H 73rd Regiment 107
Halsey, Midshipman William Edmund 180
Halson, Ordinary Seaman William 131
Hamilton, Admiral Sir Richard Vesey 58
Hamilton, Captain Frederick Tower 142
Hamilton, Captain Louis Henry Keppel 198, 211
Hamilton, Private Arthur 60th Regiment 107
Hamilton, Private Peter 74th Regiment 108
Hammick, Rear-Admiral Sir Alexander Robert, Rtd. 231

Hammond, Temporary-Lieutenant Walter James 229

Hampshire, HM 4th-rate 11, 42

Hancock, Captain Robert 37

Handley, Private James 6th Regiment 106

Handrain, Stoker Thomas 108

Hanley, Private Patrick 73rd Regiment 107

Hanlon, Private Jerome 60th Regiment 109

Hannay, Author David 18

Hannen, Private John 73rd Regiment 107

Hannibal, HM 2nd-rate 125

Hannibal, HM 3rd-rate 73

Hansard, Parliamentary Recorder Thomas Curson 2, 87

Harding, Master Jesse 72

Harding, Master's Assistant John 119

Harding, President Warren Gamaliel 179

Hardy, Captain John Oakes 75

Hardy, HM destroyer 197

Hare, Master's Assistant Charles William 104

Harmenie, French privateer 75

Harold, Sergeant John 74th Regiment 107

Harper, Stoker 1st Class Felix 175

Harpey, Private John 91st Regiment 108

Harrier, HM screw sloop 117, 119, 121, 123–125, 129

Harris, Able Seaman Samuel 108

Harris, Boatswain 3rd Class Thomas 94, 105, 108

Harris, Captain Robert 101

Harris, Mrs Eliza Ann 94

Harris, Ordinary Seaman James 126

Harris, Private Joseph 6th Regiment 106

Harris, Skipper Edward Robert, RNR 223

Harrison, Able Seaman Albert George 175

Harrison, Able Seaman Joshua 105

Harrison, Able Seaman Walter Stanley 175

Harrison, Clockmaker John 49

Harrison, Corporal Joseph 43rd Regiment 107, 113

Harrison, Mrs Elor 113

Harrison, Private George 43rd Regiment 109

Harrison, Private Thomas 74th Regiment 108

Hart, Chief Stoker John 156

Hart, Private Francis 12th Regiment 106

Hartfield, Boy 2nd Class William 131

Hartley, Private Richard 74th Regiment 110

Hartung, Correspondent Herr 106

Hartwig, *Kapitanleutnant* Paul 193

Harvester, HM destroyer 222

Harvey, Lieutenant John Douglas 134, 163

Harvie, Gun Founder Charles 3

Harwich, HM 3rd-rate 4

Haselwood, Rev Charles Baker 130

Hastings, HM 5th-rate 9, 25

Hathi, HM naval establishment, Delhi 198

Hawke, HM protected cruiser 152

Hawker Sea Hurricane 229

Hawkins, HM heavy cruiser 177, 190, 196

Hawkins, Stoker Alfred 105

Hay, Captain William 17

Hayes, Petty Officer Stoker Thomas 176

Haylock, Boy 2nd Class John 105

Haynes, Able Seaman John 87

Hayton, Harbourmaster Andre 118

Hayward, Private Henry 91st Regiment 108

Hayward, Private Samuel 12th Regiment 106

Healey, Private Michael 43rd Regiment 109

Healey, Stoker James 130

Heard, Captain Lindsay Patrick 179

Heard, Private John Royal Marines 131

Hearty, Private Michael 12th Regiment 109

Heath, Captain Thomas 9

Heaven, Reverend Hudson Grosett 134, 138, 149

Hector, HM 5th-rate 25

Heddon, Historian Victor 24, 34

Helcion, HM naval establishment Aultbea 212

Heliotrope, HM corvette 222

Hely-Hutchinson, General Lord John 76

Heming, Quartermaster James G 101, 105

Henderson, Captain William, CB 101

Henderson, Diana 111

Henderson, Private James 74th Regiment 110

Hendry, Private Alexander 74th Regiment 108

Henry Grace a Dieu, HM Great Ship 159

Henth, Gunner Charles, Royal Marine Artillery 131

Hepper, Historian David J 5

Herald, HM 6th-rate 244

Herbert, Able Seaman Thomas 129

Herbert, Admiral Arthur, Earl of Torrington 3

Herbert, Boy 2nd Class William 130

Herbert, Crown Agent Duncan Frank 94

Herbert, Deputy Paymaster General Marine Regiments Edmund 39, 45–47

Hereward, HM destroyer 231

Herin, Private John 43rd Regiment 109

Heron, HM Royal Naval Air Station Yeovilton 229

Herrick, Private John 6th Regiment 109

Hetherington, Roy Marshall 128

Hewitt, Able Seaman John 130

Hewitt, Commander George Osborne 218

Heywood, Captain Edmund 76–81

HG52, Convoy 221

Hibbert, Leading Stoker Samson David 176

Hibbs, Leading Stoker John Herbert 175

Hibiscus, HM corvette 222

Hibling, Able Seaman Horace Richard 176

Hickman, Lieutenant (later Captain) Joseph 14–15

Hicks, Sergeant William, 43rd Regiment 107

Higgins, Private Thomas 12th Regiment 109

Higham, Able Seaman John 129

Higham, Lieutenant-Commander Steve 250

Highflyer, HM frigate 101

Highlander, HM destroyer 222

Hill, Able Seaman Edward Ernest 130, 175

Hill, Able Seaman John 129

Hill, Leading Seaman George 130

Hill, Lieutenant Charles Cracnell 118, 121–122, 124, 126–127, 129

Hill, Lieutenant Ernest Edward, Royal Marine Artilley 130

Hill, Seaman James 70

Hillier, Ordinary Seaman William 131

Hills, Alexander, (AKA William Olier) 126

Hindostan, HM 4th-rate 73

Hindustan, HM battleship 142

Hines, Ordinary Seaman Daniel 131
Hinkerbein, *Hauptmann* Klaus 203
Hire, Passed Clerk George William Samuel 95, 108
Hisket, Lieutenant John 16
Hobart, Captain Henry 37
Hobbs, Gunner William Royal Marines
   Artillery 131
Hobbs, Stoker James 105
Hobson, Captain Edward 32
Hodby, Private Thomas 6th Regiment 109
Hodge, Captain Andrew 80
Hodge, Leading Seaman William Henry 176
Hodge, Private Stephen Royal Marines 131
Hodgskin, Boy 1st Class Joshua 105
Hogue, HM armoured cruiser 180
Hohenfels, German blockade runner 188
Holberry, Commander Anthony 243
Holden, Captain William 41
Holden, Private John 91st Regiment 110
Holdgate, Captain's Cook Augustus 131
Holdgate, Seaman Thomas 70
Holdstock, Ordinary Seaman Frederick William
   Tubbs 175
Holland, Captain Cedric Swinton 210
Holland, Captain Lancelot Ernest 190, 231
Holm, Master 76
Holmes, Able Seaman Henry 129
Holmes, Private Henry 73rd Regiment 107
Holt, Colonel Henry 11
Holt, Peter 7
Holtorf, *Kapitanleutnant* Erich 220
Homburg, Petty Officer Stoker Frederick
   Charles 175
Hood, Admiral Alexander, Viscount Bridport 73–74
Hood, HM battle-cruiser 187, 189, 201
Hood, Vice-Admiral Sir Samuel 51
Hope, American merchantman 72
Hope, Captain George Price Webley 157
Hope, Captain Herbert Wiles Webley 188
Hopewell, HM fire-ship 8
Hopkins, Temporary-Lieutenant Frank Clifford,
   RNR 223
Hopper, Lieutenant Humphrey Greenwood 180,
   183, 187, 189
Hore, Stoker 1st Class John Thomas 175
Horhet, Private Michael 43rd Regiment 109
Horrigan, Commodore's servant John 123, 129
Horseman, Lieutenant Andrew 49
Horsfield, Private David Royal Marines 131
Hortly, Private James Michael 6th Regiment 109
Horton, Vice-Admiral Sir Max Kennedy 197–198
Hosier, Captain Sir Francis 42
Hoskins, Stoker John 108
Hoturoa, High Priest 119
Houchen, Private Robert 73rd Regiment 107
Houghton, Private J 43rd Regiment 107
Houlden, Captain William 38
Howard, Boy 1st Class John Richards 108–109
Howard, Corporal John Royal Marines 131
Howard, Gun Room Cook John Richards 105, 109
Howard, Petty Officer Stoker Samuel 176
Howard, Private John 2nd Regiment 105

Howe, Able Seaman Albert 176
Howe, HM 1st-rate 159
Howson, Captain John Montague 197–199,
   201–204, 207–213, 215–216
Hoyle, Private Sidney Royal Marines 131
Hudson, Gunner William 130
Hudson, Lieutenant-Commander Henry Victor 218
Hudson, Master David 110
Hudson, Mrs Sarah 110
Hudson, Private Joseph 6th Regiment 106
Hudson, Private Mark 91st Regiment 110
Hughes, Sir Edward 75
Huiskes, Historian Robert 63
Hull, Surgeon-Lieutenant-Commander Herbert
   Richard Barnes 180
Humphreys, Edward 116
Humphreys, Robert 116
Humphries, Captain Kenneth Noel, CB, Rtd. 212
Hunt Class destroyers 189
Hunt Class, HM minehunters 249
Hunt Class, HM minesweeping sloops 169
Hunt, Boy 1st Class William F 131
Hunt, Captain George Percy Edward 157
Hunt, Midshipman Charles George 129
Hunt, Private Richard 6th Regiment 109
Hunter, Captain John 244
Hunter, Navigation Officer Lieutenant-Commander
   Donald Taylor 192
Hunter, Private David 74th Regiment 108
Huntley, Commander John Herbert 200
Hurlestone, Boy First Class Charles George 130
Hurley, Private Michael 73rd Regiment 107
Husky, Operation 189
Hussey, Lieutenant William Frederick Eyre 184
Hussey, Private Patrick 91st Regiment 108
Hutcheson, Commander George Moir Donan,
   Rtd 201
Hutching, Gunner's Mate John 130
Hutchins, Lord 76
Hutchins, Trooper George 12th Lancers 86, 105
Hutton, Able Seaman William M 130
Hutton, Captain Fitzroy Evelyn Patrick 214
Hutton, Midshipman Peter Coats 180, 183–184, 187
HX.14, convoy 199
HX.73, convoy 222
Hyde, Captain Richard 165
Hyde, Gunroom Stewart John 131
Hydra, HM paddle sloop 111–112, 117

Ibbott, Telegraphist Stanley Walter vii, 223–227,
   230
Ideson, Boy Second Class John D 130
Ila, Norwegian freighter 222
Implacable, HM aircraft-carrier 188
Improved Birmingham' Class, HM heavy
   cruisers 177. 194, 196
Indefatigable, HM aircraft-carrier 188–189
Indrabarah, liner 170
Ingham, Captain Augustus Henry 85
Ingham, Lieutenant Andrew Richard 238, 246,
   249–250
Ingilby, Lieutenant-Colonel William Bates 91

Innes, Major Colin Berowald vii, 104
Inspector, HM sloop 74
Inverness, Prize 72
Ireland, Historian Bernard 51
Ironclad, Operation 198
Irvin, Private John, 12th Regiment 109
Irwin, Chief Stoker Frederick George 175
Isabella, HM despatch boat 38–39
Isis, HM 4th-rate 53, 62–63
Ites, *Oberleutnant* Otto 229

Jackson, Captain Orton Porter 179
Jackson, Lieutenant-Commander John, RNR 222
Jackson, Rear-Admiral Thomas Sturges 132
Jacob, Private Henry 6th Royal Regiment 106
Jacobs, Lieutenant Thomas 49
Jacobs, Private Simon 60th Regiment 107
Jacomb, Captain Humphrey Benson 198
James, Captain Lord Dursley 37
James, Duke of York 2, 53
James, Engine Room Artificer Allan 156
James, Leading Telegraphist Ronald Robert 175
Jameson, Captain William 45
Jarvis, Stoker John 105
Jason Class, HM wooden screw corvettes 115
Jason, HM 5th-rate 80–81
Jason, HM minesweeper 222
Jason, HM wooden screw corvette 115
Jaume, *Lieutenant de Vasseau* 221
Jays, Private Thomas 91st Regiment 108
Jeffrey, Purser's Stewart James 109
Jekyll, Lieutenant Arthur John 122, 130
Jellicoe, John Rushworth, Admiral of the Fleet
    Viscount Jellicoe of Scapa 148
Jenkins, Boy 1st Class William 131
Jenkins, Captain Robert 117, 125
Jenner, Able Seaman Edward 130
Jeram, Officer's Steward Frederick 176
Jermy, Captain Seth 35
Jerrold, Historian Walter 28–29
Jersey, HM 6th-rate 35
Jervis, Captain John 66
Jesson, Captain James 35
Jeypore, Birtish cargo ship 230
Johannesson, *Korvettenkapitan* Rolf 220
Johns, Captain Adrian 250
Johns, Sir Arthur William, KCB, CBE 196
Johnson, Captain Edward John 87
Johnson, Captain John 32
Johnson, Captain of Mizzen top William 123, 129
Johnson, Captain Robert 37
Johnson, Captain Robert Warren 180
Johnson, Gunner Samuel Royal Marines
    Artillery 131
Johnson, Mrs Heather viii
Johnson, Private James, 12th Regiment 109
Johnston, Assistant Paymaster A D 130
Johnstone, Private Samuel 12th Regiment 106
Jolliffe, Able Seaman Victor 175
Jones, Captain Edward Roynon 184
Jones, Captain Lewis Tobias 101, 180
Jones, Lieutenant George Clarence, RCN 178

Jones, Lieutenant-Commander Frederick John
    Gwynn, RNR 222
Jones, Ordinary Seaman Noah 131
Jones, Seaman William 70
Jong Picter, Dutch privateer 75
Joon-Seok, Captain Lee 83
Jooste, Professor Fanie 105
Joping, Seaman Anthony 70
Jordan, Ordinary Seaman Joseph 130
Jordan, Petty Officer Philip John Marett CM 176
Joyner, Captain Joss 72
Julians, Leading Cook's Mate Samuel Martin 176
Julius Caesar, Massachusetts privateer 72
Jumper, Captain Sir William 37–39
Juno, HM 5t-rate 53
Junon, French submarine 221
Jupiter, HM battleship 142
Jupiter, HM destroyer 200
Jura, British freighter 222
Justier, Private George 91st Regiment 108

Kanimbla, HM armed merchant cruiser 188
Karimata, Dutch dredger 68
Karkas, Persian gunboat 188
Karl Galster, German destroyer 220
Kave, Gunner John Royal Marines Artillery 131
Kayle, Doctor Allan 112
Keane, Private Henry 6th Regiment 106
Keans, Private Thomas Royal Marines 109
Kearns, Private William 73rd Regiment 107
Keating, Private Adam 45th Regiment 109
Keig, Second Engineer George 193
Keir, Surgeon Commander William Wallace 170
Kelleher, Private Thomas 12th Regiment 106
Kelley, Private William 60th Regiment 107
Kelley, Stoker Felix 130
Kelley, Stoker George 108
Kelly, Boy 2nd Class John 105
Kelly, Leading Seaman Thomas 130
Kelly, Master James 104, 110
Kelly, Master Thomas 104, 110
Kelly, Mrs Honoria 104, 110
Kelly, Private John, 12th Regiment 106
Kelly, Private Michael 6th Regiment 106
Kelly, Private Patrick 91st Regiment 108
Kelly, Private Timothy 73rd Regiment 104, 107, 110
Kemp, Historian Paul 214
Kemp, Leading Stoker Frederick 130
Kemp, Private George 91st Regiment 108
Kendriksma, Novelist Martin 64
Kennedy, Captain of the Mast James 129
Kennedy, Midshipman Cecil Gordan 176
Kennedy, President John Fitzgerald 70
Kenney, Able Seaman George Frederick John 176
Kenney, Captain Thomas 11
Kent, HM 3rd-rate 26–27, 55
Kent, HM armed cutter 55
Kent, HM armoured cruiser 151–152, 155–156
Kerr, Captain Ralph 189
Kerr, Captain William 34
Kerr, Vice-Admiral William Munro 196
Kerrigan, Private Charles 12th Regiment 109

Kilberry, Paymaster Sergeant Bernard 73rd Regiment 97, 109
Kilbride, Captain Bert 81
King George V, HM battleship 176
King, Gunner George Royal Marine Artillery 131
King, Stoker John 108
King-Hall, Commander Stephen Richard 162
King-Hall, Commander William 99–100
Kingston, Boy 1st Class John 131
Kinipple, Civil Engineer Walter Robert 68
Kinneer, Lieutenant James Jervis 57
Kinneer, Superannuated Captain James 57
Kinsdale, Leading Stoker John 105
Kipling, Author Rudyard 83, 103
Kirkford, Private D 74th Regiment 110
Kirkwood, Private James 74th Regiment 108
Kirshfeloths, Master Aldred 193
Kisbee, Captain Thomas 175
Kitchen, Private John 6th Regiment 109
Kitching, Private William 6th Regiment 106
Kitchingham, Assistant Engineer 2nd Class George 89, 105
Kitty, ketch 143
Klein, Charterboat Skipper Bobby 20
Knight, Private George 2nd Regiment 105
Knowlden, Boy 2nd Class John 131
Knowles, Lieutenant Thomas 37
Koln, German light cruiser 220
Konigsberg, German light cruiser 214
Kriffe, Private John 74th Regiment 110

L-56, HM submarine 189
La Fratenite, French frigate 73
La Gentille, French frigate 73
La Gloire, French (later HM) 5th-rate 73
La Guepe, French privateer 75
La Lutine, French frigate 51, *et seq*
La Renommee, French privateer 74
La Salamandre, French frigate 37
La Valeur, HM 6th-rate 37, 39, 44
La Vengeance, French privateer 75
Lacey, Capatin Maintop James 109
Lack, Historian Clem 58
Lackie, Private Alexander 60th Regiment 109
Ladbroke, Private Thomas Royal Marines 131
Ladd, Private Joseph 60th Regiment 107
Lady Elsa, HM anti-submarine trawler 222
Laffey, Private Michael 60th Regiment 109
Laing, Sir James 170
Laing, Staff Surgeon Philip 86, 92, 108
Laird, Corporal William 74th Regiment 107
Laird, Shipbuilder John 84–85, 103, 132
Laird, Sir William 73
Lake, Captain Sir Atwell Henry, Bt, OBE 187
Laker, Historian John 29
Lamb, Historian Hubert 36
Lamb, Private John 91st Regiment 110
Lambden, Private Charles 12th Regiment 106
Lambe, Captain Charles Edward, CVO 180–181, 189–190, 198
Lambert, Richard Cornthwaite 195
Lambrest, Private Henry 6th Royal Regiment 106

Lambrest, Private Henry 6th Royal Regiment 106
Lamotte, Lieutenant-Commander Harold de Gallye 169
Lancaster, HM 3rd-rate 28
Lancaster, HM armoured cruiser 151
Lance, Captain James – (Launce, Lawnce or Lawrence) 9, 14–15
Lancey, Private John 91st Regiment 110
Landon, Lieutenant-Commander John Palmer 161
L'Andromede, French frigate 37
Lane, Captain Richard 73–74
Lane, Leading Stoker Thomas 130
Lane, Ordinary Seaman Charles 105
Lang, Oliver William 115
Langan, Private Thomas 12th Regiment 109
Langmaid, Able Seaman Thomas 108
Langridge, Petty Officer Stoker Charles James 176
Langrush, Ordinary Seaman William 130
Lanyon, Lieutenant William 55
Larkin, Private Thomas 73rd Regiment 107
Larn, Historian Richard 39
Lashbrooke, Lieutenant Walter 49
Latona, HM 5th-rate 53, 74–75
Laughton, John Knox 58
Lavery, Private Patrick 2nd Regiment 105
Lawler, Private Michael 12th Regiment 106
Lawrence, Able Seaman George 45
Lawrence, Private George 73rd Regiment 107
Lawrence, Seaman Henry 70
Lawrie, Stoker 1st Class Alexander 176
Lawson, Able Seaman Robert 176
LCT-15, HM landing craft tank 187
Le Feuvre, Master Gullaume 77
Le Fortune, French 3rd-rate 37
Le Gallais, Captain Richard 76
Le Gros, Able Seaman Ernest 175
Le Jean Bart, French privateer 73
Le Marsouin, French privateer 75
Le Riche, Master Jean Louis 75
Le Sage, French 3rd-rate 37
Le Tartare, French pirvateer 74
Lea, Lieutenant-Commander John 238, 246, 250
Leach, Captain John Catterrall 188
Leader, Operation 214
Leake, Admiral Sir John 26, 28, 30–31
Leake, Historian Stephen Martin 30–31
Lecky, Lieutenant Halton Sterling 72
L'Ecolier, Captain Jean Baptiste Louis 72
Ledgwood, Private Alexander 91st Regiment 108
Lee, Leading Signalman Jacob 176
Lee, Petty Officer Stoker Francis 175
Lee, Private Edward 12th Regiment 106
Lee, Stoker David 130
Leeds Castle, HM offshore patrol vessel 250
Leeming, Midshipman John Birch 229–230
Lees, Captain Dennis Marescaux 200
Lempriere, John 71
Lennox Historian Kerr, James 97
Lennox, HM 3rd-rate - (*Lenox*) 37–39, 43–44, 49
L'Entrepreant, French 5th-rate 10
Leonidas Z Cambanis, Greek freighter 222
Les Jeux, French 5th-rate 10

Lesk, Seaman William 70
L'Espiegle, HM cutter 60
Letchmere, Captain Edmund 35
Lethbridge, Leading Stoker George Ernest 175
Letheby, Gunner Thomas Royal Marines
    Artillery 131
Leveson-Gower, Lady Elizabeth Mary, Marchioness
    of Westminster 84
Leviathan, HM armoured cruiser 152
Lewis, Able Seaman John 101–102, 108
Lewis, Private John 6th Regiment 106
Lewis, Seaman Richard 70
Lewis, Secretary of State Sir George 116
Lewis–Lloyd, Lieutenant Robert Evan 172, 175
Leyden, Batavian 2nd-rate 53
Liefde, Dutch Greenlandsman 74
Liell, Captain Thomas 27
Lill, Stoker 1st Class Walter 156
Lillico, Stoker 1st Class John 176
Lillingston, Colonel Luke 12
Lillingston, Major Jarvis 12
Lily, HM gunboat 183–184, 193
Lind, Surgeon James FRSE, FRCPE 8
L'Indien, French 5th-rate 72
Ling, Frances 65
Linois, *Capitaine de Vaisseau* Charles 74
Lion, HM battle-cruiser 148
Lioness, schooner 91, 97–98, 101
Lister, Lieutenant Alexander Cumming, RNR 222
Litchfield Prize, HM 5th-rate 27
Littlefield, Private Thomas Royal Marines 131
Liverpool, HM destroyer 237
Lizard, HM 6th-rate 42, 44
Lloyd George, Premier David 146
Lloyd, Captain after-guard Edwin 130
Lloyd, Colonel Godfrey 11
Lloyd, Edward 57
Lloyd, Lieutenant David 14
Lloyd, Petty Officer John E 184
Lloyds of London 54, 57, 63, 65–66, 68–70
Loades, Captain Edmund 37, 45–46
Loch, Captain Granville 101
Lochard, Lieutenant Anthony 49–50
Locke, Commander Charles 74
Lockheed C-130J Hercules 242
Lockyer, Captain William 46
Lohmann, *Korvettekapitan* Dietrich 230
London, HM 2nd-rate 73
London, HM heavy cruiser 189
Long, Manager OCRSPCS Terrance P 193
Long, Captain Thomas 25
Longbottom, Lieutenant Brian Cochrane 229
Lony, Seaman George 70
Looe, HM 5th-rate 25
Loose, Leading Stoker Arthur Albert 176
Louis XIV, King of France 9
Louis XVII, King of France 51
Louis, HM destroyer 161
Louis, XVI, King of France 69
Lovegrove, Midshipman Herbert 180, 185, 189
Loveless, Petty Officer Stoker Frederick Edward 175

Lovell, Stoker William 105
Lovet, Ship's Gunner George 78
Lowrie, Private John 74th Regiment 108
Lowry, Boy 1st Class Henry 105
Lowther-Crofton, Captain Edward George 180
Lucas, Ensign Gould Arthur, 73rd Regiment 86, 88,
    92, 102
Lucas, Lieutenant John 64
Lucas, Private Charles Edward 60th Regiment 107
Luff, Corporal Jonathan Royal Marines 107
Lumsden, Captain Walter 156
Lunt, Stoker 1st Class Joseph 175
Luscomb, Gunner Fred J 156
Lutine, HM 5th-rate 51–54, 56–60, 62–66, 68–70
Lyeman, Master Leider 76
Lyme, HM 5th-rate 44
Lynch, Fisherman Samuel 19
Lynch, Journalist Jake 242
Lynch, Private Patrick 73rd Regiment 110
Lyne, Master Joseph 40, 44
Lynn, HM 5th-rate 35
Lyon, Captain Herbert 152
Lyons, Private George 43rd Regiment 109
Lyra, Norwegian freighter 222

Macdonald, Biologist Denis 244
Macgillivray, Biologist John 244
MacGregor, Captain Sir Malcolm 117
Mackay, HM destroyer 221
Mackay, William Mackintosh 92
Mackenley, Private Francis 91st Regiment 108
Mackenzie, Operations Manager Graeme 243
Mackenzie, Rod vii
Mackesy, Major-General Peirse Joseph 199
Macleod, Lieutenant-Commander Kenneth John,
    DSC, RNVR 206
Macnamara, Captain Patrick 195
Macnamara, Commander James 52
Madden, Admiral Charles Edward 173–174
Magicienne Class, French frigates 51
Maher, Private James 60th Regiment 107
Maher, Private John 73rd Regiment 107
Maher, Private Michael 73rd Regiment 107
Mahoney, Ropemaker Michael 130
Maidstone, HM submarine depot ship 234
Majestic, liner 219
Major, Private James Royal Marines 107
Makgill Crichton, Lieutenant-Commander Charles
    Lewis 168
Malan, Lieutenant-Commander Charles Caesar de
    Merindol 162–164, 175
Malay, Private Michael 2nd Regiment 109
Malaya, HM battleship 198
Malet, Commander Herbert Rivers, RNR 168
Mallard, HM destroyer 163
Mallard, Sailing Master Andrew 16
Mallock, Midshipman Arthur R 126, 130
Mallow, HM minesweeping-sloop 183
Malone, Commander Cecil L'Estrange 180
Maloney, Private Cornelius 6th Regiment 106
Maloney, Private Daniel 73rd Regiment 110
Maloney, Private James 73rd Regiment 110

Maloney, Private Patrick 6th Regiment 106
Maloney, Private Thomas 6th Regiment 106
Maltravis, Private William 12th Regiment 106
Maltravis, Private William, 12th Regiment 106
Man O'War, HM armed trawler 223
Manchester, HM destroyer 237
Manley, Captain John 74
Manly, Lieutenant John Docker Hayward 219
Mann, Captain Robert 63
Mann, Esther vii
Manning, Captain Thomas Davys 71
Mansergh, Captain Cecil Aubrey Lawson, KBE,
   CB 188
Marauder, HM tug 229
Marchant, Articifer Engineer Ernest Jacob
   William 136
Marcus, Historian Geoffrey Jules 50
Mardon, Musician Samuel 130
Marescaux, Captain Gerald Charles Adolphe 152
Marga, Norwegian freighter 222
Margate, HM 6th-rate 35
Maris, Wilhelm. 104
Mark, Able Seaman George 130
Mark, Able Seaman Harry 130
Markham, Captain John 73
Markham, Historian Clements Robert 27, 29–30
Marquess of Salisbury, James Browne William, Lord
   Privy Seal 113
Mars, Batavian 5th-rate 53
Mars, HM battleship 139, 142
Marschall, *Leutnant* Wilhelm 183
Marsh, Joan viii
Marsh, Private George 2nd Regiment 105
Marshall, Chief Stoker John 176
Marshall, Midshipman Benjamin 42
Marsham-Townshend, Robert 46–47
Marston Moor, 5th-rate 35
Martin, Amanda viii
Martin, Captain George 30–31
Martin, Captain George Bohun, CB 101
Martin, Captain Samuel 25
Martin, Captain Thomas Byam 73
Martin, Historian Frederick 55, 57
Martin, Journalist David 65
Martin, Private John 2nd Regiment 105
Martin, Private John Royal Marines 107
Martin, Roy Victor 112
Martineau, Midshipman Ian Mackenzie 180, 187
Marvell, Captain George Ralph 179
Mary Galley 44
Mary II, Queen 4
Mary Rose, 60 guns vi
Mary, HM 4th-rate 22, 28–29, 31–32
Mason, Able Seaman Charles 176
Mason, Boatswain William 129
Mason, Captain Christopher 72
Mason, Commissioner James Murray 116
Mason, May vii
Massey, Edward 232
Master, Lieutenant Streynsham 49
Masters, Private John P Royal Marines 131
Matabele, HM destroyer 202–209, 211–214

Matchless Class, HM destroyers 162
Mather, Private Henry 60th Regiment 109
Matheson, Private William 91st Regiment 109
Matheson, Attorney-at-Law Hugh Merritt 19
Matheson, Corporal Murdoch 74th Regiment 107
Matheson, Private Alexander 74th Regiment 108
Mathews, Boy 2nd Class Charles 91, 108
Mathilda, Norwegian freighter 222
Matilda, schooner 123
Matson, Captain Henry 101
Matthews, Able Seaman George Sidney 175
Matthews, Historian William Henry 88
Maud, Stoker John H 130
Maundrell, Rev. William Herbert 156
Max Schulz, German destroyer 220
Maxmin, Master Joseph Henri 60
Maxwell, Agent J P 74
Maxwell, Commander John 76–77
Maxwell, Lieutenant George B 78, 81
Maxwell, Private Thomas 74th Regiment 108
Maxwell, Quartermaster Henry 108
May, Commander William Edward 38, 49
May, Private Patrick 73rd Regiment 110
Mayers, John J 105
Mayes, Able Seaman William 129
Mayes, Engine Room Artificer Charles 175
Mayn, Private John 6th Regiment 106
Maynard, Captain Henry 42
McAcy, Private Michael John 60th Regiment 107
McAlpine, Captain Robert Kyle 179
McAnley, Private William 74th Highlanders 108
McArthur, Historian John 31
McBride, Historian Keith Donald 151, 157, 162
McBride, Historian Peter 7, 39, 46
McCabe, Stoker John 108
McCain, Lieutenant-Commander John Franklin,
   USN 192
McCann, Private Patrick 6th Regiment 106
McCarthy, Able Seaman John 108
McCarthy, Historian Lily 250
McCarthy, Scientist David J 242
McCheyne, Ordinary Seaman Francis Wallace 176
McCleary, Private Patrick 2nd Regiment 109
McCloud, Able Seaman James 130
McCluskey, Trooper William Henry, Cape Mounted
   Rifles 111
McClymont, Assistant-Engineer 2nd Class
   James 94, 105
McCracken, Sub-Lieutenant Alan Cairnhill,
   RAN 229
McDermott, Private John 12th Regiment 106
McDonald, Private John 12th Regiment 109
McDonald, Seaman Arthur 70
McDowell, Stoker 1st Class Andrew 156
McElarney, Private John 74th Regiment 108
McElligott, Stoker 1st Class William George 156
McEwan, Temporary-Lieutenant Ronald Ian
   Taylor 223
McFadden, Private Alexander 91st Regiment 108
McGee, Seaman Patrick 70
McGregor, Private James 74th Regiment 110
McGregor, Stoker 1st Class William 175

McGuyre, Private John 91st Regiment 108
McKee, Art 21
McKee, Private John 74th Regiment 110
McKee, Stoker 2nd Class Alexander 175
McKenzie, Private Thomas 2nd Regiment 105
McKinnon, Private James 74th Regiment 108
McKittrick, Stoker 1st Class John 156
McLaren, Master J C 193
McLaughlin, Captain Patrick Vivian 202
McLean, Crofter Hugh 228
McLean, Lieutenant Allan 78–79, 81
McLeod, Private Edward 74th Regiment 108
McManus, Corporal Peter 2nd Regiment 105
McMay, Private Allem 91st Regiment 110
McMenemy, Stoker 1st Class Thomas 175
McMorrow, Private Timothy 12th Regiment 106
McMullin, Private Thomas 74th Regiment 110
McMurray, Private James 73rd Regiment 107
McPartlan, Private Lackey 43rd Regiment 107
McPhee, Stoker 1st Class Alexander 175
McQuade, Private David 60th Regment 107
McQuaid, Private John 43rd Regiment 107
Meally, Private Austin 12th Regiment 106
Meara, Private Hugh 6th Royal 106
Measure, Private William 91st Regiment 108
Melbourne, British troop transport 116–117
Melita, HMS salvage vessel 168–169
Mellon, Seaman John 70
Mellows, Stoker 1st Class Walter 176
Mells, Seaman William 70
Melpomene, HM 5th-rate 53
Merchant, British freighter 222
Mercury, HM signal school Portdown 214
Meric, *Capitaine* Charles 183
Mermaid, HM 32-gun frigate 26
Mermaid, HM 5th-rate 72
Merrick, Leading Seaman George Ernest 175
Messum, Sailmaker's Mate James 109
Metcalf, Captain Chrisopher Powell, DSO 148
Metford, Ensign Lawrence Nickleson Growden, 6th
   Regiment 86, 94, 104, 106
Metford, Mrs Maria 104
Meulen, Wilhelm Hendrik ter 67–68
Meux, Vice-Admiral Sir Hedworth 156
Michael L Embiricos, Greek freighter 222
Michael Maloney, Admiralty trawler 170–171
Michou, Petty Officer Operations Mechanic (Above
   Water) 1 Alexander Stelios 242
Middleton, HM minehunter 250
Middleton, Lieutenant Commander William
   Edmund 156
Miers, Captain Anthony Cecil Capel 189
Mighells, Captain Josiah 26
Miles, Captain Roderick Bruce Tremayne 187
Milham, Private James 6th Regiment 106
Miller, Assistant Engineer Edward J 130
Miller, Captain Charles Blois 183
Miller, Lieutenant Mervyn Isdale 222
Miller, Private Alexander 74th Regiment 108
Miller, Private David 74th Regiment 108
Miller, Private George 74th Regiment 108
Miller, Translator Frank Justus 71

Milliard, Boatwain's Mates William 130
Mills, Lieutenant-Commander Robert Henry 200
Mills, Private John A 2nd Regiment 105
Milne, Biologist William 244
Miner, Private Henry Royal Marines 107
Miner, Private John Royal Marines 107
Minerve, French submarine 221
Mingles, Able Seaman Robert 176
Minniehaha, American liner 148
Minotaur Class, HM armoured cruisers 178
Minotaur, HM armoured cruiser 152, 155–157
Miranda, HM screw steam sloop 117–118, 125,
   129–130
Mirupanu, freighter 222
Mississippi, US battleship 179
Mistisloff, Russian 3rd-rate 53
Mitchell, Ben, Australian Search & Rescue 242
Mitchell, Gunroom Cook George 131
Mitchell, Leading Stoker 228
Mitchell, Seaman Robert 70
Mitchell, Stoker Petty Officer Ben 228, 242
Mitchell, Vice-Admiral Andrew 62, 63
Mitchell, Vice-Admiral Sir William 53, 62
Mitchener, Leading Signalman Eric Joseph 175
Mlanjeni, 'The Prophet' 85
Modied *Trenchant* Class, HM destroyers 217
Modified *Rosalind* Class, HM destroyers 217
Modified *Ulleswater* Class, HM destroyers 217
Mohoreasdal, Crofter Mairi 229
Monarch, cable-laying vesssel 137
Moncaul, Seaman Lawrence 70
Monck, HM 3rd-rate 26
Monck, Stoker William 105
Monckton, Captain John 52–53
Monday, Gunner George Royal Marine
   Artillery 131
Moneypenny, Captain James 37
Monmouth Class, HM armoured cruisers 151
Monmouth, HM 3rd-rate 13, 37
Monmouth, HM armoured cruiser 152, 155–156
Monroe, Jacob 19
Montagu, (ex-*Montague*) HM battleship 132–140,
   145–146, 148–150, 160
Montagu, Admiral Sir Edward 2
Montagu, John, 4th Earl of Sandwich 71
Montagu, Ralph, Baron Montagu of Boughton 132
Montague, Wireman Albert Joseph 175
Montgomery, Miss Isobel (?) 110
Montgomery, Miss Jean (?) 110
Montgomery, Mrs S W 110
Montgomery, Private Alexander 91st Regiment 108,
   110
Montgomery, Surgeon Walter 57
Montrose, liner 185
Moody, Stoker 1st Class Henry 175
Moon, Private James 91st Regiment 108
Mooney, Private Charles, 2nd Regiment 105
Moor, HM 4th-rate 44
Moore, Private James 60th Regiment 107
Moore, Private John 2nd Regiment 109
Moore, Private John 91st Regiment 108
Moore, Stoker John 130

Moorsom, Captain Robert 73
Moran, Private John 12th Regiment 106
Morby, Ordinary Seaman John 130
Morgan, Private Michael 6th Regiment 106
Morley, Captain of the Fo'c'sle John 129
Morny, Private Christopher 2nd Regiment 105
Morris, Captain Salmon 35
Morris, Petty Officer Stoker Richard 176
Morrison, Private Robert 12th Regiment 106
Mortar, HM 5th-rate 34
Mortimer, Stoker 2nd Class Leonard Albert 175
Morton, Private James 74th Regiment 108
Mounsey, HM destroyer 168
Mudge, Lieutenant William Tertius
    Fitzwilliam 121, 124, 130
Mullany, Private John 12th Regiment 106
Mullins, Miss Bridget 110
Mullins, Miss Lawry 110
Mullins, Miss Mary 110
Mullins, Mrs Anne 110–111
Mullins, Private Patrick 91st Regiment 110–111
Mumford, Mary 46
Mumper, Admiral Shovell's Newfoundland dog 46
Munden, Captain John 3
Munns, Private Robert 12th Regiment 106
Munro, Author Neil 207
Munro, Private Donald 74th Regiment 110
Murdoch, Historian Graeme 119, 129
Murdoch, Private Alexander Donald 74th
    Regiment 108
Murphy, Boy 1st Class Jeremiah 131
Murphy, Private John 73rd Regiment 107
Murray, Able Seaman John James 175
Murray, Captain George 73
Murray, Commander Robert 72
Murray, Confederate Commissioner James 116
Murray, HM destroyer 161
Murray, Private Thomas 73rd Regiment 107
Murray, Sir Oswyn Alexander Ruthaven 174
Murray, Stoker 1st Class Joseph 175
Muskerry, HM minesweeping sloop 169
Musketeer, HM destroyer 168
Myrtle, HM minesweeping sloop 166

Napier, Lieutenant -Colonel George Thomas
    Conolly, CB 113
Napier, Lieutenant George Levack Mackay 161
Napier, Vice-Admiral Sir Trevylyan Dacres
    Willes 180
Narborough, Admiral Sir John 45–46, 48
Narborough, HM destroyer 159, 162–166, 172–173,
    175, 217, 225
Narborough, James 45
Narborough, John 45
Naseby, Parliamentary 1st rate 2
Nash, Lieutenant (CC) Philip David 238, 250
Naskell, Master M 75
Nason, Private James 2nd Regiment 105
Nathaniel, Private Archibald 74th Regiment 110
Neale, Captain's Mate William 109
Neel, Lieutenant de Vaisseau Louis-Balthasa 73
Neelam, Archivist Manjunath vii

Neep, Able Seaman Henry Douglas 175
Neilson, Private Nathaniel John 74th
    Highlanders 108
Nelson, HM battleship 198
Nelson, Vice-Admiral Horatio, Lord 133.159, 226,
    250
Nepean, Sir Evan 66
Neptune, HM 1st-rate 101
Neptunus, Danaish galliot 74
Nesbit, Quartermaster-General Alexander 110
Nesbitt, Master Henry 110
Nesbitt, Master Richard Athol 110
Nesbitt, Miss Mary Anne 110
Nesbitt, Mrs Elizabeth 110
Nether, Hans viii
Nevada, US battleship 179
Newcastle, HM 4th-rate 27
Newcastle, HM destroyer 237
Newcastle, HM light cruiser 202
Newhaven, HM anti-submarine trawler 209
Newman, Ordinary Seaman Henry 130
Newman, Ordinary Seaman Peter 131
Newrick, Publisher Henry 69
Newton Ash, British freighter 222
Nichol, Able Seaman Robert Liddell 175
Nicholls, Lieutenant-Commander Harry Ernest
    Huston 209
Nichols, John Bowyer (*Sylvanus Urban*) 57
Nichols, US destroyer 192
Nicholson, Captain Stuart 138
Nicholson, Captain Wilmot Stuart 180
Nicholson, Carpenter John 130
Nicholson, Historian Ian 111
Nicholson, Rear-Admiral Douglas Romilly
    Lothian 170–171, 173
Nicholson, Rear-Admiral William Coldingham
    Masters 169
Nicholson, Stoker 2nd Class Lawrence Edward
    176
Nicks, Able Seaman Hector Redvers 176
Nicolson, Commodore Sir Frederick 116
Niger, HM screw corvette 119–120
Nightingale, HM 6th-rate 35
Nile, HM armed cutter 55, 61, 67
Noble, Able Seaman Charles 108
Noble, Admiral Sir Percy 198
Nolan, Master Daniel Percy 193
Noll, *Hauptmann* Gunther 203
Nolte, Historian Vincent 62
Norcliffe, Miles 28
Norfolk, HM 3rd-rate 13
Norfolk, HM heavy cruiser 189
Norris, Lieutenant-Commander Stephen
    Hugh 209, 236
Norris, Rear-Admiral Sir John 37, 41
Norris, Ship's Caulker David 130
Northoven, Private John Royal Marines 109
Northover, Able Seaman Joseph 130
Northumberland, HM 3rd-rate 5, 28, 31–32, 33
Norton-Taylor, Journalist Richard 243
Nottingham, HM destroyer 235, 237–244, 246–249
Nubia, steamer 155

Nugent, Captain Raymond Agnew 160
Nutall, Private Thomas 60th Rifles 109
Nymphe, HM 5th-rate 60, 73

O-21, Dutch submarine 222
OB229, convoy 221
O'Brien, Private Michael 73rd Regiment 107, 110
O'Brien, Private Patrick 60th Regiment 107
O'Callaghan, Lieutenant Denys Patrick 180, 187
Ocean, HM amphibious warfare ship 250
Ockman, Captain William 38
O'Connell, Private Michael 2nd Regiment 105
O'Connell, Private William 45th Regiment 107
O'Connell, Private William 73rd Regiment 107
O'Connor, Able Seaman John Joseph 175
O'Connor, Private Dennis 12th Regiment 106
Odiham, HM inshore minesweeper 49
OL009, convoy 222
Oldenburg, motor vessel 149
Oldham, Captain Ronald Wolseley 189
Oliert, Signalman William (aka Alexander
    Hills) 126, 129
Olorenshaw, Private John 6th Regiment 106
Ommanney, Crown Agent Octavius 94
O'Neil, Corporal John 91st Regiment 110
Onslaught, HM destroyer 234
Opal, HM corvette 162
Opal, HM destroyer 159, 162, 164–176, 217
Ophelia, HM destroyer 164
Orange, Able Seaman Percy 176
Orchard, Boy 1st Class William Thomas 131
O'Reilly, Private John 73rd Regiment 110
Orestes, HM wooden screw corvette 115
Orford, HM 3rd-rate 37, 44, 49
Orlando, HM naval base Greenock 230
Orlando, HM screw frigate 117, 126
Orotava, HM armed merchant cruiser 187
Orpheus, HM wooden screw corvette 114–118,
    120–122, 124–129
Orr-Ewing, Lieutenant David 180, 182, 189
Osborne, Midshipman Herbert Court 135
Osbourne, Ship's Corporal Thomas 130
Osbourne, Thomas, Marquess of Carmathen 4
Osburn, Lieutenant-Commander Carl
    Townsend 179
Osliabia, Russian battleship 132
Osprey, HM brig-sloop 119
Ossory, HM 2nd-rate 6
Outing, Private Edward 43rd Regiment 107
Over-yssel, HM 3rd-rate (Prize) 53
Ovidiuys Naso (Ovid) 71
Owen, Captain Frederic John 100
Owen, Private Jeremiah 12th Regiment 106
Oxley, Private James 2nd Regiment 105

P-29, HM patrol boat 163
Pacific Chieftain, tug 243
Pack, Able Seaman John Thomas 175
Packard, Commander Geoffrey Percival 201, 211
Packer, Captain Herbert Annesley 214
Paddon, Captain Henry 27
Padley, Mechanician Walter Brennan 176

Pafford, Private Peter Royal Marines 131
Page, Editor William 5
Page, Private Robert 2nd Regiment 109
Paine, Historian Ralph Delahye 59
Pakenham, Vice-Admiral Sir William
    Christopher 178
Palin, Able Seaman William 129
Palmer, Ordinary Seaman William 131
Palmer, Captain Irving Montgomery, DSO 199
Palmer, Petty Officer John Henry 139
Palmer, Private William 12th Regiment 106
Palmerston, Lord 116
Paluma, HMQ survey vessel 129
Pandora, HM brig 119
Pankhurst, Lieutenant-Commander Richard Dixon
    Herbert Stephen 221
Panther, HM 4th-rate 37–38
Parke, Able Seaman Thomas 130
Parker, Seaman Thomas 70
Parker, Stoker 2nd Class Harry Edward 176
Parkes, Doctor Oscar, OBE 133
Parkes, Engine Room Artificer Harry Howard 176
Parklin, Private Michael M, 43rd Regiment 107
Parr, Commander Anthony Jonathan, RNZN 241
Parry, Captain Henry 185
Parsons, Ordinary Seaman Edward 175
Parsons, Ordinary Seaman James 130
Parthenon, Greek freighter 222
Pascoe, Boatswain's Mate John 130
Passenger, Lieutenant William 6
Pathfinder, HM scout-cruiser 187
Patrician, HMC destroyer 178
Patriot, HMC destroyer 178
Patten, Captain Frederick 119
Patterson, Captain Wilfred Rupert 196
Patterson, Ordinary Seaman John 105
Pattinson, Lieutenant Frank 177
Paul Jacobi, German destroyer 220
Paulet, Captain Lord Henry 73
Pawle, Lieutenant Richard 81
Paxton, Thomas 46–47
Pay, Carpenter John 130
Payne, Able Seaman Edmund Gordon 175
Payne, Private Isaac Royal Marines 107
Peacock, Private Thomas 60th Regiment 107
Pearin, Private Henry Royal Marines 131
Pechell, Rear-Admiral Sir George Brooke 87
Pedestal, Operation 198
Pegg, Able Seaman James Thomas 176
Peirse, Captain Richard Henry 152
Pelham, Able Seaman Edwin 130
Pelham-Clinton, Henry Pelham Fiennes, Duke of
    Newcastle 125
Pelly, Captain Henry Bertram 139
Pelter, HM gun-brig 64
Pembroke, HM Depot ship, Chatham 158
Penelope, HM light cruiser 203
Penneck, Rev. Henry 46
Pennefather, Lieutenant William 161
Penning, Private Joseph 43rd Regiment 107
Penolver, British freighter 222
Pepys, Diarist Samuel 2, 33

Percy, Admiral Algernon, Duke of Northumberland, First Lord of the Admiralty 113
Percy, Captain Francis 19
Peresviet, Russian battleship 132
Perry, Historian Fairfax 90
Perth, RAN light cruiser 188, 199
Peters, Private George 43rd Regiment 109
Peters, Private John 2nd Regiment 109
Peters, Private Patrick 2nd Regiment 109
Petroleum, HM fleet oiler 140
Pettet, Able Seaman Pat 184
Pettifer, Private John 12th Regiment 106
Peyton, HM destroyer 168, 171–172
Pfundheller, Kapitan zur See Hans 163
Phalan, Able Seaman John 108
Philip T Dodge, US freighter 222
Phillimore, Captain Augustus 125
Phillips, Captain Christopher Hooper, Rtd. 212
Phillips, Engineer's Cook John 131
Phillips, Temporary-Lieutenant Sidney George, RNVR 222
Phoenix, HM 5th-rate 37, 39, 42–45
Phoenix, HM Damage Repair Instructional Unit 243
Pichegru, *Generale* Jean-Charles 52
Piercy, Captain Francis 37, 42, 48
Pilbeam, Ordinary Seaman Alfred 130
Pincher, HM destroyer 161
Pinfold, Military Doctor of Laws Surrogate Thomas 6
Pink, Able Seaman William Stephen 176
Piper, Private Sidney Royal Marines 107
Play, HM 6th-rate 11
PLM27, British freighter 222
Plover, HM sloop 74
Plover, Salvage vessel 140
Plowman, Captain after guard John 130
Plowman, Historian Peter 123
Pobieda, Russian battleship 132
Poland, Captain Albert Lawrence, DSC 200
Politician, British cargo ship 138
Popham, Master William 143
Portal, Captain Reginald Henry, DSC 200
Portbury, Able Seaman Henry 129
Porter, Lieutenant John Mansel 168
Portland, HM 4th-rate 35
Portlock, Captain Nathaniel 58, 61–62
Portsmouth, HM bomb ketch 24
Potts, Boy Telegraphist Alfred George 176
Pound, Admiral-of-the-Fleet Sir Alfred Dudley Pickman Rogers, GCB, OM, CVO 232–234
Power, Captain Arthur John 189, 231
Powney, Engine Room Artificer Sidney George 176
Pratley, Able Seaman Robert Edgar 175
Pratt, Ordinary Seaman Charles 105
Pratt, Private David 91st Regiment 108
Pratt, Stoker 1st Class William 175
Prescott, Rear-Admiral Henry 101
President, HM training ship 158, 169
Preston, Seaman George (aka Young, James) 70
Price, Able Seaman William Edward 176
Price, Captain John 37, 48

Price, Commander Andrew 249
Price, Private George 2nd Regiment 105
Pride, Private Thomas 74th Regiment 108
Pridham, Captain Arthur Francis 189
Prien, *Korvettekapitan* Gunther 220, 222
Prince Ernest, Mail Packet Boat 77
Prince George, HM 2nd-rate 28, 30, 33
Prince of Orange, Packet Boat 56
Prince of Wales, HM 1st-rate 159
Prince of Wales, HM battleship 188
Prince Regent, HM 1st-rate 101
Prince Royal, HM 1st rate 2
Prince, Private Charles 6th Regiment 106
Pringle, Lieutenant George 80
Proby, John Joshua, Lord Carysfort 17
Probyn, Lieutenant William 42
Prole, Master John 72
Propontis, Mail Steamer 100
Psyche, HMA gun-brig 236
Purcell, Private Thomas 12th Regiment 106
Pury, Ship's Chaplain Peter 45
Puttenham, HM inshore minesweeper 49
Pyper, Seaman James 70
Python, HM destroyer 177

Quebec, HM frigate 72
Queen Anne 22–23, 48
Queen Elizabeth II 69, 186
Queen Elizabeth the Queen Mother 70
Queen Elizabeth, HM battlleship 174
Queen Mary II 4
Queen Victoria 69, 73, 113, 128
Queen, HM 1st-rate 101
Queen's Cross, tug 221
Quigley, Petty Officer Stoker John 175
Quin, Private Edward 43rd Regiment 107
Quinn, Private John 2nd Regiment 105
Quinton, Captain of the Foretop John 129
Quisling, Vidkun Abraham Lauritz Jonsson 214

R4, Operation 199
Rabb, Private William 2nd Regiment 109
Racoon, HM destroyer 161
Rainier, Captain Peter 72
Raleigh, HM heavy cruiser 177-194, 217
Raleigh, Sir Walter 177
Ramiliies, HM battleship 145. 189
Ramillies, HM 3rd-rate 81
Ramsden, Master Thomas Emmanuel 91, 97–98
Ramsden, Miss Christiana 97–98
Ramsden, Mrs Mary Ann 91, 97–98
Ramsey, Vice-Admiral Sir Charles Gordon 212
Randall, Leading Cook's Mate Harold Douglas 175
Randall, Private George 73rd Regiment 107
Randall, Stoker George 107
Randall, Stoker Robert 130
Ranger, Salvage vessel 137–139
Ranger, US aircraft carrier 214
Ranshaw, Private Charles 43rd Regiment 107
Ransome, Author Arthur Mitchell 1
Ratsey, Commander Franklin 219
Rattler, collier 61

Rattler, HM composite screw gunboat 185
Rattlesnake, HM wooden screw corvette 115
Ratwiesan, Russian 1st-rate 53
Rayment, Novelist Sean 244–245
Raymond, Captain Beaumont 34
Raymond, Lieutenant-Commander Hugh
    Evelyn 188
Rechel, *Korvettenkapitan* Kurt 220
Reddall, Captain Finch 38, 41
Redman, Armourer George 130
Redman, Sickberth attendant Henry 130
Reed, Quartermaster Roger 105
Reed, Seaman Ebenezer 70
Rees, Able Seaman Thomas 131
Rees, Private John 60th Regiment 107
Reid, Stoker 1st Class George Bagnall 176
Reinhold, Captain Harold Owen 185
Reliance, HM fleet oiler 140
Renner, Captain Frederick 123
Rennie, Engineer John 67
Rennington, Private John 6th Regiment 106
Renwick, Chief Engineer Charles Kerr 89, 95–96,
    101–102, 108
Repulse, HM battle-cruiser 188
Reserve, HM 4th-rate 9, 11
Resolution, HM 3rd-rate 27
Resolution, HM battleship 169, 200–202, 210
Resolution, Parliamentary 1st rate 2
Restoration, HM 3rd-rate 28, 30–34
Retribution, HM frigate 101
Reunion, dive boat 112
Revenge, HM 3rd-rate 34
Revenge, HM battleship 173, 187, 231
Reyne, Captain Cecil Nugent 195
Reynolds, Able Seaman Herbert R 183
Reynolds, Private George C 12th Regiment 106
Rhadamanthus, HM transport 89, 97–98
Rhododendron, HM corvette 226, 229–230
Ribouleau, Captain Peter 75
Richard and John, merchant vessel 24
Richard, Lieutenant Geoffrey Edward 129
Richard, Parliamentary 1st rate 2
Richards, Captain George Henry 119
Richards, Master's Assistant Roland Bevan 88, 91,
    94, 96, 99, 101–103, 108
Richards, Ordinary Seaman Thomas Abraham 176
Richards, Stoker 1st Class Samuel 175
Richardson, Lieutenant-Commander Hugh Nicholas
    Aubyn 222
Richie, Captain Sir Lewis Anselmo
    ('*Bartimeus*') 161
Riddle, Captain Finch 26
Riddleston, Private John 43rd Regiment 107
Rider, Private John 6th Regiment 106
Rijnders, Johannes Arnoldus Hermann 59
Ringdove, HM gunboat 168
Ringhorn, British freighter 222
Riordan, Private Daniel 43rd Regiment 107
Ritter, Ordinary Seaman Henry Percival 176
River Class, HM destroyers 163
River Class, HM offshore patrol vessels 250
River Plate, Battle of 233

Rivett, Ordinary Seaman John Herbert 228
Rivett-Carnac, Captain James William, DSC 188
Robbe, Wreck Receiver Frederik Pieter 66–67
Roberts, Carpenter 3rd Class James 94, 105
Roberts, First Lieutenant John 75
Roberts, Mrs Elizabeth 94
Roberts, Ordinary Seaman George 130
Robertson, Able Seaman James 175
Robertson, Private Thomas 74th Regiment 108
Robertson, Seaman James 70
Robinson, Assistant Surgeon Frederick 86, 108
Robinson, Captain Robert 101
Robinson, Lieutenant William Charles 73rd
    Regiment 86, 107
Robust, HM 3rd-rate 73
Roche, Private John 12th Regiment 106
Rockett, Able Seaman Joseph James 130
Rodgers, Nicholas Andrew Martin 64
Rodney, HM battleship 188
Roe, Private Richard Royal Marines 130
Roesch, Lieutenant-Commander Herbert Otto,
    USN 192
Roffey, Captain Kerrit 25
Rogers, Able Seaman John 63–64
Rogers, Leading Stoker John Charles 176
Rohmer, Major-General Richard 186
Rokus, Greek freighter 78
Rollinson, Able Seaman Francis Joseph 175
Rolt, Cornet, John 12th Lancers 86, 94, 105
Romney, HM 4th-rate 37, 39, 44–45
Romney, HM 4th-rate 53
Roosevelt, President Franklin Delano 70
Ross, Commander Harry Leith 177
Rotchell, Ordinary Seaman Frederick James 175
Rothwell, Seaman Richard 70
Rover Class, HM tugs 166
Rowe, Captain Gordon, USN 214
Rowe, Carpenter Charles E 130
Rowland, Ordinary Seaman William 131
Rowley, Private James 2nd Regiment 105
Royal Anne, HM 1st-rate 37, 39–40
Royal Charles, HM 1st rate 2
Royal James, HM 1st rate 2
Royal Oak, HM 3rd-rate 5
Royal Oak, HM battleship 109,
Royal Oak, HM battleship 220
Royal Sovereign, HM 1st-rate 4
Ruby, HM 5th-rate 10, 11
Ruby, HM screw-corvette 179
Rundell & Bridges Goldsmiths 57
Rusgel, Ordinary Seaman Thomas 130
Rush, Petty Officer William Joseph 175
Rushbrooke, Midshipman John Charles 210
Rushpool, British freighter 222
Russell, Able Seaman Thomas 129
Russell, Able Seaman William 130
Russell, Admiral Edward, Earl of Orford 2, 4–5
Russell, Captain Gerald Walter 183
Russell, Editor Jesse 21
Russell, Engineer Alexander 91
Russell, Ensign Alexander Cumming 74th
    Regiment 86, 94, 107

Russell, HM 3rd-rate 34
Russell, HM battleship 132
Russell, Lieutenant Somerville Peregrine
　Brownlow 137
Russell, Lieutenant-Commander Archibald
　Boyd 221
Russell, Ordinary Seaman John 175
Russell, Ordinary Seaman William 130
Russell, Private William 60th Regiment 107
Ruth, Able Seaman Martin 108
Rutherford, Private Ebenezer 74th Regiment 108
Ryan, Private Patrick 6th Regiment 106
Ryan, Seaman Philip 70
Rye, HM 6th-rate 25, 37

S P Lee, US destroyer 192
Sabre, HM destroyer 211
Safeguard, HM shore establishment Rosyth 234
Sainsbury, Editor William Noel 11
Saker, HM naval establishment Washington DC 214
Salisbury, HM 4th rate 42–43, 45, 47
Salisbury, Lady Cicely 195
Salmon, Officer's Stewart Jack 175
Salmond, Master Commanding Robert 86–89, 94,
　96, 99, 102, 104
Samarang, HM survey vessel 154
Sampson, HM frigate 101
Samwells, Petty Officer Walter Joseph 228
San Jacinto, Federal steam frigate 116
Sanders, Lieutenant-Commander Harry Marcus
　Crews, RNR 222
Sandford, Fisherman George 7
Sandwich, HM sloop 222
Sandys, Captain Jordan 25
Sansom, Captain Michael 37, 43–44
Santa Margarita, HM 5th-rate 73
Sardonyx, HM destroyer 221
Saturnus, Dutch freighter 222
Sawler, Novelist Harvey 186
Saxton, Fifer Thomas Royal Marines 107
Sayer, Captain George 80
SC008, convoy 222
Scarborough, HM sloop 201
Schabracq, Hartog Isaac Levy 58, 61, 64–65
Schemmel, *Korvettenkapitan* Alfred 220
Schepke, *Korvettekapitan* Joachim 222
Schettino, Captain Francesco 83
Schofield, Trooper M 12th Lancers 109
Schomberg, Commander Geoffrey, CB, DSC 188
Scimgeour, Diarist Alexander 160
Scimitar, HM destroyer 222
Scorpion, HM destroyer 234
Scorpion, HM sloop 75
Scotsman, HM destroyer 219
Scotstoun, HM armed merchant cruiser 212
Scott, Able Seaman Norman 176
Scott, Admiral Lord Charles Montagu Douglas 132
Scott, Captain Edward Hinton 101
Scott, Captain Francis 117, 125
Scott, Commander Humphrey Gilbert 201
Scott, Historian John Burridge 106
Scott, Lady Ada Mary 132

Scott, Private Phillip 73rd Regiment 107
Scott, Rear-Admiral Richard James Rodney, AM,
　CP, MD 185
Scott, Stoker Charles 105
Scotts Shipbuilding & Engineering Company 187,
　218
Scourge, HM sloop 108
Scrymgeour-Wedderburn, Captain William Ogilvy,
　DSC 212
Scutt, Engineer's Servant Samuel 131
Scutts, Private Horace Thomas 60th Regiment 107
Seafire, HM destroyer 219
Seagrove, American schooner 72
Seale, Ordinary Seaman John George 130
Searcher, HM destroyer 219
Searle, Boy 1st Class John 131
Searle, Lieutenant Thomas 75
Seawolf, HM destroyer 188
Seccombe, Captain John 125
Sedgewood, Private William 91st Regiment 108
Seed, Lieutenant-Commander Walter Dudley, Jr,
　USN 192
Sen Soskende, Dutch privateer 75
Senator, HM destroyer 218
Sepoy, HM destroyer 188
Serene, HM destroyer 219
Serpent, HM torpedo-cruiser 177
Seton, Lieutenant-Colonel Alexander 74th
　Regiment 86, 91–92, 94, 98, 107
Severn, HM offshore patrol vessel 250
Seward, Secretary of State William Henry 116
Sewol, South Korean ferry 83
Sex Soskendi, French privateer 75
Seymour, Admiral Sir Michael 128
Seymour, Edward, Duke of Somerset 125
Shabaaz, Persian gunboat 188
Shadwell, Captain Lancelot Milman 234
Shales, Captain John 37
Shamrock, HM destroyer 219
Shannon, HM 5th-rate 53
Shannon, HM screw frigate 125
Sharbaaz, Persian gunboat 188
Sharp, Private William 43rd Regiment 109
Sharpe, Private John 74th Regiment 110
Shaughnessey, Private Francis G, 2nd Regiment 105
Shaw, Private Daniel 74th Regiment 110
Shaw, Private Duncan 74th Regiment 108
Shaw, Sub-Lieutenant Henry Stavely
　Pilkington 172, 175
Shea, Private Daniel 73rd Regiment 107
Sheargold, Able Seaman Henry 130
Sheehan, Private Timothy 73rd Regiment 107
Sheffield, HM destroyer 237
Shelmerdine, Able Seaman Sydney 175
Shephard, Private Robert 12th Regiment 106
Shepherd, Private Robert 73rd Regiment 107
Sheppard, Gunner's Mate Edward William 176
Sheppard, Petty Officer Edward William 130
Sheppard, Private George 43rd Regiment 107
Sherman, Captain Thomas 9
Shigeto, Admiral Dewa 157
Shikari, HM destroyer 219, 222–224, 233

Shipham, HM inshore minesweeper 49
Sholto, Historian Percy 90
Shorthouse, Private John Royal Marines 131
Shovell, Admiral Sir Cloudesley (Clowdisley) 28, 33, 35, 37–40, 45–50
Shovell, Lady Elizabeth 46
Shrewsbury, HM 3rd-rate 28–29, 32
Shuldham, Lieutenant Molyneux 177
Sidall, Confederate Commissioner John 116
Siemon, Historian Rosamund 58
Sim, Lieutenant-Commander Edward William Boyd 188
Simmonds, Boy 1st Class John 131
Simmonds, Private Thomas 2nd Regiment 105
Simon, Private John, 12th Regiment 109
Sinclair, Captain Claude Hamilton 179
Sinclair, Captain Donald Campbell (*Domhnall an Ban*) 229
Sinclair, Rear-Admiral Hugh Francis Paget, KCB 186
Sir Edward Hughes, East Indiaman 75
Sirce II, British freighter 222
Sirius, HM 10-gun ship, Flagship First Fleet 244
Sissons, Able Seaman William 171–174, 176
Sixtus V, Pope 20
Skate, HM destroyer 210
Skelton, Captain Charles 4–6, 7
Skidsey, Captain William 75
Skua, Blackburn 210, 220
Skynner, Captain Lancelott 53, 56–60
Slade, Captain James 60
Smales, Captain Thomas 93, 96
Smedden, Able Seaman Thomas 129
Smeeton, Sub-Lieutenant (later Admiral Sir) Richard Michael 219
Smith, Able Seaman Albert Edward 175
Smith, Able Seaman E J RNVR 228–229
Smith, Able Seaman John 108
Smith, Able Seaman Robert 70
Smith, Captain George Walter 152
Smith, Captain John 35
Smith, Corporal Thomas 6th Royal Regiment 106
Smith, Corporal William 6th Regiment 106
Smith, Corporal William E 12th Regiment 85, 98, 106, 109
Smith, Jeanie viii
Smith, Lieutenant Bosworth 177
Smith, Lieutenant-Commander Andy 250
Smith, Lieutenant-General Sir Henry George Wakelyn 'Harry' 85
Smith, Private George 73rd Regiment 107
Smith, Private James 6th Regiment 106
Smith, Private John 2nd Regiment 109
Smith, Private John 91st Regiment 90, 108
Smith, Private Luke 91st Regiment 108
Smith, Private Patrick 91st Regiment 108
Smith, Private Robert 74th Regiment 108
Smith, Private Thomas 60th Regiment 109
Smith, Private William 74th Regiment 108
Smith, Private William S 91st Regiment 108
Smith, Sailmaker Thomas 130
Smith, Stonemason Bernie 234

Smith-Cumming, Sir Mansfield 186
Smith-Stanley, Prime Minister Edward, 14th Earl of Derby 113
Smyth, Captain Sidney Keith, OBE 212
Snake, HM brig-sloop 177
Snudden, Able Seaman Thomas 130
Soames, Director Joseph East India Company 113
Soanes, Captain Joseph 25–26, 42
Sobieski, Polish troopship 211
Somers, Signalman Frank William 175
Somers, US destroyer 192
Somerset, HM 3rd-rate 37, 40, 44, 48
Somerville, Captain James Fownes 189
Somerville, Rev. Thomas 29
Sooter, Private William 60th Regiment 109
Sotheron, Captain Frank 74
Soule, Captain John 10, 14–15, 18
South Carolina, American frigate 72
South Wales, British freighter 193
Southam, Able Seaman Alfred George Thomas 176
Southampton, HM 4th-rate 42, 44–45
Southampton, HM destroyer 237
Sovereign of the Seas, HM 1st-rate 4
Sowden, Leading Stoker William J 184
Spanker, HM hospital ship 63
Sparshott, Ordinary Seaman William James 130
Spartivento, Battle of 214
Spear, Commander Joseph 81
Speedwell, HM fireship 11
Speedy, HM destroyer 218
Speer, Second Master Robert David 94
Speke, Lieutenant William 177
Spencer, Boy 1st Class Samuel F 131
Spicer, Private Thomas 6th Regiment 106
Spindrift, HM destroyer 219
Sportive, HM destroyer 219
Sprague, Diver Mark 193
Springer, Able Seaman Edward 131
Springett, Historian Dawn Gillian vii, 221
Springett, Leading Seaman Harry 220–221, 224–228, 231
Springs, Private William 12th Regiment 106
Spruce, Mrs Jane 110
Spruce, Sergeant Charles 12th Regiment 110
Spurgeon, Commander Stanley Herbert King, RAN vii, 202, 205–206, 208, 210–213, 215–216
Squires, Captain Matthew 72
St. Albans, steamer 155
St. George, HM 2nd-rate 37, 39–41, 49
St. John the Baptist (Saint Jean) 69
St. John, Captain Francis Gerald 187
St. Lawrence, Lieutenant-Commander Gaisford 180
St. Paul, US liner 148
Stafford, First Secretary of the Admiralty Augustus 87
Stanfield, Private John 60th Regiment 109
Stanley, Private John 91st Regiment 110
Starkay, Gunner Bradley Royal Marines Artillery 131
Starr, Private Michael Thomas 6th Regiment 106
Starrs, Private Francis Royal Marines 131
Stella Capella, HM armed trawler 223

Stephens, Chief Engineer Samuel 130
Stephenson, Able Seaman William 131
Sterry, Mrs Elizabeth 6
Sterry, Shipwright John 6
Stevens, Master Thomas 230
Stevenson, Commodore Charles, CBE 234
Stewart, Private Robert 74th Regiment 108
Stewart, Private William 74th Regiment 108
Stirling Castle, HM 3-rate 29–33
Stokes, Captain John Lort 119
Stokes, Commander Graham Henry 221
Stokes, Private Patrick 60th Regiment 107
Stone, Able Seaman James Charles 176
Stone, Boy 2nd Class Samuel 105
Stone, Historian Russell Cyril James 119
Stone, Lieutenant-Commander Reginald Guy 161
Stone, Ordinary Seaman Abel 87–88, 101–103, 105, 108
Stone, Private William Royal Marines 107
Stoneham, Wardroom Cook Thomas 131
Stonehenge, HM destroyer 218
Stoodley, Leding Stoker Samuel 105
Stopford, Captain The Hon. Walter George 142
Storey, Private James 60th Regiment 107
Storey, Seaman William 70
Story, Batavian Rear-Admiral Samuel 53
Story, Surgeon Probationer Louis Percival St.John 175
Stovell, Petty Officer Stoker Charles William 175
Straight, Dr. William Marcellus 20
Strange, Leading Seaman Frank Arthur 176
Strath Class, HM anti-submarine trawlers 209
Strath Derry, HM anti-submarine trawler 209
Strath Devon, HM anti-submarine trawler 209
Straw, Sergeant John Abraham 12th Lancers 86, 105
Strenuous, HM destroyer 218
Strong, Master William D 130
Strong, Ship's Stewart John 57
Stronghold, HM destroyer 218
Strout, Cabinet Maker Thomas 148
Strutt, Captain Arthur Charles 178, 185
Stuart, HM destroyer 190
Stuiver, Dutch privateer 74
Stupple, Boatswain's Mate Henry 129
Sturdee, Captain (later Admiral Sir) Frederick Charles Doveton 152, 169
Sturdee, Master Commander Frederick Rannie 89
Sturdy, HM destroyer 217, 234
Sturnfels, German blockade runner 188
Styles, Ship's Master Thomas 42, 45
Styx, HM paddle-sloop 99–100
Success, HM destroyer 161
Suecia, Swedish freighter 222
Suevic, White Star line 138
Suffolk, HM 3-rate 24–25
Suffolk, HM armoured cruiser 151
Sullivan, Private Daniel 73rd Regiment 110
Sullivan, Private James 73rd Regiment 107
Sullivan, Private John 73rd Regiment 110
Sullivan, Private Timothy 43rd Regiment 107
Sultan, HM naval establishment Singapore 211
Summers, Ordinary Seaman James 130

Summers, Seaman George 70
Summerton, Private Mark 6th Regiment 106
Supply, HM brig 244
Surveillante, HM 5th-rate 76
Sutton, Commander John Gilbert, Rtd. 224
Sutton, Duncan vii
Swain, Stoker William 130
Swan, heavy lift vessel 243–244
Swan, HM 6th-rate 10, 11
Sweeny, Private John 91st Regiment 108
Swiftsure, HM 3rd-rate 8, 37, 39, 41, 49
Swinger, HM gun-brig 64
Syfret, Vice-Admiral Sir Neville 198
Symonds, Captain Thomas 11
Symonds, Captain Thomas Matthew 101
Symonds, Seaman William 70

Tactician, HM destroyer 219
Tait, Lieutenant-Commander Arthur Andre 209
Talbot, Charles, Duke of Shrewsbury 11
Tapscott, Leading Stoker James 105
Taranaki War 118
Tarney, Private James 91st Regiment 108
Tartar, HM 6th-rate 73
Tate, Captain Francis Alban Arthur Gifford 142
Taurel, Louis Jean Marie 67
Tautra, Norwegian freighter 222
Taylor, 1st Class Stoker Charles Frederick 176
Taylor, Able Seaman William 70
Taylor, Assistant Master William J 130
Taylor, Private George 74th Regiment 110
Taylor, Private Patrick 73rd Regiment 110
Taylor, Stoker James 130
Taylor, Stoker Petty Officer William Horner 156
TB-30, HM torpedo-boat 163
Te Mana, HMNZ frigate 241
Telemachus, HM destroyer 161
Telima, salvage ship 168
Temeraire, HM battleship 173
Tennant, Captain Sir William George 188, 212
Tennant, Lieutenant-Commander Robert Basil Stewart 221
Tennant, Marine Engineer Charles 115
Terbe, Sergeant Isiah 6th Regiment 106
Termagant, HM sloop 75
Terrible, HM fire-ship 10–11, 13, 15, 18–19, 45
Terry, Lieutenant-Commander Reginald Ernest 222
Terry, Stoker 1st Class Charles Edward 175
Tetenrei Maru, Japanese cargo ship 154
Tetley, Squadron-Leader Dean, RAAF 242
Thalia, HM 5th-rate 73
Thanet, HM destroyer 219
Thatcher, Surgeon-Captain Charles Malcolm Russell, MB, ChB 187
The *Trent* Crisis' 115–116
Theobald, Boy 1st Class Charles 131
Theseus, HM light carrier 189
Thetis, HM submarine 138
Thielsen, Master 76
Thisbe, HM destroyer 219
Thistleglen, British freighter 222
Thomas & Mary, Thames trading vessel 244

Thomas, Able Seaman Peter 105
Thomas, Carpenter Henry 130
Thomas, Private Henry 73rd Regiment 107
Thomas, Private Nathaniel 2nd Regiment 105
Thompson, Admiral Sir Charles 53
Thompson, Boy 1st Class Isaiah 131
Thompson, James David Anthony 67
Thompson, Private Adam 74th Regiment 108
Thompson, Private James 60th Regiment 107
Thompson, Private John 12th Regiment 106
Thomson, Illustrator Hugh 29
Thomson, Interviewer Alistair 162
Thomson, Private John 74th Regiment 108
Thomson, Sir William (Lord Kelvin) 232
Thornbrough, Captain Edward 73
Thornhill, Stoker 1st Class George Mafeking 184
Thornton, Commander Edward Bruce
    Chichelley 230
Thornycroft, Shipbuilder John Isaac 160
Thorton, Lieutenant-Commander Mark 222
Three Brothers, Danish merchantman 76
Threlfall, Master Arthur 56
Thunderbolt, HM paddle sloop 109
Tibbits, Captain Charles 170
Tierney, Private John 6th Regiment 106
Tiger, HM destroyer 156
Tiger, HM paddle sloop 109
Tiggle, Able Seaman Richard 108
Tigne, Private William 12th Regiment 106
Tigre, French 3rd-rate 74
Till, Able Seaman George 91, 101–102, 108
Till, Captain Hugh 38
Till, Engine Room Artificer James 176
Tilley, Ordinary Seaman Arthur S 130
Tippett, Stoker 1st Class George Henry 175
Tirpitz, German battleship 214
Tobago, HM destroyer 218
Todhunter, Midshipman Robin Charles 180,
    188–189
Tokiwa, Japanese armoured cruiser 157
Tomahawk, HM destroyer 234
Toms, Able Seaman George 176
Tonen, Private Michael 73rd Regiment 107
Tonen, Private Michael, 73rd Regiment 107
Took, Trooper John 86, 105, 113
Torbay, HM 3rd-rate 37, 39–41, 49
Torbay, HM destroyer 218
Toreador, HM destroyer 218
Torless, Captain Henry Holland 152
Torpy, Private Edward 6th Regiment 106
Torrid, HM destroyer 219
Tortoise, HM troopship 75
Tottenham, Captain Henry Loftus 139
Tottenham, Major William Heathcot 113
Town Class, HM light cruisers 196
Townsend, Captain Isaac 34
Townsend, Lieutenant Michael Southcote 222
Townsend, Stewart George 130
Tozer, Master's Assistant John J 130
Tracey, Seaman John 70
Trahearn, Leading Stoker Albert Thomas 228
Tramfedach, *Korvettenkapitan* Claus 220

Tranter, Sergeant William Royal Marines 131
Trautman, Carpenter's Mate John 130
Trelawny, Brigadier-General Henry 45
Trelawny, Sir Jonathan, Bishop of Winchester 45
Trenchard, Sir John 12
Trent, Royal Mail Steam Packet 116
Trevelyan, George Macaulay 22
Trevor, Captain Trudor 35
Trimmer, Ordinary Seaman Ernest 176
Tripp, Leading Stoker Sydney George 184
Triton, HM 4th-rate 35
Trojan, HM destroyer 219
Trompenberg, Dutch freighter 222
Trott, Private George Royal Marines 131
Troubridge, Captain Thomas Hope 188
Trusty, HM 4th-rate 75
Trusty, HM destroyer 219
Tryphon, HM destroyer 218
Tuck, Private William 45th Regiment 109
Tucker, Private Henry William 43rd Regiment 107
Tucker, Private Thomas Royal Marines 131
Tudge, Mrs Mary 135
Tudge, Valet 135
Tully, Private George 6th Regiment 106
Turner, Boy 1st Class Benjamin 108
Turner, Commander Errol Concannon Lloyd 230
Turner, Private Francis 74th Regiment 108
Turtle, Ordinary Seaman George 130
Tweedie, Commodore Hugh Justin 160, 172
Two Sisters, Danish merchantman 76
Tyger, HM 4th-rate 9, 11
Tyler, Lieutenant-Commander Trevor St.Vincent
    Frederick 219
Tyler, Stoker 1st Class Reuben 184
Tyrant, HM destroyer 219

U-9, German submarine 180
U-38, German submarine 200, 222
U-46, German submarine 222
U-47, German submarine 220, 222
U-48, German submarine 222
U-89, German submarine 230
U-94, German submarine 229
U-100, German submarine 222
U-517, German submarine 193
UB-105, German submarine 183
Ulster Prince, HM landing ship infantry 212
Underhill, Captain Edwin Veale 173
Ungoed, Lieutenant Daniel Will 229
Urgent, HM troopship 109
Usher, Commander William Arthur 188
Utrecht, Batavian 5th-rate 53

Valerian, HM sloop 188
Valhalla, HM destroyer 164, 167
Valiant, HM battleship 187
van der Molen, Professor Sense Jan 59
van Dulm, *Luitenant ter Zee 1st Klasse* Johannes
    Frans 222
Van Keulen, Fisherman Jan 67
Van Sand, Systems Engineer Bruce 77
Vancouver, HM destroyer 176

Vanessa, HM destroyer 176
Vanguard, HM 2nd-rate 3, 35
Vanoc, HM destroyer 221
Vansittart, HM destroyer 202
Vassilios A Polemis, Greek freighter 222
Veal, Boy 1st Class Robert H 131
Veich, Ship's Master Alfred James 119–120, 126
Velox, HM destroyer 177
Venables, Midshipman Harry Adrian 176
Vendetta, HM destroyer 188
Venerable, HM 3rd-rate 52
Venerable, HM battleship 139, 152
Verner, Midshipman George H 130
Vernon, Captain Edward 37
Vernon, HM Mine & Torpedo Establishment, Portsmouth 142, 176
Vernon, Private Henry 2nd Regiment 109
Verulam, HM destroyer 163
Verwagting, Dutch privateer 75
Vespasian, Norwegian freighter 222
Vesse, Private Samuel 2nd Regiment 105
Vestal, HM 6th-rate 72
Vesuvius, HM fire-ship 27
Veteran, HM 3rd-rate 53
Vickery, Assistant Engineer John H 130
Vickery, Private Edward 43rd Light Infantry 107
Victor, HM sloop 53
Victoria and Albert, HM royal yacht 179, 198
Victoria, HM 1st-rate 159
Victoria, Queen vi, 69, 73, 113, 128, 159
Victory, HM 1st-rate 133, 142
Vigo, HM 4th-rate 25
Vince, Gunner John Royal Marines Artillery 131
Vincent, Caulker's Mate George 130
Vindictive, HM aircraft-carrier (later repair ship) 178, 189, 200
Vindictive, HM block-ship 148
Vinnern, Dutch privateer 75
Viper, HM destroyer 177
Viscount, HM destroyer 222
Visser, Fisherman Jan Folkerts 59–60, 62, 65
Vivacious, HM destroyer 176
Vivian, Rear-Admiral John Guy Protheroe 202–204, 206–209, 210, 213, 215
Vizalma, HM armed trawler 223
Vlieter Incident 53
Voice, Coxswain Abraham 130
von Donop, Commander Edward Pelham Brenton 108
von Mauchenheim, *Korvettenkapitan* Theodor Freiherr 220
von Pufendorf, *Korvettenkapitan* Rudolf 220
Vrow Alyda, Dutch privateer 75
Vulcan, HM 5th-rate 38
Vulcan, HM steam frigate 84
Vulcan, HM troopship 108
Vyse, Lieutenant Michael 229

Waachzamghheer, Dutch Greenlandsman 74
Wade, Private James 6th Regiment 109
Wainwright, Captain James Francis Ballard 125
Wake, Captain Drury St.Aubyn 152

Walcott, Miss 111
Walcott, Mrs James 111
Walcott, the Masters 111
Wales, Private Thomas 12th Regiment 106
Walker, Commander Charles Frederick 71
Walker, Able Seaman Henry J 130
Walker, Able Seaman Frederick William 176
Walker, Admiral Sir Baldwin Wake 115, 117
Walker, Private Charles 74th Regiment 110
Walker, Private James 2nd Regiment 105
Walker, Private Robert S 74th Regiment 108
Walker, Sergeant George 12th Regiment 109
Wallace, Able Seaman John 105
Wallace, John vii
Waller, Captain John William Ashley 198
Waller, Private George 2nd Regiment 105
Waller, Private George 2nd Regiment 105
Wallis, Private John William James 60th Regiment 107
Walmsely, Private John 91st Regiment 110
Walpole, Home Secretary Spencer Horatio, QD, LLD 113
Walrus, Supermarine 197
Walsh, Able Seaman John Albert 176
Walsh, Lieutenant John 64
Walsh, Ordinary Seaman Edward 130
Walsh, Private James T 91st Regiment 108
Walshe, Private Edward 6th Regiment 109
Wane, Able Seaman Christopher 175
Warburton-Lee, Captain Bernard Armitage Warburton 197
Ward, Able Seaman George 129
Ward, James SALMO 243
Ward, Private Patrick 12th Regiment 109
Warden, Captain Frederick 101
Ware, Journalist Hugh 244
Wareham, Alison viii
Warn, Quartermaster George 130
Warner, Boy 1st Class Edward M 131
Warren, Admiral Sir John Borlase 75
Warren, Captain Herbert Augustus 142
Warren, Temporary-Sub-Lieutenant Arthur Lionel Waldegrave 223
Warrington-Strong, Lieutenant (N) Francis 205
Warrior Class, HM armoured cruisers 177
Warspite, HM battleship 188, 200, 214
Washington, Batavian 2nd-rate 53
Wasp, HM brig-sloop 75
Watchful, HM naval hospital Great Yarmouth 187
Watercock, tug 221
Waters, Private Daniel 12th Regiment 109
Watkins, Captain Richard 25
Watlings, John (George) 77
Watson, Captain Edward Howe, USN 192
Watson, Captain Hugh Dudley Richards 173
Watson, Private George 74th Regiment 108
Watson, Stoker 1st Class John 175
Watson, Vice-Admiral Bertram Chalmers, CB, DSO 187, 230
Watts, Boy 1st Class James 105
Waugh, Arthur Evelyn St. John 196
Waveney, HM destroyer 163

Way, Private William 2nd Regiment 105
Wealords, Shipwright John 130
Weapon Class, HM destroyers 234
Weatherstone, Ordinary Seaman Henry 131
Weaver, Able Seaman James 184
Weazel, HM sloop 38–39
Webber, Corporal Arthur Alexander 91st Regiment 108
Webster, historian Roger 110
Webster, Private Benjamin 2nd Regiment 105
Weddigen, *Kapitanleutnant* Otto 180
Weightman, Captain Frederick 10, 11
Weinholt, Daniel 58
Weir, Captain of the Mast Charles 129
Weir, Lieutenant Patrick Wylie Rose 161
Weisenfels, German blockade runner 188
Welch, Private Maurice 43rd Light Infantry 107
Welch, Private William 6th Regiment 109
Weller, Diver Robert 'Frogfoot' 19, 21
Wellington, HM sloop 224
Wells, Ordinary Seaman Noah 130
Wells, Private Charles 73rd Regiment 107
Wells, Private George 12th Regiment 109
Welstead, Ordinary Seaman Henry 131
West, Private James 43rd Regiment 109
West, Private James, 6th Regiment 106
Westerne, Gun Founder Thomas 3
Westland HMA8 *Lynx* 237
Westminster, HM frigate 21, 250
Weston, Dame Agnes 156
Weston, HM sloop 222, 224
Wever, Fisherman Cornelus 67
Weybrow, Private William 91st Regiment 108
Weymouth Class, HM light cruisers 185
Weymouth, HM 4th-rate 8
Whalley, Engine Room Artificer Herbert 175
Wheeler, Metrologist Dennis 32, 36
Wheeler, Private William Henry 2nd Regiment 105
Whemys, Able Seaman George 70
Whetham, Able Seaman Charles 131
Whicher, Private Charles (1046), 2nd Regiment 106
Whiston, Mathmatician William 50
Whitaker, Captain Edward 34
Whitaker, Captain Samuel 33, 37, 45
Whitby, Ordinary Seaman Herbert Thomas 176
White, Boy 1st Class Richard 131
White, Civil Servant Andrew 86, 108
White, Private John 2nd Regiment 109
White, Private Thomas 6th Regiment 106
White, Ship's Cook James 105
Whitehall, HM destroyer 221–222
Whitehead, Lieutenant Richard 55–56
Whitford Point, British freighter 222
Whitmey-Smith, Commander George Kelvin 202
Whitton, Able Seaman William Raynor 184
Whyham, Chief Engineer William 89, 104
Wichar, Corporal Charles 2nd Regiment 110
Wichar, Mrs G 110
Wickham, British *Charge d' Affaires* William 54
Widestone, British freighter 222
Wienholt, Agent Daniel 58, 61
Wierninga, Journalist Feige 69

Wijke, Journalist Ruiter 59, 64
Wilcocks, Commodore Philip 246
Wildenfels, German blockade runner 188
Wilford, Midshipman Edward 42
Wilhelm Heidkamp, German destroyer 220
Wilkes, Captain Charles, Federal Navy 116–117
Wilkins, Private William 60th Regiment 107
Wilkins, Stoker James 105
Wilkinsen, Private Samuel 60th Regiment 107
Wilkinson, Lieutenant-Commander Ralph Wilmot 163
William I, Dutch King 57, 67
William II, Dutch King 57
William III, Dutch King 4
William V, *Stadtholder*, Prince of Orange 52
William, King Frederic, King of Prussia 103
William-Powlett, Captain Peveril Barton Reibey Wallop 189
Williams, Ian vii
Williams, Lieutenant John Richard 140
Williams, Private John Royal Marines 131
Williams, Private Richard Royal Marines 131
Willmot, Commodore Robert 10, 12–14
Wilmott, Captain Eardley 179
Wilson, Able Seaman James 129
Wilson, Admiral Sir Arthur Knyvet 137–138, 140
Wilson, Boatswain's Mate Edward 101, 109
Wilson, Captain Alexander 75
Wilson, Captain Alexander Guy Berners 189
Wilson, Captain of the Hold Joseph W 130
Wilson, Harbourmaster Clive 240, 244
Wilson, Leading Stoker John 156
Wilson, Private James 73rd Regiment 107
Wilson, Private John 60th Regiment 107
Wilson, Private William 12th Regiment 107
Winchester, HM 4th-rate 8 *et seq*
Winder, Captain Joseph 42
Windon, Able Seaman George 108
Windsor Castle, HM 2nd-rate 6, 159
Wing, Captain Thomas 119–120, 123, 128
Wing, Signal Post Attendant Edward 128
Winkworth, Able Seaman Alfred Charles 176
Winnington, Private Alexander 91st Regiment 108
Winona, US freighter 222
Winsloe, Vice-Admiral Alfred Leigh 156
Winstanley, Engineer Henry 22
Winterbottom, Private Frederick 91st Regiment 110
Winterswijk, Dutch freighter 222
Wintz, Sophie Gertrude 156
Wiscard, Lieutenant Benjamin 40
Wise, Captain Charles 101
Wiseman, Captain Sir William Saltonstall 125
Wittock, Private James Royal Marines 107
Wolf, whaling vessel 235–236
Wolfe, Major-General James 236
Wolfhound, HM destroyer 188
Wolverine, HM brig-sloop 59–61, 64
Wolverine, HM wooden screw corvette 115
Wonga Wonga, Inter-provincial mail steamship 123–125
Woobey, Able Seaman Victor William 176
Wood, Commander Percy Frank Pilkington 231

Wood, Midshipman William Henry, BEM 180, 187
Wood, Private William 73rd Regiment 110
Woodbury, US destroyer 192
Woodfall, Private Thomas 2nd Regiment 105
Woodhouse, Able Seaman Frederick Reynolds 176
Woodman, Private William 91st Regiment 108
Woodrow, Ship's Tailor John 130
Woods, Able Seaman John 108
Woods, Author Alan 32
Woods, Private John Royal Marines 107
Woodward, Ordinary Seaman William 108
Woodward, Private James 43rd Regiment 109
Woodward, Private William 60th Regiment 107
Woollason, Commander Charles 75
Woollcombe, Captain Louis Charles Stirling 165
Wootton, Private Joseph 12th Regiment 106
Worcester, HM 4th-rate 16, 37
Worill, Private Benjamin 2nd Regiment 109
Worth, Private George 6th Regiment 106
Wren, HM destroyer 202
Wrestler, HM destroyer 209
Wright, Captain Edward William Carlile, 91st
    Regiment 86, 90–91, 93, 96, 98, 101, 104, 108
Wright, Captain Samuel Harry, RNR 117
Wright, Lieutenant-Commander Richard Noel
    John 215
Wright, Seaman George 80
Wryneck, HM destroyer 230
Wyatt, Shipbuilder William 8
Wyburd, Lieutenant-Commander Derek
    Bathurst 200
Wyer, Private Christopher 91st Regiment 108
Wylie, Commander Robert 87
Wyndham, Boy 1st Class George 108

Wyvill, Commodore Christopher 88–89, 97–99,
    103, 110

Xhosa Wars (Kaffir Wars) 85–86

Yam O, tug 243
Yates, Captain Gerald Douglas 203
Yeatman, Commander Morgan John 222
Yonge, Lieutenant Duke Doughton 126, 129
York, HM 3rd-rate 13
York, HM 4th rate (ex-*Marston Moor*) 35
York, HM destroyer 237
York, HM heavy cruiser 196, 200
Young, Able Seaman George 129
Young, Able Seaman John 131
Young, Captain Frederick William 137–141, 148
Young, Captain John Edward 222
Young, Leading Seaman Alfred Charles 175
Young, US destroyer 192
Youngman, Skipper Albert Ernest 209
Yule, Trooper John 12th Lancers 109
Yunnan, Hong Kong steam ship 157

Zebra, HM sloop 56
Zee Star, Dutch privateer 75
Zephyr, Salvage vessel 141
Zephyros, Greek freighter 222
Zimmer, *Korvettenkapitan* Hans-Georg 220
Zulu, HM destroyer 200
Zwyker, Bandmaster Herr ('Twickers') vii, 105–106
Zwyker, Master 110
Zwyker, Miss 88, 110
Zwyker, Mrs 110